Practical IoT Handbook

Programming IoT by implementing hands-on projects with Arduino, Python, and Raspberry Pi

Rodrigo J Hernandez

www.bpbonline.com

First Edition 2025

ISBN: 978-93-65892-659

LIMITS OF LIABILITY AND DISCLAIMER OF WARRANTY

To View Complete
BPB Publications Catalogue
Scan the QR Code:

www.bpbonline.com

Dedicated to

My beloved daughter, ***Ana Paula***
and
My love and supportive partner, ***Vivi***

About the Author

Rodrigo J Hernandez is an electronic engineer passionate about IoT even before it existed. He has been working on tech for more than 20 years until now. For several years he has been focusing on the IoT ecosystem. He is currently giving consultations about IoT systems to clients around the world. He also produces content online about IoT and related subjects and the content is available on his blog, YouTube channel, and social networks - mainly LinkedIn. He also writes for companies that need good-quality content about their products and services. His main objective nowaday is to help others to understand and implement IoT solutions.

About the Reviewers

- **Asim Zulfiqar** is a blogger and tech content creator who has been writing tutorials on embedded systems and IoT on his blog and YouTube channel, High Voltages. Currently, he is working as a scientific programmer for IoT research projects.

  He completed his bachelor's degree in electronic engineering at Sir Syed University of Engineering and Technology, Pakistan. After that, he completed his Erasmus Mundus joint master's degree program in Photonics Integrated Circuits, Sensors, and Networks at Scuola Superiore Sant'Anna (Italy), Aston University (U.K), and Osaka University (Japan).

- **Rodrigo A. Aliaga Velez** is a Bolivian engineer with extensive expertise in **Industrial Internet of Things** (**IIoT**), **Internet of Things** (**IoT**), automation, and industrial optimization. With a background in mechatronics engineering and a specialization in lean energy, he has developed IIoT solutions for leading global companies such as AB InBev, Nestlé Vietnam, Acwa Power UAE, and Redev AI UK. His work focuses on enhancing efficiency, safety, and real-time data-driven decision-making through smart industrial systems.

  Rodrigo is a Lean Six Sigma Black Belt certified professional and is currently pursuing a master's degree in corporate management and Industry 4.0, further strengthening his expertise in digital transformation and industrial automation. He has successfully managed IIoT and IoT projects across various industries, driving technological innovation and process optimization.

  As a technical reviewer for an IoT Handbook, Rodrigo ensured the accuracy, clarity, and real-world applicability of the book's content. His contributions focused on key areas such as microcontrollers, sensors, actuators, IoT connectivity (MQTT, CoAP, HTTP), data management, and data visualization. With his background in industrial automation and smart technologies, he provided valuable insights into practical IoT implementations, including home automation and weather station development. His dedication to advancing industrial technology makes him a key contributor to Industry 4.0.

Acknowledgement

First and foremost, I want to thank my partner, Vivi, who always encouraged me to work on the book.

My gratitude also goes to the team at BPB Publications for their support and comprehension of the long time it took me to finish the book.

Preface

This book has been written with a clear objective: to give the reader a good introduction to the IoT world.

In this book, you will learn many concepts about hardware, embedded programming, protocols, platforms, tools, and many more topics.

The book covers theoretical concepts that are later applied to practical examples.

The book will lead you from basic definitions to advanced topics that you can apply to your projects.

This book is divided into 11 chapters. Every chapter develops a specific topic, like microcontrollers, sensors and actuators, computer Raspberry Pi 4, protocols, data storage, data visualization, and home automation, among others.

Chapter 1: Meet the Boards – In this chapter, you will explore the hardware you will use through the book to implement the projects

Chapter 2: Installing the Software Environment – In this chapter, we will see how to install and configure the software needed to develop the projects.

Chapter 3: Microcontrollers, Sensors, and Actuators – This chapter covers the fundamentals of sensors and actuators. You will learn about the different types of sensors and actuators, and how you can use them.

Chapter 4: Interfacing with Raspberry Pi – In this chapter, you will learn to connect different types of sensors and actuators with the Raspberry Pi 4 computer. You will learn how to configure the computer to be able to use it. Also, you will install Node-RED on the Raspberry Pi and use it to interact with the peripherals.

Chapter 5: Connecting IoT Devices using MQTT – This chapter covers the fundamentals of the MQTT protocol. You will learn how to use it to communicate with your IoT devices and transfer data between them and the MQTT broker installed in the Raspberry Pi 4.

Chapter 6: CoAP for IoT Connectivity – In this chapter, you will learn about the CoAP protocol. You will use different methods to exchange data between devices and a CoAP server in the Raspberry Pi.

Chapter 7: Using HTTP and WebSockets in IoT – This chapter covers both HTTP and WebSockets for exchanging data between devices and the Raspberry Pi. It explains the fundamentals of both protocols and provides many examples. It also emphasizes the differences between both protocols.

Chapter 8: Storing Internet of Things Data – In this chapter, you will learn how to store IoT data using time-series databases. In particular, this chapter focuses on the InfluxDB database, which is widely used in IoT systems. This chapter covers the fundamentals and shows you how to use InfluxDB in a real project.

Chapter 9: Visualizing Internet of Things Data – In this chapter, you will learn how to install, configure, and use Grafana to visualize IoT data. You will also see how to create alarms and notifications in Grafana.

Chapter 10: Building a Weather Station – This chapter covers the implementation of a weather station using the tools that you learned to use in the previous chapters.

Chapter 11: Home Automation – In this chapter, you will learn how to implement home automation using both Home Assistant and openHAB, which are open-source systems. You will also learn to use the Tasmota and ESPHome firmware for programming the devices that will connect with the home automation platforms.

Code Bundle and Coloured Images

Please follow the link to download the
Code Bundle and the *Coloured Images* of the book:

https://rebrand.ly/hy233yt

The code bundle for the book is also hosted on GitHub at **https://github.com/bpbpublications/Practical-IoT-Handbook**. In case there's an update to the code, it will be updated on the existing GitHub repository.

We have code bundles from our rich catalogue of books and videos available at **https://github.com/bpbpublications**. Check them out!

Errata

We take immense pride in our work at BPB Publications and follow best practices to ensure the accuracy of our content to provide with an indulging reading experience to our subscribers. Our readers are our mirrors, and we use their inputs to reflect and improve upon human errors, if any, that may have occurred during the publishing processes involved. To let us maintain the quality and help us reach out to any readers who might be having difficulties due to any unforeseen errors, please write to us at :

errata@bpbonline.com

Your support, suggestions and feedbacks are highly appreciated by the BPB Publications' Family.

Piracy

If you come across any illegal copies of our works in any form on the internet, we would be grateful if you would provide us with the location address or website name. Please contact us at **business@bpbonline.com** with a link to the material.

If you are interested in becoming an author

If there is a topic that you have expertise in, and you are interested in either writing or contributing to a book, please visit **www.bpbonline.com**. We have worked with thousands of developers and tech professionals, just like you, to help them share their insights with the global tech community. You can make a general application, apply for a specific hot topic that we are recruiting an author for, or submit your own idea.

Reviews

Please leave a review. Once you have read and used this book, why not leave a review on the site that you purchased it from? Potential readers can then see and use your unbiased opinion to make purchase decisions. We at BPB can understand what you think about our products, and our authors can see your feedback on their book. Thank you!

For more information about BPB, please visit **www.bpbonline.com**.

Join our book's Discord space

Join the book's Discord Workspace for Latest updates, Offers, Tech happenings around the world, New Release and Sessions with the Authors:

https://discord.bpbonline.com

Table of Contents

CHAPTER 1
Meet the Boards

Introduction

This chapter will provide you with an overview of the boards used throughout the book. We will explore their features, capabilities, and uses. Boards are divided into three groups: Espressif devices (ESP8266 and ESP32), ARM microcontroller (Raspberry Pi Pico), and Single Board Computer (Raspberry Pi 4). As you are aware, there exists a wide array of devices. Nevertheless, incorporating a comprehensive coverage of them would introduce unwarranted intricacy into this book.

On the other hand, this book proposes popularly used boards. Exploring these boards will establish a concrete base for learning programs on other platforms.

Structure

In this chapter, we will discuss the following topics:

- Espressif devices
- Raspberry Pi Pico
- Raspberry Pi Computer

Objectives

The objective of this chapter is to obtain a first approach to the hardware that we will use during the rest of the book.

Here you will learn the features and characteristics of microcontrollers and computers that we will use to build IoT systems.

Espressif devices

Espressif is a company that develops 32-bit microcontrollers with communications capabilities. These microcontrollers include either WiFi and **Bluetooth Low Energy** (**BLE**) 102 connectivity or both. The products are divided into three categories: SoC, modules, and development boards. Let us explore each of them.

System on chip

SoC is the acronym for system on chip. This type of device is a chip that includes all the necessary components from a functional point of view, and SoC may include the following:

- A 32-bit microcontroller, RAM, and ROM
- Peripheral interfaces (GPIO) digital inputs and outputs, ADC and DAC, (serial communication) I2C, I2S, SPI, UART, (memory access) DMA - GDMA, etc.
- Cryptographic hardware
- Real-time clock
- Clocks and timers
- WiFi and BLE controllers
- Radio frequency circuit

On the other hand, an SoC lacks:

- Programming interface, like USB
- Voltage regulators
- Antennas
- Any external component that is necessary to interface or feed the SoC

You can see an example of a SoC in *Figure 1.1*:

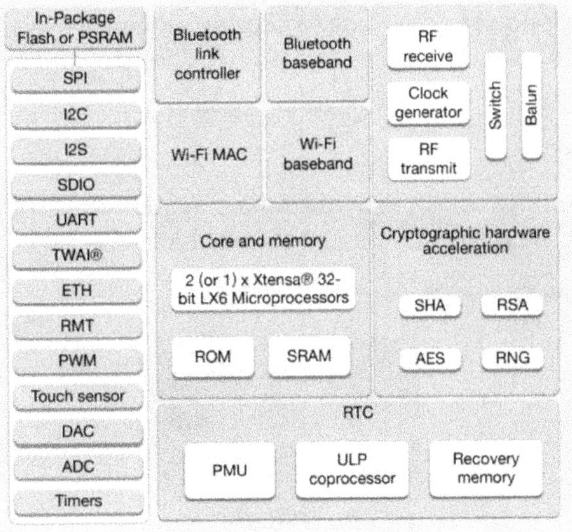

***Figure 1.1**: SoC example*[1]

Using SoCs

You may want to use a SoC for sending your product to mass production, as it is the cheapest and most efficient option to include a microcontroller in a new device. As you can see in *Figure 1.1*, a SoC has all the elements needed to obtain a fully working microcontroller with communication capabilities. However, you must design and build your **Printed Circuit Board** (**PCB**) to host the SoC accurately. This process may require several iterations. Moreover, a new PCB may require expensive certifications to be commercialized. On the other hand, you can add an SoC easily on any PCB design, given that it is a single chip.

Finally, if you are in the **proof of concept** (**PoC**) stage, you should not use an SoC as it adds unnecessary complexities.

Modules

The modules provide a higher level of integration with respect to SoCs.

The modules provide the following features:

- They include a SoC.
- They are fully certified with integrated antenna or connectors.

1 Source: **www.espressif.com**

When to use modules

Modules are a good option if you want to produce a new device without the hassle of obtaining wireless certifications. You can add the module to your board by soldering it.

While modules come at a higher cost compared to SoCs, they offer the advantage of a reduced time-to-market.

On the other hand, modules do not provide voltage regulators or programming interfaces, so you are responsible for implementing all the necessary circuits.

You can see an example of a module in *Figure 1.2*:

***Figure 1.2**: ESP32-based module*

Development boards

The development boards provide all the necessary elements to start testing a PoC or prototype immediately.

These boards typically offer some of these features:

- One or more microcontrollers or SOCs.
- They include all the circuits to bring you a programming interface. You can download your firmware using some kind of serial interface, typically in a USB format.
- Voltage regulators, and even battery chargers and energy harvesting interfaces (for example, to connect a solar panel).
- LEDs, buttons, displays, breadboards, connectors, SD card slots, etc.

Refer to *Figure 1.3* for an example of a development board:

Figure 1.3: *ESP32 development board*

When to use development boards

A development board is the best option if you need to build a PoC fast and easily.

These boards are obviously more expensive than modules, but you will not use them in mass production. However, if the project involves fewer units, perhaps you can consider using them as a final solution.

We will use development boards to show the concepts described in this book with practical examples. Regarding Espressif, we will use ESP8266 and ESP32 devices.

Note: You can choose any development board to perform the examples given in this book. Just take into consideration the characteristics of your board, like GPIO pins.

Programming environments

You can program Espressif devices using several programming environments. These include ESP-IDF, Arduino, and PlatformIO.

Regarding programming languages, you can use C, C++, Arduino, MicroPython, CircuitPython, and others.

ESP-IDF

Espressif owns a programming ecosystem, called **Espressif's IoT Development Framework** (**ESP-IDF**). With it, you can program ESP32, ESP32-S, ESP32-C, and ESP32-H SoCs.

The **Software Development Kit** (**SDK**) allows you to develop fully functional IoT applications using C or C++.

The main features of ESP-IDF are the following:

- **Open source**: It is delivered under the Apache 2.0 license, and you can obtain it freely on GitHub.

- **Compatibility**: The stack includes many modules, such as peripheral drivers, **real-time operating system (RTOS)**, network stacks, protocols, etc. You can also use these tools in officially supported IDEs, like Eclipse or **Visual Studio Code (VS Code)**.
- **Production-ready**: All the software provided in ESP-IDF goes through a release process to provide stable versions. Moreover, you get updates with important fixes and improvements.
- **Extensive documentation**: Besides the SDK itself, there is plenty of documentation, including examples to help developers achieve their objectives faster.
- **Included components**: Network Provisioning, OTA Upgrade Library, Manufacturing Utilities, Common Networking Protocols, Examples, File Systems, Object Storage, POSIX and C++ Support, Network Security, Crypto Library, IDE Plugins, Peripherals Drivers, Power Management, Wi-Fi and Bluetooth LE Mesh Networking, TCP/IP Stack, Bluetooth/Bluetooth LE Stack, Build System, RTOS Kernel, SoC Support, Software Bootloader, Wi-Fi MAC Library, Bluetooth Controller, Developer Tools.
- **Frameworks and libraries**: ESP-ADF (Audio Development Framework), ESP-MDF (Mesh Development Framework), ESP-IoT-Solution (Application examples and peripheral drivers), ESP HomeKit SDK (HomeKit-certified accessory development), Cloud Connectivity Agents (Support for AWS IoT Core, Azure IoT, Google IoT Core), ESP-Jumpstart (Framework and tutorial for building production-ready applications), ESP RainMaker (Device firmware, cloud service, mobile app solution), ESP-Arduino (Arduino IDE and libraries-based development support), AI and DSP Libraries.

Using the ESP-IDF

You can use the ESP-IDF packages employing the VSC extension, Eclipse IDE plugin, VisualGDB IDE, Arduino IDE, and PlatformIO IDE or CLI. For the purpose of this book, we will use VSC and Arduino to program the devices, but you can choose any other IDE you like.

Further, for compiling C/C++ code with VSC, we will install the required compilers. It is discussed in further in the next chapter.

Raspberry Pi Pico

In January 2021, the Raspberry Pi Foundation launched the Raspberry Pi Pico microcontroller (RP2040), available for just $4.

The Raspberry Pi Pico is based on the RP2040 microcontroller, designed by the Raspberry Pi Foundation. You can use the RP2040 on your own boards. However, in this book, we will use the development board because of a matter of simplicity.

You can see the Raspberry Pi Pico in *Figure 1.4*:

Figure 1.4: *Raspberry Pi Pico*[2]

Figure 1.5 displays the pinout of the Raspberry Pi Pico:

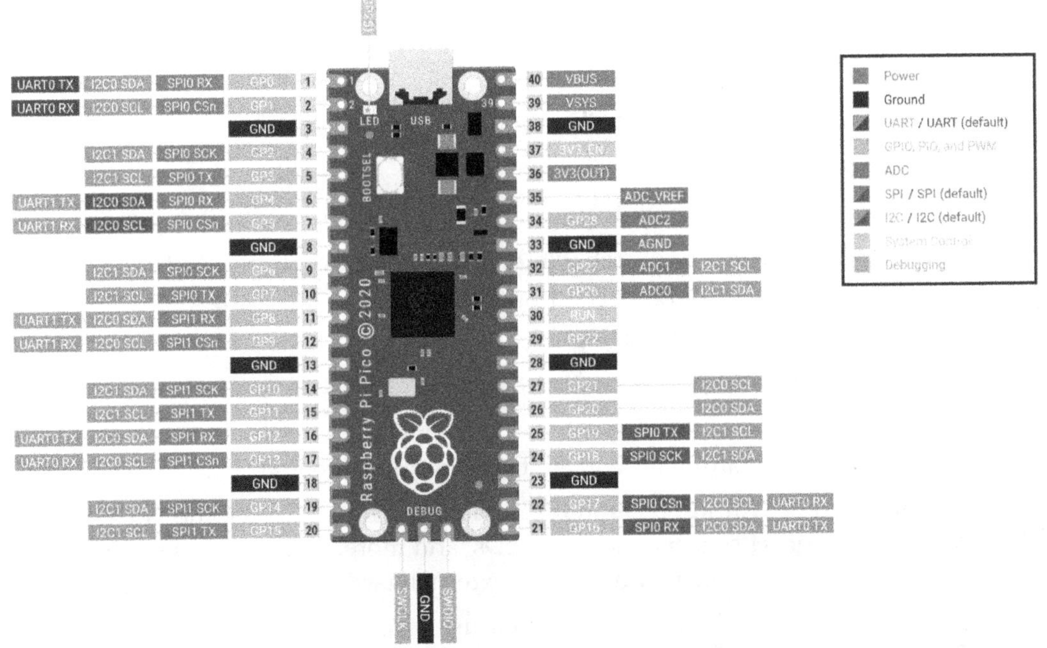

Figure 1.5: *Raspberry Pi Pico pinout*[3]

Here are the important characteristics of Raspberry Pi Pico:

- It has 264 KB of RAM and up to 16 MB of external flash memory.
- It includes two 133MHz Arm Cortex-M0+ cores.
- It comes with 2 × UART, 2 × SPI controllers, 2 × I2C controllers, 16 × PWM channels.

2 Source: **raspberrypi.com**
3 Source: **raspberrypi.com**

- It has 8 × **programmable I/O (PIO)** state machines for custom peripheral support.
- It has 1 × USB 1.1 controller and PHY, with host and device support.
- It can be programmed in various languages, including C, C++, Assembly, MicroPython, CircuitPython, and Rust.
- Drag-and-drop programming using mass storage over USB.
- Low-power sleep and dormant modes.
- Temperature sensor.
- Accelerated integer and floating-point libraries on-chip.

Collaborating with Adafruit, Pimoroni, Arduino, and SparkFun, the Raspberry Pi Foundation has created an array of accessories not only for the Raspberry Pi Pico but also for a diverse range of other boards utilizing the RP2040 Silicon Platform.

You can use this microcontroller to run simple programs and small **machine learning (ML)** models.

Pin functionalities

Let us delve further into the examination of Raspberry Pi Pico pins:

- **Power pins**:

  These pins are used to provide power to the board and to peripherals:

  - **3V3 (OUT)**: This is your reliable 3.3V power source. It is ideal for providing a steady voltage to external components.
  - **VBUS (USB power input)**: If you are using USB power, here you get 5V. It is great for keeping your board powered via USB.
  - **VSYS (External power input)**: You can connect an external power supply here to feed your board. It accepts voltages from 1.8V to 5.5V.
- **General purpose input/output (GPIO) pins**: You have 40 pins, and you can use 26 of them to connect sensors, motors, LEDs, and more. Notice that the pins work at 3.3 V. Consider this when you connect external hardware.
- **Analog input pins**: If you need to measure analog signals, the 12-bit ADC with four channels (GPIO26, GPIO27, GPIO28, GPIO29) can convert analog signals into digital data, ranging from 0 to 4095. Also, there is an ADC channel for measuring a built-in temperature sensor. You can see all these channels in *Table 1.1*:

ADC channel	GPIO	Function
ADC0	GPIO26	Input analog pin
ADC1	GPIO27	Input analog pin
ADC2	GPIO28	Input analog pin

ADC channel	GPIO	Function
ADC3	GPIO29	Voltage level of VSYS
ADC4	———	Internal temperature sensor

***Table 1.1**: ADC channels in Raspberry Pi Pico*

- **I2C pins**: I2C is a good option for connecting sensors and displays. The Raspberry Pi Pico has two I2C controllers (I2C0 and I2C1). GPIO4 (SDA) and GPIO5 (SCL) are the default pins to establish a connection with I2C devices. You can see all the available pins for I2C in *Table 1.2*:

I2C Controller	SDA	SCL
I2C0	GPIO0, GPIO4, GPIO8, GPIO12, GPIO16, GPIO20	GPIO1, GPIO5, GPIO9, GPIO13, GPIO17, GPIO21
I2C1	GPIO2, GPIO6, GPIO10, GPIO14, GPIO18, GPIO26	GPIO3, GPIO7, GPIO11, GPIO15, GPIO19, GPIO27

***Table 1.2**: I2C GPIOs in Raspberry Pi Pico*

- **PWM pins**: **Pulse Width Modulation** (**PWM**) is broadly used for controlling motors, lights, and heaters.
  - Although the Raspberry Pi Pico does not have a **Digital Analog Converter** (**DAC**), you can control a quasi-analog signal using PWM. With PWM, you can perform motor control, LED brightness adjustment, and sound modulation.
  - The Raspberry Pi Pico features eight separate PWM generators known as slices. Each of these slices combines a pair of channels labeled A and B, contributing to 16 PWM channels. In *Table 1.3*, you can see the distribution of PWM channels:

GPIO	0	1	2	3	4	5	6	7	8	9	10	11	12	13	14	15
PWM channel	0A	0B	1A	1B	2A	2B	3A	3B	4A	4B	5A	5B	6A	6B	7A	7B
GPIO	16	17	18	19	20	21	22	23	24	25	26	27	28	29		
PWM channel	0A	0B	1A	1B	2A	2B	3A	3B	4A	4B	5A	5B	6A	6B		

***Table 1.3**: PWM channels*

- **SPI pins**: SPI is useful when controlling other chips, like communication transceivers. Raspberry Pi Pico has two SPI controllers and default SPI pins at GPIO19 (TX), GPIO18 (SCK), GPIO17 (CS), and GPIO16 (RX). See *Table 1.4* for a complete list of SPI-capable pins:

SPI controller	RX GPIOs (MISO)	TX GPIOs (MOSI)	CLK GPIOs	CS GPIOs
SPI0	GPIO0, GPIO4, GPIO16	GPIO3, GPIO7, GPIO19	GPIO2, GPIO6, GPIO18	GPIO1, GPIO5, GPIO17
SPI1	GPIO8, GPIO12	GPIO11, GPIO15	GPIO10, GPIO14	GPIO9, GPIO13

***Table 1.4**: SPI pins*

- **UART pins**: If you need to communicate with other devices or even get data from your microcontroller, **universal asynchronous receiver-transmitter** (**UART**) becomes a natural option. There are two UART interfaces (UART0 and UART1). The pins GPIO0 (TX) and GPIO1 (RX) are the default UART pins. You can see a complete list in *Table 1.5*:

UART interface	TX GPIOs	RX GPIOs
UART0	GPIO0, GPIO12, GPIO16	GPIO1, GPIO13, GPIO17
UART1	GPIO4, GPIO8	GPIO5, GPIO9

***Table 1.5**: UART pins*

- **Built-in LED**: You can obtain a simple signal for debugging purposes using onboard LED (controlled by GPIO32 on Pico W or GPIO25 on Pico). It offers quick visual feedback and testing.
- **Debugging pins**: If you need additional debugging, you can use specific pins (SWDIO, GND, SWCL) to connect to a Raspberry Pi Debug Probe. It comes in handy for advanced troubleshooting.

Adding communications capabilities

On June 30, 2022, the Raspberry Pi Pico W was introduced. This board includes all the features of Raspberry Pi Pico and adds 802.11n Wi-Fi and BLE 5.2 capabilities using the chip CYW43439. This version is an ideal option for IoT projects, and we will see how to use it with several practical examples. You can see the Raspberry Pi Pico W in *Figure 1.6*. As you can notice, it includes a shielded chip, it is the CYW43439.

***Figure 1.6**: Raspberry Pi Pico W*[4]

4 Source: **raspberrypi.com**

Figure 1.7 shows the pinout of the Raspberry Pi Pico W. As you can see, most of the layout remains the same, except for the added wireless chip and the move of debug pins.

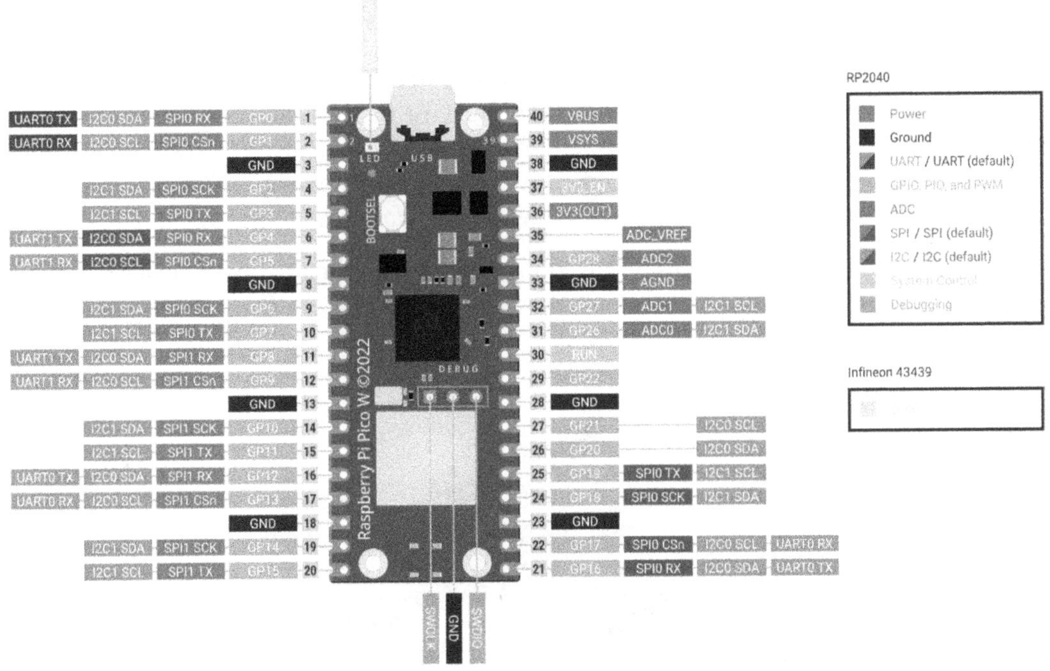

***Figure 1.7**: Raspberry Pi Pico W pinout*[5]

Programming the Raspberry Pi Pico

You can program this microcontroller using one of several languages and programming environments. In this book, we will explore some examples using Arduino, C++, and MicroPython. The selection of the right language depends on system requirements, efficiency, system integration, legacy software, and specific indications.

From easier to more complex, we can order them as follows: MicroPython, Arduino, and C++. To use MicroPython, you will have to install a specific firmware in the Raspberry Pi. This will let you execute Python commands in the microcontroller directly from your computer console. We will see how to do it in the following chapter.

Regarding Arduino, the Raspberry Pi Pico board is already integrated so that you can program it easily.

With C++, things become complex. You must install the compilers and configure the programming environment to ensure the functionality. This can be a tough path at first, but when you have everything set up and running, you can take advantage of numerous

5 Source: **raspberrypi.com**

programming resources. Moreover, you will obtain more efficiency and better control of the hardware.

Raspberry Pi Computer

The Raspberry Pi computer is a **Single Board Computer** (**SBC**). These types of computers can host a complete operating system, allowing you to run complex applications and services. The SBCs can run desktop environments, like Ubuntu Desktop; operating systems without graphical interfaces, like Raspberry Pi OS lite; server operating systems, like Ubuntu Server; or specific purpose software, like *Home Assitant*.

You can give an SBC multiple uses. In this book, we will use the Raspberry Pi 4 for building IoT projects. However, you can either use Raspberry Pi 3.

Figure 1.8 shows a Raspberry Pi 4 computer:

***Figure 1.8**: Computer Raspberry Pi 4*

Let us explore the characteristics of Raspberry Pi 4.

Raspberry Pi 4 uses and features

The Raspberry Pi 4 is a versatile hardware that allows you to run different types of applications. Some systems and applications that you can run on a Raspberry Pi 4 are:

- IoT systems
- Media centers
- Robot controllers
- Machine learning and artificial intelligent applications
- Video recording
- Home automation

Raspberry Pi 4 comes with very interesting upgrades:

- It offers better processing power, with the Quad core Broadcom BCM2711 chip.
- You can choose between four different versions, according to the memory size: 1 GB, 2 GB, 4GB, and 8 GB.
- USB 3.0 allows you to transfer data up to ten times faster than USB 2.0.
- It provides two HDMI ports, giving you the capability of connecting two 4K monitors.
- Unlike its predecessors, Raspberry Pi 4 has a 1 GB Ethernet interface. This is an important feature if you need to deal with audio and video streaming.
- It has more video processing power, with H.265 4Kp60 capabilities.

These are the full technical specifications of Raspberry Pi 4:

- Broadcom BCM2711, Quad core Cortex-A72 (ARM v8) 64-bit SoC @ 1.8GHz
- 1GB, 2GB, 4GB, or 8GB LPDDR4-3200 SDRAM (depending on model)
- 2.4 GHz and 5.0 GHz IEEE 802.11ac wireless, Bluetooth 5.0, BLE.
- Gigabit Ethernet.
- 2 USB 3.0 ports; 2 USB 2.0 ports.
- Raspberry Pi standard 40-pin GPIO header (fully backward compatible with previous boards).
- 2 × micro-HDMI® ports (up to 4kp60 supported)
- 2-lane MIPI DSI display port
- 2-lane MIPI CSI camera port
- 4-pole stereo audio and composite video port
- H.265 (4kp60 decode), H264 (1080p60 decode, 1080p30 encode)
- OpenGL ES 3.1, Vulkan 1.0
- Micro-SD card slot for loading operating system and data storage
- 5V DC via USB-C connector (minimum 3A*)
- 5V DC via GPIO header (minimum 3A*)
- Power over Ethernet (PoE) enabled (requires separate PoE HAT)
- Operating temperature: 0 – 50 degrees C ambient

Raspberry Pi 4 comes with a 40-pin header fully compatible with previous versions. You can see it in *Figure 1.9*:

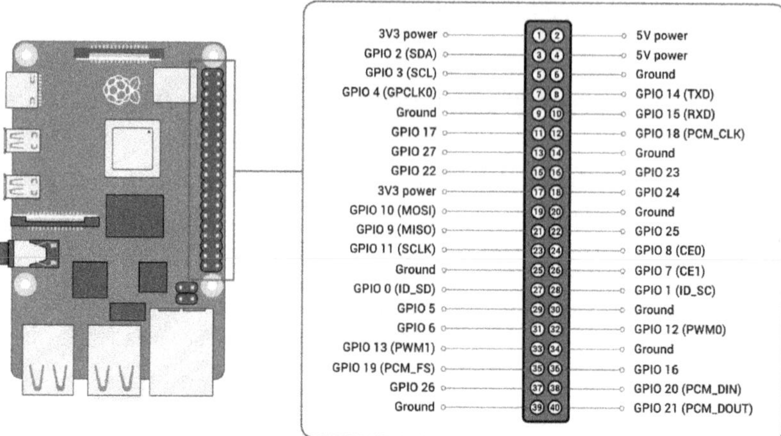

***Figure 1.9**: Raspberry Pi 4 header*[6]

Let us now proceed with the preparation of our Raspberry Pi 4 for utilization in the subsequent chapters.

Installing the Raspberry Pi OS

As we have mentioned before, you have many options regarding operating systems to choose from. However, in this book, we will use Raspberry Pi OS for building our IoT systems. This assures full compatibility with the hardware and prevents undesired issues.

Raspberry Pi Imager

The easiest way of installing Raspberry Pi OS is by using the Raspberry Pi Imager. There are three versions available: Windows, macOS, and Ubuntu x86.

To obtain the imager, go to **https://www.raspberrypi.com/software/** and select the right version for your operating system.

To install the Raspberry Pi OS, follow the given steps:

1. **Install Raspberry Pi Imager:** Install the Raspberry Pi Imager following the step-by-step procedure.
2. **Insert your SD card:** Insert your SD card into your computer's SD card reader. Use at least an 8GB card, 16 GB is recommended.
3. **Open Raspberry Pi Imager:** Launch the Raspberry Pi Imager software as shown in *Figure 1.10*:

6 Source: **raspberrypi.com**

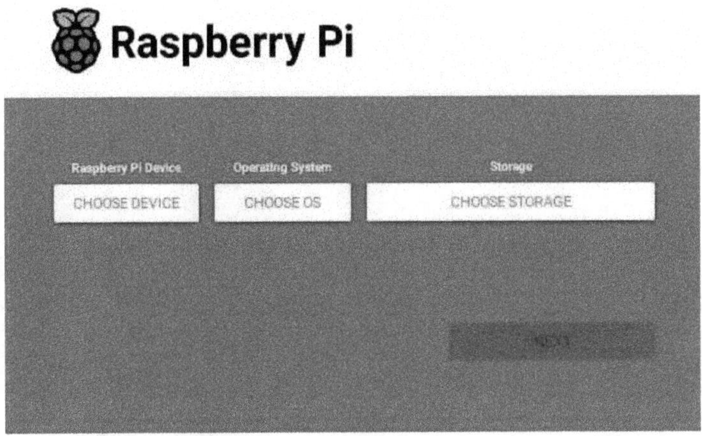

Figure 1.10: *Raspberry Pi Imager*

4. **Choose device:** Click **CHOOSE DEVICE** and select your Raspberry Pi model. See *Figure 1.11*:

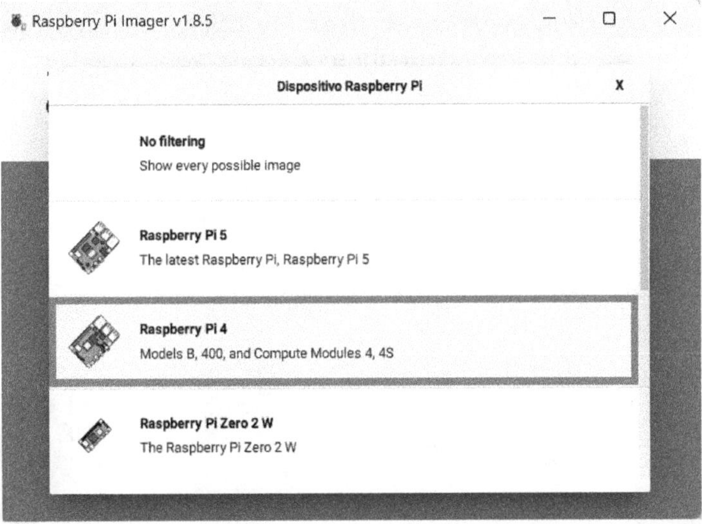

Figure 1.11: *Selecting Raspberry Pi OS (other)*

5. **Select Raspberry Pi OS Lite: After selecting the device click on CHOOSE OS | Raspberry Pi OS (Other) | Raspberry Pi OS Lite (64-bit)**. See *Figure 1.12*:

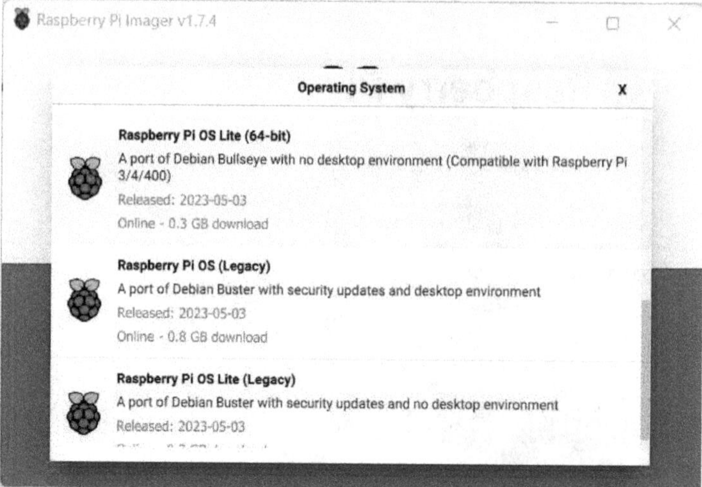

Figure 1.12: Selecting Raspberry Pi OS Lite 64-bit

6. **Choose an SD card:** Pick the target SD card you want to use.
7. **Enable SSH:** Click on the gear icon to configure the image. This will open a new window. Check the box next to **SSH** to enable it. Select the password authentication option. This will allow you to remotely access your Raspberry Pi via SSH. See *Figure 1.13*:

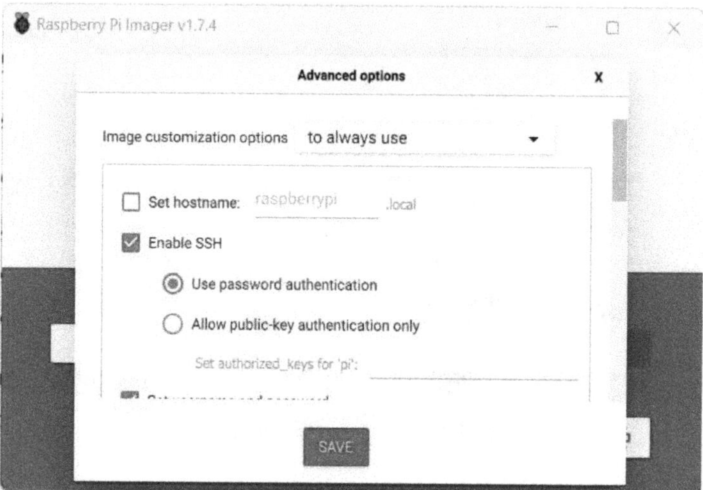

Figure 1.13: Enabling SSH

8. **Configure username and password:** In the **User** section, set your desired username and password. Make sure to confirm the password. This will create your account on the Raspberry Pi. See *Figure 1.14*:

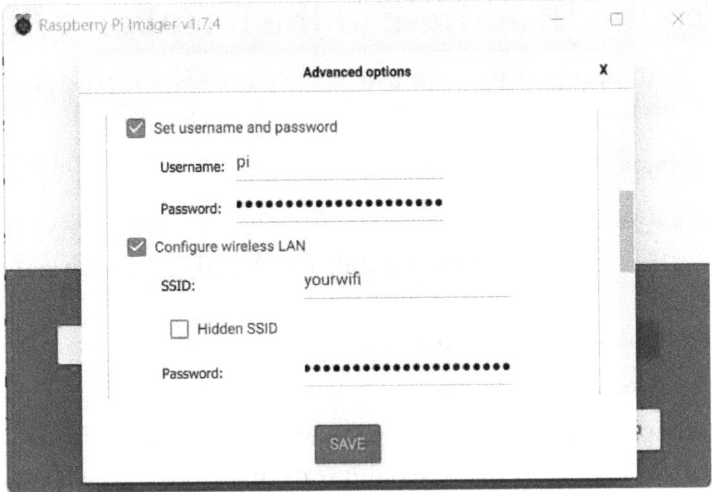

***Figure 1.14**: Configure user and WiFi*

9. **Configure WiFi:** In the **Configure wireless LAN**, enter the **SSID** (the name of your WiFi network), and the password. This will write the Wi-Fi configuration directly to the SD card. See *Figure 1.12*.
10. **Save the configuration**: Click on the **SAVE** button to save the configuration and close the windows.
11. **Start flashing:** Click the **Write** button to copy the Raspberry Pi OS Lite image and your configuration settings to the SD card.
12. **Wait for completion:** Wait for the flashing process to complete. The progress bar will show the status.
13. **Eject SD card:** Safely eject the SD card from your computer.
14. **Insert SD card into the Raspberry Pi 4:** Insert the SD card into your Raspberry Pi's SD card slot.
15. **Power up your Raspberry Pi**: Power up your Raspberry Pi. It will boot into the configuration settings you specified.
16. **Access your Raspberry Pi:** As you enable SSH, you can remotely access your Raspberry Pi using an SSH client on another device.

Your Raspberry Pi is now set up with WiFi, your chosen username and password, and SSH access.

We will use SSH access to perform most of the configurations and programming tasks. Let us see some SSH clients that you can use.

Discovering the IP address of the Raspberry Pi

There is a tool called `nmap` that you can use to discover IPs, devices, services, and ports. You can use this app to discover the IP address of your Raspberry Pi.

Let us see how to install `nmap` in your system.

Installing Nmap on Windows:

1. Download the latest stable Nmap installer for Windows from **nmap.org/download.html**
2. Run the downloaded `.exe` file as administrator.
3. Accept the license agreement.
4. Choose components to install (selecting all is recommended).
5. Select the installation location (default is `C:\Program Files (x86)\Nmap`).
6. Click Install to begin installation.
7. After Nmap installs, the Npcap setup will appear. Follow the prompts to install Npcap as well.
8. Once complete, you will have Nmap and Zenmap (GUI) installed.

Installing Nmap on Linux:

There are different ways to install Nmap in Linux, depending on your operating system.

- **Using package manager (recommended):**

  For Debian/Ubuntu:

  ```
  $ sudo apt update
  $ sudo apt install nmap
  For Red Hat/Fedora:
  $ sudo yum install nmap
  ```

- **Compiling from source**

  1. Install prerequisites:

     ```
     $ sudo apt install build-essential libssl-dev
     ```

  2. Download the latest Nmap source code:

     ```
     $ wget https://nmap.org/dist/nmap-[version].tar.bz2
     ```

  3. Extract the archive:

     ```
     $ tar jxvf nmap-[version].tar.bz2
     ```

  4. Navigate to the extracted directory:

     ```
     $ cd nmap-[version]
     ```

5. Compile and install:

```
$ ./configure && make && sudo make install
```

- **Using Snap (Ubuntu)**

```
$ sudo snap install nmap
```

After installation on either OS, verify by running:

```
nmap -version
```

Remember that on Linux, you may need to run Nmap with **sudo** privileges for certain scan types. On Windows, run the command prompt as administrator when needed.

Detecting the Raspberry Pi

To detect the Raspberry Pi using **nmap** follow these steps:

1. Open a command prompt as administrator
2. Determine your network subnet (e.g. 192.168.1.0/24)
3. Run an **nmap** ping scan on your subnet (use your network subnet):

   ```
   nmap -sn 192.168.1.0/24
   ```

4. Look for entries in the results with:
   - Hostname "**raspberrypi**"
   - MAC address starting with "**B8:27:EB**" or "**DC:A6:32**" (Raspberry Pi Foundation prefixes)
5. The IP address of your Raspberry Pi will be listed next to the matching entry.

Some additional tips:

- You may need to add the **nmap** installation directory to your system PATH to run it from any location.
- Use the **-p-** option to scan all ports if needed.
- The **-sV** option can provide additional OS/version detection.
- Zenmap provides a GUI interface for **nmap** on Windows if preferred.

SSH clients

There are many SSH clients that you can use to connect to the Raspberry Pi. The first option is using the client included in most operating systems. Windows 11, any Linux distribution, and macOS have clients available through the console.

To connect to the Raspberry Pi, enter the following in the CLI:

```
ssh <your-pi-user>@<raspberry pi IP address>
```

Example:

```
ssh pi@192.168.0.10
```

After entering this command, you will be prompted to enter the password. If the authentication is successful, you will see a screen like the one shown in *Figure 1.15*:

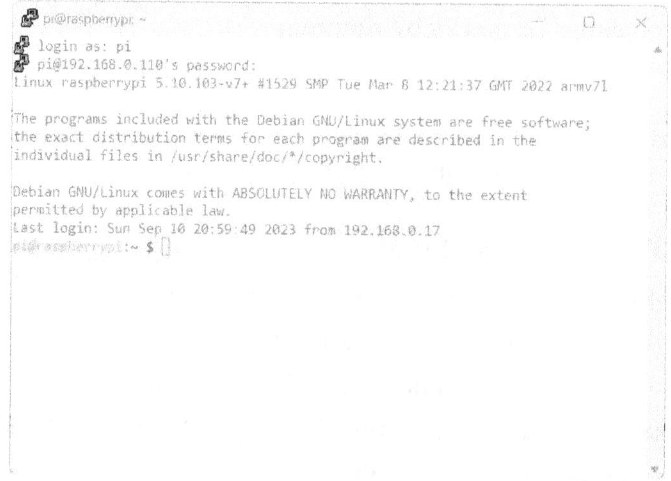

***Figure 1.15:** Raspberry Pi CLI*

If you prefer SSH clients with a graphical user interface, you can use PuTTY. To download it, go to **https://www.putty.org/** and select the right version for your operating system.

PuTTY has a very simple interface, as you can see in *Figure 1.16*:

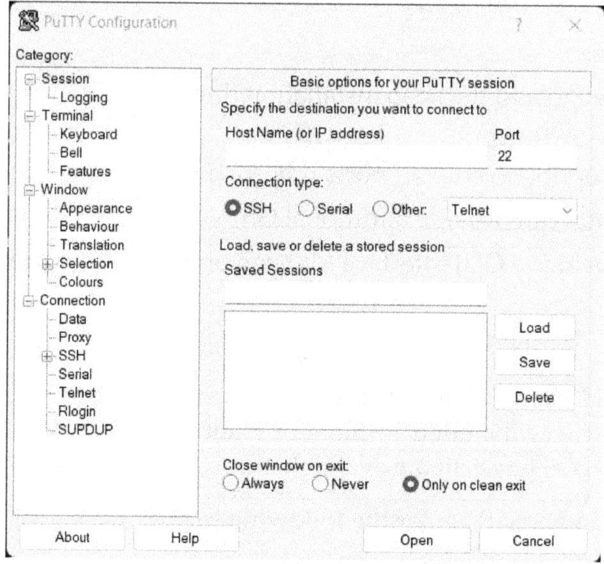

***Figure 1.16:** PuTTY interface*

To transfer files between your computer and the Raspberry Pi, you can use any of the following software:

- **FileZilla**: The FileZilla Client supports not just FTP but also FTP over TLS (FTPS) and SFTP. It operates as open-source software, distributed at no cost under the GNU General Public License. It is available for Windows, macOS, and Linux. You can download it from **https://filezilla-project.org/**.
- **WinSCP**: It is a widely used SFTP and FTP client designed for Microsoft Windows and facilitates seamless file transfers between local computers and remote servers. It supports an array of file transfer protocols such as FTP, FTPS, SCP, SFTP, WebDAV, and S3. You can download it from **https://winscp.net/**.

Conclusion

In this chapter, we have explored several boards we will use in this book to implement IoT systems. We looked through the Espressif hardware and software ecosystem. In the next chapters, we will work with ESP32 and ESP8266 microcontrollers using Arduino and VSC. Moreover, we analyzed the two versions of the Raspberry Pi Pico development board. As this is a book about IoT, we will use the W version to communicate the devices with IoT platforms. We will program this device using both Arduino and VSC.

Finally, we explored the Raspberry Pi 4 computer. In the following chapters, we will use it to connect to sensors and actuators and to run IoT platforms. The Raspberry Pi will become our IoT gateway or hub for performing edge computing.

CHAPTER 2
Installing the Software Environment

Introduction

In this chapter, we will learn about installing all the necessary software. This includes **interface development environments** (**IDEs**), compilers, interpreters, and libraries.

In particular, we will use Arduino IDE, Arduino libraries, Visual Studio Code (VS Code), and complements, C/C++ compilers: GCC and CMake, Python3 and MicroPython environments, and libraries from Espressif.

We will start by installing the software, and then we will implement some projects using Python on a Raspberry Pi.

Structure

The chapter covers the following topics:

- Installing Arduino
- Visual Studio Code
- Python for embedded development

Objectives

In this chapter, you will prepare the software ecosystem for the chapters to come. Further, we will write some simple programs in Python to test the environment. After finishing this chapter, you will have installed all the software needed to implement the projects described in this book.

Installing Arduino

Installing the Arduino IDE is easy. Just follow the steps given:

1. **Download**: Go to the following link **https://www.arduino.cc/en/software**. Once you are there, look for the Arduino IDE 2.X.X. This is the renewed IDE, recommended for new developments.
2. **Select the version**: Since you are using your computer, find the right version for your operating system. There are packages for Windows, macOS, and Linux. Refer to *Figure 2.1*:

Downloads

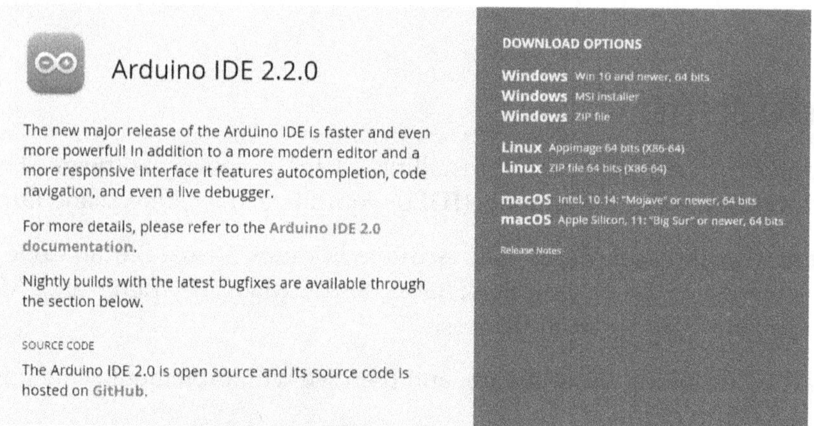

***Figure 2.1**: Arduino IDE download options*

3. **Install**: Once you have downloaded the installer, run it by following the installation steps. The installer might ask you where you want to install the Arduino IDE. Unless you have a reason to change it, just stick with the default location. Click **Next** or **Continue**.
4. **Drivers (Windows only)**: If you are using Windows, you might see a prompt about drivers. Do not worry, the installer should handle this for you. Just let it do its thing. If you are on macOS or Linux, you can skip this step.
5. **Launch Arduino IDE**: Now that you have installed it, go ahead and find Arduino IDE in your applications or programs list. Click on it to launch.

6. **Explore the user interface**: Now that the Arduino IDE is installed, look at the menus and options. Arduino comes with many features, including board packages, libraries, code examples, a serial monitor, etc. We will use these features in many projects. Refer to *Figure 2.2*:

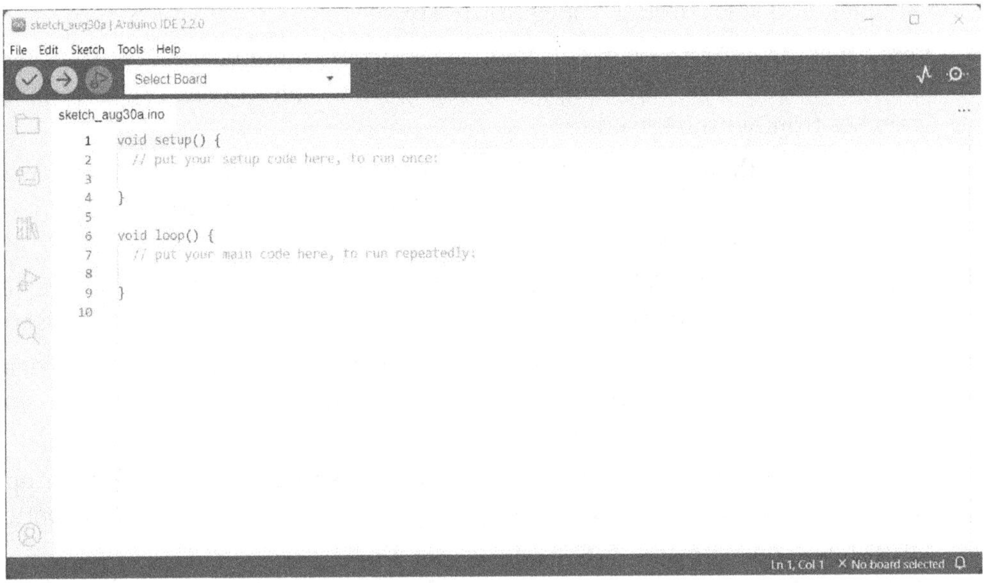

***Figure 2.2**: Arduino IDE*

Later in the book, we will install additional packages for programming boards and add specific libraries.

Now, let us see how to install VS Code.

Visual Studio Code

VS Code is a versatile programming environment. You can build applications, web pages, microcontroller programs, or even build containers, to name a few things.

Before installing it, let us see some of the standout features of VS Code:

- **Intelligent code editing**: VS Code offers intelligent code completion, suggestions, and error checking as you type, thanks to its language service integrations.
- **Extensions marketplace**: You can extend VS Code's functionality with a wide range of extensions from the marketplace. These can add support for various languages, tools, themes, and more.
- **Integrated terminal**: No need to switch between your code editor and terminal. VS Code has an integrated terminal right inside the interface for executing commands without leaving the editor.

- **Git integration**: Git is seamlessly integrated into VS Code. You can manage repositories, commit changes, and even resolve merge conflicts within the editor.
- **Debugging made easy**: VS Code provides powerful debugging capabilities with support for multiple programming languages. You can set breakpoints, inspect variables, and step through code effortlessly.
- **Version control**: Apart from Git, VS Code supports other version control systems like Subversion. You can compare changes, view commit history, and manage branches from within the editor.
- **Customizable themes and icons**: Personalize the look of VS Code with a variety of themes and icon packs available in the marketplace. Make your coding environment match your style.
- **IntelliSense**: VS Code's IntelliSense feature provides context-aware code suggestions, making coding faster and reducing the chances of making mistakes.
- **Live share**: Collaborate with others in real time using the Live Share extension. You can share your code and even co-debug, which is incredibly useful for remote teamwork.
- **Snippet support**: Save time by creating and using snippet code. VS Code supports both built-in and custom snippets to quickly insert commonly used code patterns.
- **Multi-language support**: VS Code is not limited to a specific programming language. It supports a wide variety of languages and frameworks, making it versatile for developers working on different projects.
- **Task automation**: Define and run tasks directly within VS Code using the integrated task runner. This can be handy for compiling code, running tests, and more.
- **Multiple cursors and selections**: You can place multiple cursors in your code and edit them simultaneously, which speeds up repetitive tasks.
- **Workspaces**: Organize your projects into workspaces, each with its own settings, extensions, and folder structures.
- **Extensions for remote development**: VS Code provides extensions for remote development, enabling you to work on code hosted on remote machines, containers, or virtual machines.

These are just a few of the many features that make V S Code a favorite among developers. Its flexibility, user-friendly interface, and extensive customization options make it a powerful tool for various coding needs.

Installing VS Code

Now, let us see how to install VS Code on your computer.

Download VS Code

To download VS Code, follow the given steps:

1. Go to the official website: **https://code.visualstudio.com/**.
2. Click on the **Download for [Your Operating System]** button. Refer to *Figure* 2.3.
3. If you are using Windows, you will get an installer EXE file, for Mac, it is a DMG file, and for Linux, it is a DEB/RPM file. Download the one that matches your system.

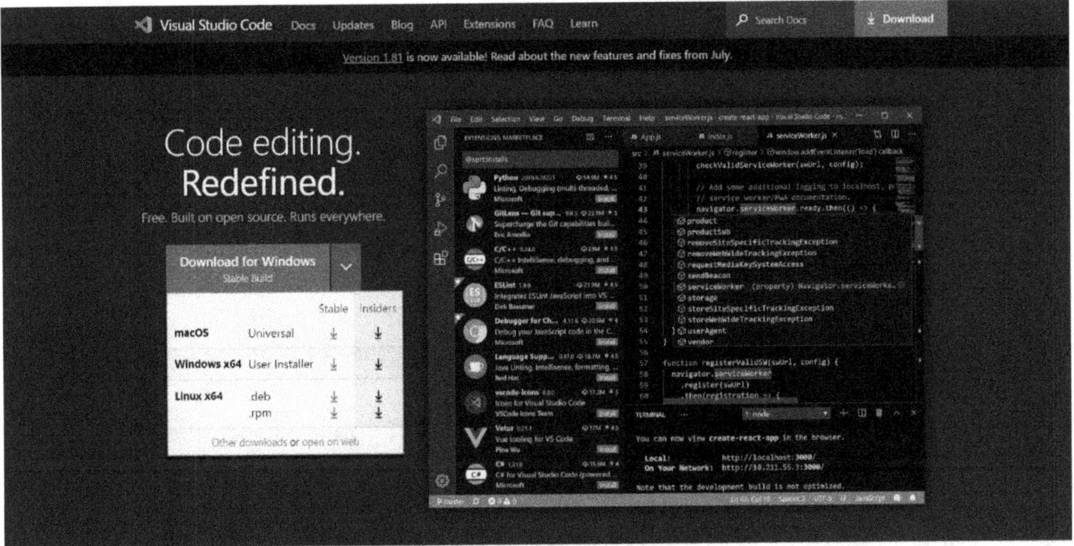

Figure 2.3: *VS Code download page*

Installing on Windows

Follow these steps to install VS Code on Windows:

1. Open the EXE file you downloaded.
2. You might see a security warning. Do not worry, VS Code is legit. Click **Run** or **Yes** to proceed.
3. The installer will guide you through the process. Just follow the on-screen instructions.
4. You might be asked to select some installation options. You can usually stick with the defaults.
5. Click **Install** and let the magic happen.

Installing on Mac

To install it on a Mac, follow the given steps:

1. Open the DMG file you downloaded.
2. Drag and drop the VS Code icon into the **Applications** folder.
3. Eject the DMG file like a pro (by dragging it to the trash or right-clicking and selecting **Eject**).
4. Go to your **Applications** folder and find VS Code. Double-click to open it.

Installing on Linux

If you are using Linux, follow these steps:

1. Open your terminal.
2. Navigate to the folder where you downloaded the DEB/RPM file. Use the **`cd`** command to get there.
3. Now, use your package manager to install the file. For example, if it is a DEB file, you might use **`sudo dpkg -i <filename.deb>`**. If it is an RPM file, you might use **`sudo rpm -i <filename.rpm>`**. Remember to replace **`<filename>`** with the actual filename.
4. You might need to resolve some dependencies. If you are lucky, the terminal will guide you on what to do.
5. Once everything is set, you can launch VS Code by searching for it in your applications or by typing **`code`** in the terminal.

Now, let us configure VS Code and add some extensions.

VS Code extensions

VS Code extensions are add-on components that enhance and customize the functionality of the VS Code editor for you. You can install these extensions from the VS Code Marketplace (see *Figure 2.4*) to extend the editor's capabilities, provide language support, add new features, and integrate with various programming languages, frameworks, and tools.

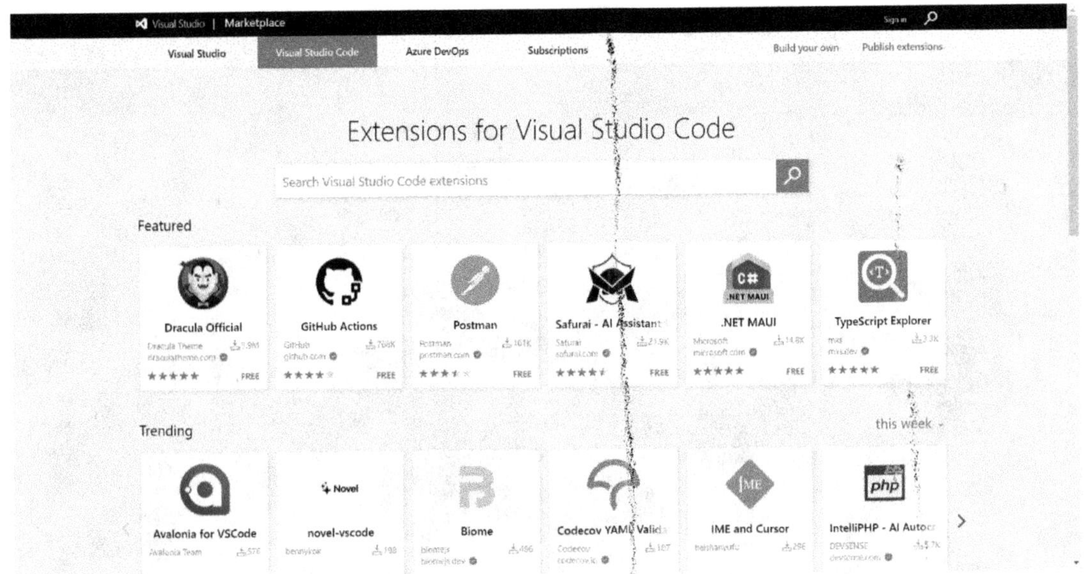

Figure 2.4: Extensions Marketplace for VS Code

Here are some key features of VS Code extensions that we will use:

- **Extensions enhance functionality**: Extensions add features and functionalities to VS Code that are not available by default. For example, they provide code linting, debugging support, version control integration, and more to make your coding experience smoother.
- **Language support**: Many extensions are designed to provide support for specific programming languages. These extensions often include syntax highlighting, autocompletion, code formatting, and debugging features tailored to that language, making it easier for you to write code.
- **Development tools**: Extensions offer development tools and integrations with popular programming platforms and frameworks. For instance, extensions like Python and C/C++ provide language-specific tools and support tailored to your needs.
- **Debugging and testing**: Extensions add debugging and testing capabilities for different languages and platforms, seamlessly integrating with popular debugging tools and testing frameworks that you might use.

VS Code extensions provide a lot more features, but these are the most important to us.

The easiest way to install an extension is to open VS Code and select the extensions panel. There, you can install, update, or remove any extension. Refer to *Figure 2.5:*

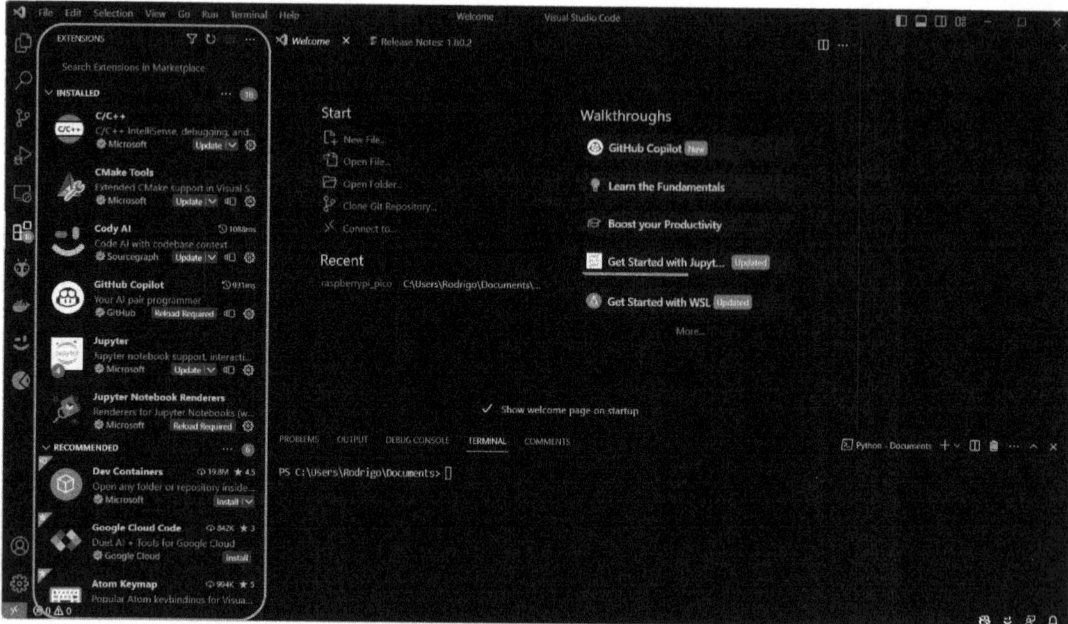

Figure 2.5: Extensions panel on VS Code

We will install a few extensions to develop our projects.

Installing Espressif extension

To install the Espressif extension for VS Code, follow these step-by-step instructions:

1. **Open VS Code**: Launch the VS Code application on your computer.
2. **Navigate to extensions**: Click on the Extensions icon located in the left sidebar. It looks like a square icon made of four small boxes, or can be accessed using the shortcut *Ctrl+Shift+X* (Windows/Linux) or *Cmd+Shift+X* (macOS).
3. **Search for Espressif**: In the Extensions view, you will see a search bar at the top. Type `Espressif` into the search bar and press *Enter*. Refer to *Figure 2.6*.
4. **Locate the extension**: Look through the search results to find the official Espressif extension for VS Code. It should have Espressif Systems as the publisher.
5. **Install the extension**: Click the **Install** button next to the Espressif extension in the search results.
6. **Reload VS Code**: After the installation is complete, a **Reload** button will appear. Click this button to restart VS Code and activate the extension.
7. **Wait for installation**: VS Code will download and install the extension. You will see a progress bar during this process.

***Figure 2.6**: Installing Espressif VS Code extension*

Before you can use the extension, it is essential to ensure that your system has the necessary dependencies available in the environment variable PATH. You can refer to the following documentation for specific requirements:

- **Windows system requirements**: **https://docs.espressif.com/projects/esp-idf/en/latest/esp32/get-started/windows-setup.html**
- **Linux and MacOS system requirements**: **https://docs.espressif.com/projects/esp-idf/en/latest/esp32/get-started/linux-macos-setup.html**

If you are using Windows, please note that you may need to install the C++ Build Tools as a prerequisite: **https://visualstudio.microsoft.com/visual-cpp-build-tools**

Now you can program, download, and debug ESP32 development boards. See the updated list of boards at **https://www.espressif.com/en/products/devkits**

Installing PlatformIO extension

PlatformIO is an open-source ecosystem, and a development platform designed to simplify the process of embedded and **Internet of Things** (**IoT**) software development. It provides a unified and cross-platform environment for programming microcontrollers, single-board computers, and other embedded systems. See the homepage at **https://platformio.org**.

These are the main features of PlatformIO:

- **Multi-platform support**: PlatformIO supports a wide range of microcontroller platforms, including Arduino, ESP8266, ESP32, Raspberry Pi, STM32, and more.

This versatility allows developers to work with different hardware platforms without switching between multiple development environments.

- **Cross-platform compatibility**: PlatformIO is compatible with various operating systems, such as Windows, macOS, and Linux. It offers a consistent development experience regardless of the platform you are using.
- **Integrated development environment (IDE)**: PlatformIO can be seamlessly integrated into popular code editors like VS Code and Atom. This integration enhances the development workflow with features like code auto-completion, project management, and debugging.
- **Library manager**: PlatformIO includes a library manager that simplifies the process of adding and managing libraries for your embedded projects. You can easily search, install, and update libraries from a centralized repository.
- **Project management**: You can create and manage projects within PlatformIO, making it easier to organize code, dependencies, and configuration settings. This project-centric approach streamlines the development process.
- **Unified build system**: PlatformIO uses a unified build system that can compile code for multiple platforms and architectures. This means you can write your code once and compile it for various target devices without major modifications.
- **Debugging and testing**: PlatformIO provides debugging tools and integration with hardware debugging platforms like GDB, making it easier to identify and fix issues in your embedded code. It also supports unit testing for embedded systems.
- **Package manager**: PlatformIO features a package manager that allows you to install development platforms and toolchains for different microcontrollers and boards. This ensures that you have the necessary tools and configurations for your specific hardware. You can see the complete list of boards here **https://docs.platformio.org/en/latest/boards/index.html.**
- **Community and documentation**: PlatformIO has an active and supportive community of developers. It offers comprehensive documentation, tutorials, and examples to help users get started and solve common problems.

Overall, PlatformIO simplifies the complexities of embedded and IoT development by providing a user-friendly, integrated environment that supports a wide range of hardware platforms and streamlines the development workflow. It is a valuable tool for both beginners and experienced developers working on embedded projects.

To install the PlatformIO extension in VS Code, follow these step-by-step instructions:

1. **Open VS Code**: Launch VS Code on your computer if it is not already open.
2. **Go to extensions**: Click on the square icon on the left sidebar, which is the Extensions icon. Alternatively, you can press *Ctrl+Shift+X* (Windows/Linux) or *Cmd+Shift+X* (macOS) to open the **Extensions** view.

3. **Search for PlatformIO**: In the Extensions view, you will see a search bar at the top. Type **`PlatformIO`** into the search bar and press *Enter*.
8. **Install PlatformIO**: Look for the **PlatformIO IDE** extension in the search results. When you find it, click the **Install** button next to it.
9. **Reload VS Code**: After installation is complete, you will see a **Reload** button next to the **PlatformIO IDE** extension. Click this button to reload VS Code and activate the extension.
10. **Verify installation**: To confirm that PlatformIO is installed correctly, you can go to the **Extensions** view again and ensure that the **PlatformIO IDE** extension is listed as installed. Refer to *Figure 2.7*:

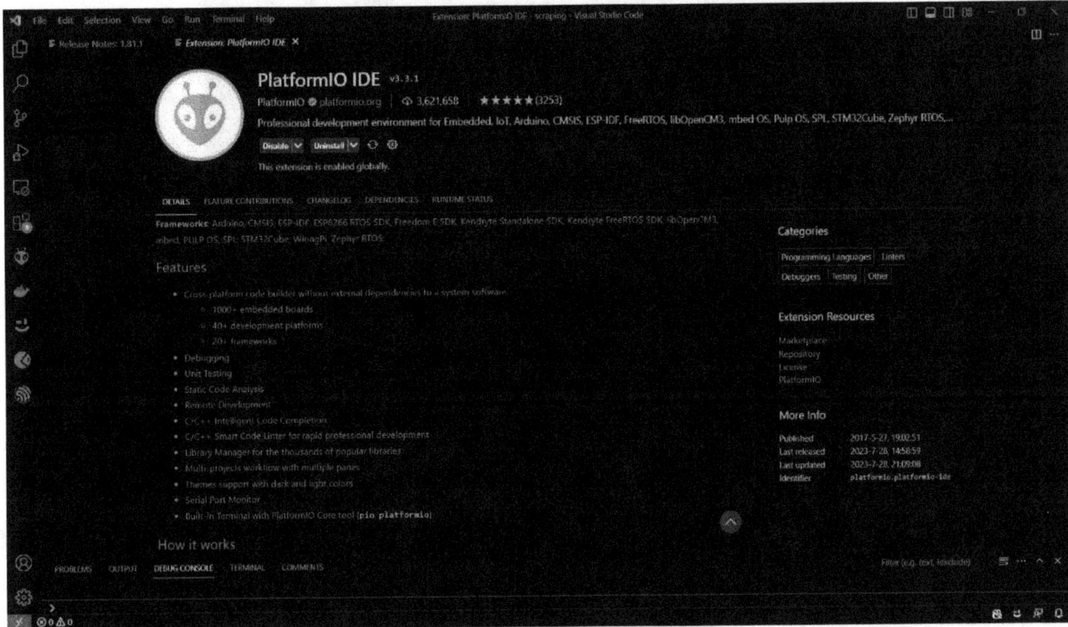

***Figure 2.7:** PlatformIO in VS Code*

Python for embedded development

We will write Python code for building some scripts and small apps on a Raspberry Pi. On the other hand, we will write firmware for embedded devices using CircuitPython.

Python in Raspberry Pi

The Raspberry Pi OS comes with Python preinstalled. We will use **`Python3`**, as **`Python2`** was deprecated years ago. Also, we will use **`pip3`** for managing Python packages.

To verify the version installed in your Raspberry Pi of **`Python3`** and **`pip3`**, run the following commands:

```
$ python3 -version
$ pip3 -version
```

You can see the results of running these commands in *Figure 2.8*:

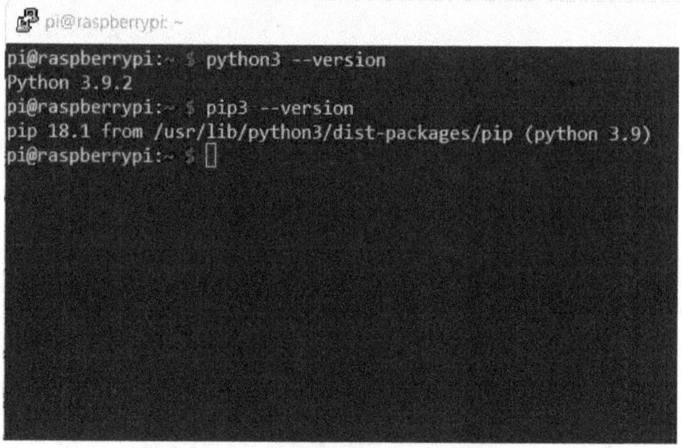

```
pi@raspberrypi: ~
pi@raspberrypi:~ $ python3 --version
Python 3.9.2
pi@raspberrypi:~ $ pip3 --version
pip 18.1 from /usr/lib/python3/dist-packages/pip (python 3.9)
pi@raspberrypi:~ $ 
```

***Figure 2.8**: Python and Pip on Raspberry Pi*

Using virtual environments in Python

Using virtual environments in Python is always a good idea. These are some of the advantages os using virtual environments:

- **Dependency isolation**: Each project has its own set of packages, preventing conflicts between different projects.
- **Reproducibility**: Ensures consistent behavior across different machines by specifying exact package versions.
- **Simplified dependency management**: Allows easy installation, updating, and removal of project-specific packages.
- **Project portability**: Environments can be easily moved or copied to different machines.
- **Clean global environment**: Keeps the system-wide Python installation uncluttered.
- **Easier experimentation**: Facilitates testing with different package versions without affecting other projects.
- **Version control**: Enables control over both package and Python versions for each project.
- **Easy cleanup**: When a project is no longer needed, its environment can be simply deleted.

These benefits contribute to a more organized, maintainable, and reliable Python development process.

To create a virtual environment in Python for a Raspberry Pi 4, follow these brief instructions:

1. Open a terminal window on your Raspberry Pi.
2. Ensure you have the venv module installed by running:

   `$ sudo apt install python3-venv`
3. Navigate to the directory where you want to create your virtual environment. For example:

   `$ cd /your_project_directory`
4. Create the virtual environment by running:

   `$ python3 -m venv --system-site-packages your_env_name`
5. Replace **your_env_name** with a name of your choice, for **example pi_env**
6. Activate the virtual environment:

   `$ source your_env_name/bin/activate`
7. Your terminal prompt should now show the name of your virtual environment, indicating it is active, as shown in the following:

   `(your_env_name) pi@raspberrypi: /your-project-directory $`
8. You can now install packages using **pip** without affecting the system-wide Python installation.
9. To deactivate the virtual environment when you are done, simply type:

   `$ deactivate`
10. Remember to activate the virtual environment each time you want to work on your project.

Running a web app with Python

There are many ways of building a web app with Python. You can choose from several modules and environments.

In this case, we will use one of the most popular modules, Flask.

To install the Flask module, run the following command in the console:

```
$ pip3 install flask
```

After installing Flask, you can start building web apps. Let us start with a simple web page with static content.

1. Use any text editor to create a new file, and use any name you want. In this case, we name it **app.py**. You can build this app on any operating system, but in this case, we are developing it in Raspberry Pi OS. So, we will use **nano** as the text editor.

2. You can run the nano editor by running the following command:

   $ nano app.py

   This will create an **app.py** file and open it. Then, you can copy and paste the code shown in the following.

3. The following code builds a web page showing the text **"Hello, Flask"**:

```
from flask import Flask

# Create an instance of the Flask class
app = Flask(__name__)

# Define a route and the associated function
@app.route('/')
def hello_flask():
    return 'Hello, Flask!'

# Run the Flask application
if __name__ == '__main__':
    app.run(host='YOUR-RASP-IP-ADDRESS', port=8080)
```

   Notice you have to specify the IP address of your Raspberry Pi in the host variable.

4. After pasting the code, press *Ctrl* + *O* to save the file and press *Enter* to confirm. Now you can run the command **ls** to verify that the file was created.

5. Then, run the app using the following command:

   $ python3 app.py

6. You will obtain a text similar to the following:

```
pi@raspberrypi:~ $ python3 app.py
 * Serving Flask app "app" (lazy loading)
 * Environment: production
   WARNING: Do not use the development server in a production environment.
   Use a production WSGI server instead.
 * Debug mode: off
 * Running on http://192.168.0.110:8080/ (Press CTRL+C to quit)
```

7. Then, go to a browser and enter the URL (**http://192.168.0.110:8080/** in the example) of your server app. You will access the webpage with the text **"Hello, Flask!"**.

8. In the Raspberry console, you will see something like the following:

```
192.168.0.17 - - [02/Oct/2023 11:09:51] "GET / HTTP/1.1" 200 -
192.168.0.17 - - [02/Oct/2023 11:09:54] "GET /favicon.ico HTTP/1.1"
404 -
```

If you pay attention to the warning message, you will notice it states that you should avoid using the Flask web server in production environments. You can improve the security of your app by using a production-ready **Web Server Gateway Interface** (**WSGI**) server like Gunicorn, uWSGI, or mod_wsgi to serve your Flask application. These servers are better equipped to handle production traffic and offer features like process management, load balancing, and improved security.

Here is how you can set up Gunicorn, a popular choice, to run your Flask application in a production environment:

1. Install Gunicorn, if it is not already installed by running:

   ```
   $ pip3 install gunicorn
   ```

2. Start your Flask application using Gunicorn. Replace **`your_app`** with the name of your Flask application file (without the **`.py`** extension):

   ```
   $ gunicorn -w 4 -b YOUR_IP:8000 your_app:app
   ```

   Here you have the description of each parameter:

   - **-w 4**: Specifies the number of worker processes. Adjust this number based on the available CPU cores on your server.
   - **-b YOUR_IP:8000**: Binds Gunicorn to listen on the specified interface at port 8000.
   - **your_app:app**: Specifies the name of your Flask application object (**`app`** in this case).

3. Your Flask application will now be served by Gunicorn, which is suitable for production use.

In our case, we can deploy the web application by running the following command from the app's directory.

See the following example and its associated console output:

```
$ gunicorn -w 1 -b 192.168.0.110:8080 app:app
[2023-10-02 12:12:21 -0300] [15687] [INFO] Starting gunicorn 21.2.0
[2023-10-02 12:12:21 -0300] [15687] [INFO] Listening at: http://192.168.0.110:8080
(15687)
[2023-10-02 12:12:21 -0300] [15687] [INFO] Using worker: sync
[2023-10-02 12:12:21 -0300] [15688] [INFO] Booting worker with pid: 15688
```

Pointing your web browser to **http://YOUR-IP-ADDRESS:8080**, you will obtain the same result as before.

Building an app to connect to ChatGPT

Now, let us experiment with a little more sophisticated app. In this case, we will build an app to run ChatGPT prompts.

Note: To run this app, you will need either a paid account on OpenAI or an active trial period.

This app will provide the user interface to enter the prompts. On the other hand, it will use the ChatGPT API to send the prompts and obtain responses from the AI.

Before using the ChatGPT Python module, you have to install it using the following command:

```
$ pip3 install openai
```

Now, you can use the OpenAI module in your app.

However, to use the ChatGPT API, you need to generate an authentication token.

Let us see how to do it step by step:

1. First, login to **https://platform.openai.com/**. You will see a page like that in *Figure 2.9*:

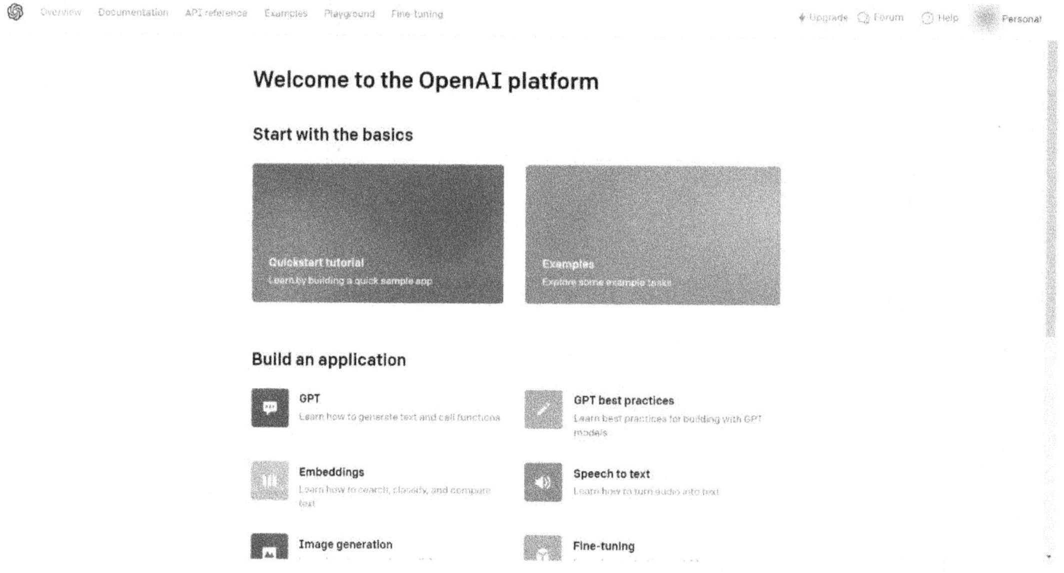

***Figure 2.9**: OpenAI platform*

2. Then, go to your personal menu, on the top left of the page, and click on the **View API keys**. Refer to *Figure 2.10*:

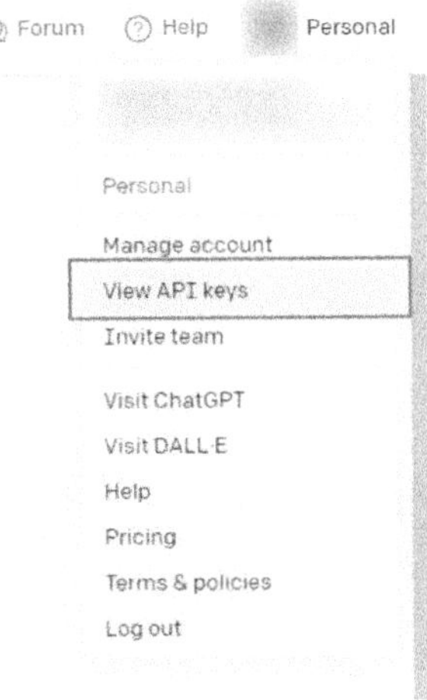

***Figure 2.10**: Click on View API keys*

3. The previous step will lead you to the **API keys** page, where you can see their list. If you have not created any key, the page will only show you the button **Create a new secret key**. Click on it to create a new API key. Refer to *Figure 2.11*:

API keys

Your secret API keys are listed below. Please note that we do not display your secret API keys again after you generate them.

Do not share your API key with others, or expose it in the browser or other client-side code. In order to protect the security of your account, OpenAI may also automatically disable any API key that we've found has leaked publicly.

NAME	KEY	CREATED	LAST USED

+ Create new secret key

Default organization

If you belong to multiple organizations, this setting controls which organization is used by default when making requests with the API keys above.

Personal

Note: You can also specify which organization to use for each API request. See Authentication to learn more.

***Figure 2.11**: Create a new secret key*

4. Enter a name for your key and click on the **Create secret key** button.

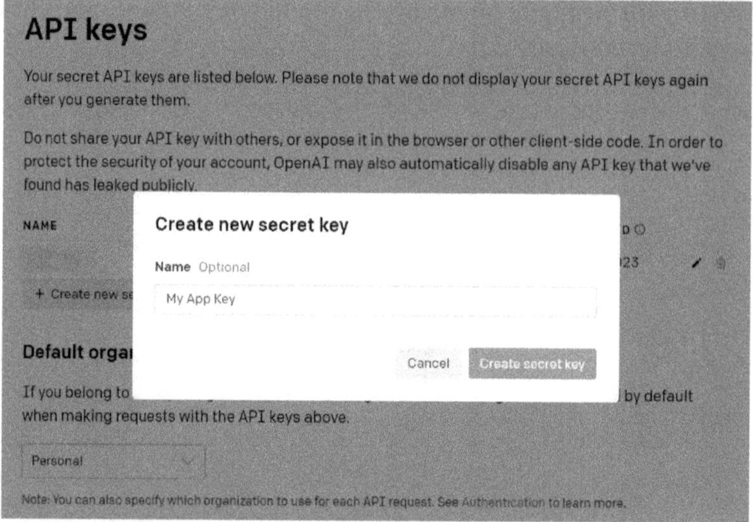

Figure 2.12: Create a new secret key

5. Be sure to copy the secret key, as you will not see it again. Save it in a secure place. Refer to *Figure 2.13*:

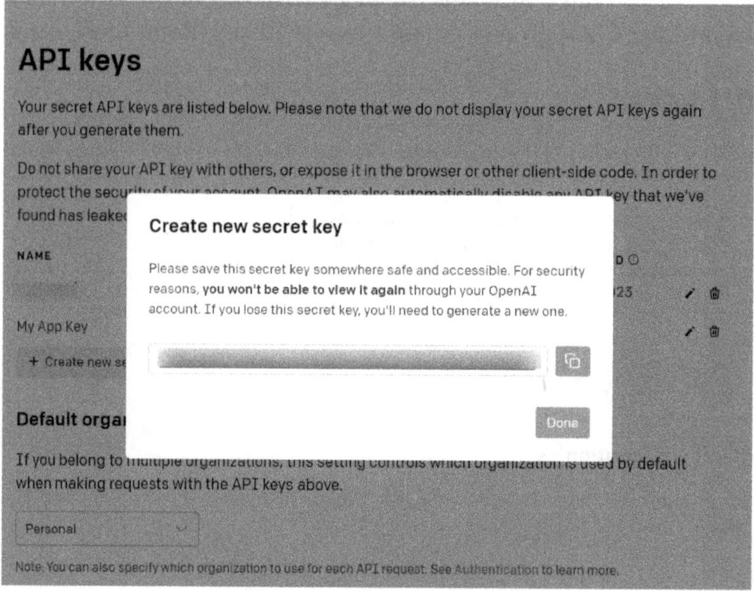

Figure 2.13: Copy the secret key

Now that you already have the secret key from ChatGPT, you can interact with it from your app.

Let us explore the code of our application. You will have to create two files, one for the application (**app.py**), and the other for the web page (**index.html**).

This app needs a directory structure as follows:

```
myproject/
    app.py
    templates/
        index.html
```

Create the **app.py** file and paste the following code:

```
from flask import Flask, render_template, request
import openai

app = Flask(__name__)

# Set your OpenAI API key here
openai.api_key = YOUR-API-KEY'

@app.route('/')
def index():
    return render_template('index.html', chat_history="")

@app.route('/chat', methods=['POST'])
def chat():
    user_message = request.form['user_message']
    chat_history = request.form['chat_history']

    # Append the user's message to the chat history
    chat_history += f"You: {user_message}\n"

    # Make an API call to ChatGPT
    response = openai.chat.completion.create(
        engine="gpt-3.5-turbo",  # Or another engine like "text-davinci-003"
        prompt=chat_history,
        max_tokens=50
    )

    # Append ChatGPT's reply to the chat history
    chat_history += f"ChatGPT: {response.choices[0].text.strip()}\n"
```

```
    return render_template('index.html', chat_history=chat_history)

if __name__ == '__main__':
    app.run(host='YOUR-IP-ADDRESS', port=8080)
```

Then, create an **.html** file in the template directory with the following code.

```
<!DOCTYPE html>
<html>
<head>
    <title>ChatGPT Web Interface</title>
</head>
<body>
    <h1>Chat with ChatGPT</h1>
    <form action="/chat" method="post">
          <textarea name="chat_history" rows="10" cols="50">{{ chat_history
}}</textarea>
        <br>
        <input type="text" name="user_message" placeholder="Your message">
        <input type="submit" value="Send">
    </form>
</body>
</html>
```

Once you have created both files, you can run your app from the project directory using the following command:

```
$ python3 app.py
```

Then, open a web browser and point it to the URL **http://YOUR-IP-ADDRES:8080**

You will obtain a page like the one shown in *Figure 2.14*:

***Figure 2.14**: App for interacting with ChatGPT from your Raspberry Pi*

Reading and writing log files with Python

Now, we will create two Python scripts. One for writing lines in a text file, and another for reading it.

There are certain circumstances where you may want to register some activity in log files. This type of file consists of plain text, where new data is added in a new line.

You can use the scripts provided here to add the log functionality to other scripts. Maybe you want to register successful and unsuccessful connections to a service or save sensor values to keep a local record.

In any case, you can include these scripts in your code with the necessary modifications according to the case.

The following code writes a new line of text to a file:

```
def write_to_file(file_name, data):
    try:
        with open(file_name, 'a') as file:
            file.write(data + '\n')  # Append data to the file with a newline
character
        print(f"Data '{data}' has been successfully written to {file_name}.")
    except Exception as e:
        print(f"An error occurred while writing to the file: {e}")


# Example usage:
data_to_write = "This is some new data."
file_name = "data.txt"
write_to_file(file_name, data_to_write)
```

This code uses the function **`write_to_file()`** to write new data in a text file. Take into consideration that you have to provide the entire path to the file, or run the script from the directory where the file is.

On the other hand, we have the script for reading data from the file:

```
def read_file(file_name):
    try:
        with open(file_name, 'r') as file:
            content = file.read()
            print(f"Contents of {file_name}:\n{content}")
    except FileNotFoundError:
```

```
        print(f"The file '{file_name}' does not exist.")
    except Exception as e:
        print(f"An error occurred while reading the file: {e}")

# Example usage:
file_name = "data.txt"
read_file(file_name)
```

The same execution conditions apply here.

Sending an e-mail using Python

Now, we will use a Python script to send emails. This script can be useful for sending data collected by sensors or sending alarm-related notifications.

You can see the script in the following code block:

```
import os
import sys
import smtplib
from email.mime.text import MIMEText
from dotenv import load_dotenv

# Load environment variables from a .env file
load_dotenv()

def send_email(subject, body, to_email):
    # Create a MIMEText object with the email body
    msg = MIMEText(body)

    # Set the subject, sender, and recipient
    msg[«Subject»] = subject
    msg[«From»] = os.getenv(«SMTP_USERNAME»)
    msg[«To»] = to_email

    # Connect to the SMTP server
    with smtplib.SMTP(os.getenv(«SMTP_SERVER»), int(os.getenv(«SMTP_PORT»)))
as server:
        # Login to the SMTP server (if required)
```

```
#   server.login(os.getenv(«SMTP_USERNAME»), os.getenv(«SMTP_PASSWORD»))

     # Send the email
    server.sendmail(os.getenv("SMTP_USERNAME"), to_email, msg.as_string())

   print(«Email sent successfully to», to_email)

if __name__ == "__main__":
    # Check if all command line arguments are provided
    if len(sys.argv) != 4:
        print(«Usage: python script.py <subject> <body> <destination_email>»)
        sys.exit(1)

    # Extract command line arguments
    subject = sys.argv[1]
    body = sys.argv[2]
    to_email = sys.argv[3]

    # Send the email
    send_email(subject, body, to_email)
```

This code uses environmental variables to specify connection parameters. So you need to create an **.env** file with the following lines.

```
SMTP_SERVER=your_smtp_server
SMTP_PORT=your_smtp_port
SMTP_USERNAME=your_email_address
SMTP_PASSWORD=your_email_password
```

Notice that the Python script and the **.env** file must be in the same directory.

To read the environment file we are using the python-dotenv module. To install it you have to run the following command.

```
$ pip install python-dotenv
```

Once you have the module installed, the script, and the environment file, you can test the program by running the following command.

```
$ python script.py "Your Subject" "Your Email Body" destination@example.com
```

Replace each parameter in the command line with the respective value.

To test this script, you can use many free services available on the internet. For example, you can use the SMTP service hosted at **https://www.wpoven.com/tools/free-smtp-server-for-testing**. This service lets you send emails without authentication. Also, it allows you to read the e-mails on its web, by specifying the destination address.

Take into consideration that this service is only recommended for testing purposes. Also, notice that you probably will not be able to send emails to services like Gmail, as this kind of service does not comply with their security directives.

CircuitPython

CircuitPython was primarily developed and maintained by *Adafruit Industries* (**https://www.adafruit.com**), an open-source hardware company known for its electronics and educational products.

CircuitPython is a user-friendly way to program and interact with hardware. It simplifies the process of working with microcontrollers, allowing you to focus more on your projects and less on complex programming details. With CircuitPython, you can write code in Python, a language known for its simplicity and readability, making it accessible even if you are new to programming.

CircuitPython includes pre-written code for various sensors, displays, and other hardware components. This means you do not have to start from scratch when working on your projects. You can easily import libraries to use in your code, saving you time and effort.

You can reach the CircuitPython repository at **https://github.com/adafruit/circuitpython** and a bundle of libraries and code examples at **https://github.com/adafruit/Adafruit_CircuitPython_Bundle**.

Furthermore, CircuitPython provides a convenient way to interact with your microcontroller through a serial connection. This means you can write and upload code directly to your hardware, making it a breeze to iterate on your projects and see immediate results.

Also, you can program your microcontrollers using CircuitPython directly from VS Code by installing the extension. Let us see how to install it.

Installing CircuitPython extension in VS Code

To install the CircuitPython extension in VS Code, follow these step-by-step instructions:

1. **Open VS Code**: Launch VS Code on your computer.
2. **Access the Extensions view**: You can do this by clicking on the square icon on the left sidebar or by pressing *Ctrl+Shift+X* (or *Cmd+Shift+X* on Mac) to open the **Extensions** view.
3. **Search for the CircuitPython extension**: In the **Extensions** view, there is a search bar at the top. Type `CircuitPython` into the search bar and press *Enter*.

4. **Install the extension**: Locate the **CircuitPython** extension in the search results and click the **Install** button next to it. Wait for the installation process to be completed. Refer to *Figure 2.9*.
5. **Restart VS Code (if prompted)**: Sometimes, VS Code will ask you to restart to complete the installation. If you see a prompt to do so, click the **Restart** button.

We will use this extension in the following chapters.

MicroPython

MicroPython is similar to CircuitPython. It offers a lightweight and efficient implementation of the Python 3 programming language that is designed to run on microcontrollers and small embedded systems.

With MicroPython, you can write code to control hardware components and interact with sensors, making it a great choice for IoT projects and other embedded systems. You will appreciate how it simplifies the process of coding for microcontrollers, as it does not require as much memory or processing power as traditional Python.

MicroPython is compatible with a wide range of microcontroller boards, making it a versatile choice for programming various embedded systems.

Some of the popular microcontroller boards that you can program with MicroPython include ESP8266, ESP32, Arduino-compatible boards (for example, Adafruit Feather M0), Raspberry Pi Pico, BBC micro:bit, Pyboard series, STM32 boards, Adafruit CircuitPython boards (for example, Circuit Playground Express), M5Stack, NodeMCU, etc.

In most cases, you will need to install the MicroPython firmware on your microcontroller board or device to use MicroPython. The firmware is a specialized software image that enables the microcontroller to interpret and run Python code.

PyMakr

One of the best ways to use MicroPython is by employing PyMakr.

PyMakr is a VS Code extension that you can use to easily develop and manage MicroPython projects on your compatible microcontroller boards. With PyMakr, you can upload code, manage files, and interact with your MicroPython-enabled devices.

To install PyMakr in VS Code, follow these steps:

1. **Open VS Code**: Launch VS Code on your computer if it is not already open.
2. **Navigate to Extensions**: Click on the **Extensions** icon located in the **Activity** bar on the side of the window (it looks like four squares).
3. **Search for PyMakr**: In the **Extensions** view, you will see a search bar at the top. Type `PyMakr` into the search bar and press *Enter*.

4. **Find and install PyMakr**: Look for the **PyMakr** extension in the search results. It is the one developed by Pycom. Click the **Install** button next to it.
5. **Wait for installation**: VS Code will download and install the PyMakr extension. You may need to wait a moment for the installation process to be completed.
6. **Activate PyMakr**: After installation, you will see an **Activate** button next to the **PyMakr** extension. Click this button to activate PyMakr.
7. **Restart VS Code**: To ensure that the extension is fully integrated, it is a good idea to restart VS Code. Close and reopen the application.

That is all for now regarding MicroPython. We will see detailed instructions on how to use MicroPython in our projects in the following chapters.

Conclusion

In this chapter, we saw all the software tools we will use in this book. This includes Arduino and VS Code with its extensions. This covers all the basic software and packages we need to start. However, in the following chapters, we will install additional libraries to build our projects. Also, we saw some examples of Python that you can build on your Raspberry Pi or any system that supports Python.

In the next chapter, we will start working with microcontrollers, sensors, and actuators.

CHAPTER 3
Microcontrollers, Sensors, and Actuators

Introduction

In this chapter, we will learn about different types of sensors and actuators and how to use them with microcontrollers.

We will explore the features of sensors by classifying them by measurement, interface, and characteristics.

Regarding actuators, we will learn about relays and motor drives.

You will learn how to interface and use some sensors and actuators with microcontrollers. We will use both MicroPython and Arduino for programming the devices.

Structure

The structure of this chapter is as follows:

- Sensors
- Actuators
- Basic projects with microcontrollers

Objectives

By the end of this chapter you will get an overview of sensors and actuators. The readers will know the features involved in the selection of sensors, connecting and using sensors and actuators with microcontrollers and implementing sensor applications using both MicroPython and Arduino.

Sensors

Sensors play a vital role in modern electronics, enabling microcontrollers to gather data from the physical world. Whether it is monitoring temperature, measuring humidity, detecting motion, or capturing light levels, sensors are the eyes and ears of microcontroller-based systems. In this section, we will explore different types of sensors, categorizing them based on the type of measurement, interface, and their unique characteristics.

Types of sensors by measurement

There are uncountable types of sensors to measure a wide range of variables: temperature, humidity, light, sound, PH, motion, voltage, current, etc.

We will use some of these sensors to build our projects.

Temperature sensors

Temperature sensors are among the most common types used with microcontrollers. They measure temperature, making them essential for climate control, industrial processes, and weather stations.

Here are some key types of temperature sensors:

- **Thermocouples**: These sensors work based on the Seebeck effect and are known for their wide temperature range and high accuracy. They are commonly used in aerospace, industrial applications, air conditioning systems, food processing, etc.
- **Resistance Temperature Detectors** (**RTDs**): RTDs rely on the change in electrical resistance with temperature and are known for their stability and precision. They are commonly used in laboratories, pharmacy, medical devices, automotive industry, environmental monitoring, etc.
- **Thermistors**: Thermistors are semiconductor-based sensors that vary their resistance significantly with temperature, providing a cost-effective option for temperature sensing. They are commonly used in the thermal management of electronics, home appliances, the automotive industry, refrigeration systems, medical applications, etc.

Humidity sensors

Humidity sensors, also known as hygrometers, measure the moisture content in the air. They find applications in climate control, agriculture, and industrial processes. Common types include:

- **Capacitive humidity sensors**: These sensors use changes in capacitance to measure humidity. Capacitive humidity sensors are known for their high accuracy, wide measurement range, and low power consumption, making them suitable for various applications, especially where precision is essential. However, they can be sensitive to contaminants.
- **Resistive humidity sensors**: Similar to thermistors, resistive humidity sensors change resistance with moisture levels and are cost-effective solutions for humidity monitoring. Resistive humidity sensors, are more robust than capacitive sensors and can handle extreme conditions but may sacrifice some accuracy and have slower response times.
- **Chemical humidity sensors**: Chemical humidity sensors, often referred to as chemo-resistive or chemo-capacitive humidity sensors, are a distinct category of humidity sensors that measure **relative humidity** (**RH**) by detecting changes in the electrical properties of certain materials in response to moisture absorption or desorption. Chemical humidity sensors offer high sensitivity and customization options but may require calibration and have limited measurement ranges. They are suitable for a range of applications where precise humidity measurements are essential and can be particularly advantageous in scenarios requiring compact, low-power, and cost-effective solutions.

Pressure sensors

Pressure sensors gauge pressure variations, critical for applications like weather forecasting, altitude measurements, and industrial processes.

They can be categorized into:

- **Piezoelectric sensors**: Piezoelectric sensors are a specialized type of sensor that harness the piezoelectric effect to measure mechanical changes or vibrations in their environment. The piezoelectric effect is the property of certain materials to generate an electrical charge or voltage in response to mechanical deformation or stress. Piezoelectric sensors typically consist of a piezoelectric crystal or material, such as quartz or certain ceramics, sandwiched between electrodes. Some applications are high-pressure measurements, ultrasonic sensors, acoustic sensors, vibration sensors, energy harvesting, impact sensors, etc.
- **Strain gauge pressure sensors**: Strain gauge pressure sensors, also known as resistive pressure sensors, rely on the deformation of materials under pressure to measure changes in electrical resistance. As pressure is applied to the sensor, the material experiences strain, causing a proportional change in resistance. This

change in resistance is then converted into a pressure measurement. Strain gauge sensors offer accuracy and long-term stability, making them suitable for a wide range of industrial and automotive applications.

- **Piezoresistive sensors**: Piezoresistive sensors are a type of sensor that uses piezoresistors, which are materials that change their electrical resistance when subjected to mechanical stress. Unlike strain gauges, which typically measure deformation in a material, piezoresistive sensors are often used to directly measure forces or pressures applied to them. These sensors contain piezoresistive materials, usually doped silicon, which change resistance when pressure or force is applied. These sensors are typically used to measure atmospheric pressure and altitude.

Light sensors

Light sensors, also known as photodetectors or photodiodes, detect light intensity or illumination levels. They find applications in ambient light control, distance sensors, obstacle sensors, optical communication, etc.

Notable types include:

- **Photovoltaic cells**: A photovoltaic sensor, often referred to as a solar cell or photodiode, is a semiconductor device that converts light energy into electrical energy when exposed to photons (light particles). The fundamental principle behind photovoltaic sensors is the photovoltaic effect, which generates a voltage and current in response to incident light. These sensors typically consist of a semiconductor material, such as silicon, with p-n junctions. As you may guess, solar panels are built with this type of material. They are also used for light-sensing applications, like light management.
- **Phototransistors**: A phototransistor sensor is a type of photosensitive transistor that amplifies the current generated by incident light. It is a semiconductor device with three layers: the emitter, base, and collector. Phototransistors are used to detect and amplify light signals, making them suitable for various applications where light intensity needs to be converted into an electrical signal. Typical uses are optoisolators, optical switches, proximity sensors, remote control receivers, light barriers, etc.

Motion sensors

Motion sensors are designed to detect movement, making them integral for security systems, gaming controllers, and automated lighting.

They can be divided into:

- **Passive infrared (PIR) sensors**: PIR sensors are motion sensors that detect changes in infrared radiation emitted by objects within their field of view. These sensors are commonly used for detecting human or animal motion and are widely employed in various applications, particularly in security systems and automatic lighting control. PIR sensors operate based on the principle that all objects with a temperature above absolute zero emit infrared radiation. PIR sensors contain one or more passive infrared detectors, typically pyroelectric materials or sensors, which are sensitive to changes in infrared radiation. Typical uses are security systems, automatic lighting control, smart home devices, occupancy sensing, etc.

- **Ultrasonic sensors**: Ultrasonic sensors are devices that use sound waves at frequencies higher than the upper limit of human hearing (typically above 20,000 Hz) to measure distances and detect objects. They use sound waves to determine the distance to an object by measuring the time it takes for sound to bounce back. These sensors are commonly used for proximity sensing, object detection, and distance measurement in a variety of applications. Many animals, like bats and dolphings, use ultrasonic sensing for navigating.

Types of sensors by interface

The interface of a sensor determines how it communicates with a microcontroller. Different interfaces cater to various applications and system requirements. Let us see some of them.

Analog sensors

Analog sensors provide a continuous output signal proportional to the measured quantity. Microcontrollers can read this analog signal using **analog-to-digital converters** (**ADCs**). Examples include thermistors, piezoelectric sensors, and resistive humidity sensors. Refer to *Figure 3.1* for an illustration of the concept:

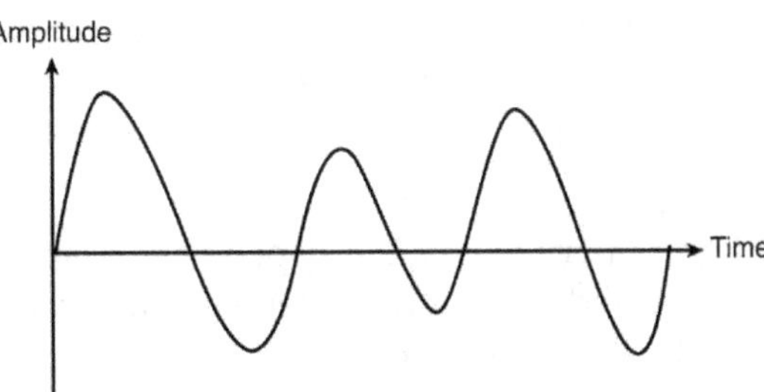

***Figure 3.1**: Example of analog signal*

Digital sensors

Digital sensors, on the other hand, provide a discrete digital signal representing the measured quantity. They are straightforward to interface with microcontrollers, providing binary states (ON/OFF, 0/1, True/False). These states are associated with specific voltage levels, depending on the working voltage range of the microcontroller. The most common digital sensors are buttons, switches, door sensors, position sensors, etc.

Inter-Integrated Circuit sensors

Inter-Integrated Circuit (**I2C**) is a popular communication protocol for sensors. I2C sensors use a two-wire serial bus to transmit data to the microcontroller. This interface is commonly employed in sensors like digital temperature and humidity sensors, accelerometers, and gyroscopes.

Serial Peripheral Interface sensors

Serial Peripheral Interface (**SPI**) is another common digital communication protocol for sensors. SPI sensors use multiple wires to transmit data, offering high-speed and full-duplex communication. Accelerometers, pressure sensors, and some motion sensors often use SPI.

1-Wire sensors

1-Wire sensors are a type of digital sensor communication protocol developed by *Dallas Semiconductor* (now Maxim Integrated) that allows multiple sensors to communicate with a microcontroller or host device using just a single data wire. This communication protocol simplifies wiring and reduces the number of pins needed on the microcontroller, making it a convenient choice for various sensor applications.

Characteristics of sensors

Each sensor has unique characteristics that influence its suitability for specific applications. Here are some important characteristics to consider:

- **Measurement range**: The measurement range defines the minimum and maximum values a sensor can accurately measure. For instance, a temperature sensor may have a range of -40°C to 125°C, making it suitable for both extremely cold and hot environments.
- **Accuracy**: Accuracy is a crucial factor, especially in applications where precise measurements are required. Sensor datasheets often specify accuracy in terms of a percentage of the full-scale measurement.
- **Resolution**: Resolution is a crucial characteristic of sensors because it directly impacts the accuracy and reliability of the data they provide. Higher-resolution sensors are capable of detecting smaller changes in the measured quantity, which means they can provide more precise and detailed information.

  For example, consider a temperature sensor with high resolution. It can detect even minute temperature variations, such as fractions of a degree Celsius. This level of precision is valuable in applications where precise temperature control or monitoring is essential, such as in scientific research, industrial processes, or medical devices.

- **Sensitivity**: Sensitivity indicates how much the sensor's output changes in response to a change in the measured quantity. High-sensitivity sensors are capable of detecting subtle changes but may also be more susceptible to noise.
- **Linearity**: Linearity measures how closely a sensor's response follows a straight line when the input varies linearly. A perfectly linear sensor provides an output directly proportional to the input.
- **Isolation**: Isolation is crucial in applications where electrical separation is necessary to prevent interference or protect the microcontroller. Some sensors, like optocouplers, provide electrical isolation.
- **Response time**: Response time is the time it takes for a sensor to react to a change in the measured quantity. Fast response times are essential in dynamic applications, while slower responses may be acceptable in stable environments.
- **Repeatability**: Repeatability is a key characteristic of a sensor that measures its ability to produce consistent and consistent results when exposed to the same input or measurement conditions over multiple trials. In essence, repeatability assesses the sensor's ability to provide nearly identical measurements or responses when the same input or stimulus is applied repeatedly. The repeatability is a crucial factor in gas sensors, whose characteristics vary over time.

Sensors are essential components in microcontroller-based systems, enabling them to interact with the physical world. Understanding the different types of sensors based on their measurement, interface, and characteristics is crucial for selecting the right sensor for your specific application. Whether you need to measure temperature, humidity, pressure, light, or motion, there is likely a sensor that fits your requirements, allowing your microcontroller-based project to gather valuable data and respond intelligently to its environment.

Actuators

Actuators are devices that convert electrical signals from microcontrollers into physical motion, making them a crucial component in various electronic and automation systems. There are several types of actuators commonly used with microcontrollers, each with its characteristics and applications.

Let us see the types of actuators we will use in this book.

Electromagnetic relays

Electromagnetic relays are switches that use an electromagnet to open or close electrical contacts when a control signal is applied. They are commonly used for high-power applications such as controlling motors, heaters, and lights. They provide electrical isolation between the microcontroller and the load, making them suitable for controlling high-voltage and high-current devices.

They can be noisy due to the mechanical switching action and have a limited switching speed.

Solid State Relays

Solid State Relays (**SSRs**) are semiconductor devices that perform the same switching function as electromagnetic relays but without moving parts. They use optocouplers and power semiconductor devices to isolate and control the load. They are quieter, faster, and have a longer lifespan compared to electromagnetic relays. They are often used for applications requiring high-speed switching, such as in industrial automation and temperature control systems.

Motor drivers

Motor drivers are specialized actuators designed to control the speed and direction of electric motors. They come in various configurations, including H-bridge, L298N, and stepper motor drivers. They are essential for robotics, CNC machines, drones, and other systems that involve motor control. They can handle various types of motors, including DC motors, stepper motors, and **brushless DC** (**BLDC**) motors.

Basic projects with microcontrollers

In this section, we will start working with microcontrollers, digital sensors, and some actuators. These projects will allow us to understand the basic concepts behind embedded systems.

We will program the microcontrollers using MicroPython and Arduino. For MicroPython, we will use **Visual Studio Code** (**VS Code**), and the Arduino IDE.

You will start blinking an LED. Then you will learn about interfacing ON/OFF sensors, actuators, and 1-Wire devices.

Also, we will see how to read an analog sensor, control a relay, and manage a motor driver.

Using MicroPython in Raspberry Pi Pico

In this section, we will work on some small projects with Raspberry Pi Pico and MicroPython. We will use VS Code and the Pymakr extension to program the microcontroller. However, first, let us prepare our microcontroller and the software environment.

Installing the MicroPython firmware

To be able to run MicroPython code in any microcontroller, you need first to install the corresponding firmware.

Let us see the steps to do it:

1. **Get the MicroPython firmware**: Download the MicroPython firmware for the Raspberry Pi Pico from the official website (**https://micropython.org/download/rp2-pico/**). Choose the appropriate version and select the UF2 format.
2. **Prepare the Raspberry Pi Pico**: Connect your Pico to your computer using a USB cable. Put your Pico into Boot mode by holding down the **BOOTSEL** button while plugging it in. See *Figure 3.1*.
3. **Flash the Firmware**: Use the UF2 method (drag and drop the firmware UF2 file onto the Pico's USB drive). The Pico will automatically restart with MicroPython.
4. **Access the MicroPython REPL**: After flashing the firmware, you can access the MicroPython **Read-Eval-Print Loop** (**REPL**) by opening a terminal on your computer and connecting to the Pico's serial port (usually named something like `/dev/ttyACM0` on Linux or COMx on Windows). We will use the terminal included in VSC to do this.

Accessing the microcontroller from VS Code

For programming the microcontroller from VS Code, follow these steps:

1. After installing the firmware, open VS Code and click on the **Pymakr** extension on the left panel. Refer to *Figure 3.2*.
2. You may see some serial ports available. Select the one that corresponds to the microcontroller.

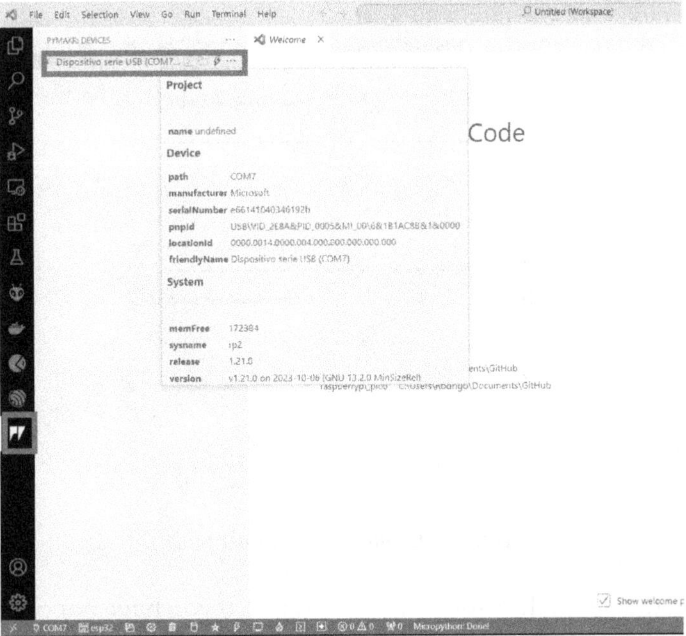

Figure 3.2: Device view in Pymakr VS Code

3. Now, you can connect to the microcontroller to be able to program and debug it. For that, just click on the lightning icon, as shown in *Figure 3.3*:

Figure 3.3: *Connecting to the microcontroller from VS Code*

4. Now that we have connected to our microcontroller that hosts the MicroPython firmware, we can start to program it.

Creating a new project

To create a new project, go to the top dialog box in VS Code and click on **Show** and **Run** commands. This will list all the available commands. Then type **`Pymakr`** to filter them.

Finally, select **Create new project**, as shown in *Figure 3.4*:

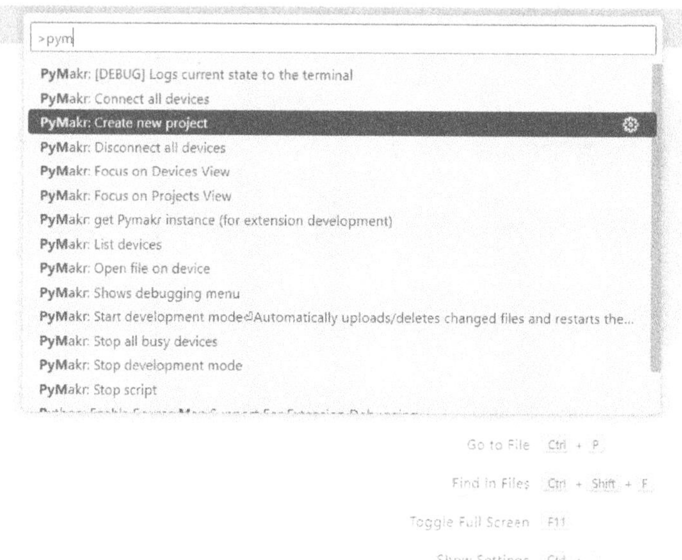

Figure 3.4: *Create a new PyMakr project*

This will lead you to select a directory for your project. If you have not created the directory, you should do it now.

Now that we have created a project, let us start by blinking an LED.

Blinking a LED

You now have a new project and the Raspberry Pi Pico connected to the environment.

Create a new file (**main.py**) in your project directory and add the following code.

```
import machine
import time

led_pin = machine.Pin('LED', machine.Pin.OUT)
while True:
    led_pin.value(1)
    print("Turning ON...")
    time.sleep(1)
    led_pin.value(0)
    print("Turning OFF...")
    time.sleep(1)
```

You may have noticed we used the LED constant to specify the address of the onboard LED pin. This constant is defined in the **picozero.py** file, inside the microcontroller memory. You can see this in *Figure 3.5*:

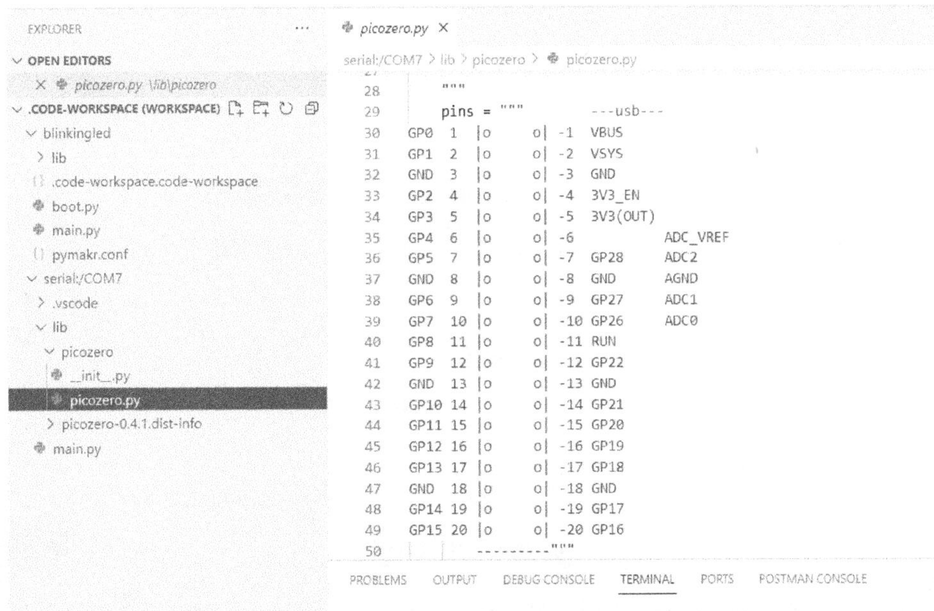

Figure 3.5: *Raspberry Pi objects*

Now, you can upload the **main.py** file to the microcontroller. To do this, go to the **Pymakr** panel and click on **Sync project to device**, as shown in *Figure 3.6:*

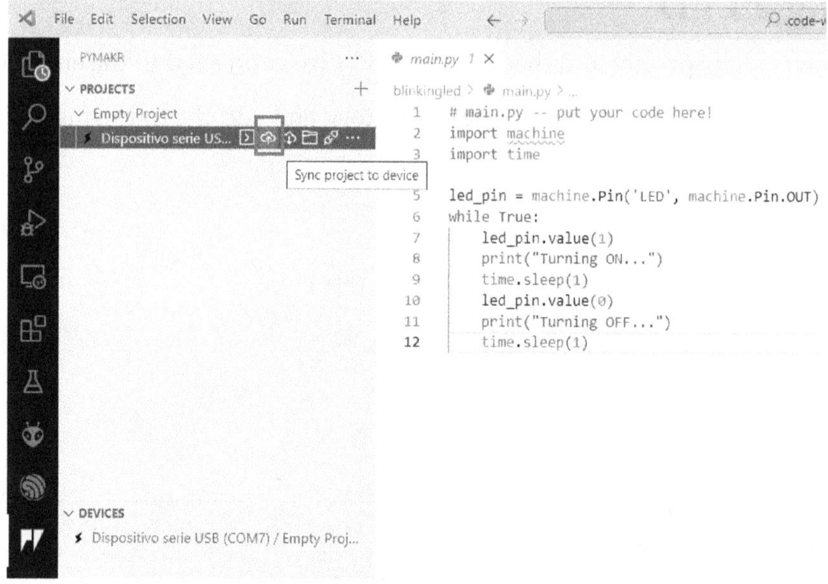

Figure 3.6: Uploading the project to the device

Now, perform a hard reset to make the microcontroller run the script. Refer to *Figure 3.7*:

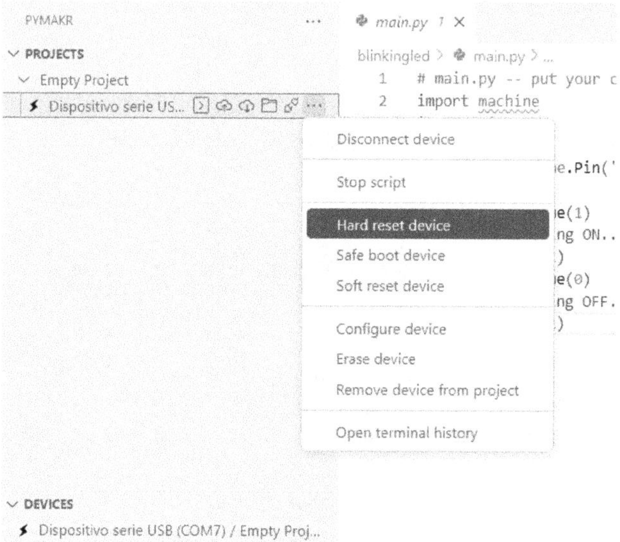

Figure 3.7: Hard reset

After rebooting, the microcontroller will start to run the program. You can connect to it to see the messages printed in the console. Refer to *Figure 3.8*:

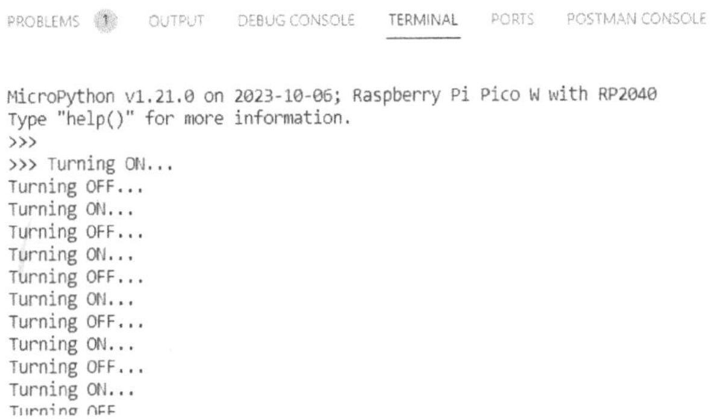

```
PROBLEMS 1   OUTPUT   DEBUG CONSOLE   TERMINAL   PORTS   POSTMAN CONSOLE

MicroPython v1.21.0 on 2023-10-06; Raspberry Pi Pico W with RP2040
Type "help()" for more information.
>>>
>>> Turning ON...
Turning OFF...
Turning ON...
Turning OFF...
Turning ON...
Turning OFF...
Turning ON...
Turning OFF...
Turning ON...
Turning OFF...
Turning ON...
Turning OFF
```

Figure 3.8: *Console messages*

This simple project taught us to create and deploy a MicroPython project using VS Code and Pymakr. In the following sections, we will use the same procedure to build other projects.

Using ON/OFF sensors

ON/OFF sensors, from a microcontroller's perspective, are sensors that provide binary or digital information typically represented as two distinct states: ON (high or logical 1) and OFF (low or logical 0).

These sensors are fundamental in digital electronics and microcontroller-based systems as they simplify the interpretation of sensor data, making it easy to implement decision-making logic. To understand these sensors better, it is essential to consider voltage levels and pull-up/pull-down configurations.

Voltage levels

The ON and OFF states are determined by the voltage levels of the pin:

- **ON state (High)**: In a microcontroller context, the ON state usually corresponds to a voltage level that is interpreted as **high** or **1** by the microcontroller. This voltage level is typically close to the microcontroller's supply voltage (Vcc). For a standard digital logic system using 5V logic, an ON state might be represented as a voltage close to 5V. The same logic applies to other Vcc voltages, like the commonly used 3.3 V.
- **OFF state (Low)**: Conversely, the OFF state corresponds to a voltage level that is interpreted as **low** or **0** by the microcontroller. In digital logic systems, this voltage level is close to 0V or ground (GND).

Refer to *Figure 3.9* for an example of OFF and ON states:

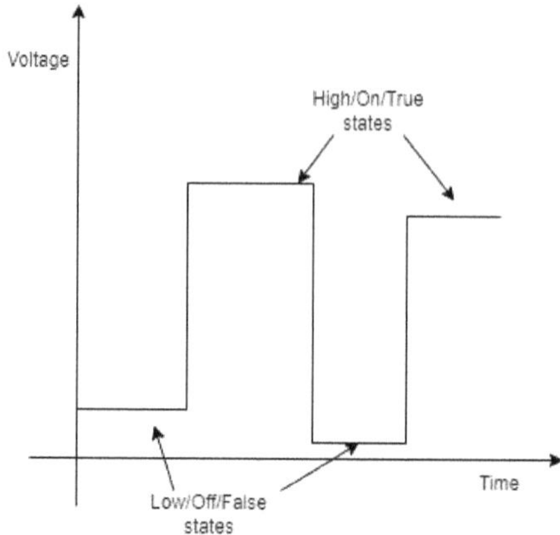

Figure 3.9: Logic states

Pull-up and pull-down configurations

The concept of pull-up and pull-down configurations is essential when working with ON/OFF sensors. These configurations ensure that the voltage level at the sensor's output is well-defined when the sensor is not actively driving it.

Let us see each of them:

- **Pull-up configuration**: In a pull-up configuration, a resistor (typically called a pull-up resistor) is connected between the sensor output and Vcc. When the sensor is in its OFF state (open or not actively driving the output), the pull-up resistor pulls the voltage level at the sensor output to Vcc, which corresponds to the OFF state (logical 0) as interpreted by the microcontroller. See *Figure 3.8*.
- **Pull-down configuration**: In a pull-down configuration, a resistor (known as a pull-down resistor) is connected between the sensor output and ground (GND). When the sensor is in its OFF state, the pull-down resistor pulls the voltage level at the sensor output to the ground, which represents the OFF state (logical 0) to the microcontroller. Refer to *Figure 3.10*:

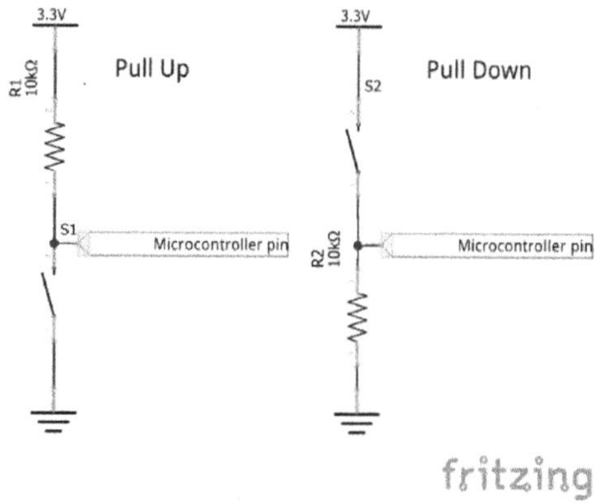

Figure 3.10: Pull-up and pull-down configurations

From a microcontroller's perspective, ON/OFF sensors with clear voltage levels and pull-up/pull-down configurations simplify the interface and data interpretation, allowing the microcontroller to make logical decisions based on the sensor's state with ease. These sensors are fundamental in numerous applications, from simple button interfaces to complex industrial control systems.

In general, it is a good practice to add pull resistors to ON/OFF sensors. However, many microcontrollers have internal pull resistors. This is the case of Raspberry Pi Pico. So, in the following example, we will not use pull resistors.

Polling versus interrupt

Polling and interrupt techniques are two common methods for obtaining values from on/off sensors connected to a microcontroller. These techniques differ in how they interact with sensors and handle sensor data.

Here is a description of each technique:

- **Polling technique**: Polling is a method in which the microcontroller periodically checks the state of the sensor to determine if it has changed. It involves the microcontroller repeatedly querying the sensor to see if there is a transition from the OFF state to the ON state or vice versa.
- **Interrupt technique**: Interrupts are signals sent by a sensor to the microcontroller when the sensor's state changes. Instead of actively checking the sensor, the microcontroller waits for an interrupt signal from the sensor. When the sensor experiences a change, it generates an interrupt to notify the microcontroller.

The choice between polling and interrupt techniques depends on factors such as the sensor's characteristics, application requirements, and the microcontroller's capabilities. In some cases, a combination of both techniques is used to optimize resource utilization and responsiveness. Polling is suitable for simple, low-demand applications, while interrupts are preferred for responsive, resource-efficient, and time-critical applications.

You can see the hardware configuration in *Figure 3.11*:

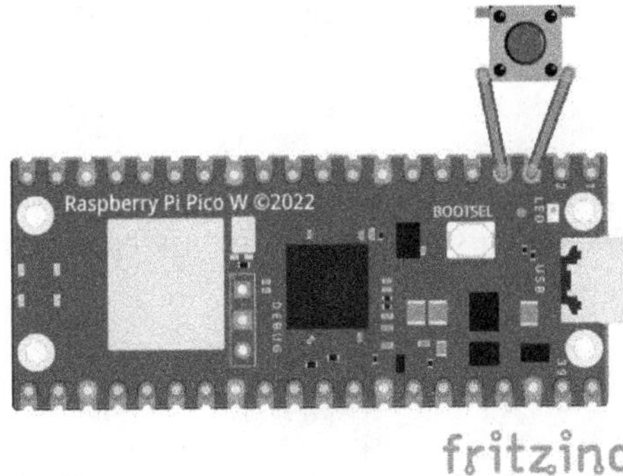

***Figure 3.11**: Button connected to Raspberry Pi Pico W*

Now that we know about pull-up/pull-down and polling/interrupt configurations, let us start coding.

Sensing a button with the polling technique

The code in the following shows a simple routine for polling the pin where the button is connected:

```
# Import necessary modules
from machine import Pin  # For hardware pin control
from time import sleep   # For introducing delays

# Initialize the LED pin as an output
led = Pin('LED', Pin.OUT)

# Initialize the push button pin as an input (connected to GPIO pin 2)
push_button = Pin(2, Pin.IN)

# Enter an infinite loop for continuous monitoring
while True:
    # Read the current state of the push button
    logic_state = push_button.value()

    # Check if the push button is pressed (logic_state is True)
    if logic_state == True:
        # Turn the LED on (set LED pin to 1)
        led.value(1)
    else:
         # If the push button is not pressed, turn the LED off (set LED pin
to 0)
        led.value(0)
```

Notice that the LED will turn off every time you press the button, and it will remain on while the button is not pressed. This is because we are connecting the input pin to GND, as you can see in *Figure 3.9*.

Bouncing effect

In the context of switches or buttons, bouncing, also known as switch bounce or button bounce, refers to a temporary and unintended fluctuation in the electrical contact state when the switch or button is actuated (pressed or released). This phenomenon occurs due to the physical characteristics of mechanical switches and their inherent electrical properties.

When a switch is physically pressed or released, the mechanical components inside the switch (such as the contacts or springs) undergo a rapid but temporary series of make-break connections. These mechanical movements can cause the electrical contacts to physically oscillate and make and break contact multiple times in a very short duration (milliseconds).

Also, the rapid and unintended contact closures and openings during bouncing generate electrical noise, leading to multiple electrical pulses or transients. These pulses can be misinterpreted by electronic circuits, such as microcontrollers, as multiple button presses or releases when, in reality, there was only one.

Bouncing can lead to erratic or unreliable behavior in applications that rely on accurate and stable switch input.

To address switch bouncing, debouncing techniques are employed. These techniques aim to eliminate or mitigate the effects of switch bounce and ensure that only a single, clean transition is recognized.

Debouncing can be achieved through hardware solutions (using capacitors, resistors, or special debouncing components) or software techniques (adding delay or filtering to the switch signal).

To handle switch bounce in digital systems, developers often use software debouncing routines or components:

- Software debouncing may involve adding a small delay after a switch state change to ensure that the bouncing settles before the state is read. We will use this technique in our code.
- Alternatively, digital filters can be used to smooth out the transitions in the switch signal.

Refer to the following code with the debouncing delay:

```
from machine import Pin
from time import sleep_ms

led = Pin('LED', Pin.OUT)
push_button = Pin(2, Pin.IN)

# Initialize variables for debounce
button_state = push_button.value()  # Initial state
debounce_delay = 50  # Adjust as needed (in milliseconds)
```

```
while True:
    # Read the current state of the push button
    current_state = push_button.value()

    # Check if the current state is different from the previous state
    if current_state != button_state:
        # Introduce a debounce delay
        sleep_ms(debounce_delay)

        # Read the button state again after the delay
        current_state = push_button.value()

        # If it remains the same, update the LED
        if current_state == button_state:
            if current_state == 1:
                led.value(0)  # Turn off the LED
            else:
                led.value(1)  # Turn on the LED

    # Update the previous state
    button_state = current_state
```

Sensing a button with interruptions

Now, let us see how we can get button states using interruptions in MicroPython.

The following code shows how to do it. The code uses the same hardware connection as with the previous example.

```
from machine import Pin
import time

led = Pin('LED', Pin.OUT)
push_button = Pin(2, Pin.IN, Pin.PULL_UP)  # Configure pull-up resistor

# Initialize a variable to track button press events
button_pressed = False
```

```
# Define an interrupt callback function
def button_callback(pin):
    global button_pressed
    button_pressed = True

# Attach the callback to the button's falling edge (button press)
push_button.irq(trigger=Pin.IRQ_FALLING, handler=button_callback)

while True:
    if button_pressed:
        # Turn on the LED
        led.value(1)
        button_pressed = False  # Reset the flag
        time.sleep(1)  # Add a delay to avoid rapid LED flicker
    else:
        # Turn off the LED
        led.value(0)
```

With this code, every time you press the button, the LED will light on for a second, and then it will light off.

Until here, we have learned a lot about dealing with buttons and microcontrollers. From hardware configurations to software techniques, we have covered the most important aspects of ON/OFF sensors.

Now, let us see how to connect and use analog sensors.

Reading an analog sensor

In this project, we will use a variable resistor (a potentiometer) to generate an analog signal. See *Figure 3.12*.

The potentiometer is connected between GND and 3.3 V, while the variable pin is connected to GPIO 26 of the microcontroller. The GPIO 26 corresponds to ADC0, which is the channel zero of the analog-to-digital converter of the Raspberry Pi Pico.

With this configuration, every time you move the knob of the potentiometer, you are changing the voltage of the middle pin. If the variable resistor has a linear characteristic, the change in the output voltage will follow a linear variation too.

As the ADC of the Raspberry Pi Pico has 12 bits of resolution, you will obtain a range of 0 to 4095 values. Then, to convert the number to the corresponding voltage, you have to apply the following formula:

$$Vout = Vcc * N/R$$

Where *Vcc* is the supply voltage, *N* is the number obtained by the *ADC*, and *R* is the *ADC* resolution.

So, if we have *Vcc* = 3.3 V, N = 1024, and *R* = 4096, the voltage measured by the ADC is calculated as follows:

$$Vout = 3.3\,V * \frac{1024}{4096} = 0.825\,V$$

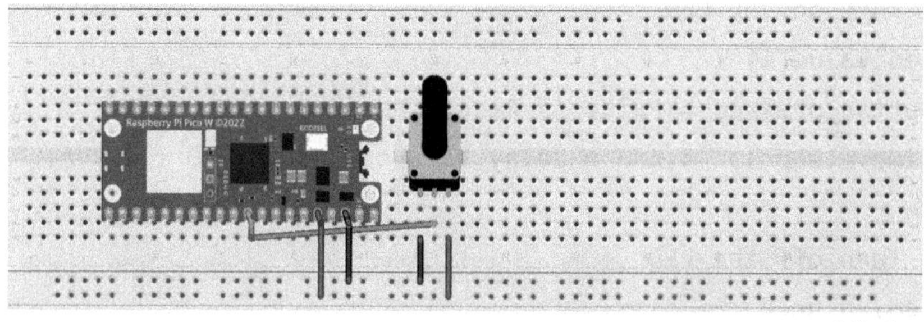

***Figure 3.12:** Connecting a variable resistor to Raspberry Pi Pico*

In the following, you can see the code implementing the reading of the analog value and its conversion to a voltage value:

```
import machine
import time

# Initialize the ADC (Analog-to-Digital Converter)
adc = machine.ADC(machine.Pin(26))  # Use the appropriate GPIO pin number

# Main loop for reading and printing the analog value
while True:
    # Read the analog value (0-4095 for 12-bit ADC)
    analog_value = adc.read()

    # Calculate the voltage measured using the formula
    voltage_measured = (3.3 * analog_value) / 4096
```

```
    # Print the analog value and the calculated voltage
    print("Analog Value:", analog_value)
    print("Voltage Measured (V):", voltage_measured)

    # Add a delay to control the reading frequency
    time.sleep(1)  # You can adjust the delay as needed
```

Reading a 1-Wire temperature sensor

In this project, we will obtain temperature values from a DS18B20 sensor.

The DS18B20 is a popular and widely used digital temperature sensor that utilizes the 1-Wire protocol for communication. It is known for its accuracy, versatility, and ease of integration into various projects.

The DS18B20 communicates with the host device (for example, a microcontroller) using the 1-Wire protocol. This protocol allows multiple DS18B20 sensors to be connected in parallel on a single data line, making it suitable for multi-sensor applications.

These sensors are known for their high accuracy in temperature measurement. They can provide temperature readings with a resolution of up to 12 bits, offering precision of +/- 0.5 °C in the range of -55°C to 125°C.

Each DS18B20 sensor has a unique 64-bit ROM code that distinguishes it from other sensors on the same bus. This feature allows you to identify a sensor in multi-sensor setups.

Other interesting characteristics of these sensors are the package. They come in various packaging options, including TO-92 (similar to a transistor package) and waterproof versions. The waterproof version is often used in applications where the sensor needs to be submerged in liquid or exposed to harsh environments.

These sensors are known for their low power consumption, making them suitable for battery-powered and low-power applications.

You can use the DS18B20 in **Internet of Things** (**IoT**) projects, environmental monitoring, temperature control systems, and embedded systems where accurate temperature measurements are required.

The integration of these sensors is easy, as there are many libraries available for Arduino, MicroPython, CircuitPython, and many other platforms and languages.

In *Figure 3.13*, you can see the connection diagram of a DS18B20 to the Raspberry Pi Pico:

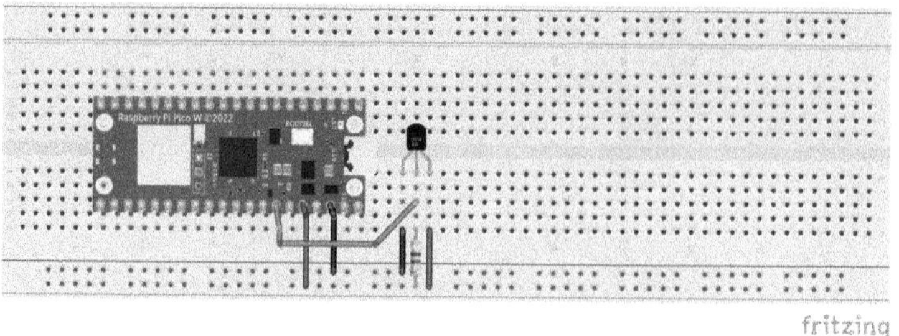

Figure 3.13: DS18B20 connection. Red = VCC, Black = GND, Blue = Signal.

In the case that you are using the waterproof version of the sensor, the pins are connected as shown in *Figure 3.14*:

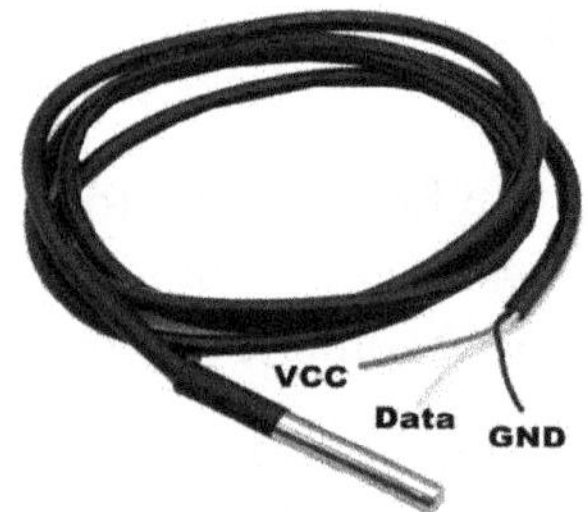

Figure 3.14: Pins connections for the waterproof version of DS18B20

Pull-up resistor

The resistor connected between the signal line and VCC (power supply) in the DS18B20 temperature sensor circuit is called a pull-up resistor. Its use is crucial for the proper functioning of the 1-Wire communication protocol used by the DS18B20.

The following is the purpose of the pull-up resistor:

- **Idle state definition**: The pull-up resistor ensures that the data line remains in a known state (high) when no device is actively driving it low.
- **Open-drain configuration**: The DS18B20 uses an open-drain (or open-collector) output, which can only pull the line low or leave it floating. The pull-up resistor provides the means to pull the line high when needed.
- **Signal integrity**: It helps maintain signal integrity by providing a defined high level and reducing noise susceptibility on the data line.
- **Multiple device support**: The pull-up resistor allows multiple 1-Wire devices to be connected to the same bus without signal conflicts.
- **Recommended value**: The datasheet typically recommends a 4.7kΩ resistor, though values between 4.7kΩ and 5kΩ are generally acceptable.

The following MicroPython code reads all the DS18B20 sensors connected to the microcontroller and shows the values in the console:

```
import time
from machine import Pin
from onewire import OneWire
from ds18x20 import DS18X20

# Define the 1-Wire bus pin (replace with your actual GPIO pin)
ow_pin = Pin(12)  # Example: Pin 12 is used as the 1-Wire data pin

# Create a OneWire bus object
ow = OneWire(ow_pin)

# Create a DS18X20 temperature sensor object
ds = DS18X20(ow)

# Scan for available DS18B20 sensors on the bus
roms = ds.scan()

if not roms:
    print("No DS18B20 sensors found")
else:
    print(f"Found {len(roms)} DS18B20 sensor(s)")

# Main loop to read and display temperature
while True:
    for rom in roms:
        ds.convert_temp()
        time.sleep_ms(750)
        temp_c = ds.read_temp(rom)
        temp_f = (temp_c * 9.0 / 5.0) + 32.0 #Convert to Farenheit
       print(f"Sensor {rom} - Temperature: {temp_c:.2f}°C | {temp_f:.2f}°F")
    time.sleep(5)  # Adjust the delay as needed
```

This code will discover all the sensors connected to the microcontroller, so you do not have to know the address of each sensor. Also, if you change or add a new sensor, the script will discover it automatically.

Using MicroPython with other boards

Until here, we have used MicroPython to program a Raspberry Pi Pico microcontroller. However, the same code that we have used is valid for other boards under the following considerations:

- Change the pin numbers according to the microcontroller you are using.
- Take note of hardware characteristics, like voltage supply, clock frequency, etc.
- Pay attention to the interfacing options of the microcontroller, like serial communications, number of ADC channels, resolution of ADC, etc.
- Consider the type and amount of memory available to store the program and additional data.

There may be further considerations beyond the ones listed before. However, they are the most important for most basic microcontroller projects. We will explore these topics more in deep in the following chapters.

Using Arduino with Raspberry Pi Pico

Now, let us see how we can program the Raspberry Pi Pico by using the Arduino IDE.

To be able to program the Raspberry Pi Pico from the Arduino IDE, we first need to add the board libraries to Arduino.

To do this, copy the following URL: **https://github.com/earlephilhower/arduino-pico/releases/download/global/package_rp2040_index.json**

Now, open the **Arduino IDE** and go to the **Preferences** option in the **File** menu. Then, paste the URL to the box **Additional boards manager URLs**, as shown in *Figure 3.15*, and click **OK**.

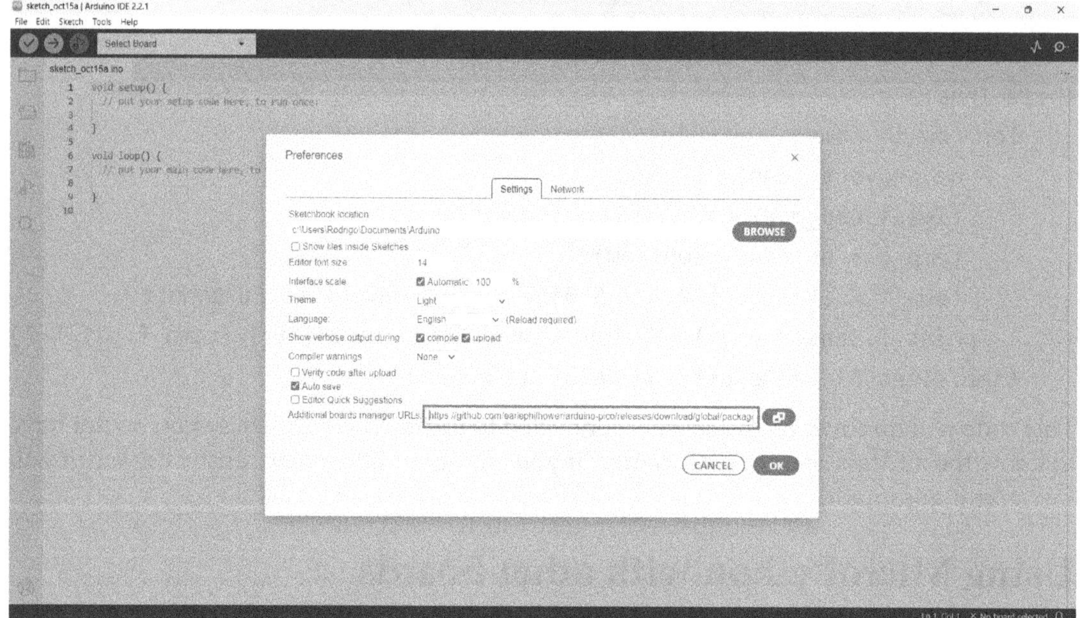

***Figure 3.15:** Adding the board to Arduino*

Now, go to the board manager on the left panel of the Arduino IDE, and search for Raspberry. You will find several board packages. Select the one that says Raspberry Pi Pico/RP2040 by *Earl F. Philhower*, as shown in *Figure 3.16*:

Note: All the examples in this book use the 2.x version of the Arduino IDE.

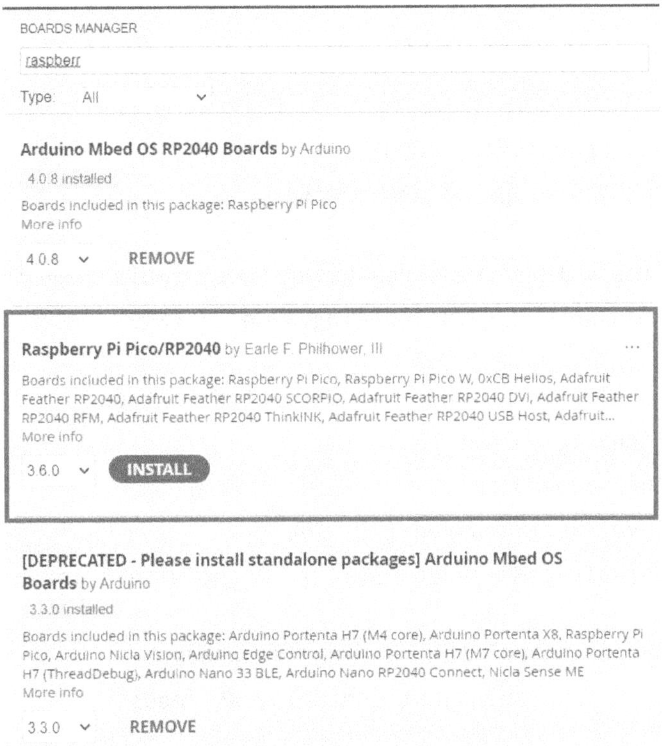

BOARDS MANAGER

raspberr

Type: All

Arduino Mbed OS RP2040 Boards by Arduino

4.0.8 installed

Boards included in this package: Raspberry Pi Pico

More info

4.0.8 REMOVE

Raspberry Pi Pico/RP2040 by Earle F. Philhower, III

Boards included in this package: Raspberry Pi Pico, Raspberry Pi Pico W, 0xCB Helios, Adafruit Feather RP2040, Adafruit Feather RP2040 SCORPIO, Adafruit Feather RP2040 DVI, Adafruit Feather RP2040 RFM, Adafruit Feather RP2040 ThinkINK, Adafruit Feather RP2040 USB Host, Adafruit...

More info

3.6.0 INSTALL

[DEPRECATED - Please install standalone packages] Arduino Mbed OS Boards by Arduino

3.3.0 installed

Boards included in this package: Arduino Portenta H7 (M4 core), Arduino Portenta X8, Raspberry Pi Pico, Arduino Nicla Vision, Arduino Edge Control, Arduino Portenta H7 (M7 core), Arduino Portenta H7 (ThreadDebug), Arduino Nano 33 BLE, Arduino Nano RP2040 Connect, Nicla Sense ME

More info

3.3.0 REMOVE

Figure 3.16: *Installing the board package*

Now, you have the required package to program a variety of boards based on the RP2040.

Reading an analog sensor

We will start by reading an analog sensor. You can use the same hardware configuration shown in *Figure 3.10*.

All the calculations and assumptions we used for the MicroPython project are still valid. This is because the theory is the same, and we are just changing the programming language.

```
// Define the analog pin for reading
const int analogPin = 26;

void setup() {
```

```
  // Initialize the serial communication for output
  Serial.begin(9600);

  // Set the ADC resolution to 12 bits (0-4095)
  analogReadResolution(12);
}

void loop() {
  // Read the analog value (0-4095)
  int analogValue = analogRead(analogPin);

  // Calculate the voltage measured using the formula
  float voltageMeasured = (5.0 * analogValue) / 4096;

  // Print the analog value and the calculated voltage
  Serial.print("Analog Value: ");
  Serial.println(analogValue);
  Serial.print("Voltage Measured (V): ");
  Serial.println(voltageMeasured, 3);  // Print with 3 decimal places

  // Add a delay to control the reading frequency
  delay(1000);  // You can adjust the delay as needed
}
```

Notice that we set the ADC resolution using the instruction **`analogReadResolution(12)`**. This is because Arduino uses a default setting of 10 bits.

Using Arduino with ESP8266 and ESP32

To be able to use ESP8266 and ESP32 devices, we need to add some board packages to the Arduino IDE, as we did with RP2040.

The procedure is the same as we did for the Raspberry Pi Pico.

1. Add **http://arduino.esp8266.com/stable/package_esp8266com_index.json** and **https://raw.githubusercontent.com/espressif/arduino-esp32/gh-pages/package_esp32_index.json** to the Addition board manager URLs.

   As you already have a board, to add these two click on the right button for a better user experience. See *Figure 3.17:*

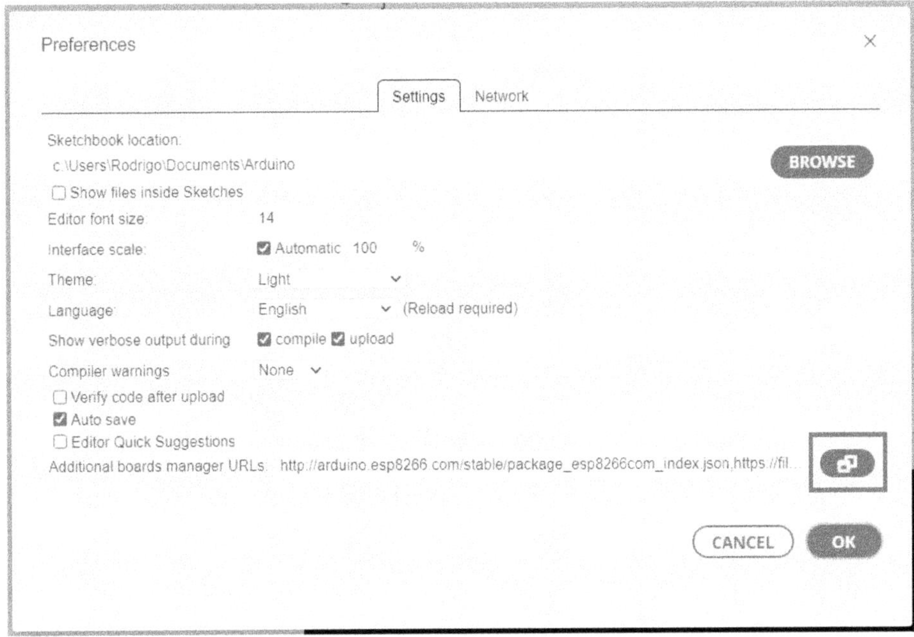

Figure 3.17: Add new boards to Arduino

2. This will open a new window with a text box. You can add the two URLs using a new line for each of them, as shown in *Figure 3.18*:

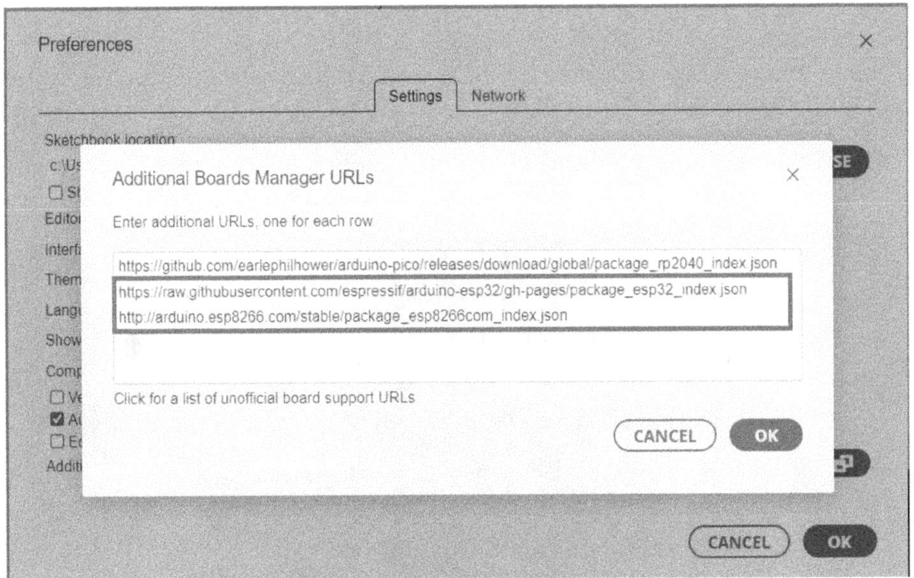

Figure 3.18: Adding the URLs

3. After adding the URLs, the packages from these devices will be available to download, as you can see in *Figure 3.19*:

Figure 3.19: ESP boards packages in Arduino IDE

4. Click on the buttons to install the packages and you will be able to use them in the Arduino IDE.

Now, we will use these microcontrollers to build the last two projects of this chapter.

Controlling a relay

In this project, we will control a relay from an ESP8266 device.

Many boards use the ESP8266 microcontroller. Also, there are many versions of the ESP8266.

You will have to adapt the code and the hardware configuration to your specific board. However, all the instructions depicted here are valid for any board and microcontroller.

In this case, we are using a NodeMCU board. This is a very popular and cheap board based on the ESP8266. You can see the pinout of the NodeMCU in *Figure 3.20*:

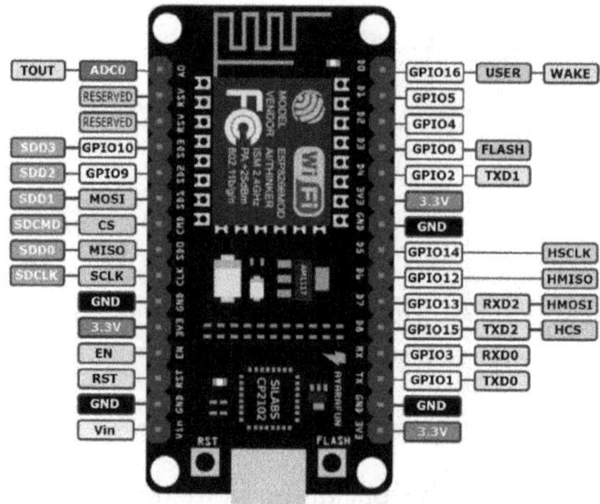

Figure 3.20: Pinout of NodeMCU

We are using the pin D8, which corresponds to GPIO 15, to control the relay.

On the other hand, we are feeding the NodeMCU using the Vin pin. This pin goes to the voltage regulator included in the board. We can apply a wide range of voltages here.

As you can see in *Figure 3.20* and *Figure 3.21*, you can use a voltage converter or batteries to feed both the board and the relay. It is important to consider the power supply here because the coil of the relay consumes quite a lot of energy when you enable it.

Notice that the input signal of the relay goes to an optocoupled switch, which in turn, activates the coil. So, even when the microcontroller can provide the current to enable the optocoupler, you need a high current to feed the coil of the relay.

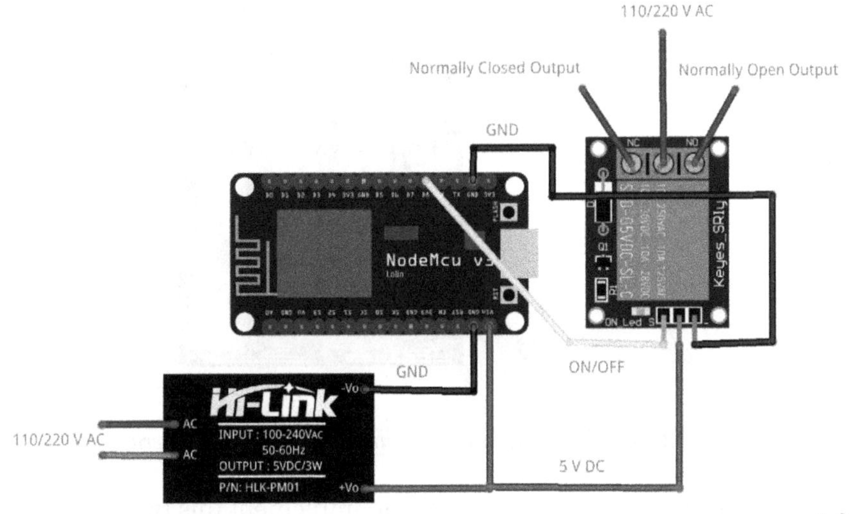

***Figure 3.21**: Feeding the relay and the microcontroller with a power converter*

Selecting the type of power source depends on the type of device or project you are developing. For example, if you want to control a light connected to the power mains, you may use a power converter. On the other hand, if you want to control a remote appliance, the battery-powered device will be a better option.

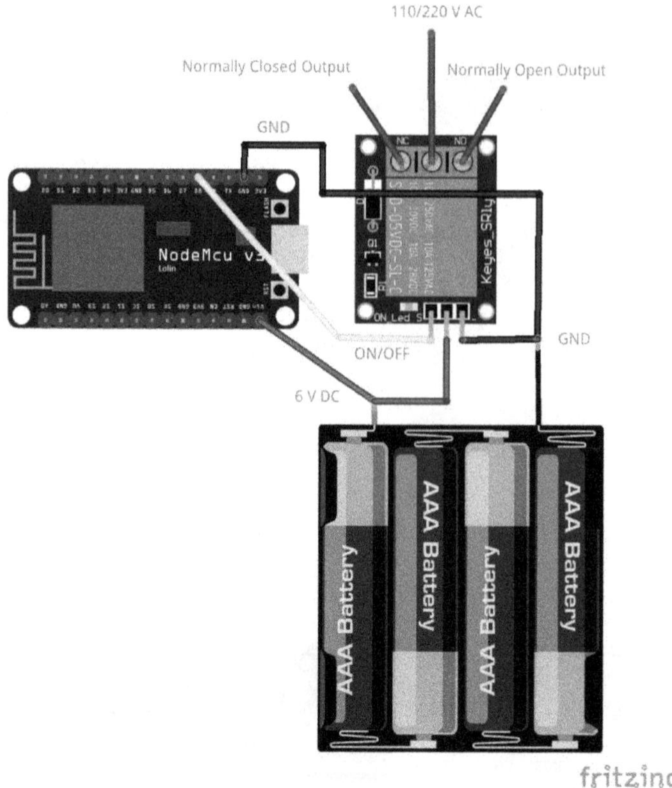

Figure 3.22: Feeding the relay and the microcontroller with batteries

Now that we have the circuit, let us see the code to implement this project.

```
// Define the GPIO pin connected to the relay module
const int relayPin = 15;  // Use the appropriate GPIO pin

void setup() {
  // Set the relayPin as an OUTPUT
  pinMode(relayPin, OUTPUT);

  // Initialize the relay in the OFF state
  digitalWrite(relayPin, LOW);
}

void loop() {
  // Turn the relay ON (close the switch) for 2 seconds
  digitalWrite(relayPin, HIGH);
```

```
  delay(2000);

  // Turn the relay OFF (open the switch) for 2 seconds
  digitalWrite(relayPin, LOW);
  delay(2000);
}
```

The next project is the last of this chapter. We will see what a motor driver is and how to use it.

Controlling a motor driver

As we have seen in the first section of this book, a motor driver is a circuit that allows us to control motors in a precise way.

In this project, we will use the popular L298N to control a **direct current** (**DC**) motor. You can see the circuit in *Figure 3.23*:

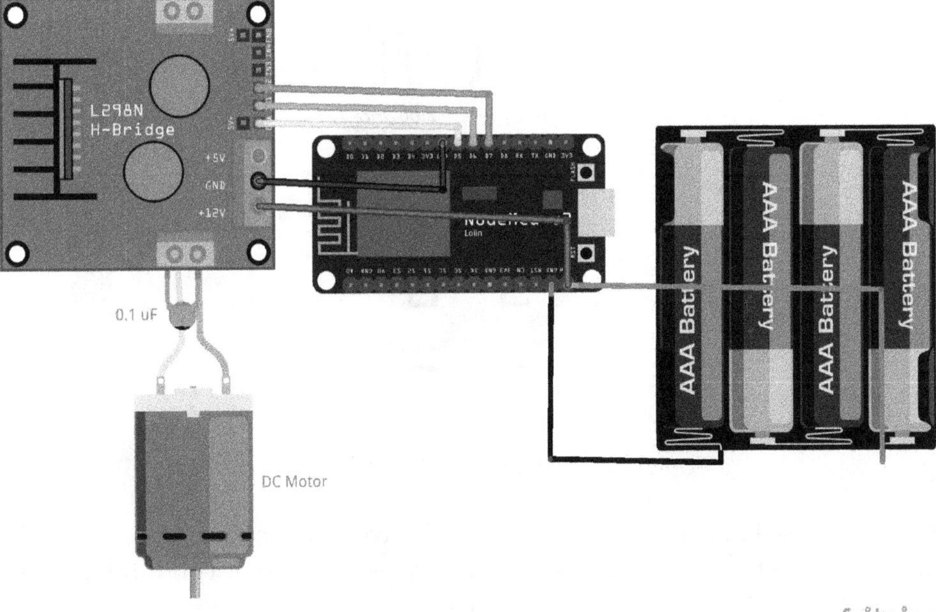

Figure 3.23*: Motor control with L298N and NodeMCU*

The L298N is a dual H-bridge motor driver that you can use to control two DC motors.

Before going to the code, let us see what **Pulse-Width Modulation** (**PWM**) is.

PWM is a technique used to modulate or control the average voltage level of a DC signal by rapidly switching it on and off at a fixed frequency. The width of the "on" or "high" portion of each cycle, known as the duty cycle, determines the average voltage applied to the load, allowing for precise control of the output.

PWM uses a rapid ON-OFF switching. The input voltage is switched on and off at a high frequency. This switching occurs in cycles, with each cycle consisting of a fixed period.

The duty cycle is the ratio of the time the signal is in the "on" state to the total cycle time. It is typically expressed as a percentage. For example, a 50% duty cycle means the signal is on for half of the cycle time.

By varying the duty cycle, you can control the average voltage applied to the load. A higher duty cycle results in a higher average voltage, while a lower duty cycle results in a lower average voltage. You can see several examples of PWM signals with different duty cycles in *Figure 3.24*. Notice that the duty cycle in Arduino varies from 0 to 255.

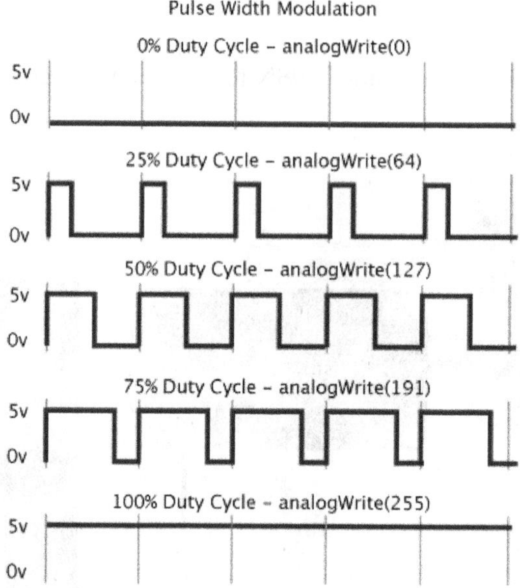

***Figure 3.24**: PWM signals with different duty cycles*

PWM is widely used in applications where precise control of motor speed, light intensity, and other parameters is required. It is commonly used in motor control, LED dimming, audio amplifiers, and many other applications.

PWM offers several advantages, including efficiency, precise control, and minimal heat generation. It is particularly effective for controlling devices that require variable power levels.

PWM typically operates at a fixed and high frequency, which is much higher than what the human eye or ear can perceive. This constant switching creates the illusion of varying voltage levels.

In some applications, a low-pass filter is used to smooth out the PWM signal, effectively converting it into an analog-like voltage. This filtered output is used to control the load, resulting in a stable and controlled response. In *Figure 3.23,* you can see that a ceramic capacitor was added to filter out high-frequency signals.

The following Arduino code lets you perform a basic control of a motor driver.

```
// Motor A connections
const int enableA = 14;  // Enable pin for motor A
const int in1 = 12;      // Input 1 for motor A
const int in2 = 13;      // Input 2 for motor A

void setup() {
  // Define the motor control pins as OUTPUT
  pinMode(enableA, OUTPUT);
  pinMode(in1, OUTPUT);
  pinMode(in2, OUTPUT);

  // Initialize the motor control pins
  digitalWrite(in1, LOW);
  digitalWrite(in2, LOW);

  // Enable the motor by applying a PWM signal to the enable pin
  analogWrite(enableA, 255);  // 255 is full speed; you can adjust it
}

void loop() {
  // Move the motor forward
  digitalWrite(in1, HIGH);
  digitalWrite(in2, LOW);
  delay(2000);  // Run for 2 seconds

  // Stop the motor
  digitalWrite(in1, LOW);
  digitalWrite(in2, LOW);
  delay(1000);  // Pause for 1 second

  // Move the motor backward
```

```
  digitalWrite(in1, LOW);
  digitalWrite(in2, HIGH);
  delay(2000);  // Run for 2 seconds

  // Stop the motor
  digitalWrite(in1, LOW);
  digitalWrite(in2, LOW);
  delay(1000);  // Pause for 1 second
}
```

Conclusions

In this chapter, we have learned about many topics. Firstly, we saw the different types of sensors available, classifying them by measurements, interfaces, and characteristics. Then we learned how to use MicroPython, building many sensor projects using the Raspberry Pi Pico. We also saw some examples using the Arduino IDE.

We learned about interfacing sensors, using pull-up and pull-down configurations, 1-Wire connections, and ADC calculations. Finally, we built two actuator projects using the NodeMCU board, a relay, and a DC motor driver. This was an extensive chapter, where we learned a lot about microcontrollers, sensors, actuators, connections, and programming.

In the next chapter, we will explore the GPIO pins, their functions, and how to harness their potential to interact with various sensors and actuators.

Join our book's Discord space

Join the book's Discord Workspace for Latest updates, Offers, Tech happenings around the world, New Release and Sessions with the Authors:

https://discord.bpbonline.com

Chapter 4
Interfacing with Raspberry Pi

Introduction

One of the key features that makes the Raspberry Pi so adaptable is its **general-purpose input/output** (**GPIO**) pins. These pins provide a means to interface with sensors and actuators, opening the door to endless possibilities for monitoring and controlling the physical world.

In this chapter, we will explore the GPIO pins, their functions, and how to harness their potential to interact with various sensors and actuators. You will discover that by combining the computing power of the Raspberry Pi with the sensory capabilities of external devices, you can create innovative solutions, automate tasks, and collect data for analysis.

Throughout this chapter, we will focus on using Python as the primary programming language. We will cover different methods and techniques to ensure you have a comprehensive understanding of how to integrate sensors into your Raspberry Pi projects.

Structure

The chapter covers the following topics:

- Raspberry Pi GPIO
- Using the filesystem to access the GPIOs

- Controlling GPIO with Python
- Using Node-RED

Objectives

By the end of this chapter, you will know how to interface with the Raspberry Pi computer by using many tools. First, you will see how to interact with the GPIO from the command line by using *Sysfs* and *libgpiod*. Then, you will learn to write scripts in C by using libgpiod to manage the pins of the Raspberry Pi. Also, you will write scripts using the RPi.GPIO library. This will let you control the GPIOs using Python. The last section of the chapter teaches you how to read and write pin states using Node-RED. Also, you will learn to export and import flows in Node-RED.

Raspberry Pi GPIO

In *Chapter 1, Meet the Boards,* we saw the fundamentals of Raspberry Pi pins. Let us remember the GPIO configuration. The pinout of the Raspberry Pi is shown in *Figure 4.1*:

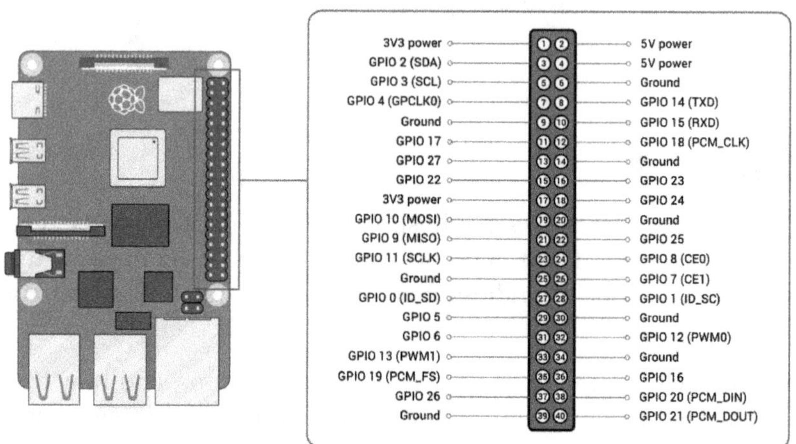

***Figure 4.1:** Raspberry Pi GPIO*
(Source: raspberrypi.org)

Refer to *Chapter 1, Meet the Boards,* for a detailed description of pins. In the following sections, we will see how to interact with and control the Raspberry Pi's GPIO.

Numbering GPIO

Figure 4.1 shows that the pin numbers on the board do not match the actual GPIO numbers.

The GPIO numbers indicated on both sides of the header correspond to the microprocessor chip. They are called **BCM pin numbers** because the chip is manufactured by *Broadcom*.

So, whenever you specify a pin number in Raspberry Pi, you must use this numbering.

Using the filesystem to access the GPIOs

You can manage the Raspberry Pi GPIOs by using the Linux filesystem. But before doing that, let us see the kernel space and the user space.

Kernel space and user space

In the Linux operating system, there are two distinct memory spaces: kernel space and user space. The Linux kernel operates in a protected area called **kernel space**, while regular user applications run in the user space.

A strict separation between these spaces serves several essential purposes:

- **Security**: It prevents user applications from accessing memory and resources required by the Linux kernel, safeguarding critical system components from unintended interference.
- **Stability**: The division prevents the Linux kernel from crashing due to poorly written or malfunctioning user code. Kernel space is isolated from user space, so one issue does not affect the other.
- **Isolation**: It ensures that one user's applications cannot interfere with another user's. This isolation is crucial in multi-user environments to maintain the integrity of each user's environment.

You can see the user and kernel space diagram in *Figure 4.2*:

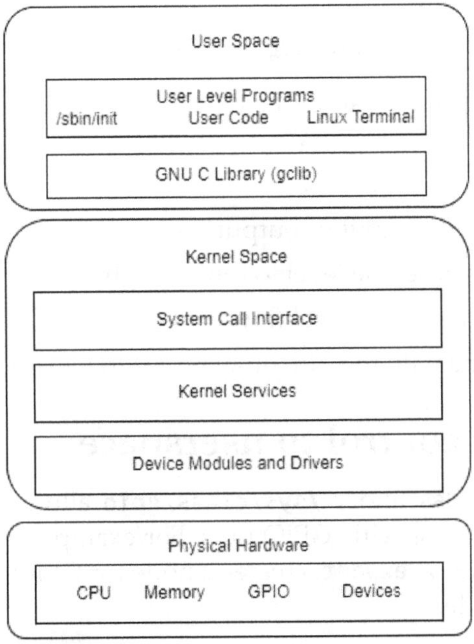

***Figure 4.2**: User and Kernel Space in Linux*

Using Sysfs

You can use Sysfs to access and control the Raspberry Pi's GPIO. However, Sysfs is a legacy system, and newer Linux kernels offer a better option. Anyway, we will see how to use Sysfs as it is still used.

Sysfs is a pseudo-filesystem in the Linux kernel that provides an interface to kernel data structures. It exposes a structured representation of kernel objects in a file-based hierarchy. This allows userspace applications to interact with and retrieve information about devices, kernel modules, filesystems, and other kernel components in a user-friendly manner.

Sysfs structure

Sysfs organizes kernel objects into a structured hierarchy. In the context of GPIO control, paths like `/sys/class/gpio` provide control interfaces to manage GPIO pins and GPIO controllers (known as `gpio_chip` instances). Each GPIO signal typically has the following paths:

- **/sys/class/gpio/gpioN/direction**: Reads as either *in* or *out*.
- **/sys/class/gpio/gpioN/value**: Reads as either 0 (low) or 1 (high).
- **/sys/class/gpio/gpioN/edge**: Reads as either *none, rising, falling,* or *both.*
- **/sys/class/gpio/gpioN/active_low**: Reads as either 0 (false) or 1 (true).

Notice that *N* in gpioN represents the GPIO number.

Steps to perform I/O using Sysfs

To perform input and output operations using `sysfs` for GPIO pins, you can follow these steps:

1. Export the desired GPIO pin.
2. Set the pin's direction (input or output).
3. If it is an output pin, set the level to low or high.
4. If it is an input pin, read its level (low or high).
5. When you are done with the pin, un-export it to release control.

Exporting GPIO control to userspace

The *export* and *unexport* files under `/sys/class/gpio` allow userspace applications to request or release control of specific GPIO pins. For example, writing the pin number to the *export* file, like `echo 19 > export`, creates a node for GPIO #19. Similarly, `echo 19 > unexport` removes the node.

Controlling GPIO with Sysfs

The following are the steps on how you can control a GPIO pin by using **sysfs** in a Linux terminal:

1. Become the superuser using the following command:
```
$ sudo su
```
2. Navigate to the GPIO folder using the following command:
```
# cd /sys/class/gpio/
```
3. Export the desired GPIO pin (in this case, GPIO4). This will create a new directory. Refer to the following command:
```
# echo 4 > export
```
4. Go to the new directory by using the following command:
```
# cd gpio4
```
5. You can list all the files with the following command:
```
# ls
# active_low device direction edge power subsystem uevent value
```
6. Set the pin's direction (in this case, out direction) using the following command:
```
# echo out > direction
```
7. Change the pin's value to turn it on. Refer to the following command to do so:
```
# echo 1 > value
```
8. To turn it off, set the value to 0 using the following command:
```
# echo 0 > value
```
9. You can check the pin's status using *cat direction* and *cat value*. Refer to the following command for clarity:
```
# cat /sys/class/gpio/gpio4/direction
# cat /sys/class/gpio/gpio4/value
```
10. When done, unexport the GPIO pin using the following command:
```
# echo 4 > unexport
```

This process demonstrates how **sysfs** allows users to manage GPIO pins directly from userspace, making it a convenient tool for interacting with hardware on a Linux system.

Managing GPIO with libgpiod

Starting with *version 4.8*, the Linux kernel introduces a user-friendly API using character devices to manage and control GPIOs effectively.

libgpiod is a C library and tool set that provides a user-level interface for interacting with GPIO pins on Linux-based systems. It is designed to work with the GPIO character device in the Linux kernel. It follows the Sysfs-based GPIO interface, making it a valuable tool for controlling and managing GPIO pins from user space.

Let us see the most relevant features of libgpiod:

- **GPIO access**: libgpiod offers a straightforward and efficient way to control and monitor GPIO pins. It allows users to configure GPIO pins, read and write their values, and set other parameters like pull-up/pull-down resistors and edge-triggered events.
- **Cross-platform**: libgpiod is not limited to a specific hardware platform. It is designed to work with various embedded systems and single-board computers running Linux. It provides a consistent API for GPIO control, regardless of the underlying hardware.
- **API features**: The library provides a C API for GPIO access. It supports features like setting pin directions (input or output), reading and writing pin values, retrieving pin information, configuring edge detection for interrupts, and more.
- **Command-line tools**: In addition to the C library, libgpiod includes command-line tools (for example, **`gpioinfo`**, **`gpiomon`**, and **`gpioget`**) that allow you to perform GPIO-related tasks from the terminal. This makes it easy to script GPIO operations and check the status of GPIO pins without writing custom code.
- **Integration with device tree**: libgpiod can be integrated with the device tree mechanism in Linux, allowing for flexible and dynamic configuration of GPIO pins. This is particularly useful for embedded systems and single-board computers.
- **User and group permissions**: It provides user and group permissions for GPIO access, allowing you to control who can manipulate GPIO pins. This enhances security and access control.
- **Efficient GPIO handling**: libgpiod is designed for efficiency and minimizes context switches between user and kernel space, making it suitable for real-time applications and low-latency GPIO operations.

Installation of libgpiod tools

On *Raspbian 10 Buster* with a *5.10 Kernel*, both **`libgpiod`** and **`gpiod`** are not pre-packaged, and manual installation is required. Fortunately, the installation process is straightforward.

To install the library and the binaries, follow these steps:

1. Use the package manager to install the binaries. Refer to the following command for clarity:

   ```
   $ sudo apt install gpiod
   ```

2. Check the correct installation of **`gpiod`** packages by running the following command:

```
$ gpioinfo
```

3. Run the following command to install the libraries:

```
$ sudo apt install libgpiod-dev
```

In the following sections, we will use these libraries to manage the GPIOs using code. This will show you an output like the one in *Figure 4.3*:

```
pi@raspberrypi:~ $ gpioinfo
gpiochip0 - 58 lines:
        line   0:      "ID_SDA"       unused   input  active-high
        line   1:      "ID_SCL"       unused   input  active-high
        line   2:        "SDA1"       unused   input  active-high
        line   3:        "SCL1"       unused   input  active-high
        line   4:   "GPIO_GCLK"       unused   input  active-high
        line   5:       "GPIO5"       unused   input  active-high
        line   6:       "GPIO6"       unused   input  active-high
        line   7:   "SPI_CE1_N"       unused   input  active-high
        line   8:   "SPI_CE0_N"       unused   input  active-high
        line   9:    "SPI_MISO"       unused   input  active-high
        line  10:    "SPI_MOSI"       unused   input  active-high
        line  11:    "SPI_SCLK"       unused   input  active-high
        line  12:      "GPIO12"       unused   input  active-high
        line  13:      "GPIO13"       unused   input  active-high
        line  14:        "TXD1"       unused   input  active-high
        line  15:        "RXD1"       unused   input  active-high
        line  16:      "GPIO16"       unused   input  active-high
        line  17:      "GPIO17"       unused   input  active-high
        line  18:      "GPIO18"       unused   input  active-high
        line  19:      "GPIO19"       unused   input  active-high
        line  20:      "GPIO20"       unused   input  active-high
        line  21:      "GPIO21"       unused   input  active-high
        line  22:      "GPIO22"       unused   input  active-high
        line  23:      "GPIO23"       unused   input  active-high
        line  24:      "GPIO24"       unused   input  active-high
        line  25:      "GPIO25"       unused   input  active-high
        line  26:      "GPIO26"       unused   input  active-high
        line  27:      "GPIO27"       unused   input  active-high
        line  28: "RGMII_MDIO"        unused   input  active-high
        line  29:  "RGMIO_MDC"        unused   input  active-high
        line  30:        "CTS0"       unused   input  active-high
        line  31:        "RTS0"       unused   input  active-high
        line  32:        "TXD0"       unused   input  active-high
        line  33:        "RXD0"       unused   input  active-high
        line  34:    "SD1_CLK"        unused   input  active-high
        line  35:    "SD1_CMD"        unused   input  active-high
        line  36:  "SD1_DATA0"        unused   input  active-high
        line  37:  "SD1_DATA1"        unused   input  active-high
        line  38:  "SD1_DATA2"        unused   input  active-high
        line  39:  "SD1_DATA3"        unused   input  active-high
        line  40:  "PWM0_MISO"        unused   input  active-high
        line  41:  "PWM1_MOSI"        unused   input  active-high
        line  42: "STATUS_LED_G_CLK" "ACT" output active-high [used]
        line  43: "SPIFLASH_CE_N" unused input active-high
        line  44:        "SDA0"       unused   input  active-high
        line  45:        "SCL0"       unused   input  active-high
        line  46: "RGMII_RXCLK" unused input active-high
        line  47: "RGMII_RXCTL" unused input active-high
        line  48: "RGMII_RXD0"        unused   input  active-high
        line  49: "RGMII_RXD1"        unused   input  active-high
```

***Figure 4.3**: Output of gpioinfo command (trimmed)*

Using the gpiod binaries from the command line

Using the command-line tools **gpiod**, provides a great way to perform tests and experiments.

Let us see what we can do with the **gpiod** commands:

- **gpiodetect** is a command-line tool that helps identify and list available GPIO chips and their associated GPIO lines. It provides information about the GPIO chips, their labels, and the number of GPIO lines they have.

  Running **gpiodetect** in the terminal will display a list of GPIO chips and their details. You can see the result of executing it on a Raspberry Pi 4 in *Figure 4.4:*

  ```
  pi@raspberrypi:~ $ gpiofind GPIO17
  gpiochip0 17
  pi@raspberrypi:~ $
  ```

  ***Figure 4.4:** Running gpiodetect*

- **gpiofind** is a tool that assists you in locating the GPIO line associated with a specific GPIO pin by its name or label. This can be especially helpful when you know the pin's name but need to find the corresponding GPIO line.

  In order to find the GPIO line associated with a pin named **GPIO17**, you can use the following command:

  $ gpiofind GPIO17

  You will obtain a result like the one shown in *Figure 4.5:*

  ```
  pi@raspberrypi:~ $ gpiodetect
  gpiochip0 [pinctrl-bcm2711] (58 lines)
  gpiochip1 [raspberrypi-exp-gpio] (8 lines)
  pi@raspberrypi:~ $
  ```

  ***Figure 4.5:** Running gpiofind*

- **gpioinfo** provides you with detailed information about a specific GPIO chip or all available GPIO chips in the system. This includes information about the chip's name, label, number of GPIO lines, and other chip-specific attributes. You can see an example of running this command in *Figure 4.3*.

- **gpioget** allows you to read the value (state) of a specific GPIO pin or line. You must specify the GPIO chip and the GPIO line number, and the tool will return the current state of that line (0 for low or 1 for high). You can use the command **gpioinfo** to find the correct information.

  For example, to read the value of GPIO pin 18, you can use the command:

  $ gpioget gpiochip0 18

  0

- **gpiomon** is a tool for monitoring GPIO lines and detecting changes in their state. It allows you to set up and watch GPIO lines for specific events, like rising or falling edges, providing a way to react to GPIO state changes in real-time.

- **gpioset** is a command-line tool for setting (writing) the value of a GPIO pin or line. Users can specify the GPIO line number and the desired value (0 for low or 1 for high) to set the pin's state.

  The following example will turn on and off GPIO14:

  $ gpioset gpiochip0 14=1

  $ gpioset gpiochip0 14=0

In the following example, we use **gpiomon** to monitor GPIO14 events. In the command, we configure the bias as a pull-up. Notice that **gpiomon** detects several rising and falling edge events because of the bouncing effect. Refer to the following figure for a better understanding:

```
pi@raspberrypi:~ $ gpiomon -B pull-up gpiochip0 14
event:  RISING EDGE offset: 14 timestamp: [  252980.166715198]
event:  RISING EDGE offset: 14 timestamp: [  253002.904275007]
event:  RISING EDGE offset: 14 timestamp: [  253002.904340746]
event:  RISING EDGE offset: 14 timestamp: [  253002.904340746]
event: FALLING EDGE offset: 14 timestamp: [  253002.904370005]
event: FALLING EDGE offset: 14 timestamp: [  253002.904380672]
event:  RISING EDGE offset: 14 timestamp: [  253002.904388857]
event: FALLING EDGE offset: 14 timestamp: [  253002.904398172]
event: FALLING EDGE offset: 14 timestamp: [  253002.904422634]
event: FALLING EDGE offset: 14 timestamp: [  253002.904448782]
```

Figure 4.6: *Running gpiomon*

Every **gpiod** command offers several options for executing it. The **-h** option after the command allows you to explore these options.

You can see an example in *Figure 4.7:*

```
pi@raspberrypi:~ $ gpiomon -h
Usage: gpiomon [OPTIONS] <chip name/number> <offset 1> <offset 2> ...

Wait for events on GPIO lines and print them to standard output

Options:
  -h, --help:            display this message and exit
  -v, --version:         display the version and exit
  -l, --active-low:      set the line active state to low
  -B, --bias=[as-is|disable|pull-down|pull-up] (defaults to 'as-is'):
                 set the line bias
  -n, --num-events=NUM: exit after processing NUM events
  -s, --silent:          don't print event info
  -r, --rising-edge:     only process rising edge events
  -f, --falling-edge:    only process falling edge events
  -b, --line-buffered:   set standard output as line buffered
  -F, --format=FMT       specify custom output format

Biases:
  as-is:         leave bias unchanged
  disable:       disable bias
  pull-up:       enable pull-up
  pull-down:     enable pull-down

Format specifiers:
  %o:  GPIO line offset
  %e:  event type (0 - falling edge, 1 rising edge)
  %s:  seconds part of the event timestamp
  %n:  nanoseconds part of the event timestamp
```

Figure 4.7: *Using -h to see command options*

Now, let us see some example code using the lipid library.

Controlling a pin

The following code lets you control a pin by specifying the pin number and its state (on or off).

First, declare the needed libraries.

```
//File name relay_control.c
#include <gpiod.h>
#include <stdio.h>
#include <stdlib.h>
#include <string.h>
```

The following functions initialize the hardware and configure the GPIO.

```
// Function to handle GPIO chip initialization and setup
struct gpiod_chip* initializeGPIO() {
    // Open the GPIO chip associated with /dev/gpiochip0
    // Returns a pointer to the initialized chip or NULL in case of an error
    struct gpiod_chip* chip = gpiod_chip_open("/dev/gpiochip0");
    if (!chip) {
        perror("gpiod_chip_open");
    }
    return chip;
}
// Function to set up a GPIO line and configure it as an output
struct gpiod_line_bulk setupGPIOLine(struct gpiod_chip* chip, int offset, const char* consumer) {
    // Configuration for requesting a GPIO line
    struct gpiod_line_request_config config;
    struct gpiod_line_bulk lines;
    int values[1] = {0};
    int err;
    unsigned int offsets[1] = {offset};

    // Get the GPIO line specified by 'offset'
    err = gpiod_chip_get_lines(chip, offsets, 1, &lines);
```

```
    if (err) {
        perror("gpiod_chip_get_lines");
    } else {
        // Configure the GPIO line for output and assign the specified
'consumer' name
        memset(&config, 0, sizeof(config));
        config.consumer = consumer;
        config.request_type = GPIOD_LINE_REQUEST_DIRECTION_OUTPUT;
        config.flags = 0;

        // Request the GPIO line with the given configuration
        err = gpiod_line_request_bulk(&lines, &config, values);
        if (err) {
            perror("gpiod_line_request_bulk");
            gpiod_line_release_bulk(&lines);
        }
    }

    return lines;
}
```

This function try to set the value of the pin. If it is not successful, it throws an error.

```
// Function to set the GPIO line value
void setGPIOLineValue(struct gpiod_line_bulk lines, int value) {
    int err;
    int values[1] = {value};
    // Set the value of the GPIO line(s) to the specified 'value'
    err = gpiod_line_set_value_bulk(&lines, values);
    if (err) {
        perror("gpiod_line_set_value_bulk");
    }
}
```

This is the **main** function, which runs the code of the script.

```
int main(int argc, char *argv[]) {
    if (argc != 3) {
```

```
        fprintf(stderr, "Usage: %s <GPIO_PIN> <on/off>\n", argv[0]);
        return EXIT_FAILURE;
    }

    int pinNumber = atoi(argv[1]);
    const char* action = argv[2]; // Action (on or off)

    // Initialize the GPIO chip
    struct gpiod_chip *chip = initializeGPIO();
    if (!chip) {
        return EXIT_FAILURE;
    }

     struct gpiod_line_bulk lines = setupGPIOLine(chip, pinNumber, "relay-
control");
    if (lines.num_lines == 0) {
        gpiod_chip_close(chip);
        return EXIT_FAILURE;
    }

    if (strcmp(action, "on") == 0) {
        // Turn on the relay (set the GPIO line to high)
        setGPIOLineValue(lines, 1);
        printf("Relay is ON.\n");
    } else if (strcmp(action, "off") == 0) {
        // Turn off the relay (set the GPIO line to low)
        setGPIOLineValue(lines, 0);
        printf("Relay is OFF.\n");
    } else {
        fprintf(stderr, "Invalid action. Use 'on' or 'off'.\n");
    }

    // Cleanup
    gpiod_line_release_bulk(&lines);
    gpiod_chip_close(chip);
```

```
    return EXIT_SUCCESS;
}
```

For compiling, run the following command:

`$ gcc -o relay_control relay_control.c -lgpiod`

Then, execute the binary as follows:

- **To turn the relay on: `$ ./relay_control <GPIO_PIN> on`**
- **To turn the relay off: `$ ./relay_control <GPIO_PIN> off`**

Replace **`<GPIO_PIN>`** with the actual GPIO pin number you want to control.

Reading a pin

This code example reads the state of a digital pin specified as a command-line argument (0 for low, 1 for high) and prints its state. Refer to the following code for a better understanding:

```
//File name read_pin.c
#include <gpiod.h>
#include <stdio.h>
#include <stdlib.h>
#include <string.h>

int main(int argc, char *argv[]) {
    if (argc != 2) {
        fprintf(stderr, "Usage: %s <GPIO_PIN>\n", argv[0]);
        return EXIT_FAILURE;
    }

    int pinNumber = atoi(argv[1]);

    // Open the GPIO chip
    struct gpiod_chip *chip = gpiod_chip_open("/dev/gpiochip0");
    if (!chip) {
        perror("gpiod_chip_open");
        return EXIT_FAILURE;
    }

    // Get the specified GPIO line
```

```
    struct gpiod_line *line = gpiod_chip_get_line(chip, pinNumber);
    if (!line) {
        perror("gpiod_chip_get_line");
        gpiod_chip_close(chip);
        return EXIT_FAILURE;
    }

    // Request the line for input
    if (gpiod_line_request_input(line, "digital-input") < 0) {
        perror("gpiod_line_request_input");
        gpiod_chip_close(chip);
        return EXIT_FAILURE;
    }

    // Read and print the state of the digital pin
    int value = gpiod_line_get_value(line);
     printf("Digital Pin %d is %s\n", pinNumber, (value == 0) ? "LOW" :
"HIGH");

    // Cleanup
    gpiod_line_release(line);
    gpiod_chip_close(chip);

    return EXIT_SUCCESS;
}
```

For compiling, run the following command:

`$ gcc -o pin_read pin_read.c -lgpiod`

Then, execute the binary as follows:

To turn the relay on: **`$ ./pin_read <GPIO_PIN>`**

Replace **`<GPIO_PIN>`** with the actual GPIO pin number you want to read.

Controlling GPIO with Python

There are many Python libraries for managing GPIO in the Raspberry Pi. However, most of them still need to be maintained.

In this book, we will use two libraries:

- RPi.GPIO, the most recent update at the time of writing this book, is 6 February 2022.
- GPIOZero, which has been updated on 1 September 2023.

You can reach the RPi.GPIO website at **https://sourceforge.net/projects/raspberry-gpio-python/** and the module repository at **https://pypi.org/project/RPi.GPIO/**.

Regarding GPIOZero, **you can reach it at https://pypi.org/project/gpiozero and the module repository at https://gpiozero.readthedocs.io/**.

Using RPi.GPIO

RPi.GPIO comes installed at the system level in the newest versions of *Raspberry Pi OS*.

You can check this by running the following command.

```
$ apt-cache show rpi.gpio-common
```

This will show you an output like the one shown in *Figure 4.8:*

```
pi@raspberrypi:~ $ apt-cache show rpi.gpio-common
Package: rpi.gpio-common
Source: rpi.gpio (0.7.1~a4-1)
Version: 0.7.1~a4-1+b4
Installed-Size: 19
Maintainer: Debian Raspberry Pi Maintainers <pkg-raspi-maintainers@lists.alioth.debian.org>
Architecture: arm64
Description-en: Module to control Raspberry Pi GPIO channels (common files)
 RPi.GPIO allows controlling Raspberry Pi GPIO channels in Python.
 .
 It provides all the basic functionality, but is unsuitable for
 real-time or timing critical applications. RPi.GPIO also does not
 support SPI, I²C or hardware PWM yet.
 .
 This package contains common files, for example udev rules.
Description-md5: e672a4883e87bdde1ee54ab2f819aa48
Multi-Arch: same
Homepage: http://sourceforge.net/projects/raspberry-gpio-python/
Section: python
Priority: optional
Filename: pool/main/r/rpi.gpio/rpi.gpio-common_0.7.1~a4-1+b4_arm64.deb
Size: 6808
MD5sum: 371b42ebb84719d7627f57dfc60d6580
SHA256: 4ecb1891748c3ca9de9e0d3308fa0fe43ef74ae6b2de88b3a68c7d6d71240227
```

***Figure 4.8:** Checking the rpi.gpio package installation*

If the package is installed, you can start using it in your Python scripts.

Install a system-wide package with apt

If your system does not have the package, you can install it using the **apt** packet manager.

To install RPi.GPIO, run the following commands:

- First, update the system by using the following command:

```
$ sudo apt update
$ sudo apt upgrade
```

- Then, install the package by running the command given in the following:

```
$ sudo apt install rpi.gpio-common
```

With this type of installation, you can use the package directly from the console using scripts or by entering the Python interpreter.

Install a system-wide package with pip

Before installing the Python packages, we need to install the package installer. **Package Installer for Python** (**Pip**) is the package manager for Python, simplifying the installation of libraries and modules for Python scripts on Raspberry Pi.

To install pip on the Raspberry Pi, you can use the terminal and the following commands:

- If needed, update the system packages. Refer to the following command for clarity:

```
$ sudo apt update
$ sudo apt upgrade
```

- Then, install the `pip` package by using the command given in the following:

```
$ sudo apt install python3-pip
```

- You can verify that the `pip` is installed by using the following command:

```
$ pip -version
```

This will show you the installed version of `pip`.

Now that we have installed `pip`, we can proceed with the installation of `RPi.GPIO`.

To install `RPi.GPIO`, run the following command:

```
$ pip install RPi.GPIO
```

This will download and install all the necessary libraries in your system. Notice that this is a system-wide installation, meaning this module will be available from any Python environment. Also, if you have already installed the package using apt, trying to install it with pip will lead to a conflict, and you will not be able to install it.

Install RPi.GPIO within a Python environment

Using a virtual environment is only a strict requirement for installing RPi. For several reasons, using the GPIO module or any other Python package is often recommended.

Let us see some of these reasons:

- **Isolation**: Virtual environments provide a clean and isolated environment for your Python projects. This isolation ensures that the packages you install do not interfere with system-level packages or packages used in other projects.

- **Dependency management**: Different projects may require different versions of Python packages. Virtual environments allow you to manage package dependencies independently for each project, avoiding conflicts.
- **Version control**: You can create a `requirements.txt` file in your project directory to specify which packages and their versions are required for your project. This helps ensure consistent development and deployment across different environments.
- **Cleaner system**: Installing packages system-wide, especially using `sudo` or a system package manager like `apt`, can clutter your system with many Python packages. Virtual environments keep your system clean, and you only install what is needed for a specific project.
- **Security**: Virtual environments prevent system-wide packages from being affected by potential security vulnerabilities in your project's dependencies. You can update packages in your virtual environment without affecting other projects.
- **Portability**: Virtual environments can be easily moved from one system to another. This can be useful if you need to transfer your project to a different Raspberry Pi or share it with others.

While using virtual environments is highly recommended, it is not an absolute requirement, especially for simple projects. If you only have one project and are not concerned about managing dependencies and potential conflicts, you can install packages system-wide. However, virtual environments provide better control and organization for more complex or collaborative projects.

To create a virtual environment and install the module there, follow these steps.

```
$ python3 -m venv myenv  # Create a virtual environment
$ source myenv/bin/activate  # Activate the virtual environment
(myenv) $ pip install RPi.GPIO  # Install RPi.GPIO within the virtual environment
```

Now, you can use this module within the environment you have just created.

Reading pins with RPi.GPIO

In this section, we will see several scripts for interacting with the GPIO using the RPi.GPIO module.

We can use RPi.GPIO in three different ways to read the pin's states.

Polling

This technique is the simplest but also the least efficient. It involves periodically polling the pin's state, as illustrated in *Figure 4.9:*

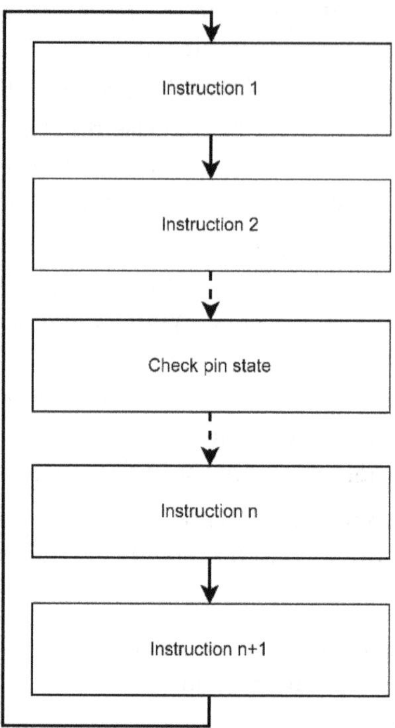

Figure 4.9: Polling technique

The polling technique offers some advantages and drawbacks:

- **Advantages**:
  - It is easy to program. You just need to include the code in a loop.
  - If the code is simple, you will have plenty of time for polling the pin.
- **Drawbacks**:
  - It is not efficient. You must run the rest of the code before polling the pin again.
  - The polling period can be variable and unpredictable. If the code is complex, interrupts and conditions can delay the pin polling. This could lead to missing events.
  - The previous point could also cause unstable behavior.

The following code implements the polling technique using the **`RPi.GPIO`** module:

```
#filename pollpin.py
import RPi.GPIO as GPIO
import time
import argparse
```

```
def poll_gpio(pin_number):
    # Set the GPIO mode to BCM
    GPIO.setmode(GPIO.BCM)

    # Set up the specified GPIO pin as an input
    GPIO.setup(pin_number, GPIO.IN)

    # Initialize the previous state of the GPIO pin
    previous_state = GPIO.input(pin_number)

    try:
        print(f"Polling GPIO pin {pin_number}")
        while True:
            # Read the current state of the GPIO pin
            current_state = GPIO.input(pin_number)

            # Check if the state has changed
            if current_state != previous_state:
                if current_state == GPIO.HIGH:
                    print(f"GPIO pin {pin_number} is HIGH")
                else:
                    print(f"GPIO pin {pin_number} is LOW")

                # Update the previous state
                previous_state = current_state

            # Delay to avoid continuous polling
            time.sleep(0.1)

    except KeyboardInterrupt:
        pass
    finally:
        # Clean up the GPIO configuration before exiting
        GPIO.cleanup()
```

```
if __name__ == "__main__":
    # Create an argument parser to handle command-line arguments
    parser = argparse.ArgumentParser(description="Poll the state of a GPIO
pin.")

    # Add a required argument for the GPIO pin number
    parser.add_argument("pin", type=int, help="GPIO pin number to poll")

    # Parse the command-line arguments
    args = parser.parse_args()

    # Call the poll_gpio function with the specified GPIO pin number
    poll_gpio(args.pin)
```

To run this Python script, execute the following command:

```
$ python pollpin.py <GPIO>
```

Where **<GPIO>** is the pin number you want to poll.

Now, let us examine the interruptions in the next section and how we can use them to detect changes in pin states.

Interruptions

Interruptions are the natural way to implement real-time systems. It can call an action almost immediately after the instruction or routine that is being executed. So, an interruption can be executed in the order of microseconds.

You can see a graphical representation of interruptions in the following figure:

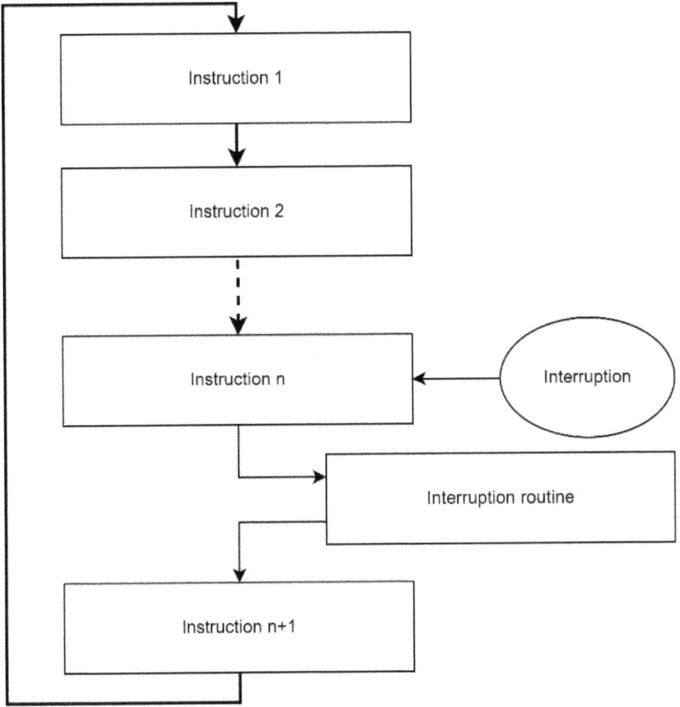

***Figure 4.10**: Interruptions*

The interruption technique offers some advantages and drawbacks:

- **Advantages**:
  - It is far more efficient than polling.
  - You obtain a faster response compared to polling. It is the recommended approach for real-time systems.
  - It is easy to program. You just need to include the code in a loop.
  - If the code is simple, you will have plenty of time for polling the pin.
- **Drawbacks**:
  - In general, it can be more complex to program than polling.
  - The interruption must be programmed with care. You must ensure that critical routines are not interrupted. This leads to the use of priorities
  - The wrong use of interruption can lead to unstable behavior.

The following code detects events in a specified pin:

```
#Filename interruptpin.py
import RPi.GPIO as GPIO
import time
import argparse

def pin_state_change(channel):
    if GPIO.input(channel) == GPIO.HIGH:
        print(f"GPIO pin {channel} is HIGH")
    else:
        print(f"GPIO pin {channel} is LOW")

if __name__ == "__main__":
    # Create an argument parser to handle command-line arguments
    parser = argparse.ArgumentParser(description="Detect the state of a GPIO
pin using interrupts.")

    # Add a required argument for the GPIO pin number
    parser.add_argument("pin", type=int, help="GPIO pin number to monitor")

    # Parse the command-line arguments
    args = parser.parse_args()

    # Set the GPIO mode to BCM
    GPIO.setmode(GPIO.BCM)

    # Set up the specified GPIO pin as an input
    GPIO.setup(args.pin, GPIO.IN)


    # Add event detection for the specified pin and configure the callback
function
    GPIO.add_event_detect(args.pin, GPIO.BOTH, callback=pin_state_change)

    try:
        print(f"Monitoring GPIO pin {args.pin}")
```

```
    while True:
        # Your main program can continue to run here
        time.sleep(1)

except KeyboardInterrupt:
    pass

# Clean up GPIO configuration
GPIO.remove_event_detect(args.pin)
GPIO.cleanup()
```

Note: You can run any code in the main loop without caring about looking for the state of the pin. Whenever a new event (rising or falling edge) occurs, the `callback` function is called, and the interruption is addressed.

To execute this script, just run the following command.

```
$ python interruptpin.py <GPIO>
```

Where **`<GPIO>`** is the pin number you want to monitor.

Using Node-RED

Node-RED is an open-source tool for visual programming. It connects devices, APIs, and online services to create IoT applications and automation workflows. The web-based interface lets you create *flows* by connecting nodes, which represent different functions or devices, using wires to define data and control the flow between them.

People often use Node-RED on the **Internet of Things** (**IoT**) and home automation fields, but its versatility makes it suitable for various applications where data integration and automation are needed. It simplifies development by offering a visual way to design and deploy applications and services. Node-RED has a wide range of nodes and a strong community that contributes to its growth and development.

Let us start by installing Node-RED on the Raspberry Pi.

Installing Node-RED

There are many ways of installing and using Node-RED, from local installations to cloud services. In this book, we will see how to install it in a Raspberry Pi.

Before installing Node-RED, you need to install Node.js and **Node Package Manager** (**nmp**). Doing this manually can be time-consuming. Fortunately, the people from Node-RED have written a script to simplify the process.

This script is also handy for upgrading your existing installation whenever a new release is available.

Simply execute the following command, which will automatically download and run the script. If you would like to inspect the script's contents before proceeding, you can view it on GitHub at **https://raw.githubusercontent.com/node-red/linux-installers/master/deb/update-nodejs-and-nodered**

```
$ bash <(curl -sL https://raw.githubusercontent.com/node-red/linux-installers/master/deb/update-nodejs-and-nodered)
```

If you need to explore additional options for the script, just add `--help` to the end of the command mentioned above.

Note: The script will ask you to install Raspberry Pi-specific packages. So, you do not have to install them later.

This script is compatible with any Debian-based operating system, including Ubuntu and Diet-Pi. To ensure that `npm` can fetch and build any necessary binary modules, you might need to run the following command first:

```
$ sudo apt install build-essential git curl
```

The script will do the following tasks:

- Remove any existing Node-RED version, if present.
- If it finds that Node.js is already installed, it will ensure it is *version 14*. If it is below version 14, it will prompt you to choose between sticking with Node-RED version 1 or upgrading Node.js to a more recent LTS version. If it does not detect Node.js, it will install the Node.js 16 LTS release using the NodeSource package.
- Install the latest Node-RED version using `npm`.
- Optionally, installing a set of Pi-specific nodes can be quite handy.
- Configure Node-RED to run as a service and provide a set of commands for managing the service.

Node-RED is also available in the Raspberry Pi OS repositories, and you can install it by using the following command:

```
$ sudo apt-get install nodered
```

However, note that it includes the Raspberry Pi OS-packaged version of Node.js but does not include `npm`. It is essential to mention that the default Node.js version included with RaspiOS Bullseye is still v12, limiting the Node-RED version that can be installed to the 2.x branch. While these packages might seem convenient initially, it is recommended to use the installation script mentioned above.

Running Node-RED

To run Node-RED in a terminal, use the following command:

```
$ node-red
```

You can stop it by pressing *Ctrl* + C or closing the terminal window.

To optimize memory usage on the Raspberry Pi (not required), you must add an extra argument instructing the underlying Node.js process to release unused memory promptly. For this, use the following command:

```
$ node-red-pi --max-old-space-size=256
```

Running Node-RED as a service

When you install Node-RED on the Pi using the script, it is automatically set up to run as a service. This allows it to run in the background and be configured to start automatically upon boot.

The commands for managing the service are given in the following:

- **node-red-start**: It initiates the Node-RED service and displays its log output. Closing the window or pressing *Ctrl* + C will not stop the service; it continues running in the background.
- **node-red-stop**: It halts the Node-RED service.
- **node-red-restart**: It stops and restarts the Node-RED service.
- **node-red-log**: It displays the service's log output.

Autostart on Boot

To have Node-RED automatically run when the Pi is powered on or rebooted, enable the service to autostart with the following command:

```
$ sudo systemctl enable nodered.service
```

To disable the service from auto starting, use the command given in the following:

```
$ sudo systemctl disable nodered.service
```

Building flows in Node-RED

To access the Node-RED interface, open a web browser (*Chrome* or *Firefox* are recommended) and point to **http://<ip-of-your-raspberry-pi>:1880**.

This will lead you to the editor of Node-RED, refer to *Figure 4.11*:

Figure 4.11: Web interface of Node-RED

Reading a pin using Node-RED

To build a flow in Node-RED to read a pin on your Raspberry Pi and display the pin's value on the debug panel, follow the steps given in the following:

1. **Install required node**: If you have not already, you might need to install the **`node-red-node-pi-gpio`** node, which allows you to access the Raspberry Pi's GPIO pins from Node-RED. You can do this from the Node-RED interface by clicking on the **Manage palette** option and then searching for and installing the **`node-red-node-pi-gpio`** node.
2. **Create a flow**:
    - Open the Node-RED web interface by accessing your Raspberry Pi's IP address, followed by port 1880 (for example, **http://your-pi-ip:1880**).
    - In the Node-RED interface, you will see a visual workspace where you can create flows. On the left side, you will find a list of nodes.
3. **Add input node**: Drag and drop a **`rpi-gpio in`** node onto the workspace. This node will read the value of a GPIO pin.
4. **Configure the input node**:
    - Double-click the **`rpi-gpio in`** node to configure it.

- o In the configuration dialog, set the **`GPIO`** field to the pin number you want to read.
- o You can also configure other options, such as the pin mode and edge detection. Play with these options and see what happens when you change them.
- o Click **Done** to save the configuration.

5. **Add debug node**: Drag and drop a **`debug`** node from the output section onto the workspace. This node will display the pin value on the debug panel.
6. **Connect nodes**: Connect the output of the **`rpi-gpio in`** node to the input of the **`debug`** node. You can do this by dragging a wire from the output of one node to the input of the other.
7. **Deploy the flow**: To deploy your flow, click the **Deploy** button in the upper-right corner of the Node-RED interface.
8. **View pin value**: You should now see the value of the GPIO pin displayed in the Node-RED debug panel, which you can access by clicking the **debug** tab in the right sidebar. Refer to the following figure for a better understanding:

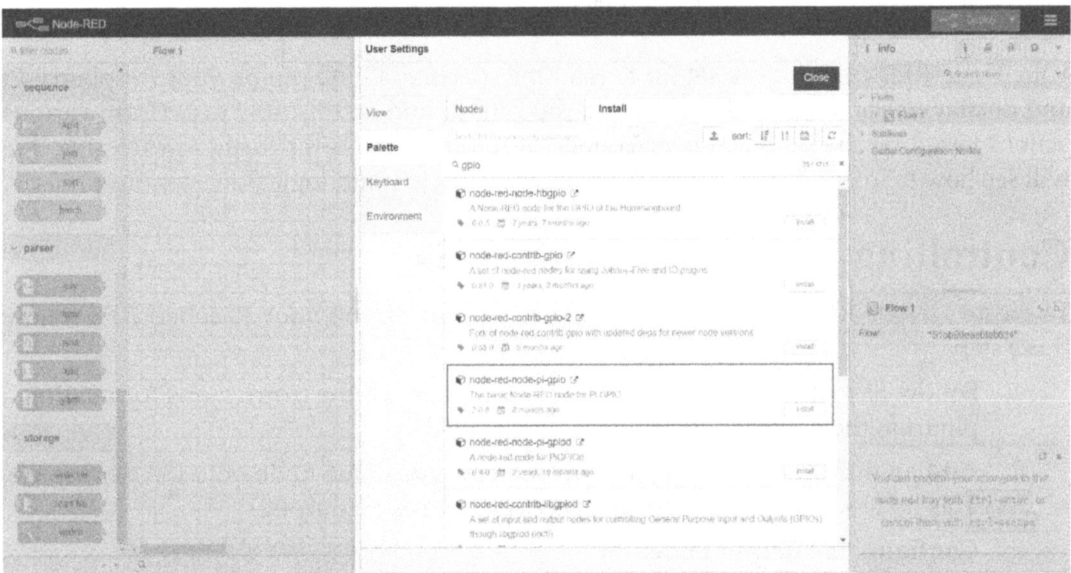

***Figure 4.12**: Installing node-red-node-pi-gpio node*

You can see the complete flow in *Figure 4.13*:

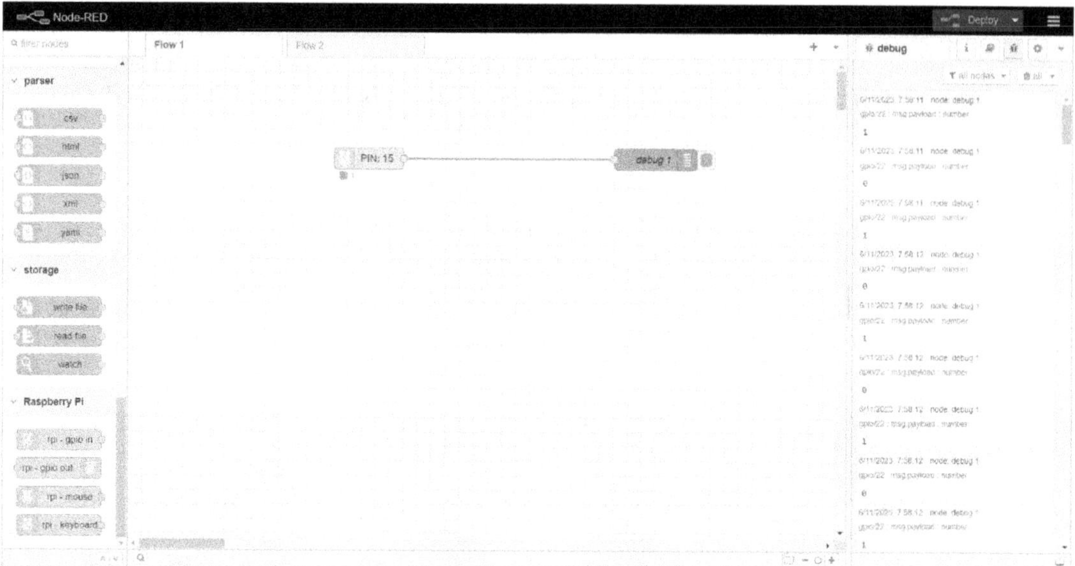

Figure 4.13: Flow for reading a pin

Your Node-RED flow is now set up to read the specified GPIO pin on your Raspberry Pi and display its value in the debug panel. You can expand on this flow to perform various actions based on the pin's value or connect it to other nodes for further processing. We will see how to integrate pin values with other blocks to build logic flows for our projects.

Controlling a pin using Node-RED

To create a Node-RED flow for controlling an output pin on your Raspberry Pi, follow these steps:

1. Follow *Steps 1* and *2* (from the previous section) of the instructions for reading a pin from the previous section.
2. **Add an output node**: Drag and drop a **`rpi-gpio out`** node onto the workspace. This node will be used to control the GPIO pin as an output.
3. **Configure the output node**:
   - Double-click the **`rpi-gpio out`** node to configure it.
   - In the configuration dialog, set the **`GPIO`** field to the pin number you want to control.
   - Configure other options as needed, such as the pin mode (for example, *output*) and initial state (for example, 1 for high or 0 for low).
   - Click **Done** to save the configuration.

4. **Add an input node**: Add two input nodes, *inject*, to control the state of the pin. Set the output value of one node to 1 and the other to 0.
5. **Connect nodes**: Connect the outputs of the inject nodes to the input of the **`rpi-gpio out`** node.
6. **Deploy the flow**: Click the **Deploy** button in the upper-right corner of the Node-RED interface to deploy your flow.
7. **Control the output pin**: You can now control the specified GPIO pin on your Raspberry Pi by triggering the input nodes. This will change the state of the output pin, turning it on or off.

You can see the complete flow in *Figure 4.14*:

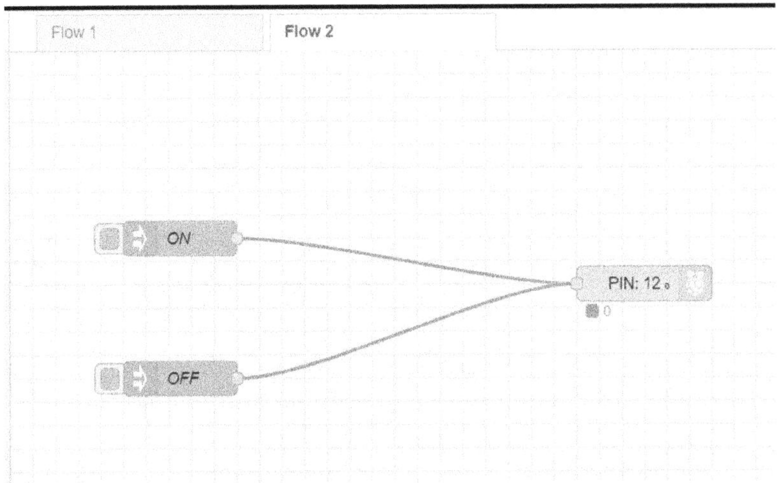

***Figure 4.14**: Controlling a pin in Node-RED*

Exporting and importing flows in Node-RED

Every flow is coded as a JSON. So, you can export and import flows using JSON files or copy and paste them into the web interface of Node-RED.

To export a flow, follow these steps:

1. **Access the Node-RED interface**: Open your web browser and enter the URL of your Node-RED instance (**http://your-pi-ip:1880** for a Raspberry Pi) to access the Node-RED web interface.
2. **Export the flow**: In the Node-RED interface, click the *hamburger* menu icon (three horizontal lines) in the upper-right corner to open the menu. From the menu, select *Export*. In the **Export nodes** dialog, click on the **Download** button to download the JSON file. See *Figure 4.15*. This is all you must do to export a flow in Node-RED.

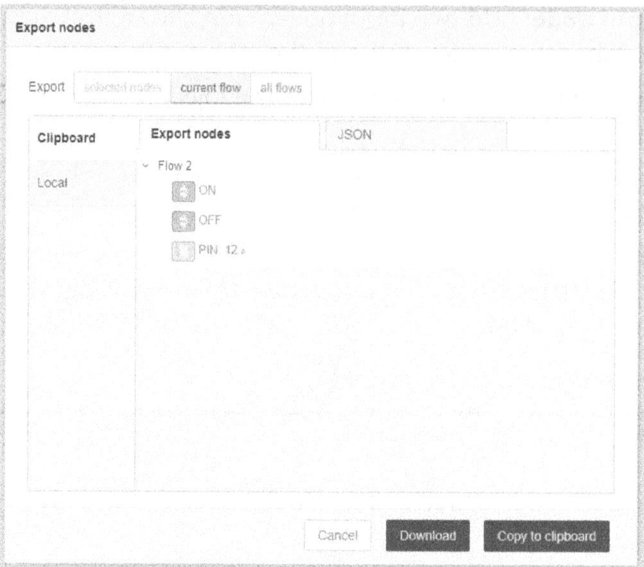

Figure 4.15: Exporting a flow in Node-RED

Now, let us see how you can import the repository flows into your Node-RED instance.

To import flows in Node-RED by copying and pasting JSON content, follow these steps:

1. **Access the Node-RED interface**: Open your web browser and enter the URL of your Node-RED instance (**http://your-pi-ip:1880** for a Raspberry Pi) to access the Node-RED web interface.
2. **Prepare the JSON content**: Open the JSON file you want to import using a text or code editor. Select the entire JSON content, including the curly braces **{}** encapsulating the flow configuration. Copy this content to your clipboard.
3. **Import the flow**: In the Node-RED interface, click the *hamburger* menu icon (three horizontal lines) in the upper-right corner to open the menu. From the menu, select **Import**. In the **Import nodes** dialog, click the text input field under **Clipboard** to place your cursor there.
4. **Paste the JSON content**: Right-click or use the keyboard shortcut (*Ctrl* + *V* on Windows or *Command* + *V* on macOS) to paste the JSON content into the input field.
5. **Review imported flow**: After successfully passing the JSON content, the imported flow will appear on your Node-RED workspace. You can drag it around, organize nodes, and make necessary adjustments.
6. **Deploy the imported flow**: Once you have reviewed and made any necessary modifications to the imported flow, click the **Deploy** button in the upper-right corner of the Node-RED interface to save and activate it.

7. **Test the imported flow**: Verify that the imported flow works as expected by testing the associated devices, services, or input sources.

You can now use, modify, and extend the imported flow for your specific application or automation tasks.

Conclusions

In this chapter, we have explored several topics about programming IoT projects in Raspberry Pi. First, we explored Raspberry Pi's GPIO features and learned to use the sysfs file system. Then, we explored libgpiod, using both the binaries and the C library.

After that, we learned how to use the RPi.GPIO Python module to read and control GPIOs. We also discussed polling and interruption techniques. Finally, we learned how to install and use Node-RED. We built two flows, one for reading GPIO pins and another for controlling them. This chapter has been a basic introduction to working with Raspberry Pi in IoT.

In the following chapter, we will build complex projects using these tools.

CHAPTER 5

Connecting IoT Devices using MQTT

Introduction

In this chapter, you will learn about the **Message Queuing Telemetry Transport** (**MQTT**) protocol and how it can be used in **Internet of Things** (**IoT**) devices. MQTT is a dedicated IoT protocol created in 1999 by *Andy Stanford-Clark* (*IBM*) and *Arlen Nipper* (*Arcom*, now *Cirrus Link*) to facilitate communication between machines (M2M). You will find MQTT widely applied in various sectors such as industry, healthcare, logistics, mobile, connected cars, smart buildings, and smart cities. It operates on short messages with a publish-subscribe mechanism.

In the following sections, we will explore the functionalities of the MQTT protocol. Also, we will implement IoT projects by using MQTT libraries.

Structure

The chapter discusses the following topics:

- MQTT features
- Mosquitto
- Using HiveMQ MQTT broker

Objectives

By reading this chapter, you will obtain good knowledge about the MQTT protocol. You will understand how it works and its main features. You will be able to install Mosquitto, an open-source MQTT broker, and communicate with IoT devices using Arduino and Python to publish and subscribe to MQTT topics. Also, you will learn how to add encryption to Mosquitto, integrate MQTT with Node-RED, and connect to cloud MQTT brokers. By completing this chapter, you will be able to build your IoT systems using the MQTT protocol.

MQTT features

MQTT is one of the most widely adopted IoT protocols. It uses a client-server architecture based on a publish-subscribe mechanism.

You can see an example of the MQTT architecture in *Figure 5.1*.

Let us look at some key features of MQTT:

- It is a lightweight and efficient use of bandwidth.
- It is designed to work well with constrained devices.
- It has low power consumption.
- It is data agnostic.
- It allows session management.
- It implements **quality of service** (**QoS**).
- It supports SSL/TLS encryption.
- It allows user and client ID management.

The fundamental concept behind MQTT is to enable data exchange between clients. Each client connects to a server running an MQTT service (broker). Clients can either send data to the broker (publish) or receive data from it (subscribe).

In this architecture, clients are independent entities, and all information is exchanged between clients and the broker. Functionally, it is quite similar to how email clients and servers operate.

Each client gains access to specific information through the use of topics, which are distinct fields in the data structure of the MQTT broker. An example of the MQTT architecture is provided in the following figure:

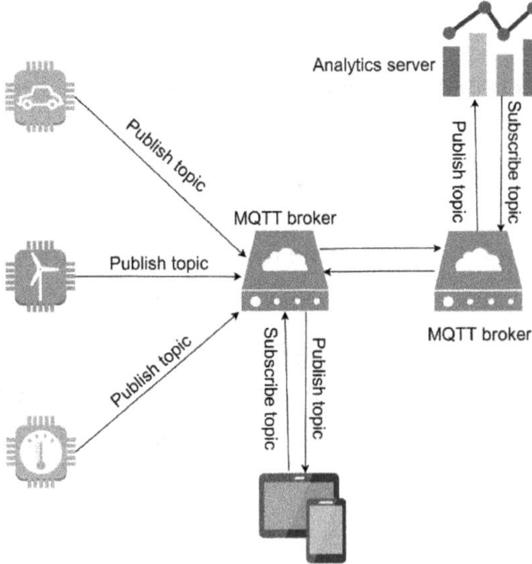

Figure. 5.1: MQTT architecture example

MQTT topics

MQTT topics are UTF-8 encoded strings used to filter and route messages between publishers and subscribers in MQTT communication. Topics are hierarchical, using forward slashes (/) to separate levels, and are case-sensitive.

Topic structure

Topics consist of one or more levels, each separated by a forward slash. For example:

- `myhome/groundfloor/livingroom/temperature`
- `USA/California/San Francisco/Silicon Valley`
- `device/001/status`

Notice the hierarchical structure of the levels, going from the bigger to the smaller.

Wildcards

MQTT supports two types of wildcards for subscribing to multiple topics:

- **Single-level (+)**: Matches any string at a single level.
  - **Example:** `myhome/groundfloor/+/temperature` will ask for all the temperature sensors located in any room on the ground floor.

- **Multi-level (#)**: Matches any number of levels, must be the last character in the topic.
  - **Example**: `device/001/sensors/#` will obtain all the values of the sensors connected to the device (for instance, temperature and humidity).

Best practices

When designing MQTT topics, consider the following recommendations:

- Keep topics short and concise whenever you can.
- Avoid leading or trailing forward slashes.
- Use ASCII characters only, avoiding spaces and non-printable characters.
- Include unique identifiers or client IDs in the topic structure.
- Use specific topics rather than general ones.
- Consider future extensibility in your topic design.

The following are the examples:

- **Temperature sensor**: `home/livingroom/temperature`
- **Device status**: `device/12345/status`
- **Command topic**: `office/lights/switch1/set`

By following these guidelines, you can create an efficient and scalable MQTT topic structure for your IoT applications.

MQTT QoS

MQTT incorporates a QoS implementation, presenting three levels of QoS for communication between clients and brokers. Let us see each one of them.

QoS 0

At this level, the sender dispatches the message without anticipating acknowledgment, constituting a best-effort delivery service. This level can be likened to applications using the UDP protocol, where acknowledgment messages are absent.

When the communication link is reliable, opting for QoS 0 can be advantageous, conserving processing power and energy in IoT devices.

You can see the operation of QoS 0 in *Figure 5.2:*

***Figure 5.2:** QoS 0 operation*

QoS 1

At this level, the message is delivered at least once. The sender retains the message until receiving a PUBACK packet from the broker. To handle multiple transmissions of the same message, a packet identifier is used, allowing the sender to correlate PUBACK packets with the corresponding packet ID.

Notice that duplicated packets must be detected and discarded by the application running over MQTT. Refer to the following figure for a better understanding:

Figure 5.3: *QoS 1 operation*

QoS 2

This level ensures that each receiver obtains the message precisely once. Although the safest, QoS 2 is the slowest in MQTT. Both the sender and receiver utilize packet IDs to match messages. The process involves the sender initiating a PUBLISH packet, the receiver responding with a PUBREC packet, and subsequent steps including message processing, acknowledgment, and prevention of duplicate packet processing. See *Figure 5.4* for a better understanding:

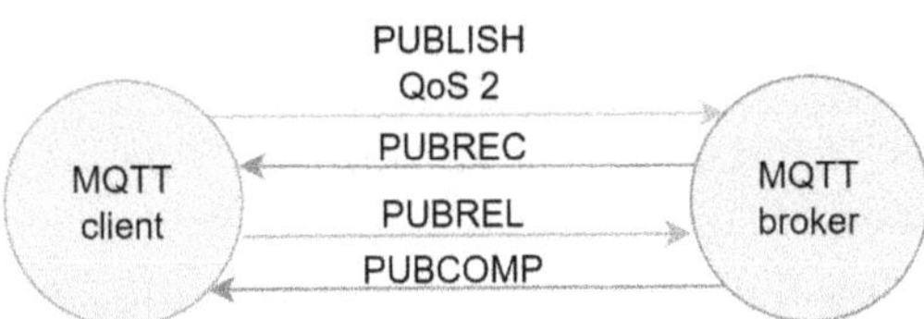

Figure 5.4: *QoS 2 operation*

MQTT versions

Two prevalent MQTT versions are in use: version 3.1.1 and version 5. These versions are not fully compatible, so it is important to decide which version are you going to use in advance.

Due to this lack of compatibility, it is recommended to use the same version of MQTT for all the IoT devices of the system. Even if you have to choose the older version (3.1.1) instead of the newest (5.0).

Let us start by examining some important features of version 3.1.1 that are still available in version 5.0.

MQTT payload

Although MQTT was designed to be used in constrained devices, it allows a maximum payload of 256 MB. MQTT does not impose a data type, so you can send unformatted bytes, binary files, JSON data, integers, strings, etc.

So, although MQTT was designed for carrying small payloads, you could use it to send images or audio files.

Wildcard filters

MQTT supports wildcard filters in topic subscriptions, providing flexible and granular control over the messages subscribers receive. There are two types of wildcards: the single-level wildcard (+), which matches a single level within a topic hierarchy, and the multi-level wildcard (#), which matches any number of levels within a topic hierarchy. Let us illustrate this feature with two examples.

Suppose you have the following topic structure: **`city/building/office/`**

If you want to obtain data from all the offices of a building, you can use the following wildcard: **`mexicocity/headquarters/#`**.

This topic will show you data from all the offices in a specific building.

On the other hand, if you want to ask for the managers' office of all the buildings, you can use **`mexicocity/+/manageroffice`**.

Retained messages

MQTT allows publishers to send messages with the *retained* flag, indicating that the message should be retained by the broker and delivered to new subscribers when they connect. This feature ensures that subscribers receive the most recent state or information upon subscription.

Every time the client publishes a new message, the retained message is overwritten.

Session persistence

MQTT brokers can be configured to maintain client sessions, enabling clients to establish persistent connections. This allows clients to resume their subscriptions and receive missed messages after reconnecting without the need to start a new session, ensuring data integrity and reliability.

Last Will and Testament

MQTT supports the concept of **Last Will and Testament** (**LWT**), which allows clients to specify a *last message* to be published on their behalf when they disconnect unexpectedly.

This feature is particularly useful for handling scenarios where clients may go offline without sending a proper disconnection message.

Security features

MQTT supports **Transport Layer Security** (**TLS**) encryption, enabling secure communication between clients and brokers. It also provides authentication mechanisms like username/password and client certificates, ensuring the confidentiality and integrity of data exchanged.

Scalability

MQTT is designed to scale horizontally, allowing the distribution of clients and brokers across multiple machines or clusters. This facilitates the handling of large-scale deployments with millions of connected devices or high message requirements.

Message expiry

MQTT supports the inclusion of an expiry time for messages. Publishers can specify a **Time-to-Live** (**TTL**) value when publishing a message, indicating how long the message should be considered valid. This feature ensures that stale or outdated messages are not delivered to subscribers.

Version 3.1.1 brought several improvements over 3.1. Here are some of the key updates:

- The new specification introduced MQTT over WebSockets.
- Client IDs were expanded significantly from 23 bytes per client to 65535 bytes.
- Now, there is no need to wait for a CONNACK response from the broker. This allows constrained devices to CONNECT, PUBLISH, and disconnect more efficiently.
- The client ID can now be set to zero byte length, specifically useful for anonymous client implementations.
- An additional error in MQTT SUBACK was included to notify clients about forbidden subscriptions.
- When a client with a persistent session connects to a broker, a flag in the CONNACK message informs that the broker already has client information. This enhances communication efficiency.

Version 5.0

The 5.0 version was a major upgrade to the protocol. It added robustness, security, and efficiency. However, versions 3.1.1 and 5.0 are not fully compatible. So, when choosing the version, take into consideration this fact.

MQTT 5 brings significant enhancements to the protocol, some of which are mentioned in the following:

- Improved scalability support.
- Enhanced error reporting for better diagnostics.
- Increased efficiency for smaller clients.
- Introduction of user properties for added customization.

Some of the added features are mentioned in the following:

- **Header properties**: MQTT 5 introduces properties in the MQTT header, enabling the assignment of custom headers to transport metadata.
- **Reason codes**: This functionality adds reason codes to MQTT, aiding in identifying the specific type of error occurring in MQTT communications.
- **Return codes**: MQTT 5 offers return codes, allowing brokers to inform clients about the specific features they support.
- **AUTH packet**: A new addition in MQTT 5, the AUTH packet, provides advanced authentication techniques, including OAuth. Additionally, it allows re-authentication of a client without terminating the current connection.
- **Connection termination**: In MQTT 5, both the client and the broker can terminate the connection. Contrastingly, in version 3.1.1, only the client could conclude the communication.
- **QoS in MQTT 5**: For reliable communication links, MQTT 5 enables the omission of MQTT message re-delivery. Both brokers and clients abstain from sending retransmissions unless TCP errors occur, thereby optimizing QoS usage.
- **Payload format**: MQTT 5 introduces the payload format indicator, determining whether the payload is in binary or text format. This feature adds versatility to the protocol.
- **Shared subscriptions**: MQTT 5.0 introduces the concept of shared subscriptions, which enables multiple subscribers to share the message load from a single topic. With shared subscriptions, a group of subscribers with the same subscription pattern can collectively receive and process messages from the subscribed topic, allowing for load balancing, high availability, and parallel processing.

Mosquitto

In this section, we will learn how to install and configure the Mosquitto broker. It is actively maintained by the *Eclipse Foundation* and is used in many IoT systems.

You can reach the website of the Mosquitto project at **https://mosquitto.org/**

Now, let us see how you can install Mosquitto on your Raspberry Pi.

Installing Mosquitto

The following step-by-step instructions will guide you through installing Mosquitto on Debian systems like Ubuntu or Raspberry Pi:

1. **Update packages**: Updating the system packages is always recommended. Run the following command to update the system.

   ```
   $ sudo apt-get update && sudo apt-get upgrade -y
   ```

2. **Install Mosquitto broker and client**: Run the following command to install Mosquitto packages.

   ```
   $ sudo apt-get install mosquitto mosquitto-clients
   ```

3. **Basic configuration**: The main configuration file is located at `/etc/mosquitto/conf.d`.

   a. Open `mosquitto.conf` in a text editor to see the configuration settings.

   b. Looking into the `mosquitto.conf` you will see something like the following.

   ```
   # Place your local configuration in /etc/mosquitto/conf.d/
   #
   # A full description of the configuration file is at
   # /usr/share/doc/mosquitto/examples/mosquitto.conf.example
   pid_file /var/run/mosquitto.pid
   persistence true
   persistence_location /var/lib/mosquitto/
   log_dest file /var/log/mosquitto/mosquitto.log
   include_dir /etc/mosquitto/conf.d
   ```

4. **Default values**: Any unspecified option in the configuration file takes its default value.

5. **Example configuration file**: You will find an example configuration file at `/usr/share/doc/mosquitto/examples/`. It is compressed as `mosquitto.conf.gz`.

6. **Unzip the file using**: `$ gunzip mosquitto.conf.gz`.

   You will get four files; the relevant one is `mosquitto.conf`. Open it with a text editor.

7. **Configuration options**: Customize settings like the default **Transport Control Protocol** (TCP) port (1883) or specify a particular interface for the broker to listen to (for example, 192.168.0.1). You can explore all available configuration options and set them according to your needs.

8. **Copy the new configuration file**: Now that you have edited your configuration file, go to the directory where you have it and copy it to the **/etc/mosquitto/conf.d** directory, refer to the following code for a better understanding:

```
$ sudo cp mosquitto.conf /etc/mosquitto/conf.d
```

9. **Restart the mosquitto service**: Restart the **mosquitto** service for the changes to take effect. Run the following command to restart Mosquitto.

```
$ sudo systemctl restart mosquitto.service
```

10. **Basic security setup**: Set a username and password for basic security, refer to the code in the following for the same:

```
$ sudo mosquitto_passwd -c /etc/mosquitto/pwfile your_user
```

11. **Change your_user**: Replace it with the desired username and follow the prompts to set the password.

Using the Mosquitto client

Now that you have installed the broker, let us connect to it by using the Mosquitto client.

Here is how to publish and subscribe to a specific topic using Mosquitto:

- **Subscription:**
  - To subscribe to a topic, run the following command:

    ```
    $ mosquitto_sub -h <ip address> -p <port number> -i <client-id-1>
    -u <user> -P '<password>' -t topic
    ```

  - This line subscribes a client to a topic. It uses the IP address, a TCP port, user credentials, a password, and a client ID.
- **Publishing:**
  - To publish to a topic, use the next command:

    ```
    $ mosquitto_pub -h <ip address> -p <port number> -i <client-id-2>
    -u <user> -P '<password>' -t topic -m "hello world"
    ```

  - This command publishes a message on the same topic. Upon publishing a message, any subscribed client will receive it. You can open two terminals, one for publishing messages and the other for subscribing and receiving them.

Using the MQTTX desktop client

In case you want a desktop MQTT client with a beautiful user interface, you could install and use the MQTTX client.

This software is developed by *EMQX*. It is open-source, and you can download it for free from **https://www.emqx.com/en/products/mqttx**.

Configure your connection by selecting the + button on the left menu bar and filling in the required fields in the form. You can see the new connection section in *Figure 5.5*:

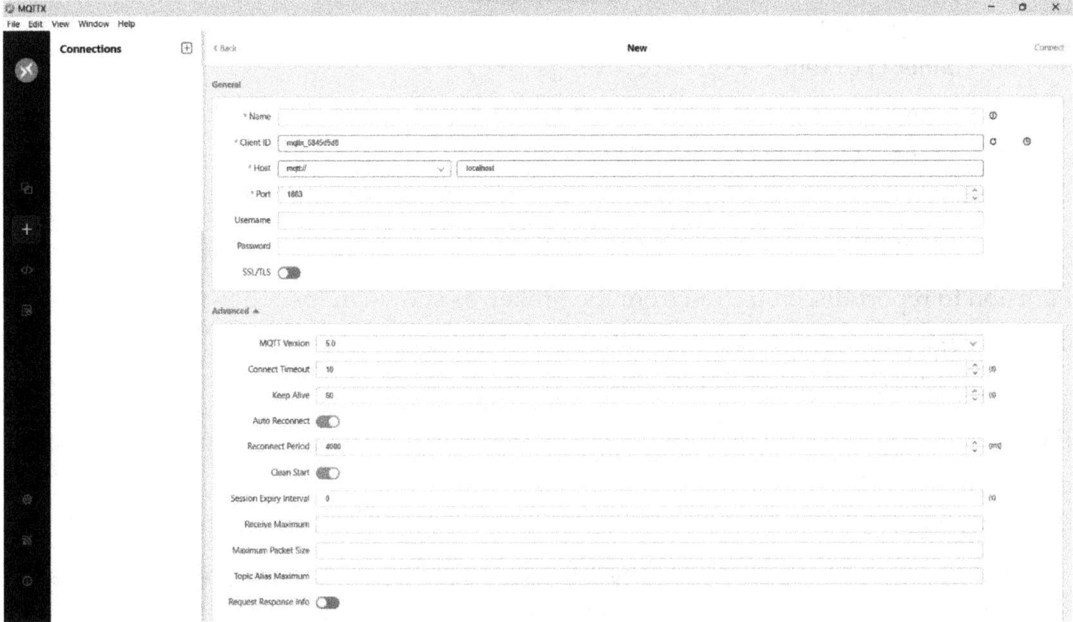

***Figure 5.5**: Connecting to a MQTT broker using MQTTX*

Once configured, click the **Connect** button in the upper right corner to establish a connection to the MQTT broker.

After you connect to MQTT, you can perform tests for publishing and subscribing to messages.

Connecting to the broker using Python

Paho was developed by the *Eclipse Foundation*, and it is available in several programming languages, including Python, Java, JavaScript, GoLang, C++, etc. You can see the complete list of languages at this link **https://eclipse.dev/paho/index.php?page=downloads.php**.

The Paho project provides open-source implementations of messaging protocols for M2M and IoT applications. It was initially focused on MQTT client implementations for embedded platforms, with plans for server support.

In this section, we will use the Python Paho library to connect to the MQTT broker.

The following script is a command-line-based MQTT client that enables you to interact with an MQTT broker by subscribing to or publishing messages on specific topics.

First, import the needed Python modules, as shown in the following:

```
import sys
import paho.mqtt.client as mqtt
```

Function to report if the connection was successful or not, as shown in the following:

```
def on_connect(client, userdata, flags, rc):
    if rc == 0:
        print("Connected to broker")
    else:
        print(f"Failed to connect, return code: {rc}")
```

Function to report disconnection from the broker, as shown in the following:

```
def on_disconnect(client, userdata, rc):
    print("Disconnected from broker")
```

Function to show the available options for executing the script, as shown in the following:

```
def print_help():
    help_text = """
    Usage: python mqtt_client.py <broker_address> <broker_port> <username>
<password> <client_id> <-s/-p> <topic_name> [payload]
    Options:
        -h, --help          Show this help message and exit
        -s, --subscribe     Subscribe to the specified topic
        -p, --publish       Publish a message to the specified topic
    """
    print(help_text)
    sys.exit()
```

Function to display received messages from the MQTT broker, as shown in the following:

```
def on_message(client, userdata, msg):
    print(f"Received message: {msg.payload.decode()} on topic {msg.topic}")
```

This is the **main** function, that calls all the other functions in the script, as shown in the following:

```
def main():
    if len(sys.argv) == 2 and (sys.argv[1] == "-h" or sys.argv[1] == "--
help"):
        print_help()
    if len(sys.argv) < 8:
        print("Usage: python mqtt_client.py <broker_address> <broker_port>
```

```
<username> <password> <client_id> <-s/-p> <topic_name> [payload]")
        sys.exit(1)
```

Get all the parameters from the arguments in the command line, as shown in the following:

```
    broker_address = sys.argv[1]
    broker_port = sys.argv[2]
    username = sys.argv[3]
    password = sys.argv[4]
    client_id = sys.argv[5]
    operation = sys.argv[6]
    topic = sys.argv[7]

    if not all([broker_address, broker_port, username, password, client_id,
operation, topic]):
        print("Missing parameter(s). Please provide all required parameters.")
        sys.exit(1)

    try:
        broker_port = int(broker_port)
    except ValueError:
        print("Broker port should be an integer.")
        sys.exit(1)
```

Create the MQTT client, as shown in the following:

```
    client = mqtt.Client(client_id)
    client.username_pw_set(username, password)
    client.on_connect = on_connect
    client.on_disconnect = on_disconnect
```

If it is a **subscribe** operation, connect to the broker and subscribe to the topic, as shown in the following:

```
    if operation == "-s" or operation == "--subscribe":
        client.on_message = on_message
        try:
            client.connect(broker_address, broker_port)
            client.subscribe(topic)
            client.loop_forever()
```

```
        except KeyboardInterrupt:
            client.disconnect()
```

If it is a **publish** operation, publish the message to the topic, as shown in the following:

```
    elif operation == "-p" or operation == "--publish":
        if len(sys.argv) < 9:
            print("Please provide a payload for the publish operation.")
            sys.exit(1)

        payload = sys.argv[8]

        try:
            client.connect(broker_address, broker_port)
            client.publish(topic, payload)
            client.disconnect()
            print(f"Published message '{payload}' to topic {topic}")
        except Exception as e:
            print(f"Error publishing message: {str(e)}")

    else:
        print("Invalid operation. Use -s/--subscribe or -p/--publish.")
        sys.exit(1)
```

This line of code calls the **main()** function when the script is executed, as shown in the following:

```
if __name__ == "__main__":
    main()
```

The following section describes what you can do with the script.

Subscribing to a topic

To subscribe to a topic, you can use the previous script with specific arguments.

You can subscribe to an MQTT topic by running the script with the following arguments:

- **<broker_address>**: It is the address (IP or name/domain) of the MQTT broker.
- **<broker_port>**: It is the TCP port number of the MQTT broker (default is 1883).
- **<username>**: It is the username for authentication with the broker.
- **<password>**: It is the password for authentication with the broker.

- **<client_id>**: It is a unique client identifier for the MQTT client.
- **-s or --subscribe**: It specifies the operation as a subscribe action.
- **<topic_name>**: It is the MQTT topic that you subscribe to.

Example: `$ python3 mqtt_client.py broker.example.com 1883 user pass client001 -s topic/example`

Publishing to a topic

To publish messages using the script, you need to specify some arguments.

You can publish a message to an MQTT topic by running the script with the following arguments:

- **<broker_address>**: It is the address of the MQTT broker.
- **<broker_port>**: It is the port number of the MQTT broker.
- **<username>**: It is the username for authentication with the broker.
- **<password>**: It is the password for authentication with the broker.
- **<client_id>**: It is a unique client identifier for the MQTT client.
- **-p or --publish**: It specifies the operation as a publish action.
- **<topic_name>**: It is the MQTT topic to publish the message to.
- **[payload]:** It is the message payload to be published to the topic.

Example: `$ python3 mqtt_client.py broker.example.com 1883 user pass client001 -p topic/example "Hello, MQTT!"`

The script also has the following features:

- The script includes a `-h` or `--help` option that displays a help message, explaining the script's usage and available options.
- It handles missing parameters and provides appropriate messages to guide users on the required arguments.
- For subscription, it prints received messages on the subscribed topic.
- For publishing, users can specify a payload to be sent along with the topic.

This script offers a simple yet versatile way to interact with an MQTT broker by subscribing to topics to receive messages or publishing messages to specific topics.

Connecting NodeMCU using Arduino IDE

Now, we will use an ESP2866 to connect to publish MQTT messages. In *Chapter 3, Microcontroller, Sensors, and Actuators,* we installed the ESP8266 package. This package comes with the ESP8266WiFi library, which we will use now to connect to a WiFi network.

Now, we need to add a new package to be able to connect to an MQTT broker. For this purpose, we will use **PubSubClient**.

In order to install the library, just go to the library manager in the Arduino IDE and select it, as shown in *Figure 5.6*:

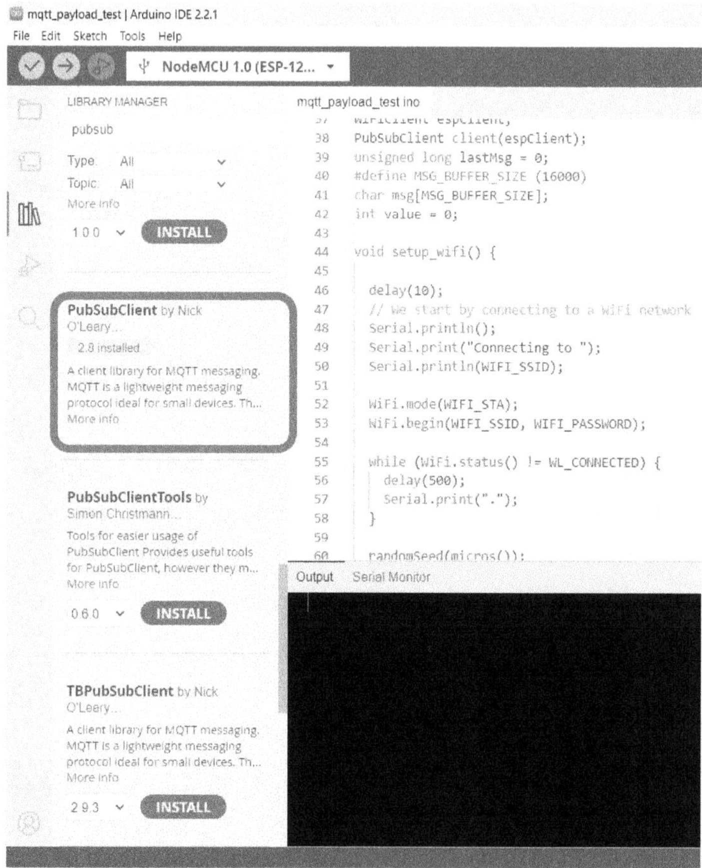

***Figure 5.6:** Installing PubSubClient library in Arduino*

Now that you have installed the **PubSubClient** library, let us program your ESP8266.

Publishing on a topic

This Arduino code is a simple program designed to connect an ESP8266 device to a Wi-Fi network and an MQTT broker and publish on a specified topic. Refer to the following code for a better understanding:

- **Libraries**: The code imports the necessary libraries:
  - o **ESP8266WiFi.h**: Library for connecting the ESP8266 to a Wi-Fi network.
  - o **PubSubClient.h**: Library for MQTT communication.

```
#include <ESP8266WiFi.h>
#include <PubSubClient.h>
```

- **Constants declaration**: Several constants are defined. Replace the values according to your configurations and credentials.
    - **Wi-Fi credentials:** (**WIFI_SSID**, **WIFI_PASSWORD**).
    - **MQTT server details**: This includes IP address, port, username, and password (**MQTT_CLIENT_ID**, **MQTT_SERVER_IP**, **MQTT_SERVER_PORT**, **MQTT_USER**, **MQTT_PASSWORD**).

```
#define MQTT_VERSION MQTT_VERSION_3_1_1

// WiFi Credentials
const char* WIFI_SSID = "WIFI_NAME";
const char* WIFI_PASSWORD = "WIFI_PASS";

// MQTT Configuration: ID, Server IP, Port, User, Password
const PROGMEM char* MQTT_CLIENT_ID = "YOUR_CLIENT_ID";
const PROGMEM char* MQTT_SERVER_IP = "YOUR_BROKER_IP";
const PROGMEM uint16_t MQTT_SERVER_PORT = YOUR_BROKER_PORT;
const PROGMEM char* MQTT_USER = "YOUR_BROKER_USER";
const PROGMEM char* MQTT_PASSWORD = "YOUR_BROKER_PASS";
```

- **Global variables**: The code uses the following global variables:
    - **WiFiClient espClient**: Object to handle the Wi-Fi connection.
    - **PubSubClient client(espClient)**: MQTT client object.
    - **lastMessageTime**: Holds the timestamp of the last message sent. Notice that we are calculating the time instead of using the **delay()** function. This avoids blocking the execution of the rest of the code and lets us maintain the MQTT connection in an active state.
    - **MSG_BUFFER_SIZE and msg**: Buffer size and message array for MQTT messages.
    - **Counter**: Holds an incremental value used in the published message:

```
WiFiClient wifiClient;
PubSubClient mqttClient(wifiClient);
unsigned long lastMessageTime = 0;
#define MAX_MSG_BUFFER_SIZE (16000)
```

```
char message[MAX_MSG_BUFFER_SIZE];
int counter = 0;
```

- **Function setup_wifi()**: Wi-Fi's setup function.
  - Function to set up and connect to the Wi-Fi network.
  - It initializes the Wi-Fi connection and prints the local IP address once connected.

```
// Establishing a WiFi Connection
void establishWiFiConnection() {
  delay(10);
  Serial.println();
  Serial.print("Connecting to ");
  Serial.println(WIFI_SSID);

  WiFi.mode(WIFI_STA);
  WiFi.begin(WIFI_SSID, WIFI_PASSWORD);

  while (WiFi.status() != WL_CONNECTED) {
    delay(500);
    Serial.print(".");
  }

  randomSeed(micros());

  Serial.println("");
  Serial.println("WiFi connected");
  Serial.println("IP address: ");
  Serial.println(WiFi.localIP());
}
```

- **Function reconnect()**: Handles the reconnection to the MQTT broker.
  - It tries to connect to the broker and, if successful, publishes an initial message and subscribes to a topic.
  - It waits for five seconds before trying again.

```
// Reconnecting to MQTT Broker
void reconnectToMQTT() {
  while (!mqttClient.connected()) {
```

```
    Serial.print("Attempting MQTT connection...");
    if (mqttClient.connect(MQTT_CLIENT_ID, MQTT_USER, MQTT_PASSWORD)) {
      Serial.println("connected");
      mqttClient.publish("outTopic", "hello world"); // Publish initial message after connection
    } else {
      Serial.print("failed, rc=");
      Serial.print(mqttClient.state());
      Serial.println(" retrying in 5 seconds");
      delay(5000);
    }
  }
}
```

- **Function setup()**: Arduino's setup function:
  - It initializes the built-in LED pin as an output.
  - It also starts the serial communication, sets up Wi-Fi, and configures the MQTT server details.

```
void setup() {
  pinMode(BUILTIN_LED, OUTPUT); // Initialize the BUILTIN_LED pin as an output
  Serial.begin(115200);
  establishWiFiConnection(); // Connect to WiFi
  mqttClient.setServer(MQTT_SERVER_IP, MQTT_SERVER_PORT); // Set MQTT server and port
}
```

- **Function loop()**: The **main** loop function.
  - It checks the MQTT connection and handles reconnection if not connected. It also handles publishing a message every two seconds.
  - The message contains an incrementing value appended to **hello world** and is sent to the **outTopic** MQTT topic.

```
void loop() {
  if (!mqttClient.connected()) {
    reconnectToMQTT(); // Reconnect to MQTT if not connected
```

```
  }
  mqttClient.loop(); // Maintain MQTT connection

  unsigned long currentTime = millis();
  if (currentTime - lastMessageTime > 2000) {
    lastMessageTime = currentTime;
    ++counter;
      snprintf(message, MAX_MSG_BUFFER_SIZE, "hello world #%d", counter);
    Serial.print("Publishing message: ");
    Serial.println(message);
    mqttClient.publish("outTopic", message); // Publish message to 'outTopic'
  }
}
```

The code connects the ESP8266 to Wi-Fi, establishes an MQTT connection to a broker, and periodically publishes messages to the **outTopic** topic. It demonstrates basic MQTT functionality and showcases how to interact with Wi-Fi and MQTT using an ESP8266 device.

We will use this code to implement different projects in the following chapters.

Subscribing to a topic

Now, let us see how to subscribe to a topic from our microcontroller by using a **callback** function.

The following code connects to a WiFi network and to an MQTT broker in the same way that the previous code did. However, instead of publishing MQTT messages it subscribes to receive messages from the broker.

In the following code have been omitted the parts related to constants, global variables, WiFi connections, etc. Here you can see the details regarding the subscription process.

- **Message handling:**
  - The callback function (**callback**) handles incoming messages received on the subscribed topic (**inTopic**).
  - Whenever a message arrives on **inTopic**, the **callback** function is triggered.
  - The function prints out the received message's topic and payload.

  - Additionally, it toggles the built-in LED based on the received message's content. For instance, if the first character of the message payload is **`'1'`**, it turns on the LED; otherwise, it turns it off.

```
// Callback function for incoming MQTT messages
void handleIncomingMessage(char* topic, byte* payload, unsigned
int length) {
  Serial.print("Received message on topic [");
  Serial.print(topic);
  Serial.print("]: ");

  for (int i = 0; i < length; i++) {
    Serial.print((char)payload[i]);
  }
  Serial.println();

  if ((char)payload[0] == '1') {      // If message is "1" the LED
turns on, otherwise turns off.
    digitalWrite(BUILTIN_LED, LOW);
  } else {
    digitalWrite(BUILTIN_LED, HIGH);
  }
}
```

- **Subscription process:**
  - MQTT Reconnection (**`reconnect()`**) continuously attempts to connect to the MQTT broker until successful.
  - Once connected, the client subscribes to an MQTT topic named **`inTopic`** (**`client.subscribe(inTopic)`**).
  - This subscription is part of the successful connection process within the **`reconnect()`** function.

```
// Function to reconnect to MQTT broker
void attemptMQTTConnection() {
  while (!mqttClient.connected()) {   // While not connected, try
to connect to the MQTT broker
    Serial.print("Attempting MQTT connection...");
```

```
        if (mqttClient.connect(MQTT_CLIENT_ID, MQTT_USER, MQTT_
PASSWORD)) {
        Serial.println("MQTT connected");
        client.subscribe(MQTT_TOPIC); // Subscribe to the topic
      } else {
        Serial.print("Connection failed, return code=");
        Serial.print(mqttClient.state());
        Serial.println(" Retrying in 5 seconds...");
        delay(5000);
      }
    }
}

void setup() {
  pinMode(BUILTIN_LED, OUTPUT); // Initialize the BUILTIN_LED pin
as an output
  Serial.begin(115200);          // Set serial baudrate
  establishWiFiConnection();
    mqttClient.setServer(MQTT_SERVER_IP, MQTT_SERVER_PORT); //
Establish MQTT server
  mqttClient.setCallback(handleIncomingMessage);
}

void loop() {
  if (!mqttClient.connected()) {
    attemptMQTTConnection();
  }
  mqttClient.loop();
}
```

The code sets up the ESP8266 to connect to Wi-Fi and subscribe to an MQTT topic (**inTopic**). Upon successful connection to the broker, it subscribes to this topic and continuously listens for incoming messages.

Whenever a message is received on **inTopic**, it triggers the **callback** function to process and respond to the received message while keeping the MQTT connection active via the **main** loop.

When the message received contains the number one in the payload, the microcontroller lights on the LED. When the payload contains a zero, it turns off the LED.

Adding encryption to MQTT

In this section, we will delve into how to add encryption to our MQTT communications using the Mosquitto broker.

TLS/SSL and its usage

To begin with, TLS is a standard based on SSL, developed after vulnerabilities were discovered in SSLv3. So, when we talk about SSL today, we generally mean TLS.

The purpose of using SSL/TLS is to provide authentication, encryption, and integrity.

This means the following:

- **Authentication**: Ensures the sender is who they claim to be.
- **Encryption**: Prevents anyone along the path from reading the message.
- **Integrity**: Ensures the message cannot be altered.

To achieve this, a digital signature (certificate) and public/private keys are used to encrypt and decrypt the message. Next, we will go step by step on how to add encryption to MQTT communication.

Requirement

To implement encryption in Mosquitto, we need the following:

1. Generate a public and private key for the **certificate authority** (**CA**).
2. Create a certificate for the CA and sign it with the previously generated private key.
3. Generate a public and private key for the MQTT broker.
4. Create a certificate signing request for the keys from the previous step.
5. Use the certificate from *step* 2 to sign the request from the previous step.
6. Copy all certificates to a directory on the MQTT broker.
7. Copy the CA certificate to the client.
8. Edit the Mosquitto configuration.
9. Edit the client configuration to use TLS and the CA certificate.

This may seem complex, but let us take it step by step. First, let us install SSL on our Raspberry Pi using the following command:

```
$ sudo apt-get install openssl
```

Now, let us start with the process:

1. **Create the CA key pair**: Run the following command on the Raspberry Pi, using `sudo` for root permissions:

```
$ sudo openssl genrsa -des3 -out ca.key 2048
```

2. **Create a certificate for the CA and sign it**: Execute the following command, entering the passphrase from the previous step and then providing the required data. The most important is the common name, which can be any name. In our case, we have used the hostname **raspberry**. Ensure this name can be resolved to your Raspberry Pi.

   ```
   $ openssl req -new -x509 -days 1826 -key ca.key -out ca.crt
   ```

3. **Create the broker MQTT key pair**: Generate the key pair for the broker with:

   ```
   $ sudo openssl genrsa -out server.key 2048
   ```

4. **Create a certificate request**: Create a certificate request file (**.csr**). During creation, enter the same values as for the CA certificate but modify some to ensure they are not identical, which could disrupt the connection.

   ```
   $ sudo openssl req -new -out server.csr -key server.key
   ```

5. **Sign the certificate request**: Use the CA certificate to sign the request from the previous step, creating the **.crt** file for the broker.

   ```
   $ sudo openssl x509 -req -in server.csr -CA ca.crt -CAkey ca.key
   -CAcreateserial -out server.crt -days 360
   ```

6. **View created files**: Use **ls** to view all created files. The **ca.key** file is not copied to the broker or client, as it is only used for generating new certificates.

7. **Copy files to the broker**: Now copy **ca.crt**, **server.crt**, and **server.key** to the Mosquitto configuration directories. These directories are typically found at **/etc/mosquitto**. Place **ca.crt** in **ca_certificates** and **server.crt** and **server.key** in **certs**.

8. **Copy certificates to the client**: Copy **ca.crt** to your client. The exact location varies by client.

9. **Configure Mosquitto**: Modify the Mosquitto configuration to use SSL/TLS. Mosquitto provides an example configuration file located at **/usr/share/doc/mosquitto/examples**. Copy it to **/etc/mosquitto/conf.d** and rename it to **mosquitto.conf** if it has the **.example** suffix.

   ```
   $ sudo cp /usr/share/doc/mosquitto/examples/mosquitto.conf.example /
   etc/mosquitto/conf.d/mosquitto.conf
   ```

   ```
   $ sudo nano /etc/mosquitto/conf.d/mosquitto.conf
   ```

   Configure the port to **8883**, which is used for encrypted communications, and specify the locations of the certificate files.

10. **Test connection with the broker**: Finally, test the connection with the broker from your client. Ensure your **hosts** file (if on Windows) or equivalent is edited to resolve the hostname to your Raspberry Pi.

    To subscribe:

```
$ mqtt-cli.exe sub -t test -h raspberry -p 8883 -s --cafile ca.crt -V
3 -v
```

To publish:

```
$ mqtt-cli.exe pub -t test -m "hello" -h raspberry -p 8883 -s --cafile
ca.crt -V 3 -v
```

We have explored how to add encryption to MQTT communications. While the steps are numerous, the process itself is not overly complicated.

Using Node-RED with MQTT

As we have seen in the previous chapter, Node-RED offers great flexibility to implement IoT systems. Now, we will use it to connect the Raspberry Pi to an MQTT broker.

By default, Node-RED comes with MQTT blocks to subscribe and publish messages.

Follow these steps to connect to an MQTT broker from Node-RED:

1. In order to start, go to the web interface of Node-RED by pointing your browser to **http://your-raspberry-pi-ip:1880**
2. On the left panel, select the MQTT input block, as shown in *Figure 5.7*. Drag the block and drop it in the flow space. Then, double-click on it to configure it.

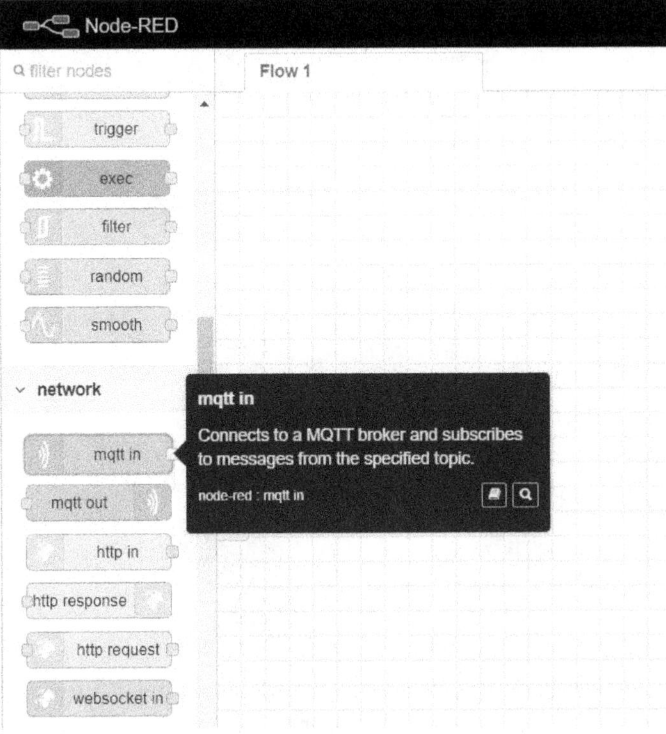

***Figure 5.7**: Add an mqtt in block*

3. In the configuration of the *MQTT in* a block, you will see the configuration options. Refer to the following figure for clarity:

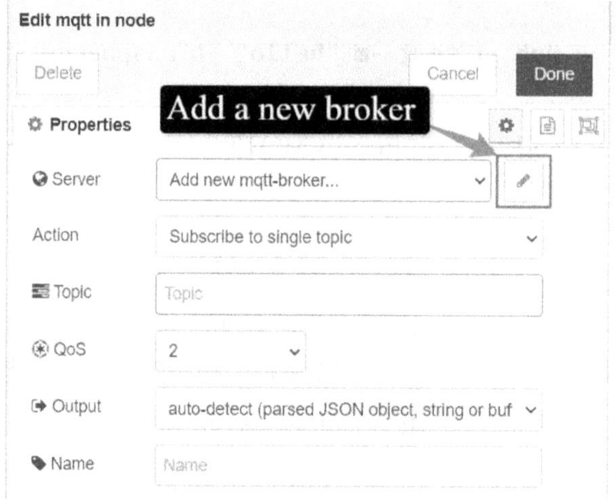

Figure 5.8*: Adding a new MQTT broker*

4. Click on the pencil icon to add a new MQTT broker. This will lead you to the interface shown in *Figure 5.9*:

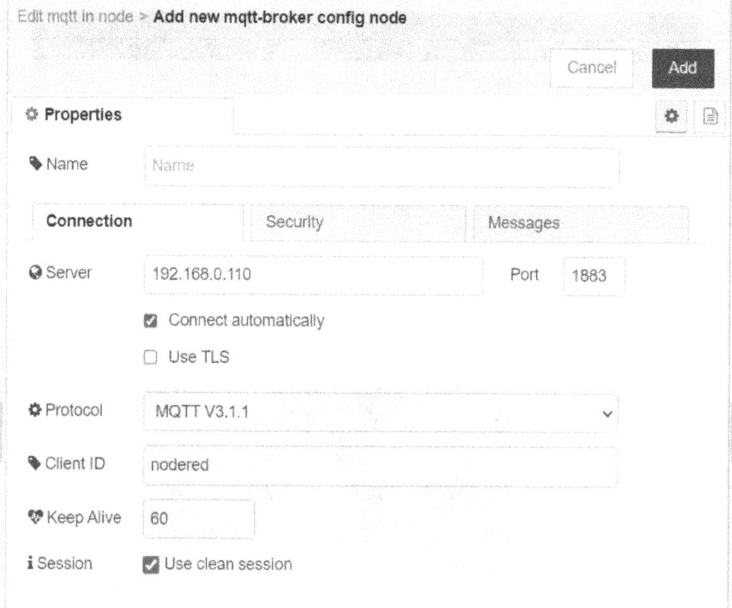

Figure 5.9*: Configuring the MQTT broker client*

5. In the connection section, enter the IP and the port of the broker you are using. Select the right version of MQTT, according to the one used by the broker. Also, specify the client-id and the keep-alive parameter. In this case, we are not using

encryption, so we do not select the **TLS** option. Refer to the following figure for a better understanding:

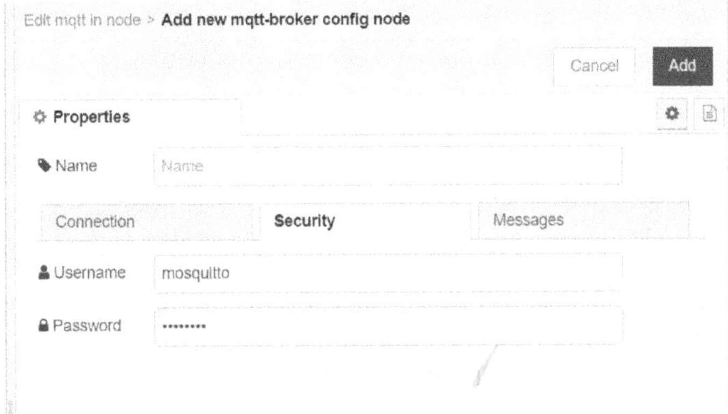

***Figure 5.10**: Configuring the security options*

6. In the **Security** section, enter the username and the password.
7. Give a name to your broker so you can identify it easily.
8. When you finish the previous steps, click on the **Add** button. This will lead you to the previous windows, where you will see something similar to *Figure 5.11*:

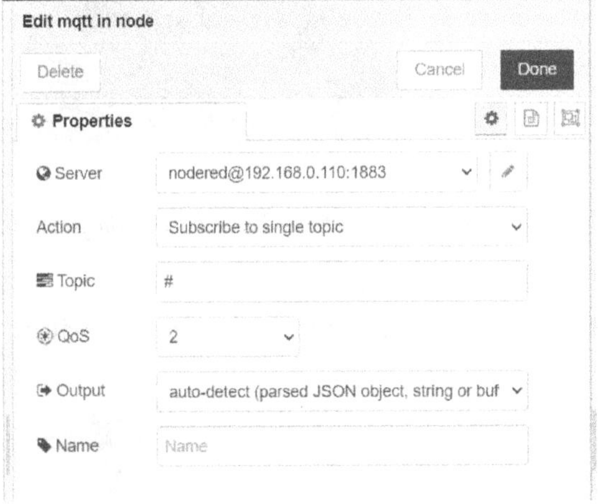

***Figure 5.11**: MQTT in the block with an MQTT server*

9. Now that you have an MQTT server to connect to, you can use it to subscribe to a topic. You can use a specific topic or a wildcard to get data from multiple topics. In *Figure 5.11*, a **#** is used to subscribe to all the topics available in the broker. Also, you can choose the **QoS** type and the payload format.
10. Finally, give a name to the block and click on the **Done** button. Then click on **Deploy**. If all the parameters are correctly configured, you will see the client connected in the flow space, as shown in *Figure 5.12*:

***Figure 5.12:** MQTT client connected to the broker, and debug block to show data received*

11. Now, add a debug block and connect the output of the *MQTT in* block to it. In this way, you will see the data received from the broker in the debug interface. You can send data from any MQTT client to test the configuration.
12. Click on **Deploy** to apply all the configurations.

Now, let us see how we can publish data to an MQTT broker using Node-RED:

1. First, go the the block section and select the MQTT out block, as shown in *Figure 5.13*:

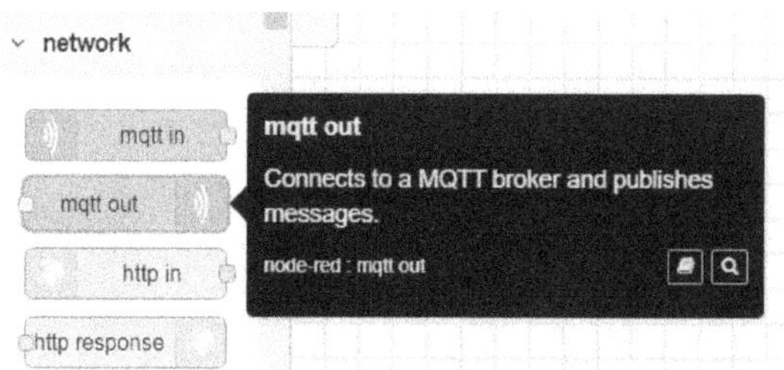

***Figure 5.13:** Add an MQTT out block to the flow*

2. Select the MQTT broker you want to use, specify a topic and QoS level, and give the block a name. Refer to the following figure for clarity:

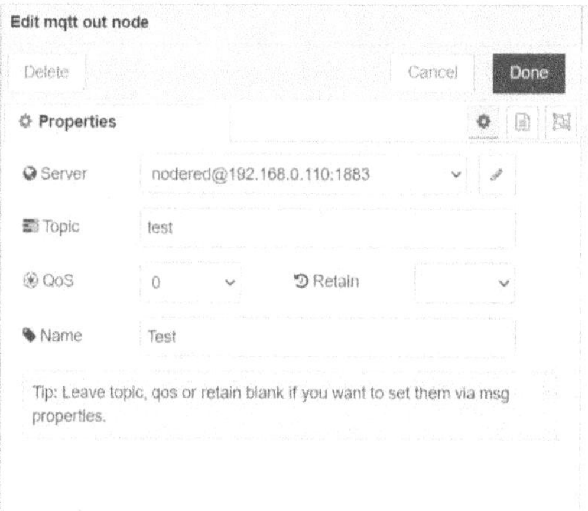

***Figure 5.14:** Configuring the MQTT out block*

3. When you are ready, click on the **Done** button.
4. Now, you will need a block to send data to the broker. Drag and drop an inject node and double-click on it to configure it. In the msg.payload field, select string as type and enter some text, as shown in *Figure 5.15*:

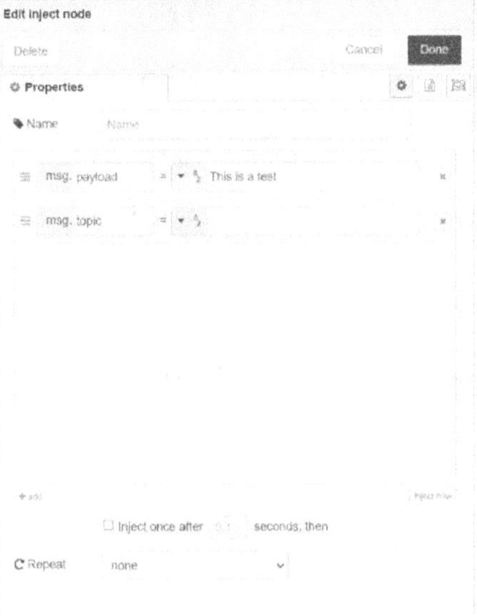

***Figure 5.15**: Configure the inject node*

5. Give the block a name and click on the **Done** button.
6. Now, connect the inject block with the MQTT out block, and click on **Deploy**. Every time you click on the inject node, you will see the message in the debug window, as shown in *Figure 5.16*:

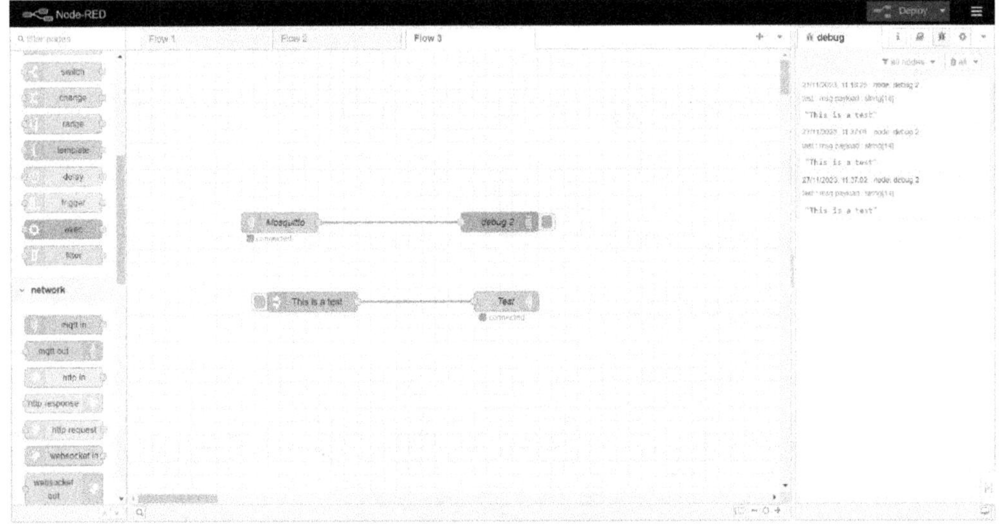

***Figure 5.16**: Complete MQTT flow*

Until here, we have learned to use the MQTT client in the Node-RED environment. We will use this configuration in the following chapters to interact with the MQTT broker from Node-RED.

Using HiveMQ MQTT broker

HiveMQ is a renowned MQTT service provider with a free tier available for unlimited use. This free tier supports up to 100 MQTT devices and allows for 10 GB of data transfer per month, which is sufficient for most IoT applications.

This means you can operate your IoT system with up to 100 devices (clients) in the HiveMQ cloud.

To start using HiveMQ, go to **https://www.hivemq.com/company/get-hivemq**

Once registered, you will need to select a service option (see *Figure 5.17*).

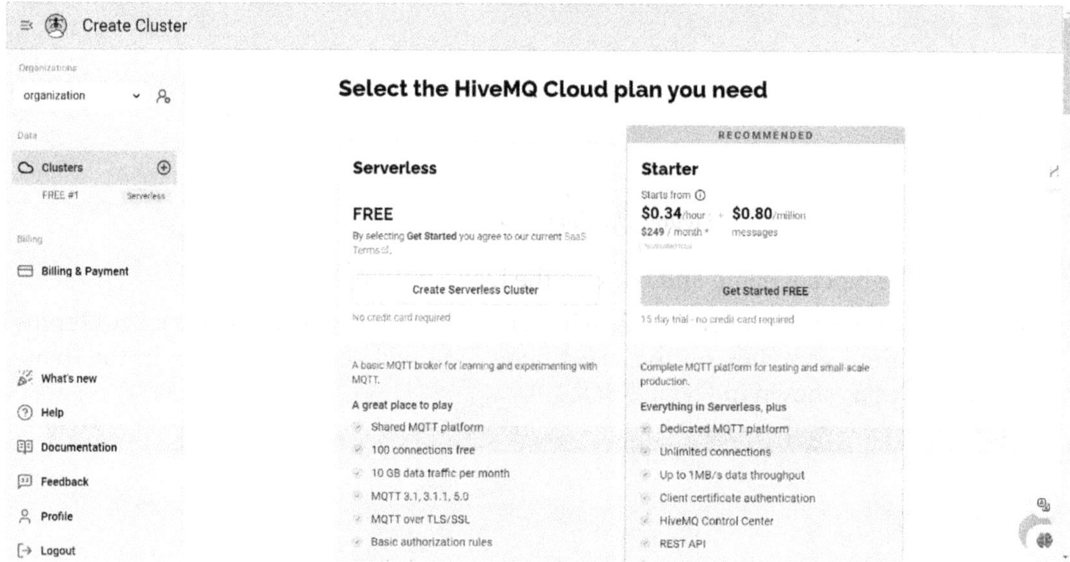

Figure 5.17: Selecting HiveMQ service

To create a cluster, choose the **Serverless FREE** service.

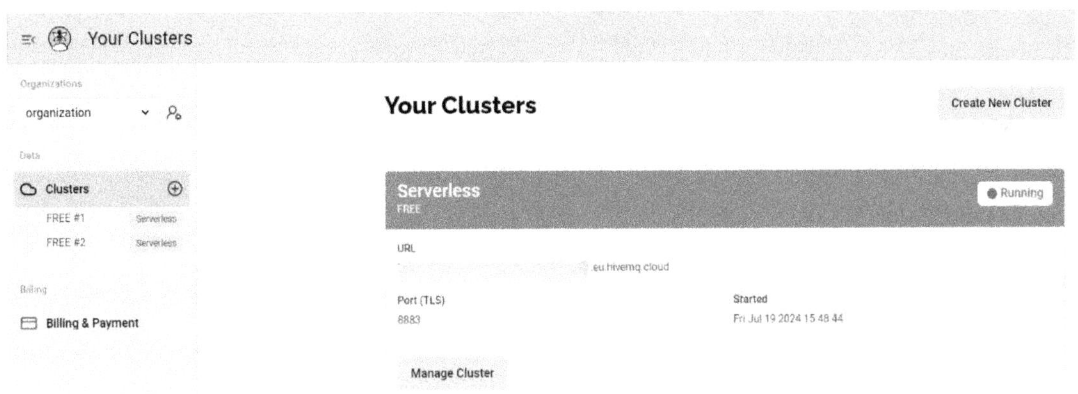

Figure 5.18: *Your cluster*

After creating the cluster, you can view its details, as shown in *Figure 5.19*:

OVERVIEW ACCESS MANAGEMENT INTEGRATIONS NEW WEB CLIENT

Cluster Details

Cluster Information

Name Current Plan Current Tier

d28 Serverless FREE

Cloud Provider

aws

▶ What is included in my plan?

Cluster URL

782 .s1.eu.hivemq.cloud

Port

8883

Websocket Port

8884

TLS MQTT URL

782 .s1.eu.hivemq.cloud:8883

TLS WebSocket URL

7828 .s1.eu.hivemq.cloud:8884/mqtt

Figure 5.19: *Cluster details*

Next, you have to create user credentials and give publish/subscribe permissions to the user. See *Figure 5.20*:

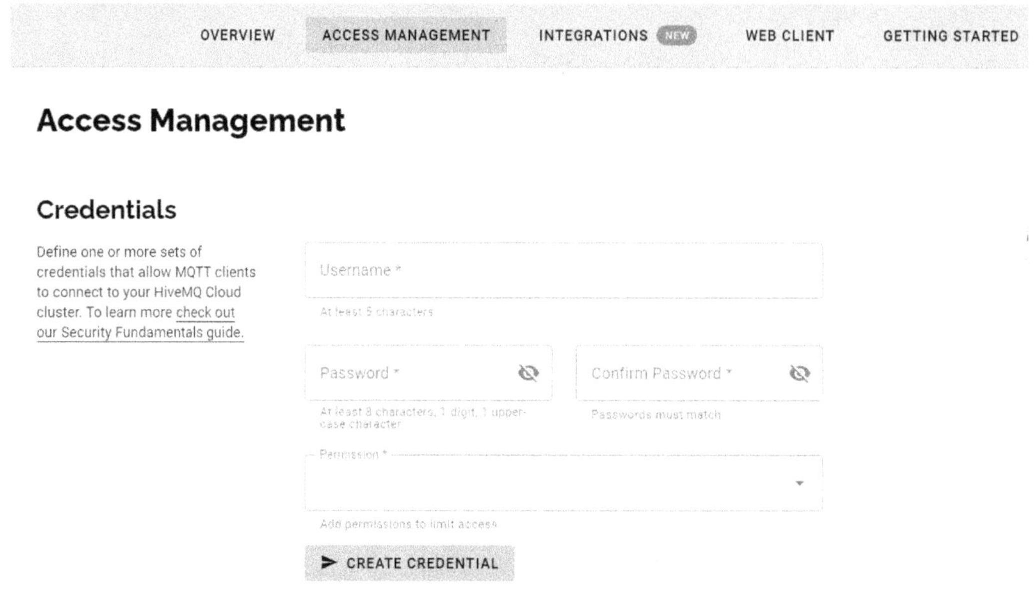

Figure 5.20: Creating user credentials

Finally, you will be able to connect to the MQTT service using a MQTT client.

Conclusion

In this chapter, we learned about using MQTT. First, we explored the MQTT architecture and how it works. Then, we learned the most important features of the protocol, like QoS levels, wildcards, retained messages, last will and testament, etc.

We also saw the main differences between MQTT versions. After having a clear view of the MQTT protocols, we installed a Mosquitto broker in the Raspberry Pi and configured it.

Then, we started to play with MQTT clients. In particular the Mosquitto CLI client and the MQTTX. The last one offers a very nice and simple user desktop interface. After testing the broker with the clients, we implemented our client using Python and the Paho library, developed by the *Eclipse Foundation*. Last but not least, we used Node-RED to connect to our broker for subscribing and publishing messages.

In the next chapter, we will learn about the CoAP protocol, a widely used IoT protocol. We will see its characteristics and will learn to use it in IoT projects.

CHAPTER 6
CoAP for IoT Connectivity

Introduction

Constrained Application Protocol (**CoAP**) is one of the most used IoT protocols for constrained devices. This protocol offers a small overhead, fast and light communications, and low power consumption.

It uses HTTP-like messages to send and receive messages. This leads to easy-to-implement solutions. Also, there are many libraries and tools that we will use throughout the chapter.

Structure

This chapter covers the following topics:

- CoAP fundamentals
- Using CoAP in Raspberry Pi
- Implementing CoAP with Node-RED
- Using CoAP with Arduino

Objectives

In this chapter, we will see the protocol fundamentals, its features, and its advantages. Also, we will look at how to use it to communicate with microcontrollers the Raspberry Pi computer.

By the end of this chapter, you will know how the protocol works and how to implement it using the tools covered here.

CoAP fundamentals

CoAP is a specialized protocol that facilitates communication between constrained devices in low-power and low-bandwidth networks. Unlike traditional protocols like HTTP, CoAP is specifically tailored to meet the unique demands of IoT devices. Let us see some of its features:

- It minimizes overhead and utilizes efficient messaging to enable reliable communication in resource-constrained scenarios.
- CoAP follows a client-server architecture like HTTP but optimized for IoT.
- Devices in a CoAP network can act as clients, servers, or both. Clients initiate communication by sending requests to servers, which respond with relevant data or actions.
- CoAP supports various request methods, such as GET, POST, PUT, and DELETE, allowing clients to retrieve data, create new resources, update resources, and remove resources.
- Servers generate responses containing the requested data or the outcome of the requested action.
- CoAP defines four primary message types: **confirmable** (**CON**), **non-confirmable** (**NON**), **acknowledgment** (**ACK**), and **reset** (**RST**).
- CoAP resources are fundamental entities in the protocol, identified using **Uniform Resource Identifiers** (**URIs**). CoAP's lightweight design and support for constrained devices make it a pivotal protocol in shaping the future of IoT applications.
- CoAP uses the **User Datagram Protocol** (**UDP**) as its transport protocol. UDP is a lightweight and connectionless transport protocol that requires less overhead compared to TCP. This makes UDP a suitable choice for constrained environments where resources such as bandwidth, processing power, and energy are limited.
- UDP does not guarantee reliable data delivery by default, but CoAP offers three levels of reliability (confirmable, non-confirmable, and acknowledgement) to cater to different use cases. CoAP's use of UDP is one of its distinguishing features that contributes to its efficiency and adaptability in constrained networks.

CoAP architecture

CoAP follows a client-server architecture like HTTP but optimized for IoT devices. In this architecture, CoAP clients initiate communication by sending requests to CoAP servers, which respond with relevant data or actions, refer to *Figure 6.1* for a better understanding:

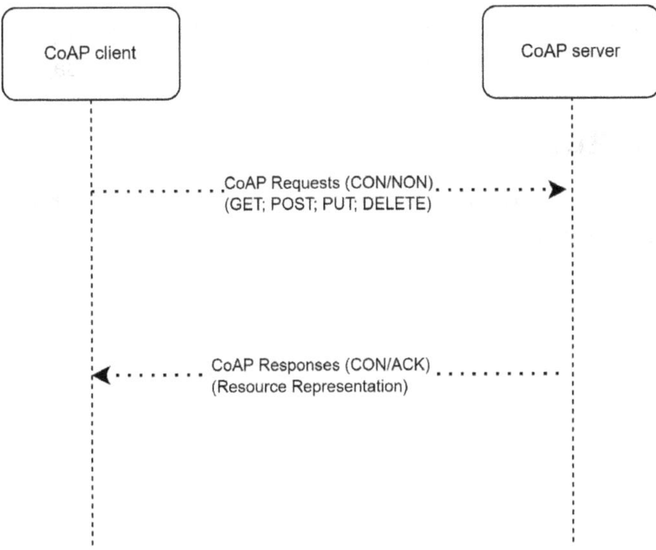

Figure 6.1: *CoAP architecture*

Let us explore some definitions of the CoAP architecture:

- **Clients**: Clients can be sensors, actuators, or any other IoT devices that require data or actions from the network.
- **Servers**: CoAP servers process incoming requests, perform relevant actions, and generate responses containing the requested data or indicating the status of the operation.
- **Proxies**: They can be used as intermediaries between clients and servers, filtering or modifying requests and responses, or caching responses to reduce network traffic.
- **CoAP resources**: They are identified using URIs and can represent data, services, or actions that a device exposes to the network. Similar to URLs in HTTP, URIs can represent data, services, or actions that a device exposes to the network. This design allows for interoperability and the application of web paradigms to IoT applications. For example, a CoAP URI could be **coap://example.com/temperature** where *example.com* is the server address and *temperature* is the resource being accessed.
- **Messages**: CoAP messages are small and lightweight, encapsulating each request and response. They can include options that provide additional information about the request or response, such as content format, observe, ETag, and Max-Age.

- **Block-wise transfers**: This feature is supported to allow large resources to be split into smaller blocks and transferred in a sequence of requests and responses. This enables devices with limited memory and bandwidth to access large resources.

CoAP messages

CoAP messages are an important part of the implementation of the protocol. In this section, we will explore the main characteristics and options of CoAP messages.

Message structure

CoAP messages have a defined structure for enabling efficient data exchange and transmission control. You can see this structure in *Figure 6.2*:

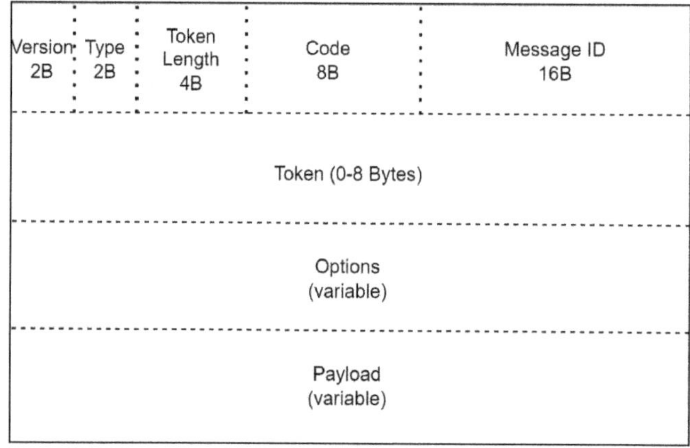

Figure 6.2*: Message structure*

CoAP message header

The header encapsulates details about the message and its attributes. It includes the following fields:

- **Version (2 bits)**: It denotes the CoAP version in use.
- **Type (2 bits)**: It specifies message types like CON, NON, ACK, or RST.
- **Token length (4 bits)**: It dictates the token field's size.
- **Code (8 bits)**: It defines the CoAP method, response, or error code.
- **Message ID (16 bits)**: It uniquely identifies the message, facilitating request-response pairing.

Token

This segment correlates related messages in a CoAP exchange. A randomly generated value, the token aids in associating interlinked requests and responses. Its length is specified within the header and can have a value between 0 and 8.

Message types

The CoAP protocol defines four message types: confirmable, non-confirmable, acknowledgment, and reset, as explained in the following:

- **Confirmable messages**: They ensure reliable communication by requiring acknowledgment and retransmission until acknowledged.
- **Non-confirmable messages**: They prioritize efficiency over reliability.
- **Acknowledgment messages**: They are sent by the recipient of a confirmable message to confirm receipt.
- **Reset messages**: They are sent when a server or client receives a message that cannot be processed.

Message options

CoAP messages can include various options that provide additional information about the request or response. Some of the common options in CoAP messages include:

- **Content-format**: It specifies the format of the payload in a CoAP message. It also indicates how the data in the payload should be interpreted or processed. For example, it can indicate that the payload contains JSON, XML, or binary data.
- **Observe**: The Observe option is used for resource observation in CoAP. It allows clients to subscribe to resources and receive real-time updates about changes to those resources. When a resource changes, the server sends an updated response to the observing clients.
- **ETag**: The ETag option is used for caching and conditional requests in CoAP. It is a unique identifier for a specific version of a resource. Clients can include the ETag value in subsequent requests to check if the resource has changed since the last request.
- **Max-Age**: The Max-Age option indicates the cache validity duration for a resource. It specifies the maximum time in seconds that a resource can be considered fresh without revalidating it with the server. After the Max-Age duration expires, the client needs to revalidate the resource with the server.
- **URI-Path and URI-Query**: The URI-Path option identifies the resource path in the URI, providing additional context to the message. It allows the client or server to specify the path to the desired resource. On the other hand, the URI-Query option provides query parameters for the resource. It allows clients to include additional

information or parameters in the request which can be used by the server to process the request or filter the response.

Payload

The payload contains the actual transmitted or received data, the payload's length and format depend on the specific use case and the content-format option specified in the header. This section might include sensor data, commands, or other pertinent information. The recommended maximum length is 1024 bytes.

CoAP security

CoAP is crafted as a streamlined and resource-effective protocol suitable for devices and networks with limited capabilities.

CoAP implements security through **Datagram Transport Layer Security** (**DTLS**) which establishes a secure communication channel between devices and ensures the confidentiality and integrity of data exchanged.

Additionally, CoAP supports lightweight security mechanisms such as **pre-shared key** (**PSK**) and **Raw Public Key** (**RPK**) to authenticate endpoints and secure communication. These security measures help protect against unauthorized access and ensure the secure transmission of data in CoAP.

However, the protocol's simplicity leaves it susceptible to specific security vulnerabilities.

The following outlines several security concerns within CoAP, along with potential remedial actions:

- **Resource discovery exploitation**: CoAP offers a straightforward method for discovering network resources, prone to exploitation by attackers seeking unauthorized access. To counter resource discovery attacks, enforce access control mechanisms on the CoAP server, restricting entry to specific resources.
- **Authentication gap**: CoAP lacks inherent authentication mechanisms, enabling anyone to send requests to a CoAP server. To mitigate this, DTLS can be employed for secure communication via UDP. DTLS delivers authentication and encryption services to safeguard communication between the CoAP client and server.
- **Message tampering risk**: CoAP messages are susceptible to interception and modification by attackers, potentially leading to unauthorized access or data compromise. You can mitigate this risk by employing message integrity measures like **message authentication code** (**MAC**) or digital signatures, ensuring message integrity during transmission.
- **DoS vulnerability**: CoAP is prone to DoS attacks wherein attackers flood the server with requests, causing it to overload and become unresponsive. Preventive

measures involve implementing rate limiting and access control mechanisms on the CoAP server.

- **Authorization deficiency**: CoAP lacks built-in authorization mechanisms, granting access to server resources for anyone sending requests. Addressing this issue involves integrating access control mechanisms on the server which limit resource access based on client identity and request type.

Now that we have explored the fundamentals of the CoAP protocol, we will see how to use it in the Raspberry Pi computer and microcontrollers.

Using CoAP in Raspberry Pi

Installing a server in a Raspberry Pi is not as easy as installing the Mosquitto broker. However, we can still do it with a minimal setup.

There are many implementations based on different languages and frameworks. You can find the list of available projects in the following link **https://coap.space/impls.html**. Some interesting projects are mentioned in the following:

- **Californium**: It is an entire CoAP ecosystem, developed by the *Eclipse Foundation*. You can reach its webpage at **https://eclipse.dev/californium/**. However, we will not use it in this book as it requires the installation of the Java environment.
- **libCoAP**: It is a library written in C that you can use in a **Portable Operating System Interface** (**POSIX**), like any *Unix*, *Linux*, or *macOS*. Also, there are versions available for embedded devices that run *Contiki*, *TinyOS*, *LwIP*, and *RIOT* operating systems. We will use this library to build a simple CoAP server in our Raspberry Pi.
- **Aiocoap**: It is a Python library that uses asynchronous mechanisms. Also, it provides command line tools for fetching and proxying resources. We will use this module to implement CoAP clients with Python.

Let us start by installing the `libcoap` library.

Installing libcoap

In order to install the `libcoap` library in the Raspberry Pi, follow these steps:

1. Connect to the Raspberry Pi through SSH using PuTTY or any other SSH client.
2. If you do not have Git installed, use the following commands to install it:

```
$ sudo apt update
$ sudo apt upgrade
$ sudo apt install git
```

3. Now, use `git` to download the source code of `libcoap` from its repository.

```
$ git clone https://github.com/obgm/libcoap.git
```

4. The previous step will create a directory called **libcoap**. Go inside the directory running the next command.

```
$ cd libcoap
```

If you run the **ls** command in the directory, you will see a list similar to the one shown in *Figure 6.3*:

***Figure 6.3**: Files obtained from the GitHub repository*

5. From within the **libcoap** directory, run the following command.

```
$ ./autogen.sh
```

6. Now, configure the repository to be able to compile it. In the following command, we can use the following four options:

   a. The option **enable-examples** installs all the provided program examples in the repository.

   b. **disable-doxygen** and **disable-manpages** options disable the installation of docs. This is advantageous as the docs require the Doxygen package. So, by disabling the **manpages**, we avoid installing it. On the other hand, it is not necessary to have the docs in our Raspberry Pi.

   c. The **disable-dtls** option gets rid of the installation of the encryption part. As we will not use encryption, we do not need this.

   To see all the available configurations, visit **https://libcoap.net/install.html**.

   Run the following command to configure the code for compilation:

```
$ ./configure --enable-examples --disable-doxygen --disable-manpages
--disable-dtls
```

7. Now that we have configured the package, we need to compile it and install it by running the following commands from the repository directory:

   $ make

   $ sudo make install

8. Once the installation finishes, you will have all the libraries, examples, and binaries to run CoAP servers and clients. Go to the **examples** directory to see all the code examples and binaries, as shown in *Figure 6.4*:

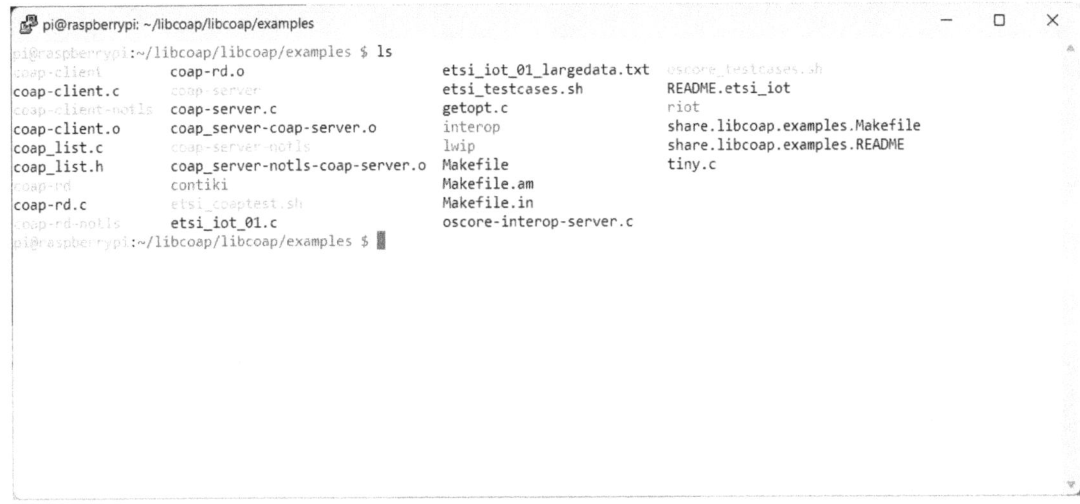

***Figure 6.4**: Code examples and executable files*

9. You can run the commands **coap-client**, **coap-client-notls**, **coap-rd**, **coap-rd-notls**, **coap-server**, and **coap-server-notls** from the **examples** directory.

Running libcoap

Now that you have **libcoap** installed on the Raspberry Pi, you can start using it.

Execute these steps for running and testing a CoAP server:

1. First, we will run a CoAP server using the **coap-server** executable. Go to the **examples** directory and run the following command:

   $ ./coap-server

2. Now, open another console by connecting to the Raspberry Pi, go to the **examples** directory, and run the following command.

   $ ./coap-client -m get coap://localhost/.well-known/core

This will show you the available resources in the CoAP server. You will get something like the screen shown in *Figure 6.5*. In our case, we have not created any resources yet, so it shows default sample data.

Figure 6.5: Showing the resources available on the server

Creating dynamic resources

In order to be able to create dynamic resources, you have to use the **-d** option in the **coap-server** command. This parameter allows resource creation during a PUT and sets a maximum limit. When this limit is reached, a 4.06 status code is sent back until some dynamic resources are deleted.

The following command allows the dynamic creation of resources with a limit of ten:

```
$ ./coap-server -d 10
```

Now, you can go to the other console and execute the client to create a new resource on the server.

The following command will create a new resource called **actuators/relay** and set its value to **1** (string):

```
$ ./coap-client -e 1 -m put coap://localhost/actuators/relay
```

Now, you can get the value of the resource by running the following command, which will show you the value of **1**:

```
$ ./coap-client -m get coap://localhost/actuators/relay
$ 1
```

In the same way, you can set the value to zero, as follows:

```
$ ./coap-client -e 0 -m put coap://localhost/actuators/relay
```

Any client can request the value of the resource and use it to control, for instance, a relay.

If the server does not allow dynamic resources, any request on a resource that does not exist will throw a 404 error.

Finally, if you run the well-known query, you will see the newly created resource, as shown in *Figure 6.6*:

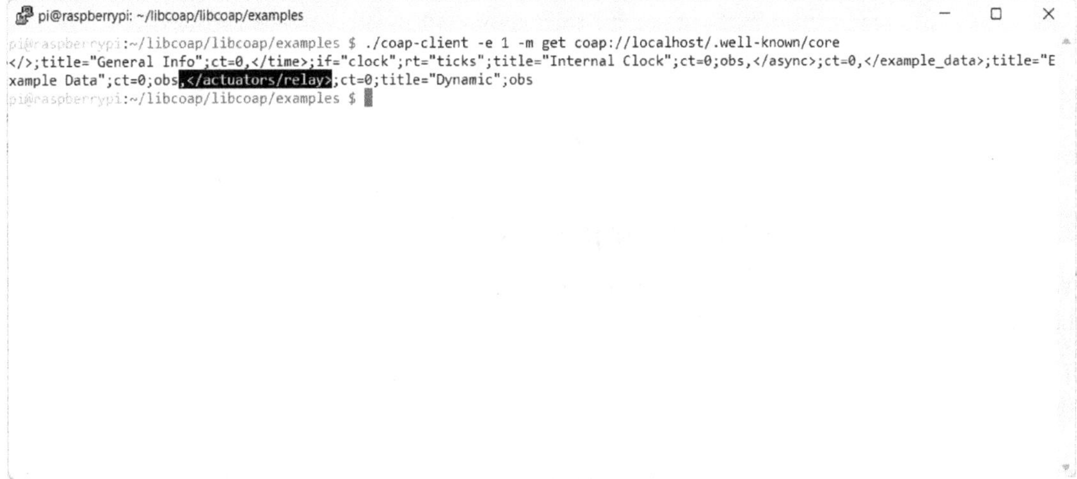

Figure 6.6*: New resource in CoAP server*

Using aiocoap

As we mentioned earlier in this section, **aiocoap** is a Python module for implementing CoAP applications.

Installing aiocoap

In order to be able to use **aiocoap**, we need to install the module first. Use the following instructions to download it from the PyPI repository (**https://pypi.org/project/aiocoap/**) and install it:

1. First, create a new Python environment (if you have not already done it). The following commands create and activate the **raspenv** Python environment:

   ```
   $ python3 -m venv raspenv
   $ source raspenv/bin/activate
   ```

   Remember that we use Python environments to keep our Python projects organized and clean. On the other hand, you cannot install the module using **pip** outside of an environment, as Python is installed system-wide in Raspberry Pi.

2. Once you are in the Python environment, you can install the module as follows:

   ```
   $ pip install aiocoap
   ```

This will download the module and install it in the environment, as shown in *Figure 6.7*:

```
(raspenv) pi@raspberrypi:~ $ pip install aiocoap
Looking in indexes: https://pypi.org/simple, https://www.piwheels.org/simple
Collecting aiocoap
  Downloading https://www.piwheels.org/simple/aiocoap/aiocoap-0.4.7-py3-none-any
.whl (208 kB)
     ━━━━━━━━━━━━━━━━━━━━━━━━━━━━━━━━━━━━━━ 208.4/208.4 kB 183.3 kB/s eta 0:00:00
Installing collected packages: aiocoap
Successfully installed aiocoap-0.4.7
(raspenv) pi@raspberrypi:~ $
```

***Figure 6.7**: Installing aiocoap using pip*

Documentation of aiocoap module

You can reach the full documentation of this module at **https://aiocoap.readthedocs.io/en/latest/index.html**.

There, you will find all the information about the module, such as several examples, and the full Python API.

Implementing CoAP clients with aiocoap

In this section, we will see how to use **aiocoap** to implement CoAP clients.

You can reach the examples provided by the project developers on this link **https://aiocoap.readthedocs.io/en/latest/examples.html.**

We will use these examples as a basis to develop our clients.

CoAP client to set a resource value

Taking the example of the relay, we used previously, the following code implements a put action to set the state of the relay to 1 or 0:

```
#filename coap_relay_control.py
import logging
import argparse
import asyncio
from aiocoap import *

logging.basicConfig(level=logging.INFO)

async def set_relay_state(state):
```

```
    context = await Context.create_client_context()

    relay_request = Message(code=PUT, uri=f'coap://<ip-of-server>/actuators/
relay', payload=str(state).encode())

    try:
        response = await context.request(relay_request).response
    except Exception as error:
        print('Failed to set relay state:')
        print(f"Encountered error: {error}")
    else:
        print('Relay state set successfully.')
        print('Response: %s\n%r' % (response.code, response.payload))

if __name__ == "__main__":
    parser = argparse.ArgumentParser(description='Set the value of the relay
resource (0 or 1).')
    parser.add_argument('state', metavar='state', type=int, choices=[0, 1],
help='Value for the relay (0 or 1)')

    args = parser.parse_args()

    asyncio.run(set_relay_state(args.state))
```

This script uses an argument to set the value of the resource to 1 or 0. To use it, execute the command as follows. Notice that you are running it from within the Python environment.

For setting the relay to 1:

(raspenv) pi@raspberrypi:~ $ python coap_relay_control.py 1

For setting the relay to 0:

(raspenv) pi@raspberrypi:~ $ python coap_relay_control.py 0

CoAP client to get a resource value

The following code gets the value of the resource we set up with the previous script:

```
# filename coap_relay_state_getter.py
import logging
import asyncio
```

```
from aiocoap import *

logging.basicConfig(level=logging.INFO)

async def get_relay_state():
    context = await Context.create_client_context()

    relay_request = Message(code=GET, uri='coap://<ip-of-server>/actuators/
relay')

    try:
        response = await context.request(relay_request).response
    except Exception as error:
        print('Failed to retrieve relay state:')
        print(f"Encountered error: {error}")
    else:
        print('Relay state retrieved successfully.')
        print('State: %s\n%r' % (response.code, response.payload.
decode('utf-8')))

if __name__ == "__main__":
    asyncio.run(get_relay_state())
```

This code gets the value of the resource **actuators/relay** and shows it on the screen. To use it, execute it as follows:

```
(raspenv) pi@raspberrypi:~ $ python coap_relay_state_getter.py
```

Implementing CoAP with Node-RED

There are many CoAP nodes available for use in Node-RED. We will use **node-red-contrib-coap**, as it is the most updated when writing this book. You can reach the page of the node at **https://flows.nodered.org/node/node-red-contrib-coap**.

Installing CoAP in Node-RED

To install CoAP in Node-RED, we will follow the procedure given in the following:

1. Access the web interface of Node-RED by pointing your browser to **http://your-raspberry-ip:1880.**

2. Once you have opened the web interface, go to the right menu and select **Manage palette**, as shown in *Figure 6.8*:

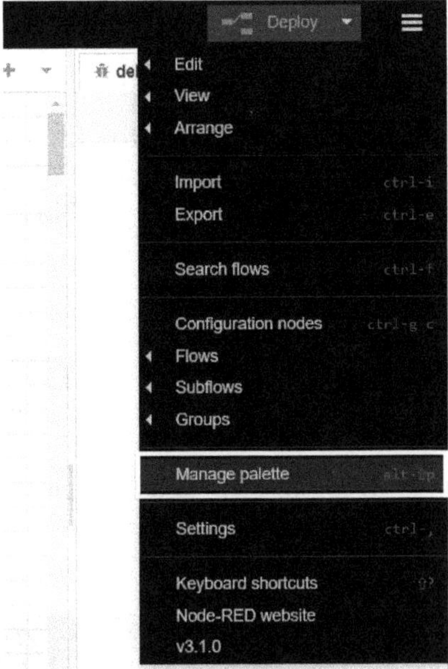

***Figure 6.8**: Manage palette in Node-RED*

3. This will lead you to the panel shown in *Figure 6.9*. Click on the **install** button of the **`node-red-contrib-coap node`** and wait for the node to be installed.

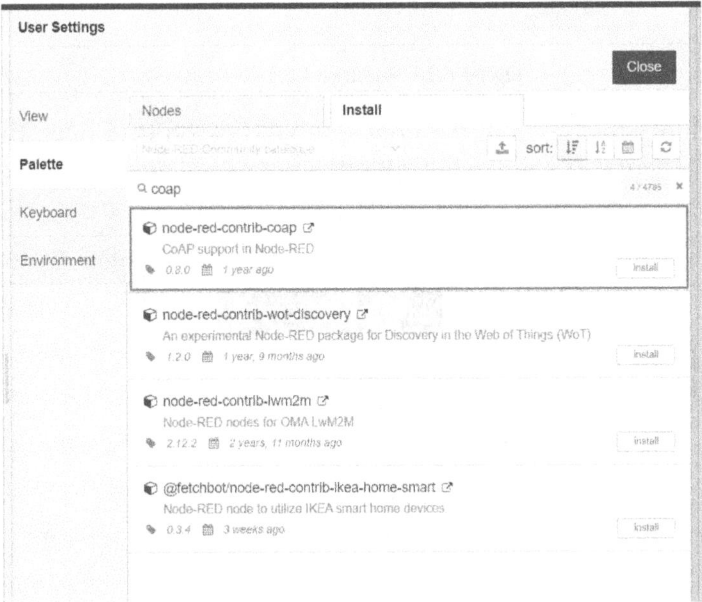

***Figure 6.9**: Installing node-red-contrib-coap node*

Now, let us see how to use these nodes to implement CoAP in Node-RED.

Implementing CoAP in Node-RED

In this section, we will implement a CoAP server in Node-RED.

You can download all the settings and code from the file located at **https://github.com/ingrjhernandez/node-red/blob/main/coap-server.json. You can implement the whole system described in this section by importing this JSON file into your Node-RED or by copying and pasting the content of the JSON file. You can refer to** *Chapter 4, Interfacing with Raspberry Pi,* for further information.

Creating a CoAP server in Node-RED

To set up a CoAP server in Node-RED, follow these steps:

1. Creating a CoAP server in Node-RED is as simple as adding a *CoAP in* node, as you can see in *Figure 6.10*:

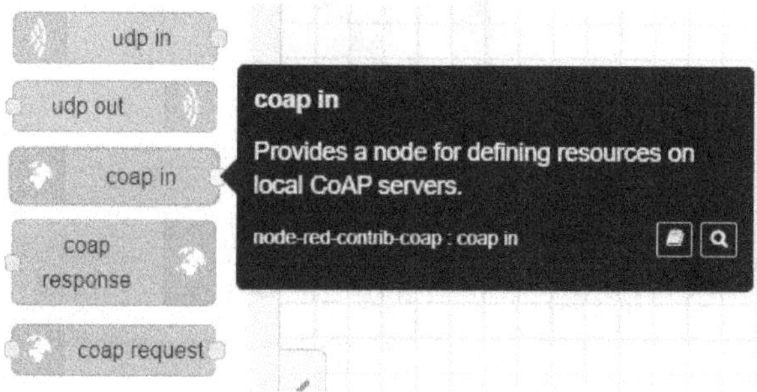

Figure 6.10*: Adding a CoAP in node*

2. After adding this node to the flow, double-click on it to open the configuration settings. There you will see the options shown in *Figure 6.11*:

Figure 6.11*: Add a new CoAP server*

3. After adding this node to the flow, double-click on it to open the configuration settings. There you will see the options shown in *Figure 6.12*:

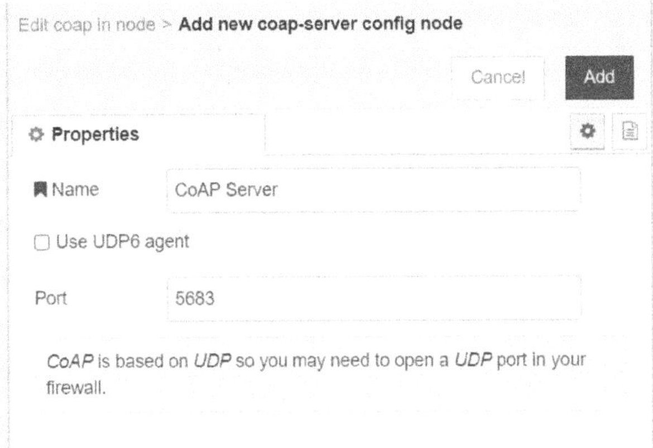

***Figure 6.12**: Configuring the CoAP server*

4. This will lead you to the CoAP server configuration, shown in *Figure 6.12*.
5. As you can see in *Figure 6.12*, there are a few options to configure the CoAP server. In this case, we will just assign a name to it, leaving the other options by default. Click on the **Add** button to return to the *CoAP in* the node.
6. In the *CoAP in*, select the CoAP server you have just created and fill in the other parameters as shown in *Figure 6.13*.

   This node will create a resource in the CoAP server with the specified URL and method. In this case, the URL is **`/actuators/relay`**, and the method is PUT. So, every request with these parameters will be processed by this node.

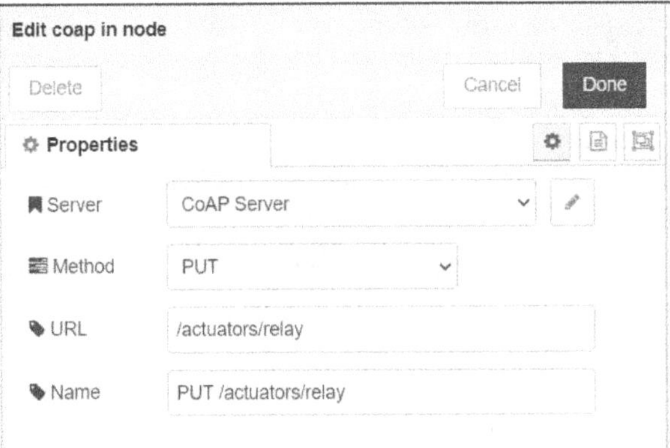

***Figure 6.13**: Configuring the CoAP in node*

7. Now, select a *CoAP response* node, drop it on the flow, and connect it to the *CoAP in* node. You can see this setup in *Figure 6.14*:

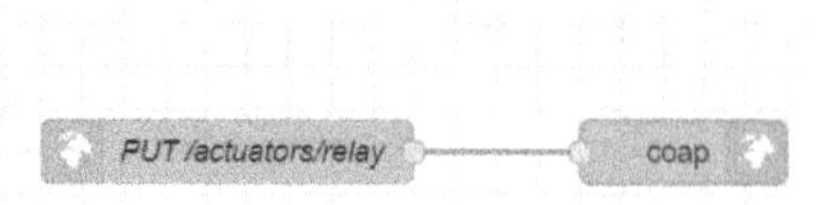

Figure 6.14: Connecting CoAP in with CoAP response

8. At this point, you have a simple setup to receive CoAP messages on the URL using the **PUT** method. Every time you send a PUT to the URL, you will receive a response from the server.
9. Now, connect a debug node to the CoAP input node, as shown in *Figure 6.15*. We will use this node to see if we receive CoAP messages.

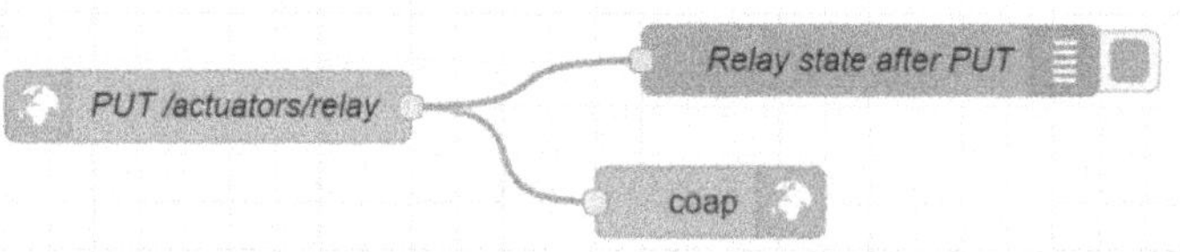

Figure 6.15: Adding a debug node

10. Finally, let us test our CoAP server using the **libcoap coap-client** by running the following command. Remember that you must run this command from the **examples** directory of the **libcoap** library.

```
$ ./coap-client -e 1 -m put coap://<your-coap-server-ip>/actuators/
relay
```

Note: Use the IP address of your Raspberry Pi instead of using localhost to avoid rejection from the CoAP server.

After executing the command, you will see the response of the server both on the command line and the debug panel of Node-RED, as shown in *Figure 6.16*:

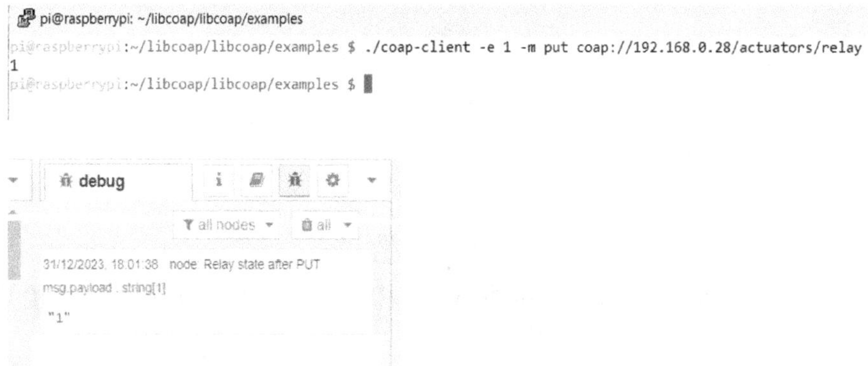

Figure 6.16: Response from the CoAP server

In the following section, we will add a new resource that uses the GET method.

Adding a GET resource

Now that we have a working CoAP server in Node-RED, let us add a new resource with the GET method. This will allow us to get the state of the resources in the CoAP server.

However, we must take into consideration that this CoAP server does not save the values of the resources, as does the **`libcoap`** implementation. So, you will have to store these values in variables to get their values later.

To implement this part of the project, follow these steps:

1. Add a new *CoAP in* node to the flow, and configure it as shown in *Figure 6.17*.

   This will create a new resource with the same URL as in the previous node but with the GET method instead of PUT.

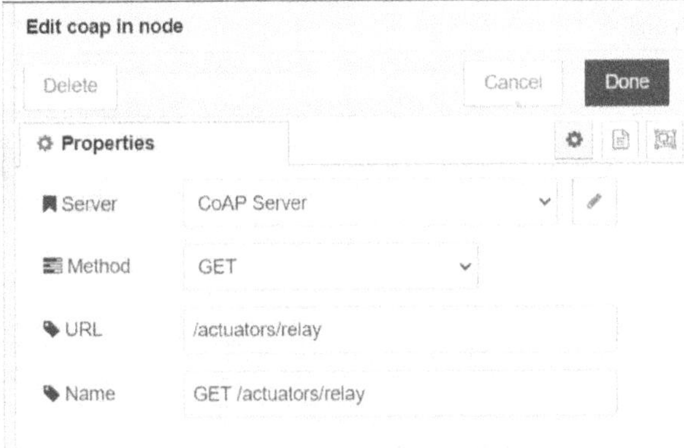

***Figure 6.17**: Creating a new CoAP in node with the GET method*

2. Create two function nodes by selecting the node from the left panel of Node-RED, as shown in *Figure 6.18*:

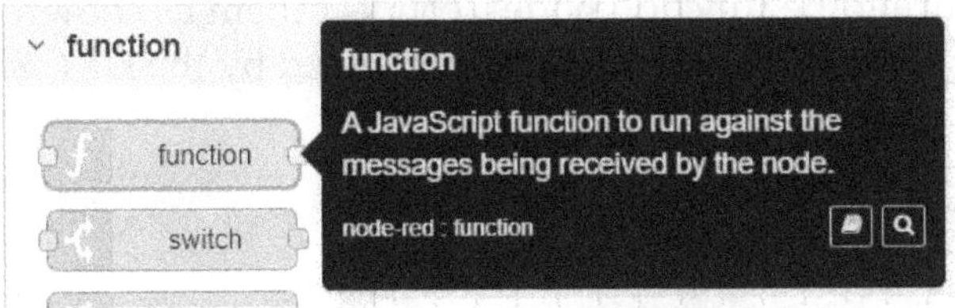

***Figure 6.18**: Select and add the function node*

3. Go inside the first function block and write the code shown in *Figure 6.19*. Click on the **Done** button when you finish.

   This function block gets the payload delivered by the *PUT actuators/relay* block and saves it on the **`relay_state`** variable. This variable has a flow reach which means that you can access it from within the same flow.

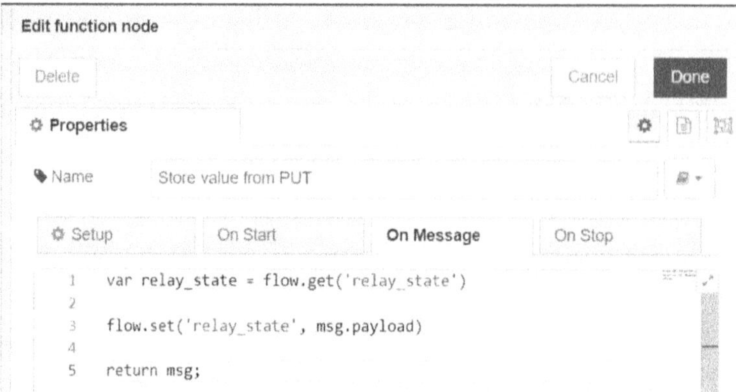

Figure 6.19: Code of Store value from PUT function node

4. Go to the other function block and configure it as shown in *Figure 6.20*. This block will get the value stored in the **`relay_state`** variable and will pass it through the message payload.

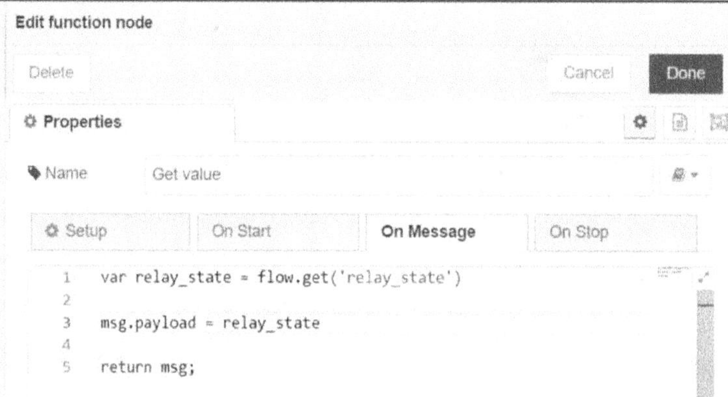

Figure 6.20: Code for getting the value of the relay-state variable

5. After configuring the function nodes, connect them as shown in *Figure 6.21*. Also, add a debug node to show the values processed by the *GET /actuators/relay* node.

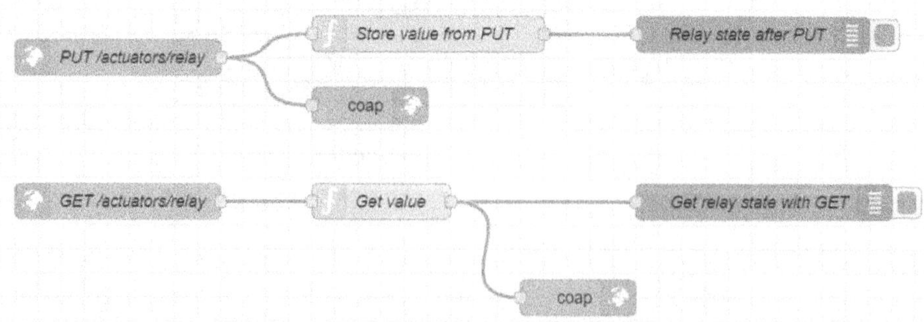

Figure 6.21: Complete CoAP system

6. Now, we can test the CoAP server by sending messages from the command line by using the **coap-client**. You can execute the following commands:

   ```
   $ ./coap-client -e 1 -m put coap://192.168.0.28/actuators/relay
   $ ./coap-client -m get coap://192.168.0.28/actuators/relay
   ```

   You will obtain the results shown in *Figure 6.22*:

```
pi@raspberrypi:~/libcoap/libcoap/examples $  ./coap-client -e 1 -m put coap://192.168.0.28/actuators/relay
1
pi@raspberrypi:~/libcoap/libcoap/examples $ ./coap-client -m get coap://192.168.0.28/actuators/relay
1
pi@raspberrypi:~/libcoap/libcoap/examples $
```

***Figure 6.22**: Responses from the CoAP server*

Meanwhile, you will see the response in the debug panel of Node-RED, as shown in *Figure 6.23*:

```
31/12/2023, 19:03:42   node: Relay state after PUT
msg.payload : string[1]
"1"
31/12/2023, 19:04:05   node: Get relay state with GET
msg.payload : string[1]
"1"
```

***Figure 6.23**: Responses in the debug panel of Node-RED*

At this point, we have a CoAP server running in Node-RED. We also have two resources, one for the PUT method and the other for the GET method. Both resources have the same URL.

You can create more resources with different methods according to your needs, and the procedure is always the same.

Remember that you need to store the values of the resources in a variable or another storage method (file, database, etc.).

Using CoAP with Arduino

In this section, we will see how to run a CoAP client from a *Raspberry Pi Pico W*. To program the board, we will use *Arduino*.

Installing the library

Before starting to program our device, we need to install the Arduino library. We will use the CoAP simple library available in the Arduino repository.

You can install it from the Arduino IDE, as shown in *Figure 6.24*:

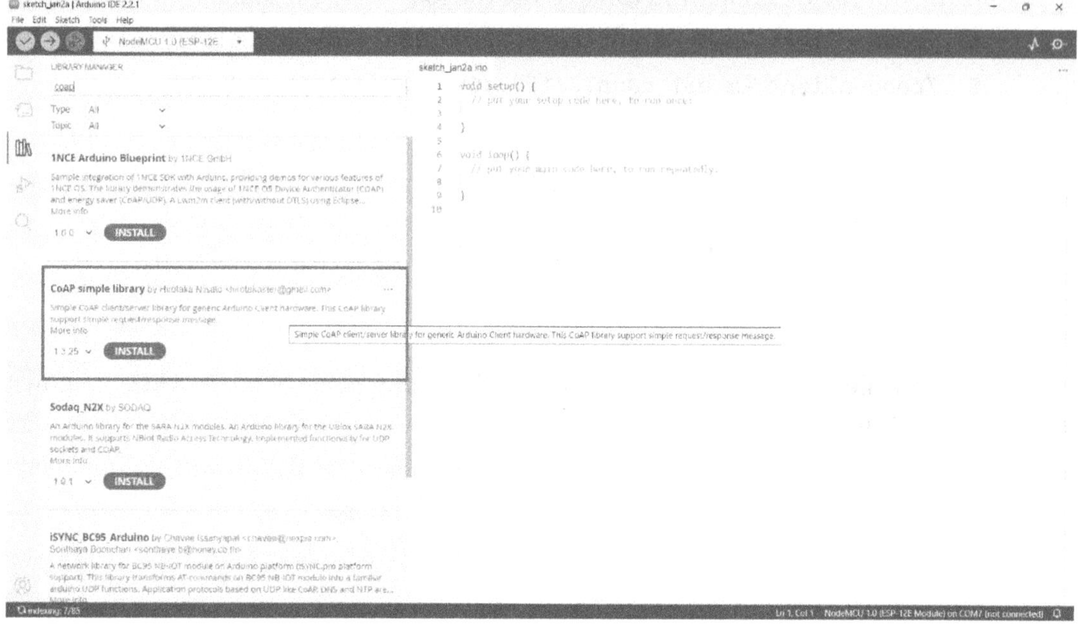

***Figure 6.24**: Installing the CoAP simple library in Arduino*

Arduino will download all the required packages. Once they are installed, you are ready to use the library.

Now, let us continue with the program.

Programming the Raspberry Pi Pico W

In this section, we will program the Raspberry Pi Pico W to interact with the CoAP server in the Raspberry Pi.

The code will perform the following operations:

1. Set up a CoAP client.
2. Connect to Wi-Fi.
3. Request data periodically from a specific CoAP server endpoint using the **GET** method.
4. React to the response by controlling the built-in LED based on the received payload. It turns on the LED if the payload is one and turns it off elsewhere.
   a. First, include the libraries needed, as shown in the following:

```
#include <WiFi.h>
#include <WiFiUdp.h>
#include <coap-simple.h>
```

b. Configure the Wi-Fi parameters, as shown in the following:

```
// WiFi credentials
const char* ssid = "WIFI-SSID";
const char* password = "WIFI-KEY";
```

c. Specify the CoAP server details, as shown in the following:

```
// Server details
IPAddress serverIP(XXX, XXX, XXX, XXX); // Replace with your server's IP
int serverPort = 5683; // Replace with server's CoAP port
const char* endpointURL = "actuators/relay"; // Replace with your server's endpoint

WiFiUDP udp; // UDP object
Coap coap(udp); // CoAP object initialized with UDP
```

d. Function to perform GET requests on the CoAP server, as shown in the following:

```
void requestDataUsingGET() {
  // Perform GET request to receive data from the server
  coap.get(serverIP, serverPort, endpointURL);
}
```

e. Function to process the response from the CoAP server, as shown in the following:

```
void callback_response(CoapPacket &packet, IPAddress ip, int port)
{
  // Handle the response received from the server after the GET request
  Serial.println("[Coap Response got]");

  // Copy the payload into a character array
  char p[packet.payloadlen + 1];
  memcpy(p, packet.payload, packet.payloadlen);
  p[packet.payloadlen] = NULL; // Null-terminate the string

  // Print the received payload
```

```
    Serial.println(p);

    // Control the built-in LED based on the received payload
    if (strcmp(p, "1") == 0) {
      digitalWrite(LED_BUILTIN, HIGH);
    } else {
      digitalWrite(LED_BUILTIN, LOW);
    }
}
```

f. Set up a function to perform the initialization of the device, as shown in the following:

```
void setup() {
  Serial.begin(9600); // Start serial communication for debugging

  // Connect to WiFi
  WiFi.begin(ssid, password);
  while (WiFi.status() != WL_CONNECTED) {
    delay(500);
    Serial.print(".");
  }

  // Set up built-in LED pin as an output and turn it on
  pinMode(LED_BUILTIN, OUTPUT);
  digitalWrite(LED_BUILTIN, HIGH);

  // Print WiFi connection details
  Serial.println("");
  Serial.println("WiFi connected");
  Serial.println("IP address: ");
  Serial.println(WiFi.localIP());

  // Set up callback function for handling server responses
  Serial.println("Setup Response Callback");
```

```
    coap.response(callback_response);

    // Start CoAP client
    coap.start();
  }
```

g. Loop function to run the CoAP operations with the server, as shown in the following:

```
void loop() {
  // Request data using GET method from the CoAP server
  requestDataUsingGET();

  coap.loop(); // Handle CoAP tasks
  delay(1000); // Add delay between loop iterations
}
```

If the Raspberry Pi Pico W board is running MicroPython, remember to press the **BOOTSEL** button to force the bootloader. If you have already done it, it is not necessary to repeat the operation. Now, you can compile and upload the code to the board.

Also, remember to specify the Wi-Fi credentials and the IP address of the CoAP server.

Testing the program

We will test this code by using the following setup:

- We will use the CoAP server running in Node-RED.
- Use the **`coap-client from libocap`** for sending PUT messages.
- We will receive the responses from the CoAP server using our Raspberry Pi Pico W.

Follow these steps to test the communication between the Raspberry Pi and Raspberry Pi Pico W using the CoAP protocol:

1. With the board connected to your computer, open the **Serial Monitor** within Arduino.
2. Connect to the Raspberry Pi and send PUT messages as we did earlier in this chapter.
3. Check the responses shown in the **Serial Monitor**.
4. Check that the LED turns on if the message is 1 and turns off if the message is 0.

You can see a screenshot of the testing in *Figure 6.25*:

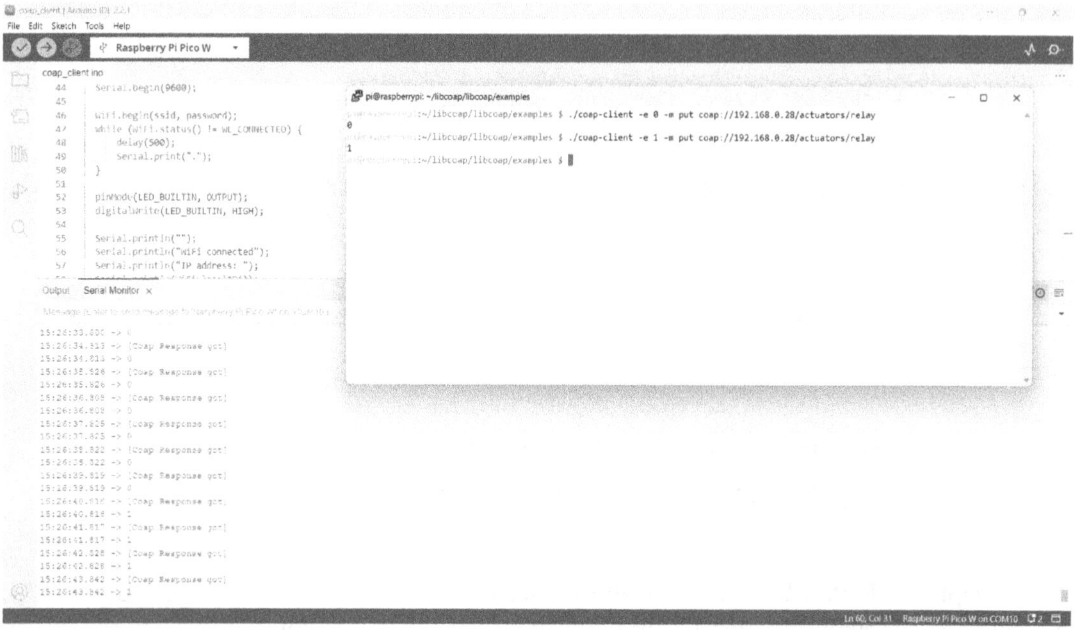

Figure 6.25: Testing the Raspberry Pi Pico W CoAP communication

Conclusion

In this chapter, we learned about the fundamentals of the CoAP protocol. We explored its characteristics and mechanisms. To implement CoAP, we used three different approaches.

First, we explored the libcoap library and used the libcoap executables to run a server and a client. Then, we used the aiocoap Python module to program a CoAP client. We also used the node-red-contrib-coap blocks in Node-RED to implement a CoAP server. Finally, we programmed a Raspberry Pi Pico W board to run a CoAP client using the CoAP simple library.

In the next chapter, we will learn how to use HTTP to connect IoT devices. You will see some similarities between CoAP and HTTP. However, there are also many differences, and each protocol is tailored to specific uses.

CHAPTER 7
Using HTTP and WebSockets in IoT

Introduction

In this chapter, we will explore the features of **Hyper Text Transfer Protocol** (**HTTP**). Also, we will see how to use this protocol in **Internet of Things** (**IoT**) projects, both from the server and client side.

The HTTP protocol was created in 1989 by *Tim Berners-Lee*, a British computer scientist who is credited with inventing the **World Wide Web** (**WWW**). The first version of the protocol, HTTP/0.9, was very simple and only allowed for the retrieval of static web pages. This first version could only return HTML files. Subsequent versions added different data types, protocol messages, conditional execution, etc.

Using HTTP in IoT systems is a natural choice, as this protocol has ruled the Internet and is widely used to transmit any kind of data. In this chapter, we will examine the advantages and drawbacks of using HTTP in IoT devices and the recommended use cases.

Structure

This chapter has the following structure:

- Hyper text transfer protocol fundamentals
- Implementing HTTP in Node-RED

- Using HTTP with microcontrollers
- WebSockets
- Implementing WebSockets in Node-RED
- Using WebSockets in microcontrollers

Objectives

In this chapter, you will learn how to use HTTP in embedded devices to send and receive data.

Also, you will learn to install and configure web servers, set and use HTTP endpoints, use headers, etc.

After reading this chapter, you will have the knowledge to design and implement HTTP communications in your IoT systems.

Hyper text transfer protocol fundamentals

To start our path with HTTP, we will explore its fundamentals. First, let us see the characteristics of the HTTP protocol.

Hyper text transfer protocol

HTTP is a fundamental protocol used for communication on the WWW. It is an application layer protocol used to exchange information between web clients (like browsers) and web servers.

The following are the key aspects of HTTP:

- **Stateless protocol**: HTTP is a stateless protocol, meaning that each request from a client to a server is independent and unrelated to previous requests. The server does not retain information about the client's previous interactions. This simplicity contributes to its widespread use and scalability.
- **Client-server architecture**: HTTP operates on a client-server model. Clients send requests to servers, and servers respond with the requested resources, such as HTML pages, images, or other content.
- **Request-response model**: Communication in HTTP is based on a request-response model. A client sends an HTTP request to a server, specifying the action it wants to perform (for example, `GET` for retrieving data), and the server responds with the requested information or an indication of success or failure.
- **Methods**: HTTP defines various methods or verbs that indicate the desired action to be performed on a resource. Common methods include `GET` (retrieve a resource), `POST` (submit data to be processed), `PUT` (update a resource), and `DELETE` (remove a resource).

- **Status codes**: HTTP responses include status codes indicating the outcome of the request. Common status codes include **`200 (OK)`**, **`404 (Not Found)`**, and **`500 (Internal Server Error)`**.
- **Uniform Resource Identifiers (URIs)**: HTTP uses URIs, commonly referred to as **Uniform Resource Locators** (**URLs**), to identify and locate resources on the web.
- **Versioning**: HTTP has gone through several versions, with HTTP/1.1 being one of the most widely used versions. The development of HTTP/2 and HTTP/3 aims to improve performance and address the limitations of earlier versions.

In the following sections, we will see each of these aspects in detail.

Architecture and communication model

As mentioned in the previous section, the HTTP protocol is based on a server-client architecture with a request-response mechanism.

In *Figure 7.1*, you can see the flow of a HTTP connection:

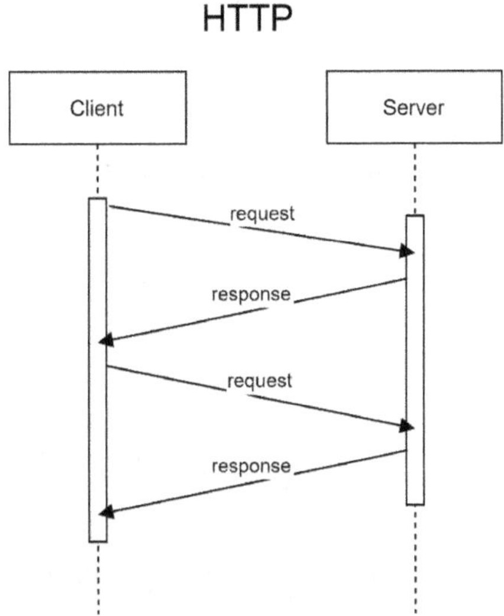

Figure 7.1*: HTTP connection and data exchange*

The operational approach of HTTP necessitates establishing a new connection or request for obtaining each new resource. This means that the protocol is better suited for efficiently transferring substantial amounts of data rather than transmitting smaller data fragments.

Therefore, if your intention is to transmit documents or images, HTTP proves to be a suitable choice. On the contrary, if you only need to send a concise **JavaScript Object Notation** (**JSON**) containing sensor data, opting for **Message Queuing Telemetry Transport** (**MQTT**) or **Constrained Application Protocol** (**CoAP**) would be more advantageous.

Methods and headers

HTTP uses methods for performing operations on the server's resources.

NOTE: In the context of HTTP methods, an operation is considered idempotent if performing it multiple times has the same effect as performing it once. In other words, making a repeated request with an idempotent method should not produce different outcomes compared to making the same request just once.

These are the more commonly used HTTP methods:

- **GET**: This method is used to get data from the server.
  - **Purpose**: Retrieve data from the server.
  - **Idempotent**: Yes (multiple identical requests have the same effect as a single request).
  - **Example**: Fetching a webpage, an image, or any resource from the server.
- **POST**: This method is used to send and receive data from the server.
  - **Purpose**: Submit data to be processed by a specified resource.
  - **Idempotent**: No (Repeated identical requests may have different effects).
  - **Example**: Submitting a form, uploading a file, or creating a new resource on the server.
- **PUT**: This method is used to create or modify data.
  - **Purpose**: Update a resource on the server or create a new resource if it doesn't exist.
  - **Idempotent**: Yes.
  - **Example**: Updating the content of a file or creating a new resource with a specific identifier.
- **DELETE**: This method is used to delete data from the server.
  - **Purpose**: Remove a resource from the server.
  - **Idempotent**: Yes.
  - **Example**: Deleting a file or removing a record from a database.
- **PATCH**: This method is used to update data on the server.
  - **Purpose**: Partially update a resource on the server.
  - **Idempotent**: No.
  - **Example**: Modifying specific fields of an existing resource without affecting the entire resource.

- **OPTIONS**: This method is used to establish options or see available methods.
  - **Purpose**: Retrieve information about the communication options available for a resource or server.
  - **Idempotent**: Yes (Multiple identical requests have the same effect as a single request).
  - **Example**: Checking which HTTP methods are supported by a server for a specific resource.
- **HEAD**: This method asks just for the headers, not the content.
  - **Purpose**: Retrieve only the headers of a resource without the actual data.
  - **Idempotent**: Yes (multiple identical requests have the same effect as a single request).
  - **Example**: Checking if a resource has been modified since a certain date without downloading the entire content.

Headers

Headers play an important role in HTTP communications, so let us explore a little more about them.

The HTTP headers are used to exchange additional information between the client and the server about the request or response.

The following are some relevant examples of HTTP headers:

- **Request headers**: These are some commonly used headers in HTTP.
  - **Host**: This is the host that the connection points to.
    - **Purpose**: Indicates the domain name of the server.
    - **Example**: Host, refer to the link **www.example.com**.
  - **User-agent**: It tells the type of HTTP client that is being used.
    - **Purpose**: Provides information about the user agent (browser or client) making the request.
    - **Example**: User-agent such as Mozilla/5.0 (Windows NT 10.0; Win64; x64) AppleWebKit/537.36 (KHTML, like Gecko) Chrome/91.0.4472.124 Safari/537.36.
  - **Authorization**: These are authorization-related elements.
    - **Purpose**: Provides credentials for authentication purposes. We will use this header to establish secure communication with platforms.
    - **Example**: Authorization such as basic YWxhZGRpbjpvcGVuc2VzYW1l

- **Response headers**: The response headers indicate the type of content and other data that is included in the response.
  - **Content-type**: It indicates the type of content.
    - **Purpose**: It specifies the media type of the resource in the response.
    - **Example**: Content-type such as text/html; charset=utf-8
  - **Location**: It provides the location of a resource.
    - **Purpose**: Used in redirections or to provide the location of a newly created resource.
    - **Example**: Location, refer to the link **https://www.example.com/new-location**.
  - **Server:**
    - **Purpose**: Identifies the software used by the origin server.
    - **Example**: Server such as Apache/2.4.29 (Ubuntu).

These headers, among many others, contribute to the proper functioning, security, and performance of HTTP transactions. They convey essential metadata and instructions for both clients and servers involved in the communication process.

Hyper Text Transfer Protocol status codes

HTTP status codes are three-digit numbers returned by a web server in response to a client's request made to the server. These codes provide information about the status of the request, indicating whether it was successful, encountered an error, or requires further action.

In other words, status codes are the language the client and server speak to know if the data exchange was successful or not.

Following is a breakdown of HTTP status codes and some of the most commonly used ones:

- **1xx-informational**: These codes are purely informational.
  - These are provisional responses indicating that the request was received, that the process is continuing, or that there is another interim response.
  - For example, **`100 Continue`**. The initial part of the request has been received, and the client should proceed with sending the rest.
- **2xx-success**: These codes indicate success in an HTTP request.
  - These codes indicate that the client's request was successfully received, understood, and accepted.

  - For example, **200 OK**. The request was successful, and the server has returned the requested data. You always expect to obtain this response, as it means that the operation was performed correctly.
- **3xx-redirection**: These codes indicate redirection.
  - These codes inform the client that further action needs to be taken to complete the request.
  - For example, **301 Moved** permanently. The requested resource has been permanently moved to a new location. This means that the request must be redirected to another URL.
- **4xx-client error**: These are client-related errors.
  - These codes indicate that the client seems to have made an error, or the request cannot be fulfilled by the server.
  - For example, **404 Not Found**. The requested resource could not be found on the server. This could happen, for instance, if a web page was deleted or moved to another path.
- **5xx-server error**: These are server-side errors.
  - These codes indicate that the server failed to fulfill a valid request. This type of error can originate from many circumstances, like an error in connecting to a database or some misconfiguration.
  - For example, **500 Internal Server Error**. A generic error message was returned when an unexpected condition was encountered on the server.

The following are commonly used HTTP status codes:

- **200 OK**: Successful request; the server successfully processed the request.
- **201 Created**: The request was successful, and a new resource was created as a result.
- **400 Bad Request**: The server cannot or will not process the request due to a client error.
- **401 Unauthorized**: The request lacks valid authentication credentials.
- **403 Forbidden**: The server understood the request, but it refuses to authorize it.
- **404 Not Found**: The requested resource could not be found on the server.
- **500 Internal Server Error**: A generic error message indicating that the server has encountered an unexpected condition.

Understanding these status codes is essential for you to diagnose and troubleshoot issues with web applications and services. They provide valuable insights into the success or failure of HTTP requests.

Hyper Text Transfer Protocol resources

The target of an HTTP request is referred to as a **resource**. This could be anything like a document, a photo, or any other item. Each resource is identified by a URI within HTTP.

Uniform Resource Identifier

The URL is a type of URI. The following are the examples:

- **https://www.linux.org**
- **https://www.linux.org/whats-new/**
- **https://www.linux.org/forums/# linux-tutorials.122**

Typing any of these URLs into your browser's address bar will prompt it to load the associated page or resource.

A URL consists of various parts, some are mandatory while others are optional. The following example shows a more complex URL:

http://www.example.com:8080/path/to/file.html?key01=value01&key02=value02# SomePlaceInThePage

Structure of a URL

Let us explore each of the parts that can be used to build a URL:

- **Protocol or scheme**: The part of a URL related to the communication protocol is known as the **scheme**. The scheme indicates the protocol or method used to access the resource specified in the URL. It comes before the colon (:) in the URL and is followed by two slashes (/ /).

  Common schemes include the following:

  - **HTTP:** Used for transmitting information on the World Wide Web. Example: **http://www.example.com**
  - **Hypertext Transfer Protocol Secure (HTTPS):** Similar to HTTP but uses a secure **Secure Session Layer** (SSL) or **Transport Layer Security** (TLS) connection for added security. Example: **https://www.example.com**
  - **File Transfer Protocol (FTP):** Used for transferring files between computers on a network. For example, **ftp://ftp.example.com**
- **Authority**: The authority part of a URL typically refers to the specific location or address on the internet where the resource is hosted. This portion of the URL comes after the scheme and the double slashes (/ /) and is followed by the path to the resource.

  For example, **http://www.example.com:8080**

The following is a breakdown of the authority or domain part. For many URLs, the authority part consists of two main components:

- o **Host**: This is the primary identifier for the server or machine that hosts the resource. It could be an IP address (for example, 192.168.0.1) or a domain name (for example, **www.example.com**).
- o **Port**: This is an optional component that specifies a specific communication endpoint on the host. If not provided, the default port for the scheme is used (for example, 80 for HTTP, 443 for HTTPS).

The following are the examples:

- o **http://www.example.com** (Here, **www.example.com** is the host.)
- o **https://api.example.org:8080** (Here, **api.example.org** is the host, and 8080 is the port.)

- **Path**: The path in a URL represents the specific location or resource on the web server, following the authority or domain part. It comes after the domain and is separated by a forward slash (/).

  The path is a series of directories or folders separated by forward slashes. It points to the specific location of the resource on the server's file system or a virtual structure created by the server. The server uses this information to retrieve the requested resource.

  The following are the examples:

  - o **http://www.example.com/page1.html** (Here, the path is **`/page1.html`**.)
  - o **https://api.example.org/data/user/profile** (Here, the path is **`/data/user/profile`**.)

- **Query**: In some cases, the URL may also include parameters or queries. These are additional information provided to the server, often used in dynamic web applications to customize or filter the content.

  Look at this example with a query parameter **https://www.example.com/search?query=example&page=1**

  In this example, the path is **`/search`**, and the query parameters are **`query=example`** and **`page=1`**.

- **Fragment:** In a URL, the fragment is a component that appears at the end of the URL and is preceded by a hash symbol (#). The fragment is used to identify and navigate to a specific section or anchor within the resource indicated by the rest of the URL. It is primarily relevant for HTML documents, where specific elements, such as headings or anchors, are assigned unique identifiers.

  For example, **http://www.example.com/page1.html#title**. This URL leads to the **title** anchor.

When a URL with a fragment is opened in a web browser, the browser will attempt to scroll to the element on the page with the corresponding identifier, making it visible to the user.

Now that we know all the parts included in a URL, we can start using HTTP in our IoT projects.

Implementing HTTP in Node-RED

Node-RED includes HTTP nodes for receiving and sending data through HTTP. You can find these nodes in the **network** section of the node panel, as shown in *Figure 7.2*:

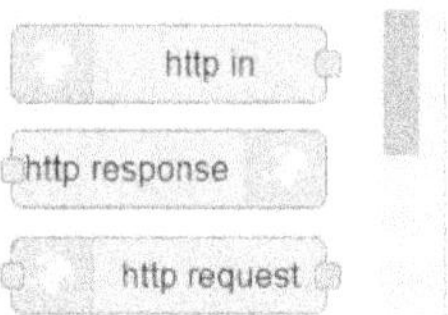

***Figure 7.2**: HTTP nodes in Node-RED*

As you can see in *Figure 7.2*, there are three nodes available:

- **http in**: This node receives HTTP requests and transmits the data to the following node.
- **http response**: This node returns the response to the request received from an HTTP input node. You need to use this node to complete a request-response behavior. Otherwise, the HTTP client will stay blocked, waiting for a response from the server.
- **http request**: This node combines both request and response. It allows you to process requests and send back responses to the client.

Let us see how we can use these nodes.

Accepting HTTP requests in Node-RED

To start receiving data through HTTP in Node-RED, we need to use the **http in** node.

To start using the HTTP nodes in Node-RED, we will use a project example. Suppose you have a door sensor that sends open and closed states using HTTP messages.

The message is a string with the value of **1** for open and **0** for closed.

To get the HTTP messages from the sensor in Node-RED, follow these steps:

1. Drag and drop an **http in** node in the flow.
2. Double-click on it to configure it.
3. In the configuration fields, fill in the **Method**, the **URL**, and the **Name**, as shown in *Figure 7.3*:

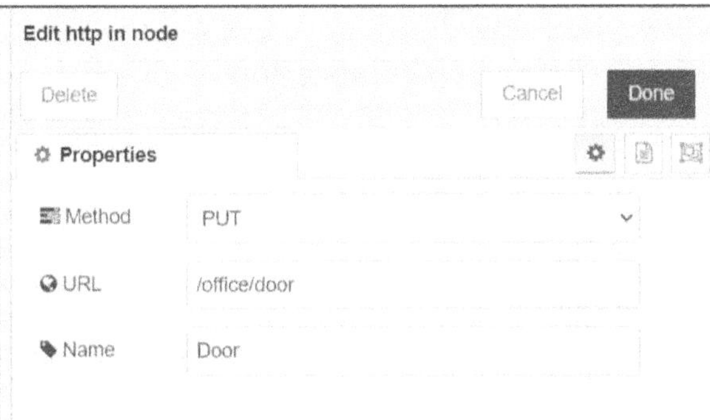

Figure 7.3: Configuring the http-in node

4. Click on the **Done** button to save the changes.
5. Now, add an **http-response** block to the flow.
6. Connect the output of the **http-in** block to the input of the **http-response** block.
7. Add a **debug** node and connect it to the **http-in** node. Name this block as **Door debug** or something meaningful.

   You can see a screen capture of the scheme in *Figure 7.4*:

Figure 7.4: Node-RED flow with HTTP-in and HTTP-out nodes

To test this implementation, you can run a curl command from the console of your Raspberry Pi.

Client URL (**cURL**) is a command-line tool that allows you to transfer data to and from a server using various protocols.

The following are the main features of the `curl` command:

- It is primarily used to retrieve data from or send data to a server without user interaction.
- Supports multiple protocols, including HTTP, HTTPS, FTP, **Secure File Transfer Protocol** (**SFTP**), **Secure Copy Protocol** (**SCP**), and more.
- Commonly used for testing **application programming interface** (**API**), downloading files, and troubleshooting network connections.
- Basic syntax such as `curl [options] [URL]`
- Without any options, `curl` will simply output the content of the specified URL (using a `GET` method).

- It offers numerous options to customize requests, such as:
    - Specifying HTTP methods (`GET`, `POST`, `PUT`, etc.)
    - Adding custom headers
    - Sending data in request bodies
    - Saving responses to files
    - Following redirects
    - Handling authentication

  In this case, we will use curl as follows.

    - `$ curl -X PUT -d "office_door=1" http://localhost:1880/office/doorx`

  This command sends the `office_door = 1` data in the body of the HTTP request. After executing this command, you will get a message from the debug block showing the `JSON {office_door: "1"}`.

Note: If you are not running the `curl` command from the computer that is running Node-RED, you will have to specify the IP address of your Node-RED instance instead of localhost.

Getting data from the internet

You can obtain data from the internet by asking an API for specific information. There are APIs for weather, space, traffic, finance, government, etc.

You can find a large list of public APIs on this site **https://publicapis.dev/**.

One of these APIs is Open-Meteo, where you can obtain weather forecast data for any place in the world. To see the API and build your query, you can visit **https://open-meteo.com/en/docs/**.

Let us see an example. The following query asks about temperature data for the next seven days in Buenos Aires, Argentina:

https://api.open-meteo.com/v1/forecast?latitude=-34.6&longitude=-58.37&hourly=temperature_2m&timezone=America%2FSao_Paulo

To run this query, you could use curl from the command line, a browser, a script, etc. In this case, we are going to use Node-RED. You can see the scheme in *Figure 7.5*:

***Figure 7.5**: Scheme for HTTP request*

To complete the configuration, follow these steps:

1. Once you have the blocks connected, double-click on the **http request** block and configure it as shown in *Figure 7.6*.
2. In the **URL** field, enter the full URL, including the path and the query.
3. In the **Return** field, select **a parsed JSON object** option to show the response as a JSON.

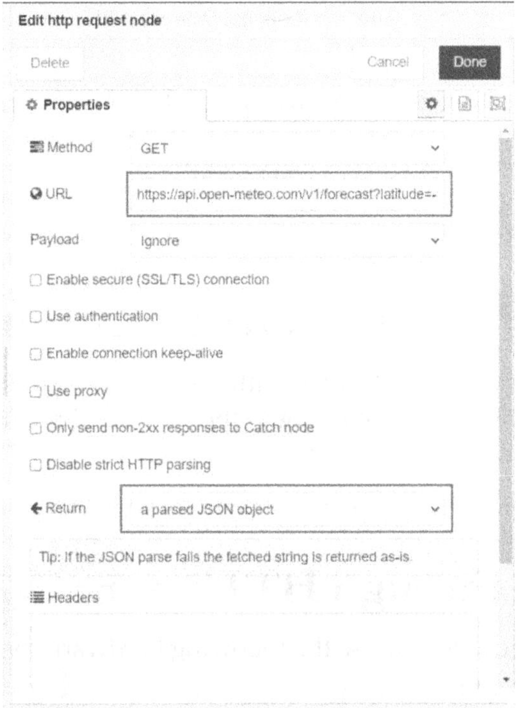

***Figure 7.6**: Configuring the http-request node*

4. Save the block by clicking on the **Done** button.
5. Deploy the flow.
6. Now, every time you click on the input button, you will obtain a response from the API that will be shown in the debug panel. You can see an example of the response in *Figure 7.7*:

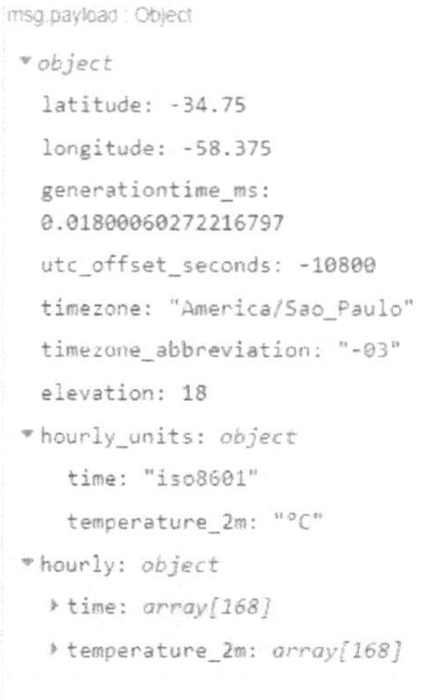

msg.payload : Object
▾object
latitude: -34.75
longitude: -58.375
generationtime_ms: 0.01800060272216797
utc_offset_seconds: -10800
timezone: "America/Sao_Paulo"
timezone_abbreviation: "-03"
elevation: 18
▾hourly_units: object
time: "iso8601"
temperature_2m: "°C"
▾hourly: object
▸time: array[168]
▸temperature_2m: array[168]

Figure 7.7: *Response from the API*

Note: You can use and route this data to other nodes to store it, transmit it, transform it, etc.

Also, you can trigger the API query using other types of inputs. You could, for instance, trigger the request by publishing an MQTT message to a certain topic.

Using HTTP with microcontrollers

There are many ways of using HTTP with microcontrollers. You can choose from different languages and libraries according to the board and the **integrated development environment** (**IDE**) you are going to use.

In this section, we will implement an HTTP client for ESP8266.

Sending data through HTTP in ESP8266

To implement this project, we will use the following hardware configuration:

- An ESP8266 NodeMCU board.

Note: You can use any other board that uses the ESP8266 microcontroller, but you will need to adjust the pin configuration as needed.

- You can use a button, a door sensor, or any other on or off sensor. This example is adapted to a reed sensor, typically used for sensing the state (open or close) of doors and windows.

Note: The code is the same for any on or off sensor.

Refer to *Figure 7.8*:

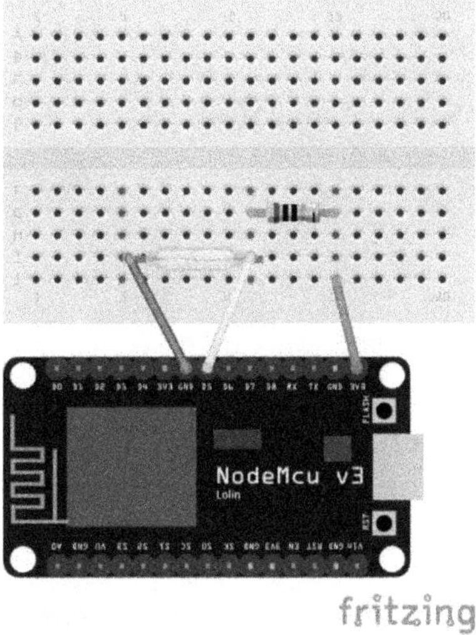

***Figure 7.8**: NodeMCU with door sensor*

The following is the explanation about the hardware:

- We used a pull-up resistor connected to the 3.3 V pin.
- The sensor is connected to GND and GPIO 14, sharing this pin with the pull-up resistor.
- You change the configuration by selecting any other pin available on your board.

Now that we have set up the hardware, let us continue with the firmware. The following code implements an on or off sensor detection. Every time a change in the sensor is detected, the corresponding value is transmitted to a web server using an HTTP PUT operation.

In the following, you can see the code the microcontroller will run.

```
#include <ESP8266WiFi.h>
#include <ESP8266HTTPClient.h>

#define SERVER "SERVER-IP:1880" //Replace SERVER-IP with the IP address of
your server
#define RESOURCE_PATH "/office/door"
#define DOOR_SENSOR_PIN 14

volatile int doorState = 0; // Variable to store the door state
```

```
volatile int state_change = 0; // Variable to trigger the HTTP publication

#define STASSID "WIFI-SSID"
#define STAPSK "WIFI-KEY"

void ICACHE_RAM_ATTR doorStateChanged();

void setup() {

  Serial.begin(115200);

  Serial.println();
  Serial.println();
  Serial.println();

  pinMode(DOOR_SENSOR_PIN, INPUT_PULLUP); // Set GPIO 14 as input for the
door sensor

  // Connect to the WiFi network
  WiFi.begin(STASSID, STAPSK);
  while (WiFi.status() != WL_CONNECTED) {
    delay(500);
    Serial.print(".");
  }
  Serial.println("");
  Serial.print("Connected! IP address: ");
  Serial.println(WiFi.localIP());

  // Attach interrupt to handle changes in door sensor state
  attachInterrupt(digitalPinToInterrupt(DOOR_SENSOR_PIN), doorStateChanged,
CHANGE);
}

// Interrupt Service Routine (ISR) for handling changes in door sensor state
void ICACHE_RAM_ATTR doorStateChanged() {
  doorState = !digitalRead(DOOR_SENSOR_PIN);
```

```
  state_change = 1;
}

void loop() {
  // Wait for WiFi connection
  if (WiFi.status() == WL_CONNECTED) {
    WiFiClient client;
    HTTPClient http;

    if (state_change == 1) {
      state_change = 0;

      Serial.print("[HTTP] begin...\n");

      // Concatenate server IP address with resource path
      String url = "http://" + String(SERVER) + String(RESOURCE_PATH);

      // Begin the HTTP PUT request to the server's URL
      http.begin(client, url);  // HTTP
      http.addHeader("Content-Type", "application/json");

      Serial.print("[HTTP] PUT...\n");

      // Prepare the payload based on the door state
      String payload = "{\"status\":\"" + String(doorState) + "\"}";

      // Start the connection and send HTTP header and body
      int httpCode = http.PUT(payload);

      // HTTP code will be negative on error
      if (httpCode > 0) {
        // HTTP header has been sent, and the server response header has been
handled
        Serial.printf("[HTTP] PUT... code: %d\n", httpCode);
        // File found at the server
        if (httpCode == HTTP_CODE_OK) {
```

```
          const String& response = http.getString();
          Serial.println("Received response:\n<<");
          Serial.println(response);
          Serial.println(">>");
        }
      } else {
              Serial.printf("[HTTP] PUT... failed, error: %s\n", http.
errorToString(httpCode).c_str());
        }

    http.end();
    }
  }
  delay(100); // Wait for 0,1 seconds before the next iteration
}
```

Most of the code has comments or we have used it before. However, there are some new topics we need to explore.

Volatile variables

You can see we are using two **volatile** variables. The volatile keyword is used to indicate to the compiler that a variable's value can be changed unexpectedly, usually by external factors beyond the program's control, like an interruption in our case. When you declare a variable as volatile, you are telling the compiler not to optimize any code involving that variable, because its value might change at any time due to external factors like hardware interrupts, memory-mapped I/O, or other threads in a multi-threaded environment.

ICACHE_RAM_ATTR parameter

The **ICACHE_RAM_ATTR** is a macro used in the ESP8266 Arduino core to specify that a function should be placed in the instruction cache RAM (**ICACHE_RAM**) and that it is also an attribute of the function. This macro is commonly used when defining **Interrupt Service Routines** (**ISRs**) or other critical functions that need to be executed quickly and reliably.

Attribute (ATTR) indicates that **ICACHE_RAM_ATTR** is a function attribute, which is a feature supported by some compilers to specify additional properties of functions. In this case, **ICACHE_RAM_ATTR** is used to specify that a function should be placed in the **ICACHE_RAM**.

Implementing and testing

To test the code, we will use the previously configured **HTTP in** a node in Node-RED as the web resource.

After programming the board with the Arduino IDE, you can play with it by pressing the button or moving the sensor door. The change in the sensor will be detected by the microcontroller, and an HTTP message will be sent to the web server.

Also, the debug node in Node-RED will show the received data in the debug panel, as shown in *Figure 7.9*:

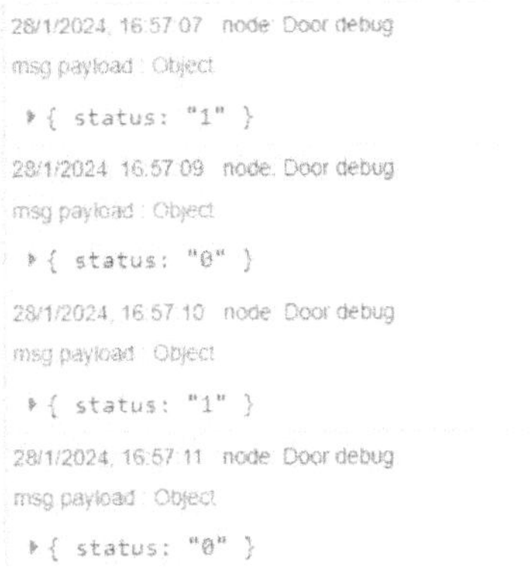

```
28/1/2024, 16:57:07   node: Door debug
msg.payload : Object
 ▸{ status: "1" }
28/1/2024, 16:57:09   node: Door debug
msg.payload : Object
 ▸{ status: "0" }
28/1/2024, 16:57:10   node: Door debug
msg.payload : Object
 ▸{ status: "1" }
28/1/2024, 16:57:11   node: Door debug
msg.payload : Object
 ▸{ status: "0" }
```

Figure 7.9*: Messages received from the microcontroller*

WebSockets

WebSockets is a communication protocol that provides a full-duplex communication channel over a single, long-lived connection between a client and a server. Unlike the traditional request-response model of protocols like HTTP, which involves a new request for each server response, WebSockets lets you establish bidirectional communication, allowing data to be sent and received in both directions in real-time.

Although WebSockets is an independent protocol, in general, it is used over HTTP.

The steps to establish a WebSocket connection over HTTP are the following:

1. When WebSockets runs over HTTP, the connection starts, as usual, with an HTTP request.
2. In the request, the HTTP header indicates that the server should perform an upgrade (in this case, to WebSockets).
3. If the server accepts the upgrade, data can be exchanged between the client and the server.
4. The WebSocket connection can be closed either by the client or the server.

Note: The data can be exchanged in both ways as long as the WebSocket connection lasts. This means a great efficiency improvement compared to HTTP, where you need a new request for each resource.

In *Figure 7.10*, you can see an example of a WebSocket communication:

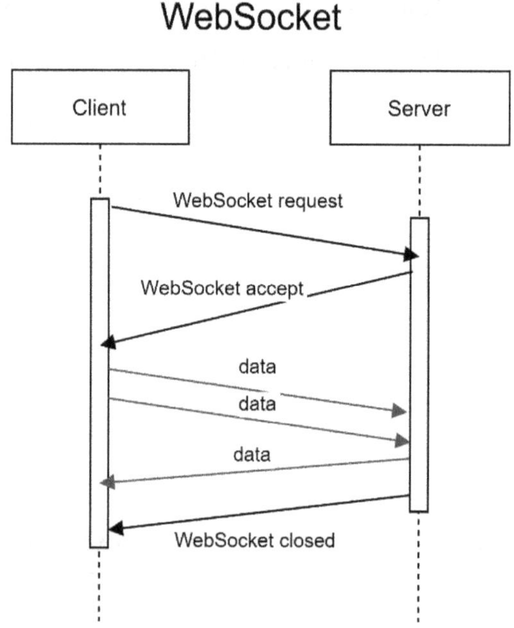

Figure 7.10: WebSocket communication

Implementing WebSockets in Node-RED

In this section, we will implement a WebSocket server using Node-RED.

Node-RED comes with a couple of WebSocket nodes, one as input and another as output. To start using WebSockets in Node-RED, we will create a flow as shown in *Figure 7.11*:

Figure 7.11: WebSockets flow

Now, let us configure each of these nodes as follows:

1. Open the **WebSocket in** node, and click on the pencil icon to add a new WebSocket service. See *Figure 7.12*:

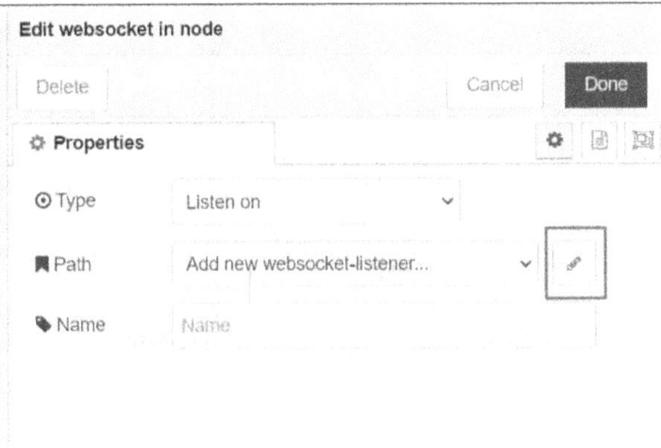

Figure 7.12: Add a new WebSocket service

2. The previous step will guide you to the configuration of the new WebSocket service. Enter the parameters as shown in *Figure 7.13*. Then, click on the **Add** button to apply the changes.

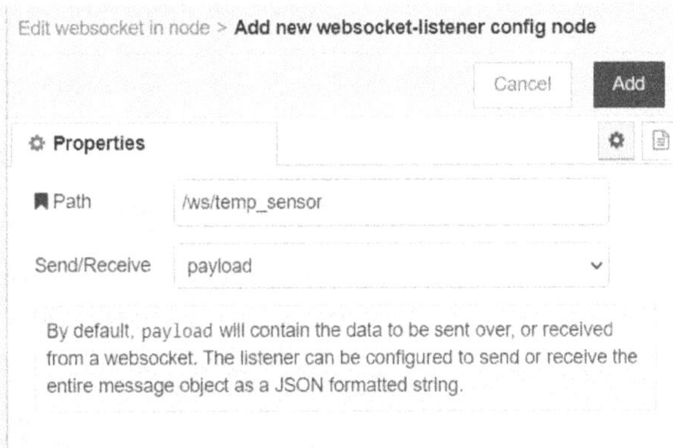

Figure 7.13: Configuring WebSocket service

3. Return to the **WebSocket in** node, give it a name to the node (in this example, **Temp Sensor WS**), and save the node.
4. Now, open the output WebSocket node and click on the pencil icon to add a new client, as shown in *Figure 7.14*:

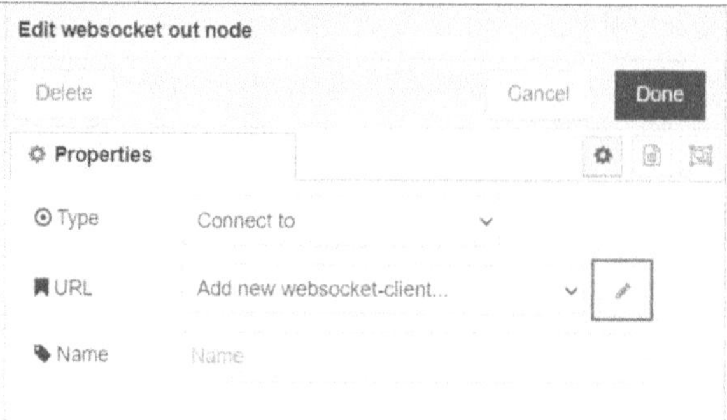

Figure 7.14: WebSocket out node configuration

5. In the client configuration, enter the details of your WebSocket resource. You can see an example in *Figure 7.15*:

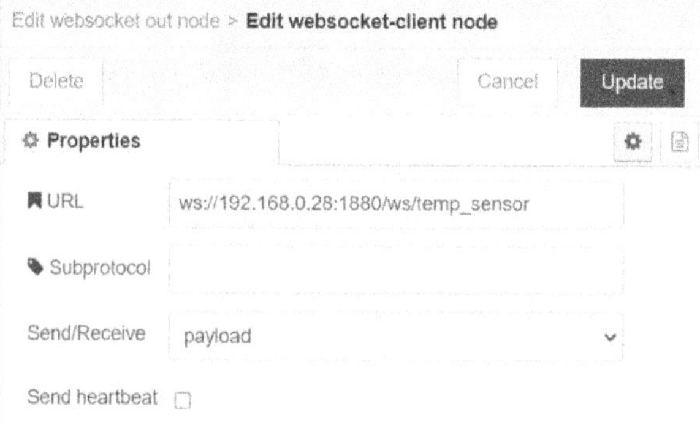

Figure 7.15: WebSocket client configuration

6. Click on the update button, and select this new client in the output node, as shown in *Figure 7.16*. Also, change the type option from **Listen to** to **Connect to**.

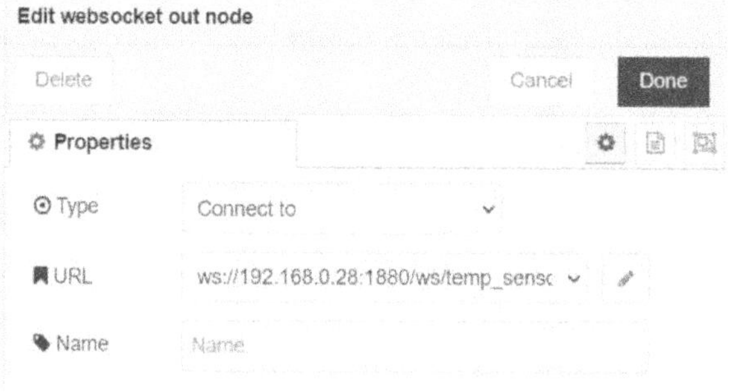

Figure 7.16: WebSocket output node configured with the new client

7. Open the input inject node and configure it, as shown in *Figure 7.17*. We will use this node later for sending data to the WebSocket client.

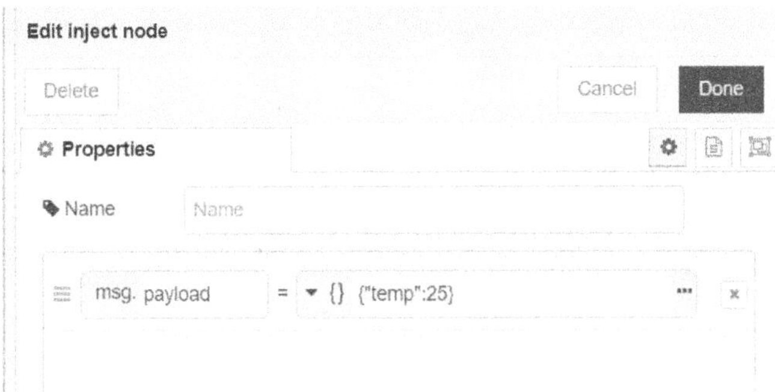

Figure 7.17: Configuring inject node

8. With all the nodes connected and configured, we can now test our implementation. Click on the input inject node, and you will see the data in the debug panel of Node-RED. This is because the WebSocket resource is receiving the data from the output WebSocket node (client).
9. Now, let us try another test. Using Chrome, go to the following URL to install the browser WebSocket client **https://chromewebstore.google.com/detail/mdmlhchldhfnfnkfmljgeinlffmdgkjo**.
10. Open the browser WebSocket client and connect to the WebSocket service, as shown in *Figure 7.18*.

Note: You have to ingress your WebSocket URL, like `ws://YOUR-SERVER-IP/ws/temp_sensor`.

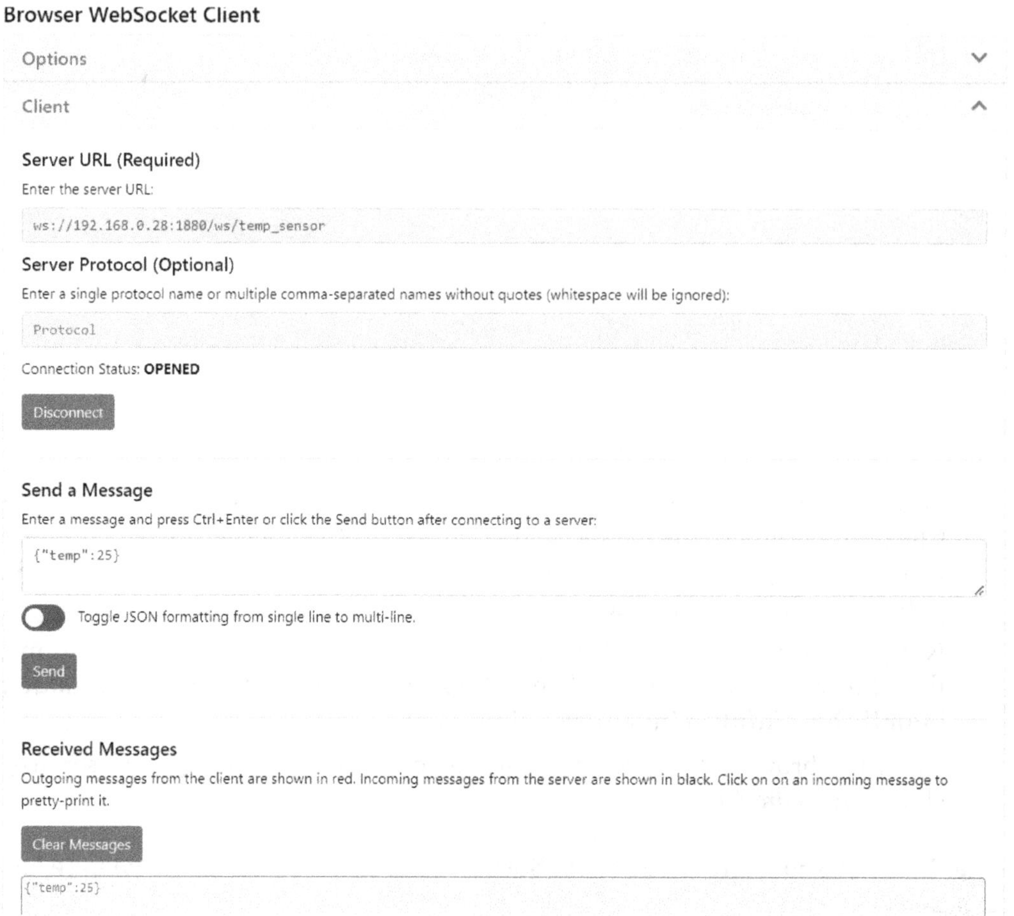

Figure 7.18: Browser WebSocket client interface

11. Enter a value into a JSON (in this case **{"temp":25}**) and click on the send button. This action will send a WebSocket message to your server, and you will be able to see it in the debug panel of Node-RED.

Note: Communications in WebSocket are bidirectional.

12. To test this, click on the inject node in Node-RED. This will send a message to the client, and you will see it in the browser WebSocket client.

This is all regarding the use of WebSockets in Node-RED. Now, let us see how to send WebSocket messages from a microcontroller.

Using WebSockets in microcontrollers

To show an example of using WebSockets in microcontrollers, we will use the Raspberry Pi Pico W.

The circuit used in *Chapter 3, Microcontrollers, Sensors, and Actuators,* is reprinted in *Figure 7.19*:

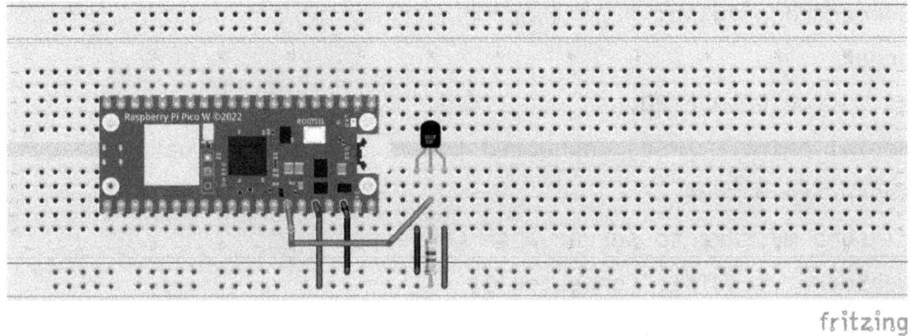

***Figure 7.19**: Connecting Raspberry Pi Pico W and DS18B20*

In this circuit, the DATA pin of the sensor is connected to the GPIO 28. We also use a GND pin and the 3.3V output pin from the board to feed the sensor.

Arduino code

In the following, you can see the Arduino code we use to read the temperature sensor and send the value to Node-RED using WebSockets:

```
#include <Arduino.h>
#include <WiFi.h>
#include <WiFiMulti.h>
#include <WebSocketsClient.h>
#include <microDS18B20.h>

// Data wire is plugged in GPIO 28
MicroDS18B20<28> sensor;

float temperature = 0;
bool connected = false;

WiFiMulti WiFiMulti;
WebSocketsClient webSocket;

void webSocketEvent(WStype_t type, uint8_t * payload, size_t length) {

  switch(type) {
```

```
    case WStype_DISCONNECTED:
      Serial.printf("[WSc] Disconnected!\n");
      connected = false;
      break;
    case WStype_CONNECTED:
      Serial.printf("[WSc] Connected to url: %s\n", payload);
      connected = true;
      // send message to server when Connected
      webSocket.sendTXT("Connected");
      break;
    case WStype_TEXT:
      Serial.printf("[WSc] get text: %s\n", payload);

      // send message to server
      webSocket.sendTXT("message here");
      break;
    case WStype_BIN:
      Serial.printf("[WSc] get binary length: %u\n", length);
      hexdump(payload, length);
      break;
    // send data to server
      // webSocket.sendBIN(payload, length);
    case WStype_PING:
      // pong will be send automatically
      Serial.printf("[WSc] get ping\n");
      break;
    case WStype_PONG:
      // answer to a ping we send
      Serial.printf("[WSc] get pong\n");
      break;
  }

}

void ds18b20_read()
```

```
{
 sensor.requestTemp();

 delay(500);
 temperature = sensor.getTemp();
 Serial.println("Temperature: ");
 Serial.print(temperature);
 Serial.println();

}

void setup() {
  // Serial.begin(921600);
  Serial.begin(115200);

  //Serial.setDebugOutput(true);
  Serial.setDebugOutput(true);

  Serial.println();
  Serial.println();
  Serial.println();

  WiFiMulti.addAP("YOUR_SSID", "YOUR_WIFI_KEY");

  //WiFi.disconnect();
  while(WiFiMulti.run() != WL_CONNECTED) {
    delay(100);
  }


  // server address, port and URL
  webSocket.begin("YOUR-SERVER-IP", 1880, "/ws/temp_sensor");

  // event handler
  webSocket.onEvent(webSocketEvent);
```

```
  // try ever 5000 again if connection has failed
  webSocket.setReconnectInterval(1000);

  webSocket.enableHeartbeat(15000, 3000, 2);

}

void loop() {
  ds18b20_read(); //Read sensor value.

  char string_temp[5];  //Create a char array to store the value.
   dtostrf(temperature,5,2,string_temp); //Convert double to char and store
it.
  webSocket.loop();   //Maintain the WebSocket client connected.
  if (!connected) return; //VERY IMPORTANT: Check the connection is active.
  webSocket.sendTXT(string_temp); //Send the value as String.
  delay(10000);
}
```

In this code, we used some libraries to read the sensor and transmit the data with WebSockets.

To be able to read the DS18B20 sensor from the Raspberry Pi Pico W we need to use a compatible library. In this case, we used the microDS18B20 library. You can install this library directly from the library manager, as it is included in the Arduino repository.

For the WebSocket part, we used the WebSocketsClient library. You can download the ZIP file from **https://github.com/Links2004/arduinoWebSockets/releases/latest** an install it using the option in the menu, as shown in *Figure 7.20*:

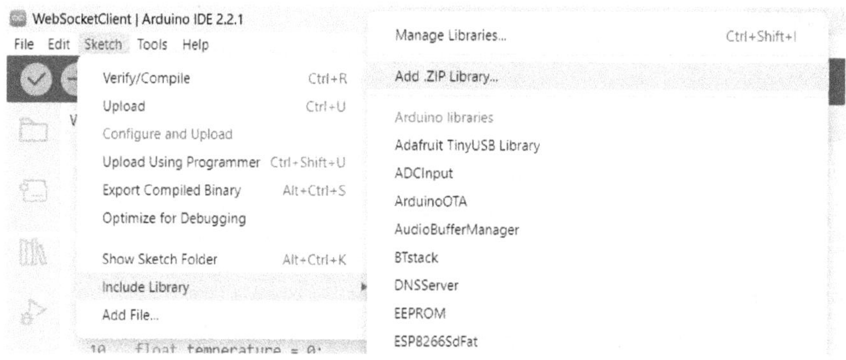

***Figure 7.20**: Installing a library with a ZIP file*

Before uploading the code to the board, check the Wi-Fi credentials and the IP address of your WebSocket server.

When executing the code, you will start seeing the data in the debug panel of Node-RED, as shown in *Figure 7.21*:

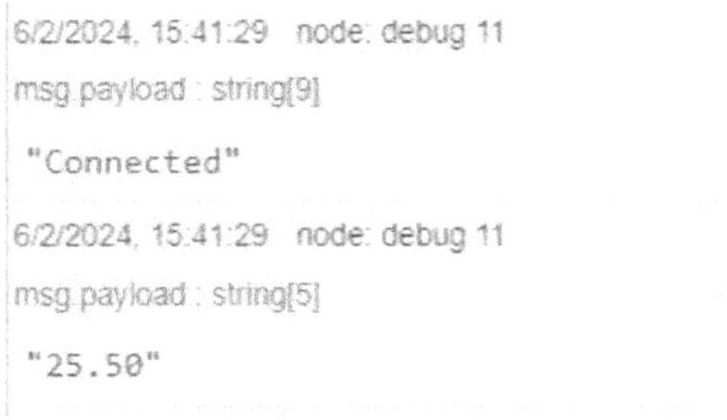

```
6/2/2024, 15:41:29   node: debug 11
msg.payload : string[9]
"Connected"

6/2/2024, 15:41:29   node: debug 11
msg.payload : string[5]
"25.50"
```

***Figure 7.21**: Message received in the WebSocket server*

Now, we have implemented a WebSocket client in a microcontroller, sending data from a sensor connected to it.

Note: You can also implement a WebSocket server in the microcontroller and send data to it from another microcontroller or any other device.

Conclusions

In this chapter, we have learned about HTTP fundamentals, including URLs, response codes, and headers. We also used Node-RED to implement HTTP web resources and to perform requests on web services. We used an ESP8266 and the Arduino IDE to send messages through HTTP to the endpoint in Node-RED.

We also covered WebSockets and saw its advantages over HTTP for exchanging data between IoT devices and servers. Then, we implemented WebSockets in Node-RED and used a Chrome extension to test it. Finally, we used a Raspberry Pi Pico W and MicroPython to implement a WebSocket client for sending sensor data.

In the next chapters, we will use HTTP to integrate platforms by using the APIs provided by the platforms. This will allow us, for example, to write or read data in a database and show it on a dashboard.

CHAPTER 8
Storing Internet of Things Data

Introduction

In this chapter, you will learn about time-series data and how to store and manage it.

The **Internet of Things** (**IoT**) data is always related to the time it was produced. Every point of data must be associated with a specific timestamp. In this way, you can use the data to show it on a dashboard, analyze trends, perform calculations, and apply predictive models.

In this chapter, you will learn about InfluxDB fundamentals, and we will see how to install and use InfluxDB, both on-premise and in the cloud.

We will also cover how to build a data structure that offers scalability.

Structure

The structure of this chapter is as follows:

- InfluxDB fundamentals
- Data standardization
- Installing InfluxDB in a Raspberry Pi
- Storing and reading data in the bucket
- Using InfluxDB Cloud service

Objectives

By the end of this chapter, you will learn to install and use the InfluxDB database. You will know how to manage IoT data using InfluxDB.

You will also be able to perform queries to write and read data in InfluxDB using Python and Node-RED, and you will learn how to create an account in the InfluxDB Cloud service.

InfluxDB fundamentals

InfluxDB is one of the most used time-series databases in the IoT world. In this section, you will learn the fundamental concepts around this technology.

It is important to understand the topics covered in this section ot obtain a solid foundation. This will allow you to design a proper data structure, according to your project needs.

Let us discuss the InfluxDB instance.

InfluxDB hierarchy

InfluxDB has a hierarchical structure. The top level of this hierarchy is the organization.

Each organization includes buckets, users, dashboards, and tasks.

A bucket consists of a database that is related to a retention period. The retention period is the time the data will last in the database.

Users in InfluxDB belong to an organization. Each user may have access to some resources with specific permissions. For example, a user can access a bucket with read-only permission.

In InfluxDB, you can create dashboards to visualize and analyze the data without the need to use an external tool. This is useful for debugging purposes because you can check if the data is being stored according to your needs.

An InfluxDB task is a scheduled Flux script that handles data manipulation. It includes task options, a data source, processing steps, and a destination, all contributing to streamlined execution. Task options specify scheduling and other details, while Flux scripts manage data retrieval and filtering, seamlessly integrating with task options for added functionality. Processed data can be stored back into InfluxDB or other destinations, with comprehensive Flux scripts providing clear implementation examples.

Data structure

The data stored in each bucket must follow a specific data structure.

This structure includes the following:

- Timestamps
- Measurements
- Fields
- Tags

Timestamps

InfluxDB has a time column that stores a time value (timestamp) for each row of the bucket.

By default, the timestamp value corresponds to the time each data point is written to the bucket. However, you can specify the timestamp independently of the current time. To do this, you can include the timestamp in the data.

The timestamp information is stored on disk using the epoch nanosecond format. This means that the timestamp is represented as the number of nanoseconds that have elapsed since January 1, 1970, at 00:00:00 UTC (Unix Epoch). InfluxDB shows the time data using **`RFC3339`**, which is a human-readable format.

Each timestamp is stored in the **`_tiempstamp`** column in the bucket.

Measurements

A measurement is a group of timestamps, fields, and tags. You need to provide the respective measurement whenever you want to read some value from an InfluxDB bucket.

InfluxDB uses the **`_measurement`** column to store the name of each measurement. You can see an example of a measurement in *Table 8.1*:

_time	**_measurement**	**location**	**_field**	**_value**
2024-02-08T10:20:00Z	environment	Office	temp	30

***Table 8.1**: Measurement example*

Fields

The fields are pairs of keys and values. The keys are stored in the **`_field`** column, whereas the values are stored in the **`_value`** column.

The keys identify the variable of interest, while the value provides the actual value.

When different fields share the same timestamp, they are called a **field set**. You can see an example of a field set in *Table 8.2*:

_time	_measurement	location	_field	_value
2024-02-08T10:20:00Z	environment	Office	temp	30
2024-02-08T10:20:00Z	environment	Lab	hum	25
2024-02-08T11:20:00Z	environment	Office	temp	35
2024-02-08T11:20:00Z	environment	Lab	hum	40

Table 8.2: Example of two field sets

You can have multiple fields on the same measurement. However, having too many fields can impact performance and storage efficiency. It is recommended to design your schema with an appropriate balance between the number of fields and the number of measurements and tags based on your data requirements and query patterns.

Tags

Tags are optional but recommended. They let you organize the data according to specific characteristics and circumstances.

A tag consists of a pair of values. It is a key to identifying the tag and a value to obtain the actual value of the tag.

You can, for instance, use tags to identify a device, a site, a type of sensor, etc. Tags are helpful for grouping and filtering data using them on the queries.

Tags are indexed, so you can run faster queries than when using fields.

The collection of tag key-value pairs makes up a tag set. You can obtain multiple tag sets by grouping different tags and their values.

The following example shows four different tag sets:

- `location = office, site = headquarters`
- `location = lab, site = branch1`
- `location = office, site = branch1`
- `location = lab, site = headquarters`

Series in InfluxDB

In InfluxDB, we have several definitions for describing series and points. They are as follows:

- **Series key**: A series key is a collection of points that share a measurement, tag set, and field key.

  The following example shows a series key:

  ```
  measurement:environment, tag: location=lab, tag: site=headquarter, field:temp
  ```

- **Series**: A series includes timestamps and field values for a given series key.

  By following the previous example, you can see a series in *Table 8.3*:

_time	_measurement	location	site	_field	_value
2024-02-08T10:20:00Z	environment	office	headquarter	temp	30
2024-02-08T11:20:00Z	environment	office	headquarter	temp	35

Table 8.3: *Series*

- **Points**: A point includes the series key, a field value, and a timestamp. You can see an example in *Table 8.4*:

_time	_measurement	location	site	_field	_value
2024-02-08T10:20:00Z	environment	office	headquarter	temp	30

Table 8.4: *A point in an InfluxDB bucket*

Data standardization

Beyond the internal structures used in InfluxDB, we need to address a complex topic, such as data standardization.

Data standardization has to do with having a predictable data model that allows you to scale your IoT system without compromising efficiency and performance.

In other words, data standardization leads to the following objectives:

- **Interoperability**: In IoT systems, you may have devices from different vendors. These devices can use different communication technologies, protocols, and data formats. If you do not have a uniform data structure, the interoperability could be compromised.
- **Scalability**: If you have a pre-defined data format, scaling the system will be far more easy than if you have different data formats.
- **Visualization and analytics**: When you want to create visualizations or perform analytics on your data, having a standard format is crucial. If you have data with different formats, you will need to pre-process it before being able to visualize or analyze it.

There are many efforts to implement data standardization in IoT systems. This is a complex topic that we cannot cover here. However, if you want to explore more about this topic, refer to the *FIWARE Foundation* website **https://www.fiware.org/**.

According to the FIWARE website, the FIWARE Foundation works with its members and partners to develop open standards for portable and interoperable smart solutions, aiming to avoid vendor lock-in scenarios and promote sustainability and innovation in the business ecosystem.

To access the data models, visit **https://www.fiware.org/smart-data-models/**.

Building a data model

When you build a data model, you have to consider all the relevant information you may want to have, besides the data obtained by the sensors.

The following **JavaSscript Object Notation** (**JSON**) shows an example of a data object defined according to FIWARE specifications:

```
{
  "id": "urn:ngsi-ld:MEASUREMENT:id:PMZY:77452386",
  "dateCreated": "2021-09-03T07:33:18Z",
  "dateModified": "2021-09-03T07:33:18Z",
  "source": "Datacenter",
  "name": "Simple measurement",
  "alternateName": "",
  "description": "DAta center measurement values",
  "dataProvider": "",
  "owner": [
    "urn:ngsi-ld:MEASUREMENT:seeAlso:owner:00001"
  ],
  "seeAlso": [
    "urn:ngsi-ld:MEASUREMENT:seeAlso:ZMHH:32977"
  ],
  "location": {
    "type": "Point",
    "coordinates": [
      60.170833,
      24.9375
    ]
  },
  "address": {
    "streetAddress": "Pohjoisesplanadi 11-13 ",
    "addressLocality": "Helsinki",
    "addressRegion": "Helsinki",
    "addressCountry": "Finland",
```

```
    "postalCode": "00099",
    "postOfficeBoxNumber": "1"
  },
  "areaServed": "Helsinki council",
  "type": "DeviceMeasurement",
  "numValue": 55.2,
  "textValue": "",
  "controlledProperty": "humidity",
  "refDevice": "urn:ngsi-ld:MEASUREMENT:refDevice:ZMHH:32871158",
  "deviceType": "sensor",
  "measurementType": "FillingLevelSensor",
  "dateObserved": "2021-09-03T07:33:18Z",
  "outlier": true,
  "unit": "UDT0000016"
}
```

This is certainly a complex data model with a lot of information about the device and the context where it is working. However, in many cases, you will not see this level of detail.

If you opt to build your models, do not just think about the measured variables, but also about all the context data that can add value to your IoT solution.

For example, the serial number of the device, installation date, battery replacement date, geolocation, postal address, floor, office number, descriptions, etc.

Now that we have explored the fundamentals of InfluxDB and the data structure, let us see how to install InfluxDB on the Raspberry Pi computer.

Installing InfluxDB in a Raspberry Pi

In this section, we will install an InfluxDB instance to be able to run it locally.

This will allow us to write and read time-series data, which we will use later to build visualizations.

We will install the latest 2.X version available for Raspberry Pi OS.

Installation steps

Let us now discuss the following steps to install InfluxDB on your Raspberry Pi:

1. **Update packages**: Start by ensuring that all currently installed packages are up to date by running the following commands in your terminal:

```
$ sudo apt update
$ sudo apt upgrade
```

2. **Adding InfluxDB repository**: Next, add the InfluxDB repository key to your Raspberry Pi to enable package verification. Use the following command:

```
$ curl https://repos.influxdata.com/influxdata-archive.key | gpg --dearmor | sudo tee /usr/share/keyrings/influxdb-archive-keyring.gpg >/dev/null
```

3. **Add repository to sources list**: Add the InfluxDB repository to your sources list by running the following command:

```
$ echo "deb [signed-by=/usr/share/keyrings/influxdb-archive-keyring.gpg] https://repos.influxdata.com/debian stable main" | sudo tee /etc/apt/sources.list.d/influxdb.list
```

4. **Update package list**: Update the package list to include the newly added repository by running the following command:

```
$sudo apt update
```

5. **Choose InfluxDB version**: You can install V1.X or V2.X. In this case, we will install V2.X because it comes with a web interface and many very useful features.

6. **Install InfluxDB**: Install the chosen version using the following appropriate command:

```
$sudo apt install influxdb2
```

7. **Start InfluxDB service**: Enable InfluxDB to start at boot and start the service with the following commands:

```
$ sudo systemctl unmask influxdb
$ sudo systemctl enable influxdb
$ sudo systemctl start influxdb
```

The initial command unmasks the InfluxDB service file, allowing us to enable and start the service. Enabling the InfluxDB service is the subsequent step, prompting the service manager to monitor the `influxdb.service` file and configure the service accordingly.

The installation process might change over time. In any case, refer to **http://docs.influxdata.com/influxdb/v2/install/** to install InfluxDB 2.x.

In the next section, we will see how to access the web interface.

Accessing the web interface

Let us access the web interface of InfluxDB V2 on your Raspberry Pi.

The following are the steps:

1. **Find your Raspberry Pi's IP address**: First, determine the local IP address of your

Raspberry Pi. You can do this by running the following command:

```
$ hostname -I
```

2. **Access the web interface**: Once you have the IP address, open your favorite web browser and enter the following URL, replacing `<IPADDRESS>` with your Raspberry Pi's IP address, **http://<IPADDRESS>:8086/**. Refer to *Figure 8.1*.

   On this page, click on the **GET STARTED** button.

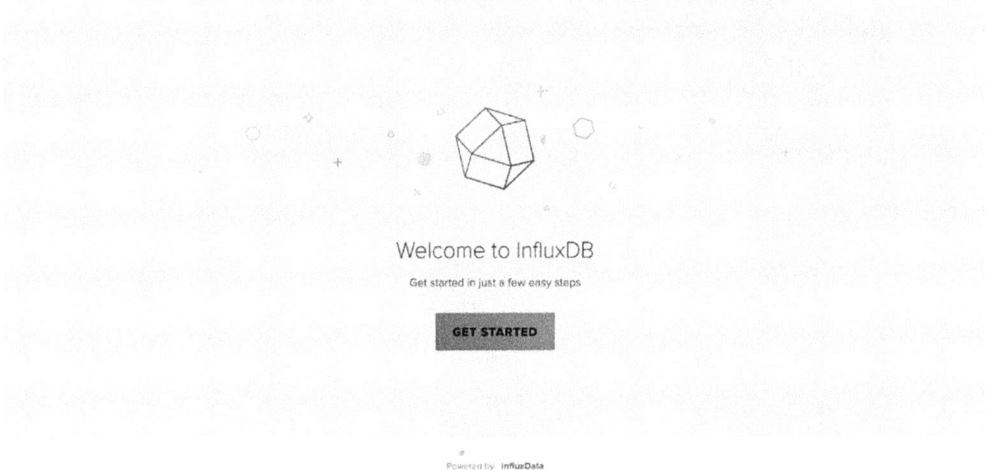

***Figure 8.1**: Starting page of InfluxDB 2*

3. **Initial setup**: Upon accessing the InfluxDB 2 interface for the first time, you will need to create an initial user. Refer to *Figure 8.2*:

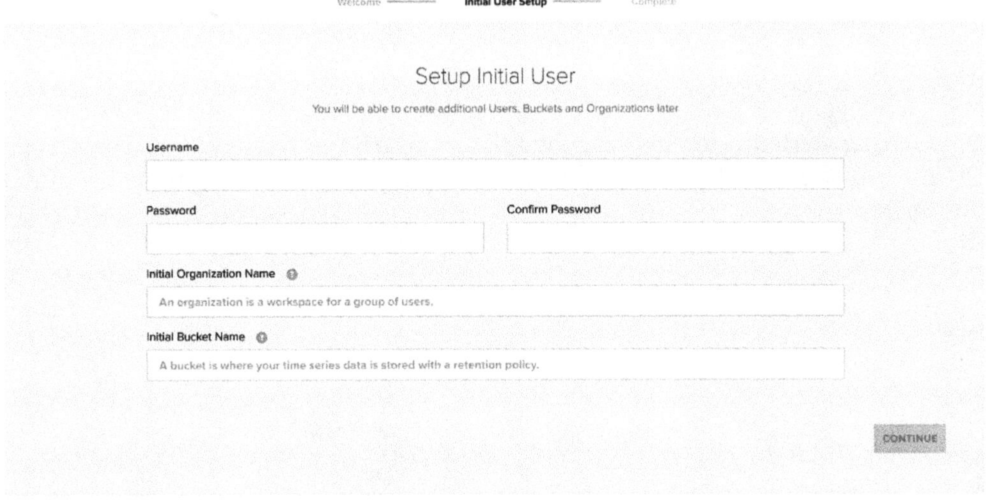

***Figure 8.2**: Initial configuration page*

Follow these steps:

a. Provide the necessary details for your user, including a strong password.

b. Give a name to your organization.

c. Enter a name for your first bucket.

d. After filling out the fields, click **CONTINUE**.

4. **Copy the application programming interface (API) token**: InfluxDB V2 will generate an API token for your Raspberry Pi. Copy this token as it grants superuser privileges and will not be shown again (see *Figure 8.3*). Before continuing, make sure the token has been copied to the clipboard. If not, copy the token manually (without using the button). Then, click **QUICK START**.

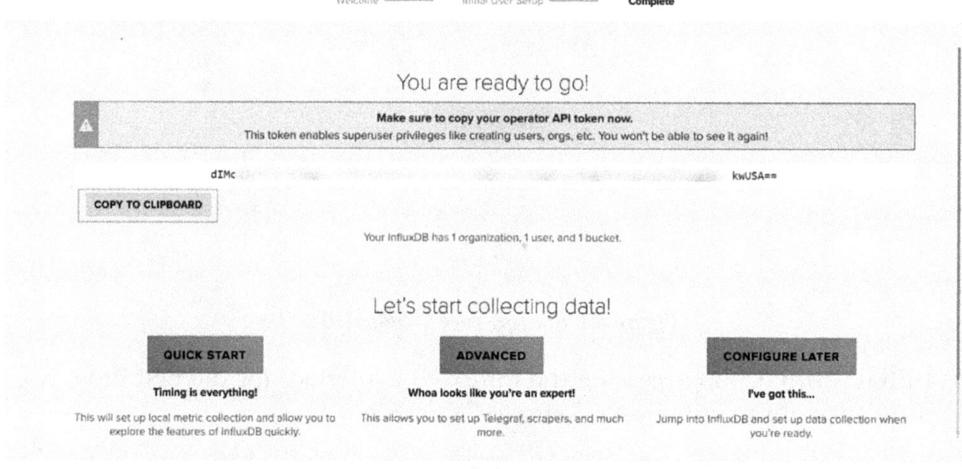

Figure 8.3: Copying the token

5. **Getting started**: After clicking the **QUICK START** button, you will see a page like the one shown in *Figure 8.4*. This is the starting point of managing your InfluxDB2 instance.

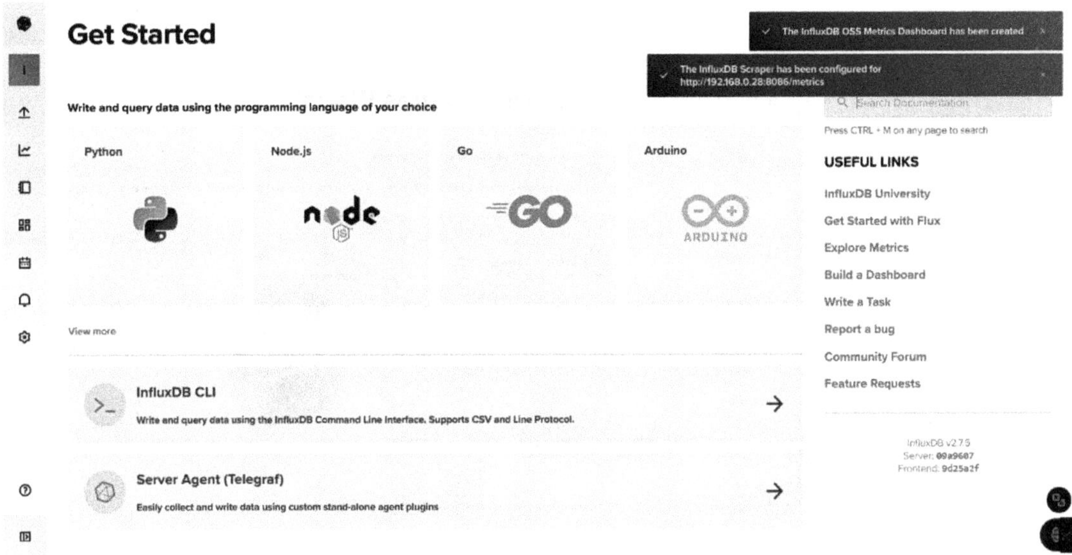

Figure 8.4: *Home page of InfluxDB 2 web interface*

In the following section, we will see several methods to store data in the InfluxDB bucket we have just created.

Storing and reading data in the bucket

There are many ways to interact with an InfluxDB bucket.

The following are some examples:

- Using one of the many libraries such as Node.js, Python, Go, or even Arduino, to name a few.
- Using the web interface to upload or download preformatted data.
- Using the **command line interface** (**CLI**) with the **influx** command.
- Using agents or brokers like Telegraf, Node-RED, Fluentbit, etc.

As you can see, there are plenty of options to interact with InfluxDB. In this chapter, we will use Python and Node-RED.

Using Python to store data in InfluxDB

In this section, we will see how to build a Python script to store data points in an InfluxDB bucket.

If you look at the home page of the InfluxDB instance, you will see a big button with the Python logo (see *Figure 8.4*). Clicking on it will lead you to the **Setting Up** Python page, as shown in *Figure 8.5*:

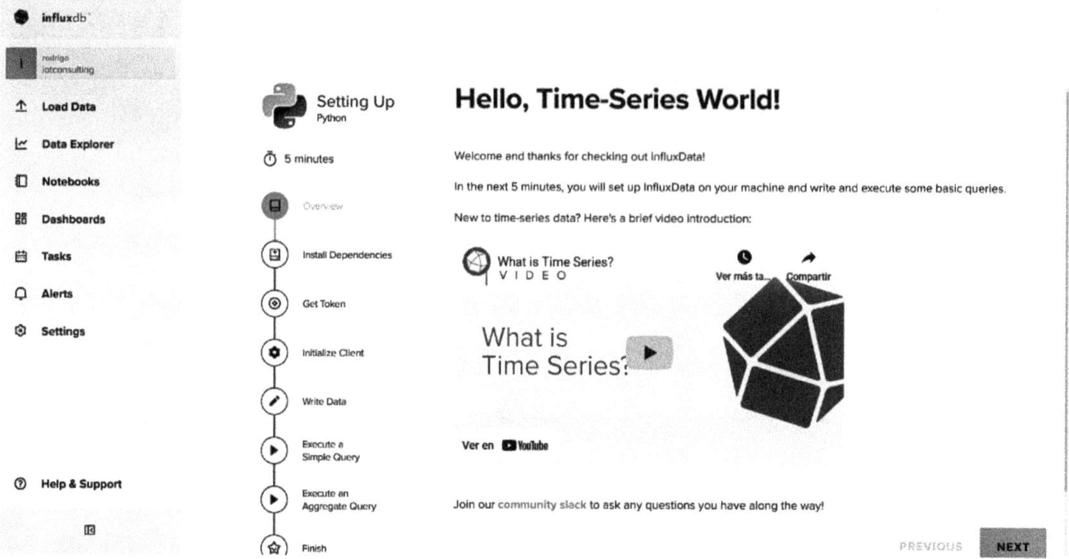

Figure 8.5:Setting Up Python page

If you follow the steps proposed on this page, you will be able to set up a Python client to write data points in the InfluxDB bucket.

To shorten the process, we will see how to do it by following a few steps:

1. First, activate the Python environment we created in *Chapter 2, Installing the Software Environment*, by running the following command.

   ```
   $ source raspenv/bin/activate
   ```

Note: If you used another name than `raspenv`, you have to change it accordingly on the path.

2. Once you are in your Python environment. Run the following command to install the InfluxDB client Python module.

   ```
   $ pip3 install influxdb-client
   ```

3. Also, install the **dotenv** module as follows.

   ```
   $ pip3 install dotenv
   ```

4. Now, go to the web interface of InfluxDB, and select the menu option **Load Data | API TOKENS**. You will see a page like the one shown in *Figure 8.6*. Then, click on the **GENERATE API TOKEN** button and select **CustomAPI Token**.

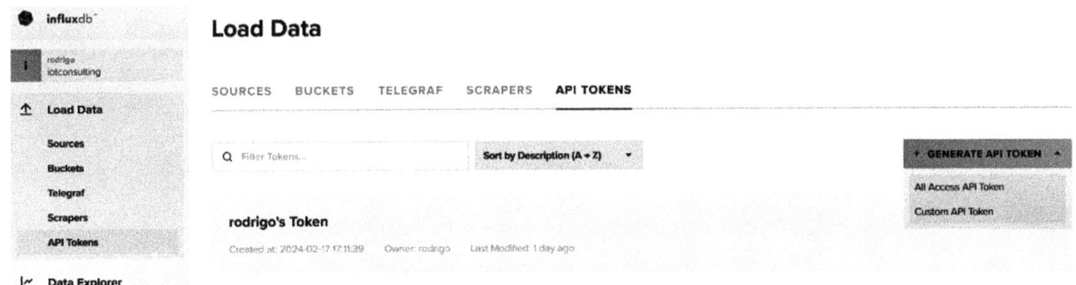

Figure 8.6: API TOKENS page

5. In the open window, select permissions to write and read on the bucket you created before. See *Figure 8.7*:

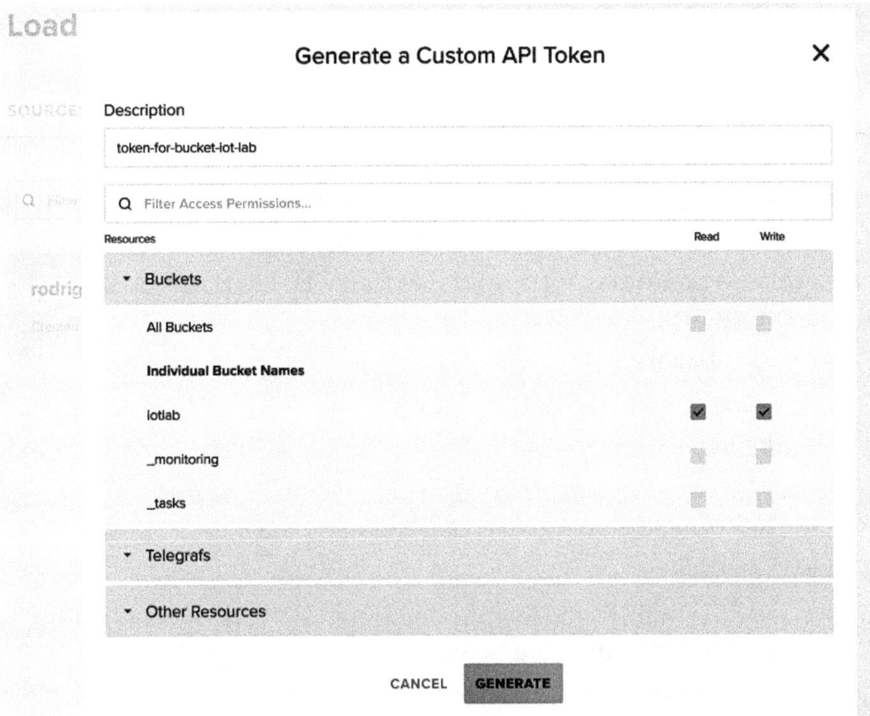

Figure 8.7: Configuring token permissions

6. The previous step will generate a new token. Copy and save it in a text file for further use. See *Figure 8.8*:

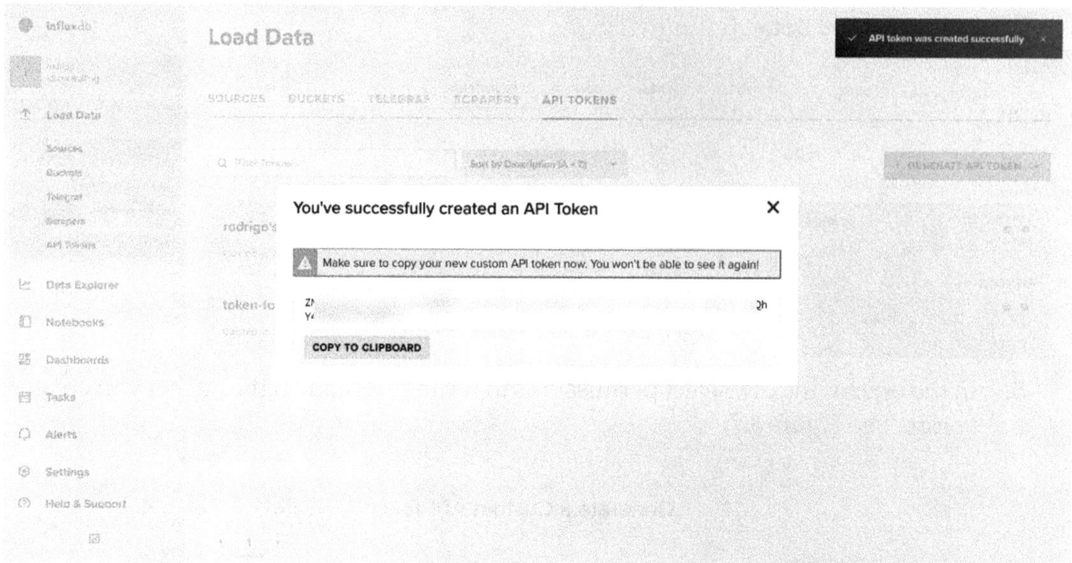

Figure 8.8: Generating new token

7. Now that you have generated a token with reading and writing permissions on the bucket, you can use it in your Python script.
8. Now, create a new directory in your Raspberry Pi, let us say **influxdb**. We will use this directory to put our files.

   ```
   $ mkdir influxdb
   ```

   After creating it, go to the new directory.

   ```
   $ cd influxdb
   ```

9. In the new directory, create a file called **.env**. We will use this file to store the token. Run the following command to create and open the file.

   ```
   $ nano .env
   ```

   In the **.env** file, add the following line (replace **<YOUR-TOKEN>** with your actual token). Use the following parameters:

   a. **INFLUXDB_TOKEN = "<YOUR-TOKEN>"**

   b. Then, press *Ctrl* + *O* to save the file and *Ctrl* + *X* to exit.

10. Now, create a new file, called **influx_client.py,** and paste the code provided in the following. Replace **YOUR_ORG**, **YOUR_IP**, and **YOUR_BUCKET** with your actual values:

   ```
   import sys
   import time
   from dotenv import Dotenv
   from influxdb_client import InfluxDBClient, Point
   ```

```
from influxdb_client.client.write_api import SYNCHRONOUS

# Load environment file
dotenv = Dotenv('.env')

# Fetch token from environment variables
token = dotenv["INFLUXDB_TOKEN"]
org = "YOUR_ORG"
url = "http://YOUR_IP:8086"

# Initialize InfluxDB client
write_client = InfluxDBClient(url=url, token=token, org=org)

# Specify bucket
bucket = "YOUR_BUCKET"

# Initialize write API
write_api = write_client.write_api(write_options=SYNCHRONOUS)

# Command-line arguments
if len(sys.argv) != 3:
    print("Usage: python script.py <field_value> <tag_value>")
    sys.exit(1)

value = int(sys.argv[1])
tag_value = sys.argv[2]

# Writing data points
point = (
    Point("temp_sensor")
    .tag("location", tag_value)
    .field("temp", value)
)
write_api.write(bucket=bucket, org=org, record=point)
```

11. Save the file by pressing *Ctrl* + *O* and exit with *Ctrl* + *X*.
12. Now, you can run this script from the command line to ingest new values in the bucket.

Note: The first argument of the command corresponds to the temperature value, whereas the second one is about the location.

You can, for example, execute the command as follows:

```
$ python influx_client.py 25.2 office
```

This will store a new point in the bucket with a `temp` field equal to `25.2` and a location tag equal to the office.

Note: In the previous command, we used 25.2 instead of an integer, like 25. This is because this creates a double (float) field value in the bucket. If you use just an integer, the field format will be an integer, and you will not be able to store float values in that field.

13. To check the correct writing of the point, you can go to the web interface and select the **Data Explorer** option in the left menu. Then, look for the `temp_sensor` measurement and the `temp` field, as shown in *Figure 8.9*. Finally, click on the **Submit** button to show the data point in the dashboard.

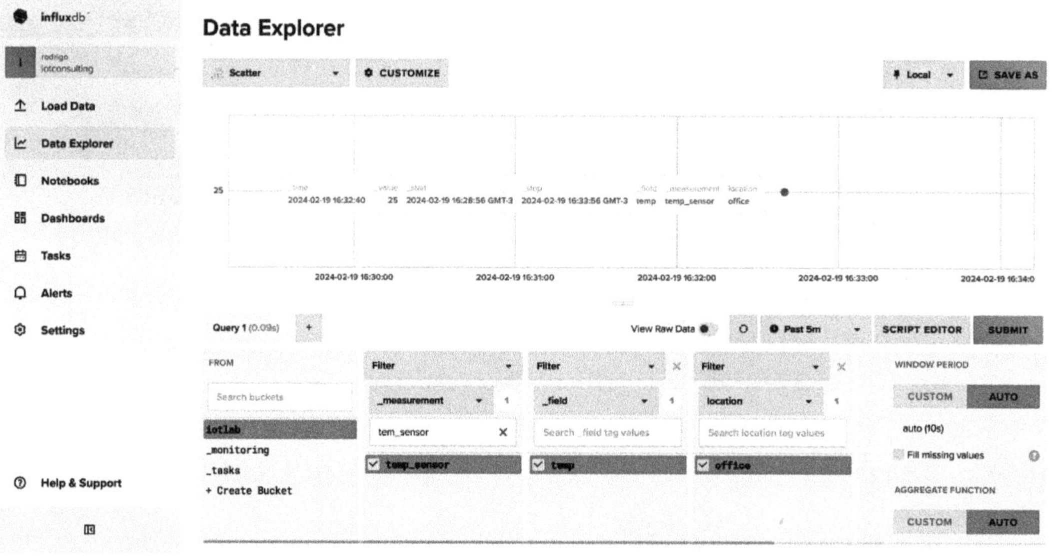

Figure 8.9: Data Explorer

Now, let us see how we can store data points using Node-RED.

Using Node-RED to write and read data points

In this section, we will see how to use Node-RED to write and read data points in an InfluxDB bucket.

Writing data points

Let us see how to write data points in the InfluxDB bucket.

To build the flow, follow these steps:

1. First, we need to install a new Node-RED node. Click on the **Manage palette** option in the Node-RED menu on the right. Then go to the **Install** tab and look for **`influxdb`**. From the list, select **`node-red-contrib-influxdb`**, as shown in *Figure 8.10*:

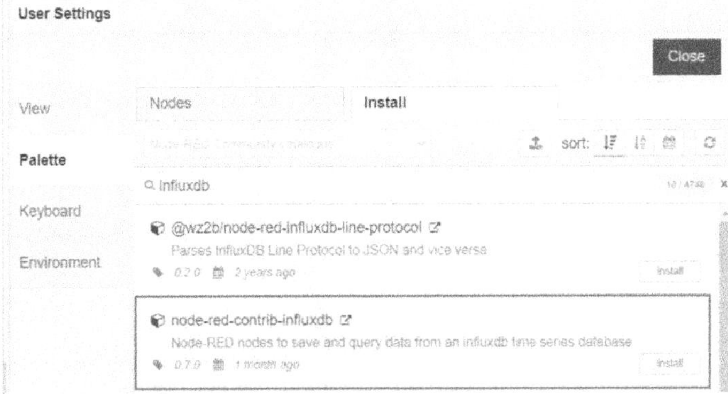

***Figure 8.10**: Installing node-red-contrib-influxdb*

2. Now that you have installed the node, let us configure the InfluxDB client. Add an **`influx-db-out`** node to the flow, and double-click on it. This will lead you to the configuration panel shown in *Figure 8.11*. There, click on the pencil to add a new InfluxDB connection.

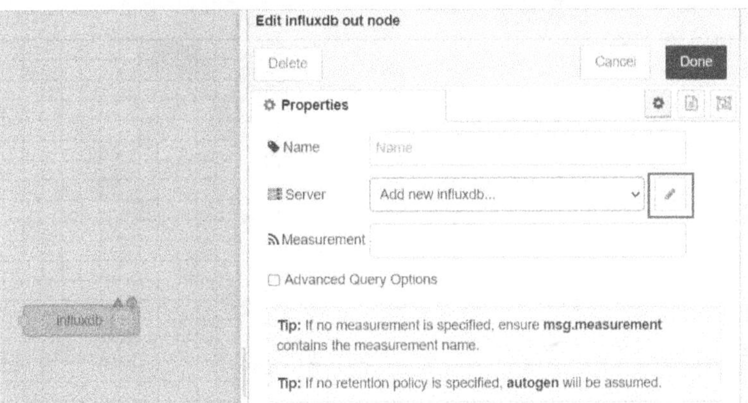

***Figure 8.11**: Creating a new InfluxDB connection*

3. Enter the connection parameters as shown in *Figure 8.12*.
   Enter a name for the block. Then select version 2.0 and enter the URL where you are running the InfluxDB instance.
   Use the token you generated earlier for the Python script. Also, unset the **Verify server certificate** option, as we have not configured encryption in the InfluxDB instance.
   After finishing the configuration, click on the **Add** button to apply the changes and return to the **`influx-db-out node`**.

Figure 8.12: *Adding a new InfluxDB connection*

4. In the **`influx-db-out node`**, enter the following parameters:
   - A name for the node.
   - Select the InfluxDB connection that you have just created.
   - Enter the name of your organization. This is the name you chose when you configured the InfluxDB instance. You can see this name below your username, in the upper-left of InfluxDB's web interface.
   - Enter the name of the bucket where you are going to write the data.
   - Finally, enter the name of the measurement.

   You can see an example in *Figure 8.13*:

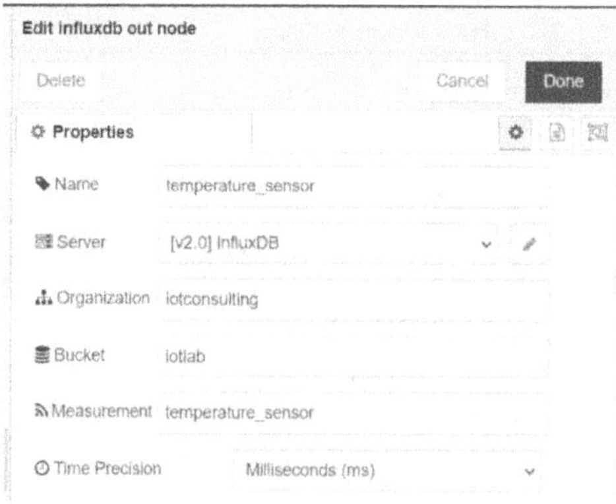

Figure 8.13: *Configuring the influx-db-out node*

5. Now that we have configured the node, let us add other nodes to write data in the database:
   - Add an input inject node.
   - Add a function node.
   - Connect the nodes as shown in *Figure 8.14*:

***Figure 8.14**: Flow for writing data in the InfluxDB bucket*

6. The code in the function is as follows:

```
msg.payload = [{
    temperature: 22.5
},
{
    location:"lab"
}];
return msg;
```

Whenever you click on the input inject node, this code sends a float value (**`22.5`** in this case) for the temperature field and a string (**`lab`**) for the **`location`** tab.

Note: This is just an example, and we will send real data from sensors in the following chapters.

Reading data points

Now that we have some data points in our bucket, let us see how we can read them from Node-RED.

To build the flow, follow these steps:

1. Grab an **`influxdb-in`** node and place it in the Node-RED flow. Then, click on it to configure it.

   In this node, you have to enter the following data:
   - A name for the node.
   - Select the InfluxDB connection.
   - Enter the organization name.

- Add a Flux script to perform the query on the bucket. We will do this in the following step. You can refer to the Flux docs at **https://docs.influxdata.com/flux/v0/**.

You can see the block configuration in *Figure 8.15*:

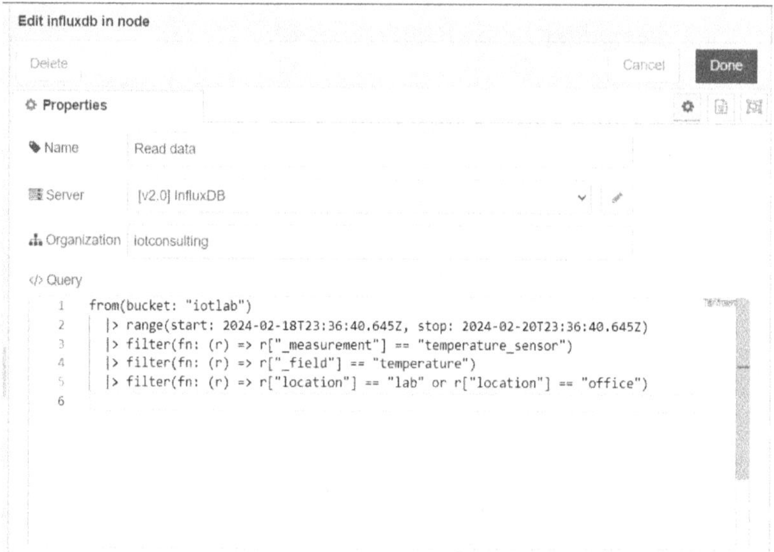

***Figure 8.15**: InfluxDB in node*

2. To get the data from the InfluxDB database, we need to run a Flux script. However, we will do it without having to learn the language (although it is quite intuitive).
   a. First, go to the web interface of InfluxDB and click on the **Data Explorer** option in the left menu.
   b. Then, use the graphic query builder to create your query. Select the bucket, the measurement, the tags, and the time interval. Then, click on the **SUBMIT** button to execute the query.
   c. Now, click on the **SCRIPT EDITOR** button to switch to the other mode. You can see this button in *Figure 8.16*:

***Figure 8.16**: Changing to script editor mode*

   d. This will lead you to the text editor, as shown in *Figure 8.17*:

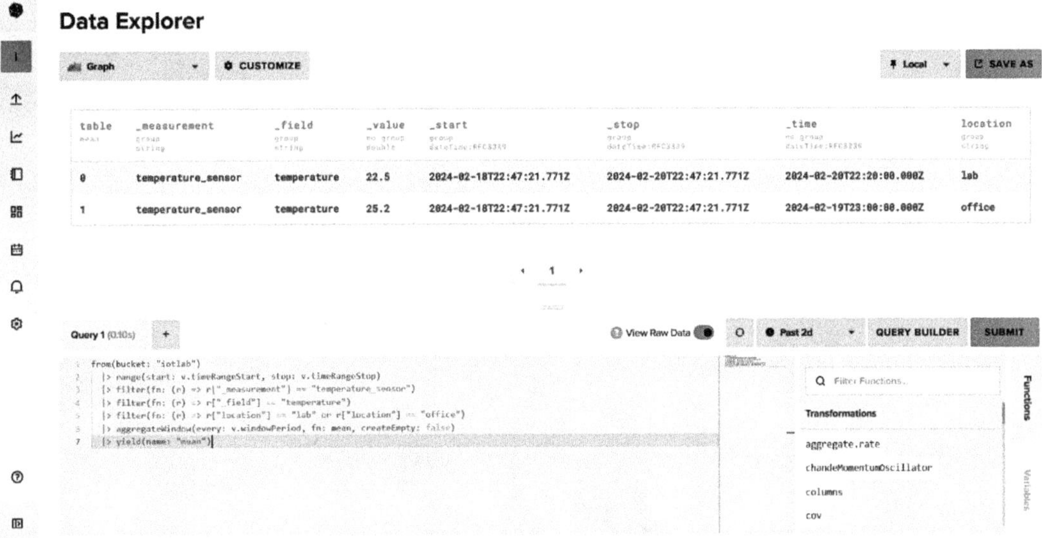

Figure 8.17: Script Editor mode

e. Following, you can use this code in the **influxdb-in** node in Node-RED. However, we first need to perform a few modifications:

   i. Replace the **v.timeRangeStart** and **v.timeRangeStop** variables for the corresponding values shown in the table of points. This is needed because these variables are not available during the query from Node-RED.

   ii. Remove the last two lines, that correspond to a mean transformation that the query builder applies by default. We do not need this and it uses the **v.windowperiod** that is not available from the Node-RED query.

f. You can see the resulting query in *Figure 8.15*. Yours should look similar to this example.

3. Now, add two blocks to the flow, such as an inject node and a debug node. Connect them as shown in *Figure 8.18*:

Figure 8.18: Flow for reading InfluxDB bucket

4. When you click on the inject node, you will get the data from the InfluxDB bucket, according to the Flux script, as shown in *Figure 8.19*:

```
msg.payload : array[2]
▾array[2]
 ▾0: object
    result: "_result"
    table: 0
    _start: "2024-02-18T23:36:40.645Z"
    _stop: "2024-02-20T23:36:40.645Z"
    _time: "2024-02-20T22:16:06.625Z"
    _value: 22.5
    _field: "temperature"
    _measurement: "temperature_sensor"
    location: "lab"
 ▾1: object
    result: "_result"
    table: 1
    _start: "2024-02-18T23:36:40.645Z"
    _stop: "2024-02-20T23:36:40.645Z"
    _time: "2024-02-
    19T22:53:10.476219843Z"
    _value: 25.2
    _field: "temperature"
    _measurement: "temperature_sensor"
    location: "office"
```


Figure 8.19: *Data from the InfluxDB bucket*

Now, we know how to write and read data from an InfluxDB bucket using Node-RED.

Using InfluxDB Cloud service

Using the cloud service of InfluxDB is quite the same as using it locally. In this section, we will see how to create and set up an account.

Follow these steps to register in the InfluxDB Cloud service 2.0:

1. **Sign up**: Perform the following actions to create an account in InfluxDB Cloud.
    a. Visit the InfluxDB Cloud Service 2.0 at **https://cloud2.influxdata.com/signup** (see *Figure 8.20*).
    b. Fill out the registration form with your email address and password.
    c. Click on the **Sign Up** button.
    d. Confirm your email address through the verification email sent to you.

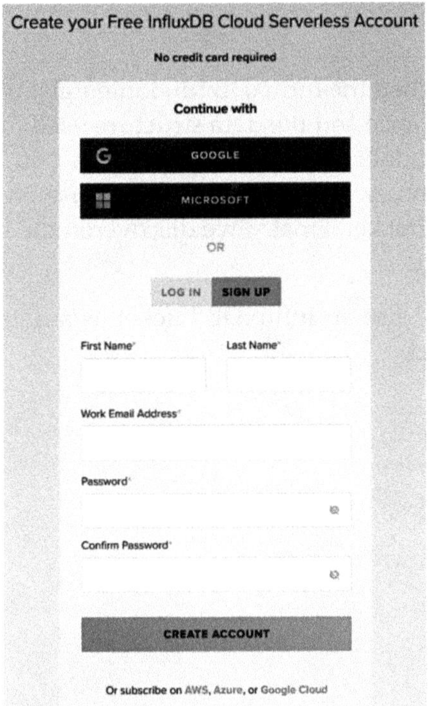

Figure 8.20: InfluxDB Cloud account registration page

2. **Create an organization**: Upon logging in, create your organization. This is where your data will be stored and managed. Give your organization a name and description.
3. **Set up a bucket**: Within your organization, create a bucket to store your time-series data. Define the retention policy for your bucket (for example, how long data will be retained).
4. **Generate tokens**: Follow these steps to create the token:
   a. Generate tokens to authenticate your applications and users.
   b. Assign appropriate permissions to these tokens based on your security needs.
5. **Write data**: Use the InfluxDB API or client libraries to write data to your bucket.

Note: Unlike with the local instance, this time you will use an encrypted connection. So, set up your clients accordingly.

6. **Query and visualize data**: Like with the local instance, you can perform queries and explore the data using the Data Explorer tool.

Now, you have a working account in the InfluxDB Cloud service. You can use it entirely for free if you run small projects or want to use it for testing purposes.

Conclusions

In this chapter, first, we learned the InfluxDB fundamentals. We saw all the main concepts regarding the InfluxDB instance and the data structure used in the buckets. We also made some considerations about data standardization. Then, you learned how to write data points using the Python library. We also saw how to use Node-RED to write and read data points in an InfluxDB bucket. Finally, we discovered the InfluxDB Cloud service and learned to create an account.

In the next chapter, we will use an InfluxDB bucket as a data source for visualizing the data in a Grafana dashboard.

CHAPTER 9

Visualizing Internet of Things Data

Introduction

In this chapter, we will use Grafana to visualize and analyze **Internet of Things** (**IoT**) data. Grafana is an open-source powerful visualization tool that you can use to visualize data in dashboards. Grafana admits a very wide range of visualizations, according to the type of data and its purpose. You can feed Grafana using different types of data sources. From spreadsheets to **Standard Query Language** (**SQL**) databases and time-series databases, to name a few. This variety of data sources brings Grafana great flexibility, as you can combine many of them on the same visualization dashboard.

Also, Grafana allows you to create data-based alarm conditions and trigger notifications using different communication channels.

Structure

This chapter has the following structure:

- Installing Grafana in Raspberry Pi
- Data sources
- Building a dashboard in Grafana
- Plugins in Grafana

- Alerts in Grafana
- Notifications in Grafana
- Users and permissions in Grafana
- Using Grafana Cloud Service

Objectives

In this chapter, you will learn how to install, configure, and use Grafana with IoT data. We will use InfluxDB as a data source to populate the dashboards. You will also learn to build data-based alarms and configure notifications.

By the end of this chapter, you will be able to build insightful dashboards using the data collected by IoT devices.

Installing Grafana in Raspberry Pi

In this section, you will learn how to install Grafana on the Raspberry Pi computer. In this case, we are going to use Raspberry Pi 4, but the procedure is similar for other versions of Raspberry Pi.

Follow these steps to install Grafana:

1. As usual, it is recommended to update the packages before starting with the installation of new software. Run the following commands to do so:

   ```
   $ sudo apt update
   $ sudo apt upgrade
   ```

2. Add the Grafana package repository by adding the **Advanced Package Tool** (**APT**) key with the following command:

   ```
   $ wget -q -O - https://packages.grafana.com/gpg.key | sudo apt-key add
   -
   ```

3. Add the Grafana repository to the list of package sources with the following command:

   ```
   $ sudo add-apt-repository "deb https://packages.grafana.com/oss/deb
   stable main"
   ```

4. Update the package list by running the following commands:

   ```
   $ sudo apt update
   ```

5. Install Grafana on your Raspberry Pi by running the following commands:

   ```
   $ sudo apt install Grafana
   ```

6. Enable Grafana to start at boot by running the following commands:

   ```
   $ sudo systemctl enable grafana-server.service
   ```

7. Start the Grafana server software by running the following commands:

```
$ sudo systemctl start grafana-server
```

8. Check that the Grafana service is running the following commands:

```
$ sudo systemctl status grafana-server
```

9. Access the Grafana web interface by pointing your browser to **http://<your-raspberry-ip>:3000**. You will see a login page like the one shown in *Figure 9.1*.
10. Enter the default credentials to access Grafana for the first time (user: admin, password: admin). Refer to *Figure 9.1*:

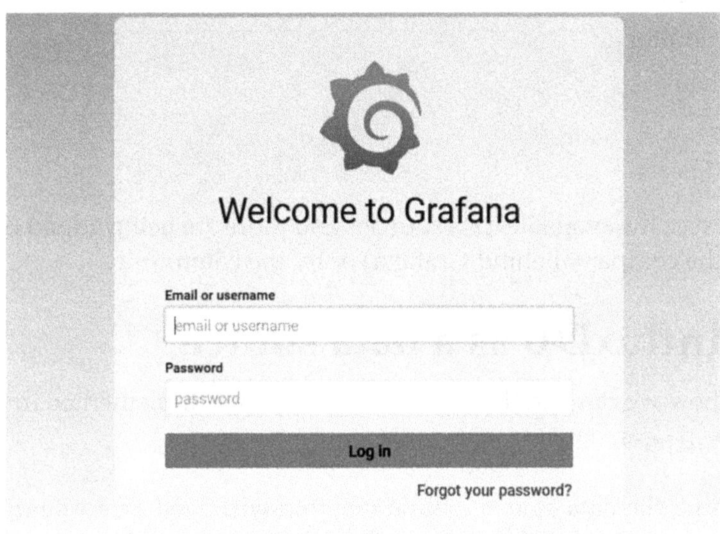

***Figure 9.1**: Login page of Grafana*

In the following sections, we will learn how to add data sources and build dashboards.

Data sources

In this section, we will learn how to add data sources to our Grafana instance.

Data sources are necessary, as they are the repositories of the data we need to build visualizations.

Note: Grafana does not store data. It just gets it by performing queries over the configured data sources.

This feature allows you to obtain data from different sources, even managed by different organizations, and show it on a single or several Grafana dashboards.

These are many of the data sources supported by Grafana. They are as follows:

- InfluxDB
- MySQL
- MongoDB
- Graphite
- OpenTSDB
- PostgreSQL
- OpenSearch
- Azure Monitor
- Prometheus
- CSV files
- Google Sheets

This is a short list of the available data sources, and more are being added continuously by Grafana Labs (the company behind Grafana) or by the community.

Adding InfluxDB as a data source

Now let us see how we can add the InfluxDB database we implemented in the last chapter as a data source in Grafana.

Note: For adding the data source to Grafana, you will need an authentication token. Refer to Chapter 8, Storing Internet of Things Data, to see how to generate a new token. In this case, consider using read-only permission on the selected bucket, as you will only read data.

Follow these steps for adding an InfluxDB bucket as a data source:

1. In the left menu, go to **Home** | **Connections** | **Data sources**. This will lead you to the **Data source** page, as shown in *Figure 9.2*:

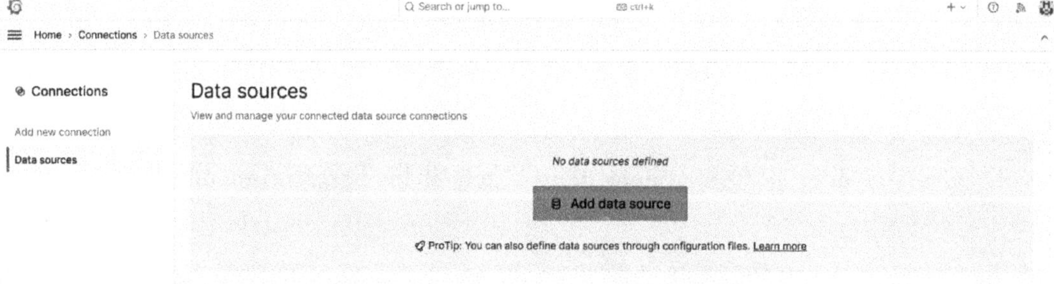

***Figure 9.2:** Data sources page in Grafana*

2. Click on the big blue button with the text **Add data source**. You will then be able to access the page to add data sources. You can see this page in *Figure 9.3*:

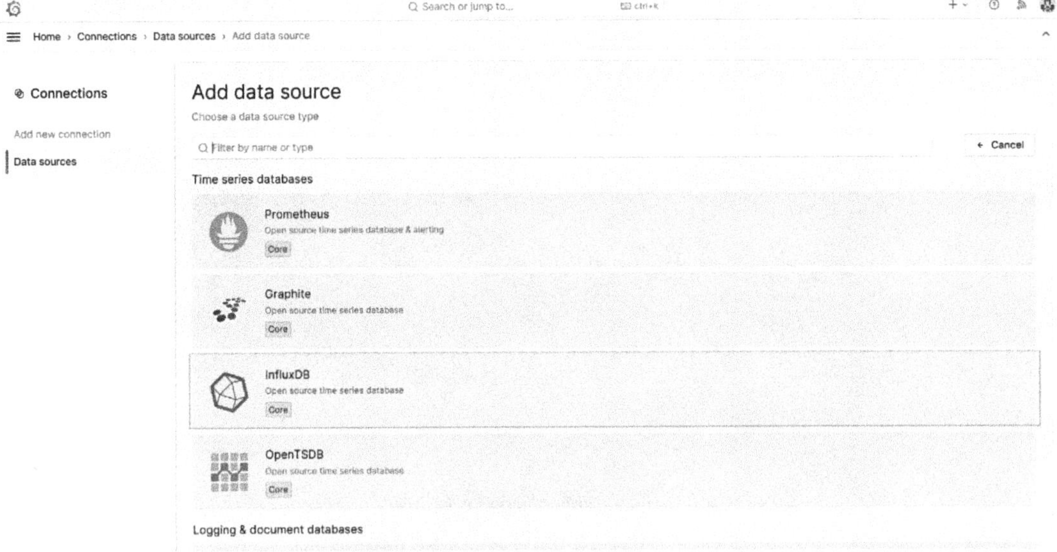

Figure 9.3: List of data sources available to add

3. Select InfluxDB from the list by clicking on the corresponding row. This will lead you to the data source configuration page.
4. In the InfluxDB data source configuration page, enter the following data:
   a. Give a name to the data source. You can, for instance, use a meaningful name related to the data of the bucket.
   b. Select Flux from the dropdown list as the query language.
   c. Enter the URL of the InfluxDB instance. In this case, we are using both InfluxDB and Grafana on the same host, so we can specify **http://localhost:8086**. You can see all these parameters in *Figure 9.4*:

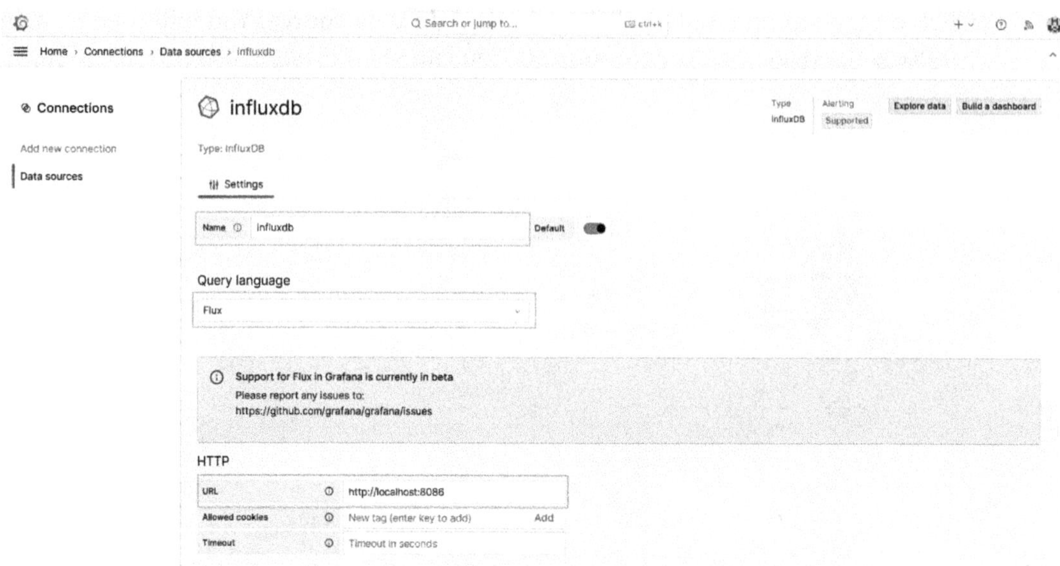

Figure 9.4: Configuration options for InfluxDB data source

d. Scroll down and configure the rest of the parameters: the InfluxDB organization, the authentication token, and the bucket to be used. You can see an example in *Figure 9.5*:

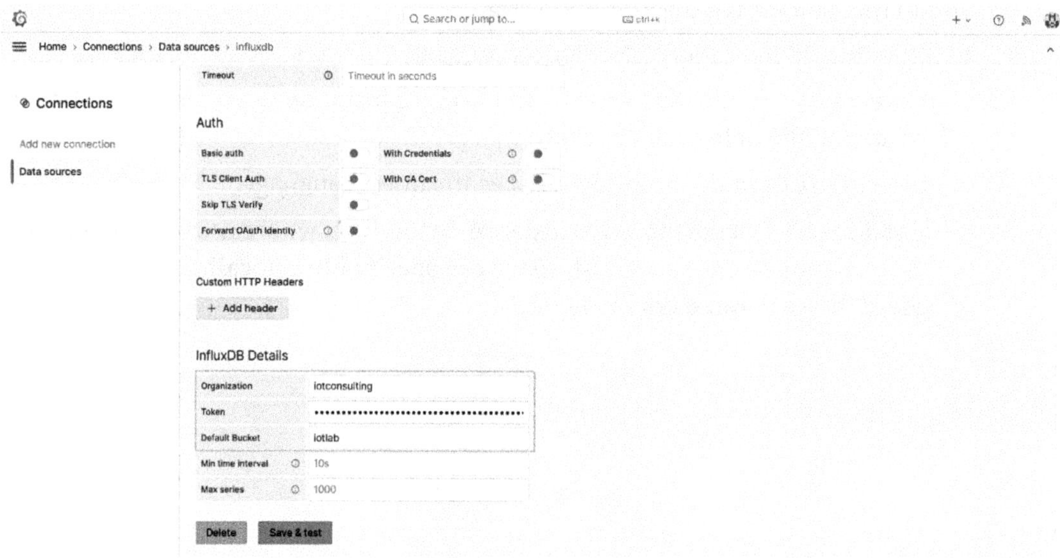

Figure 9.5: Configuration parameters for InfluxDB data source

Now, we have a working data source. In the next section, we will use it to build dashboards in Grafana.

Populating the bucket with system usage data

Before proceeding to build a dashboard, let us write some data in the InfluxDB bucket. In this case, we will use Node-RED to write the system resource usage of the Raspberry Pi.

To build the flow in Node-RED, follow these steps:

1. Open the web interface of your Node-RED instance, go to the menu, and select the **Manage palette** option. Then, click on the **Install** tab and look for the **`node-red-contrib-os node`**, as shown in *Figure 9.6*. This node lets you obtain system usage data.

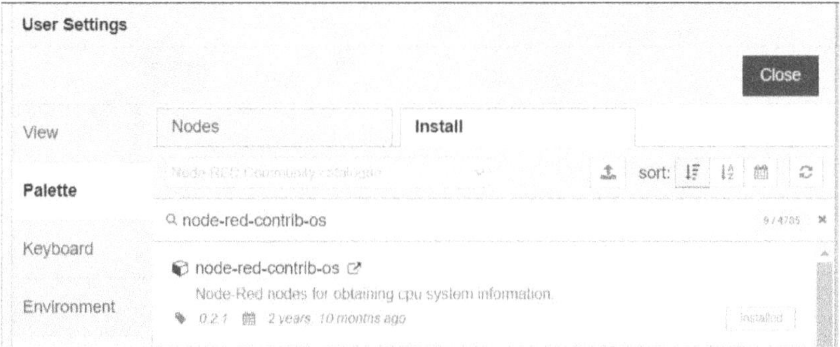

Figure 9.6*: Installing node-red-contrib-os*

2. Once the node is installed, return to the flow interface and add the following nodes:
    - One inject
    - One loadavg
    - One memory
    - Two function nodes
    - One join
    - One debug
    - One influxdb out
3. Name one function node as **`load_object`**, and the other as **`add tag`**. Also, name the influxdb out node as **`system load`**. This step is optional but recommended.
4. Connect all the nodes, as shown in *Figure 9.7*:

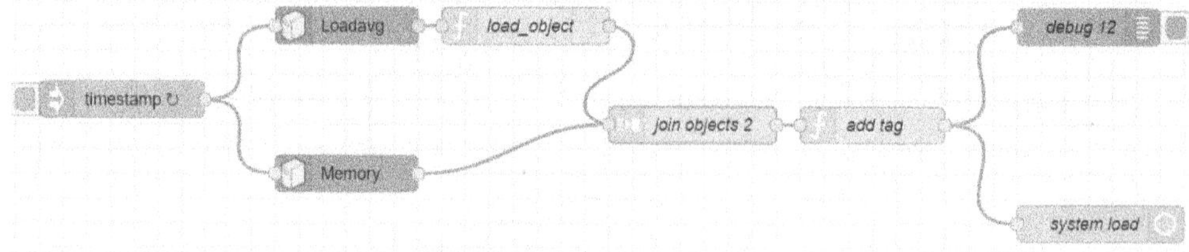

Figure 9.7: Complete flow

5. Now, let us configure each of these nodes. Open the inject node and configure it to send messages every five minutes, as shown in *Figure 9.8*:

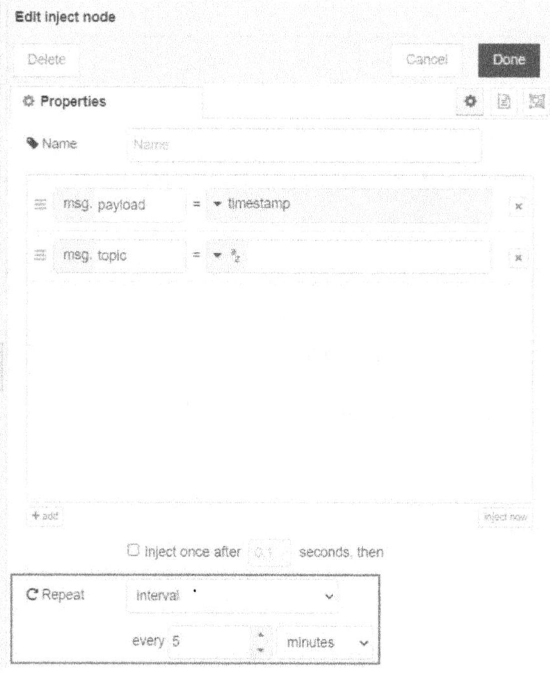

Figure 9.8: Inject node configuration

6. Open the **load_object** function, paste the following code, and save the node:

```
msg.payload = {
    "load_1": msg.payload.loadavg[0],
    "load_5": msg.payload.loadavg[1],
    "load_15": msg.payload.loadavg[2]

};

return msg;
```

7. Open the join node and configure it, as shown in *Figure 9.9*:

Note: You have to select the manual mode. Also, in the `to create` field, select `a merged Object`.

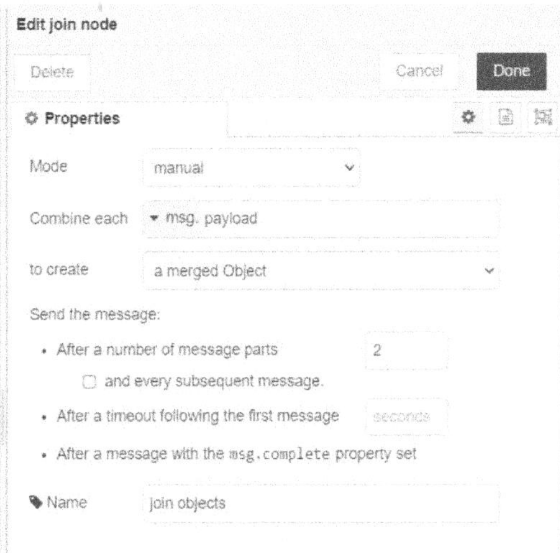

***Figure 9.9**: Configuring the join node*

8. Open the **add tag** function node and enter the following code. This code adds a tag named **device** that refers to the hostname of the computer:

```
msg.payload= [
    msg.payload
,
    {
        "device": "raspberrypi"
    }
];

return msg;
```

9. Finally, let us configure the influxdb out node. Here, you can use the same configuration you used in *Chapter 8* for the InfluxDB connection or create a new one. In any case, refer to *Chapter 8, Storing Internet of Things Data* instructions for setting up the server connection.

   In the node, enter the following information:

   a. Give a name to the node

   b. Select the InfluxDB server from the list.

c. Enter the organization, the bucket, and the measurement you are going to use. You can see an example in *Figure 9.10*:

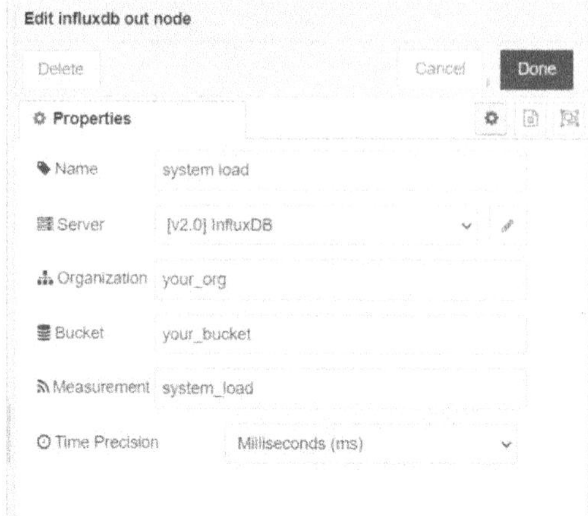

***Figure 9.10**: Configuring the influxdb out node*

10. Once everything is configured and programmed, click on **Deploy**. You should start to see the data in the debug panel, as shown in *Figure 9.11*:

```
msg.payload : array[2]
▾array[2]
▾0: object
    totalmem: 908.34
    freemem: 505.191
    memusage: 44.38
    load_1: 0.02
    load_5: 0.02
    load_15: 0.02
▾1: object
    device: "raspberrypi"
```

***Figure 9.11**: Data shown in the debug panel*

Now, let us check that the data is being stored in the InfluxDB bucket.

Exploring the data in the bucket

To see if the data is being stored in the bucket, you can use the Data Explorer of the InfluxDB instance. On the left menu, go to **Data Explorer** to access the tool.

There, you can use the query builder to select the bucket, the measurement, the fields, and the tags. Play by selecting different fields to show each of their values. Refer to *Figure 9.12*.

In this case, we have just one tag: device. If you have more than one device, you can use this tag to filter the devices by their identification.

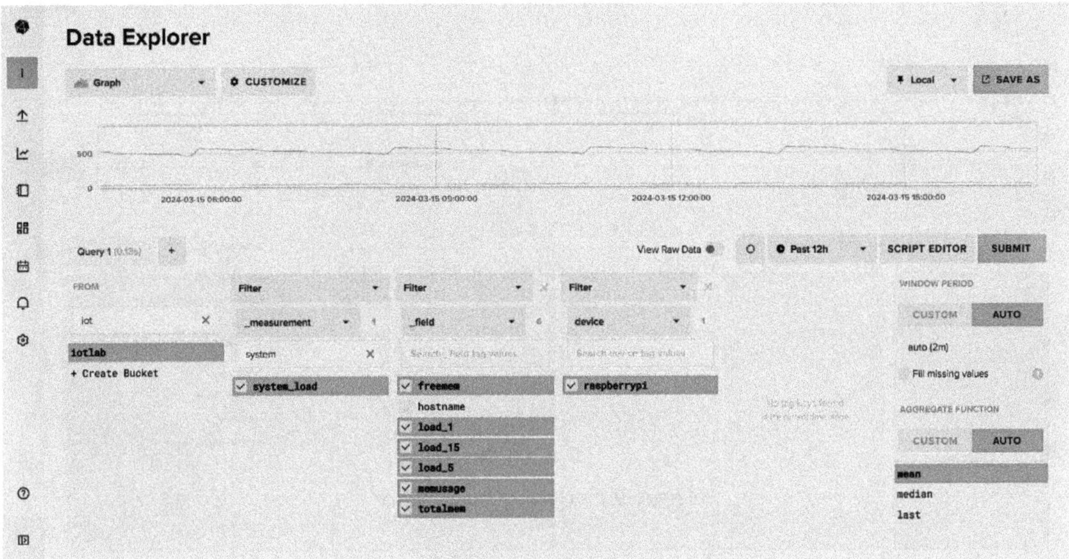

Figure 9.12: *Exploring the data and building the query*

Note: On the right panel, you can select different functions to transform the data.

Once you have the data you want, you can switch to the text format by clicking on the script editor button. The **Data Explorer** will show you the flux script, and you will be able to edit or copy it. See *Figure 9.13*.

In the next section, you will be able to copy and paste this script to use it in a Grafana dashboard.

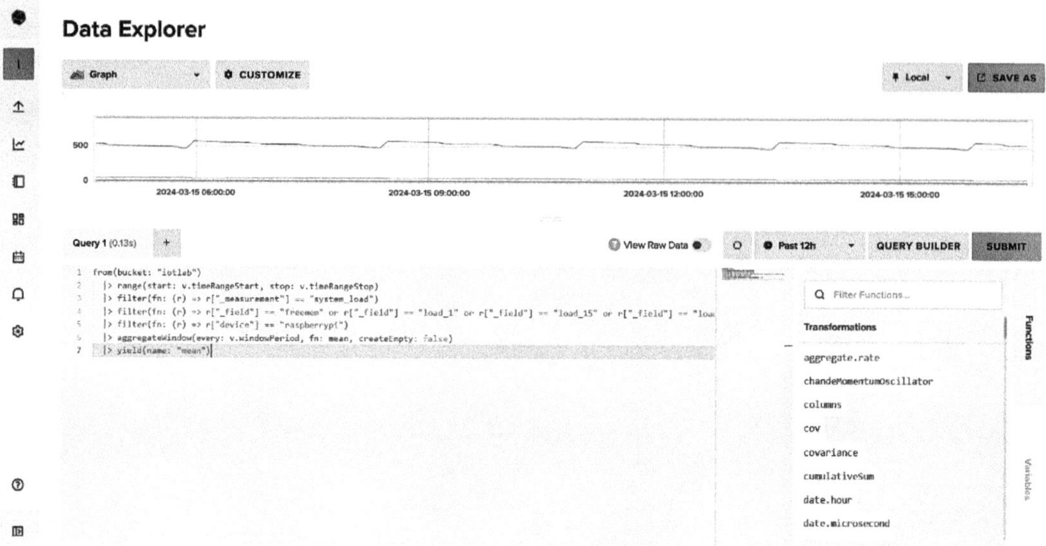

Figure 9.13: Query script in Flux

Now, let us see how you can show this data on a Grafana dashboard.

Building a dashboard in Grafana

To create a dashboard, follow these steps:

1. Go to the left menu and select **Home | Dashboards**. After clicking on it, you will see a dashboard page, like the one shown in *Figure 9.14*.
2. Click on the big blue button **Create Dashboard** or on the button **New**, on the top right corner.

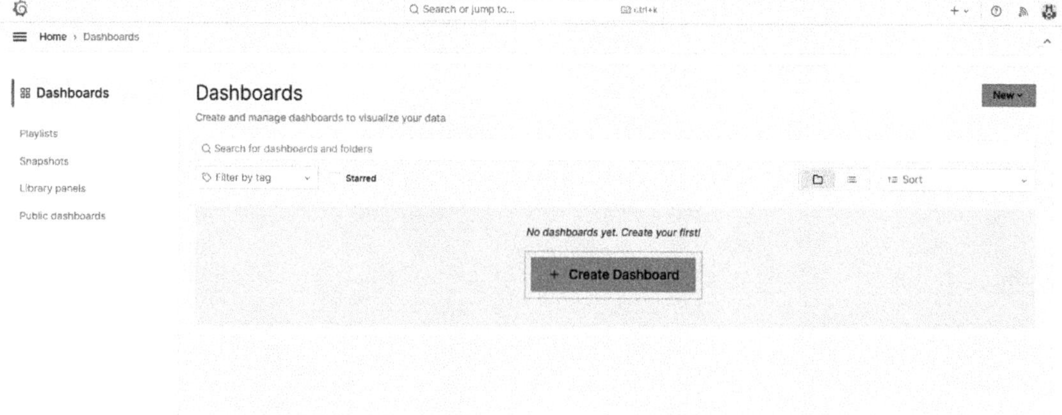

Figure 9.14: Creating a new dashboard

3. The previous step will lead you to the screen shown in *Figure 9.15*, where you can select the data source. In our case, we have just the InfluxDB data source we configured previously. Click on it to select it.
4. Notice that even after selecting the database, you can switch to another later if you need it. Also, you can configure a new one by clicking on the button **Configure a new data source**.

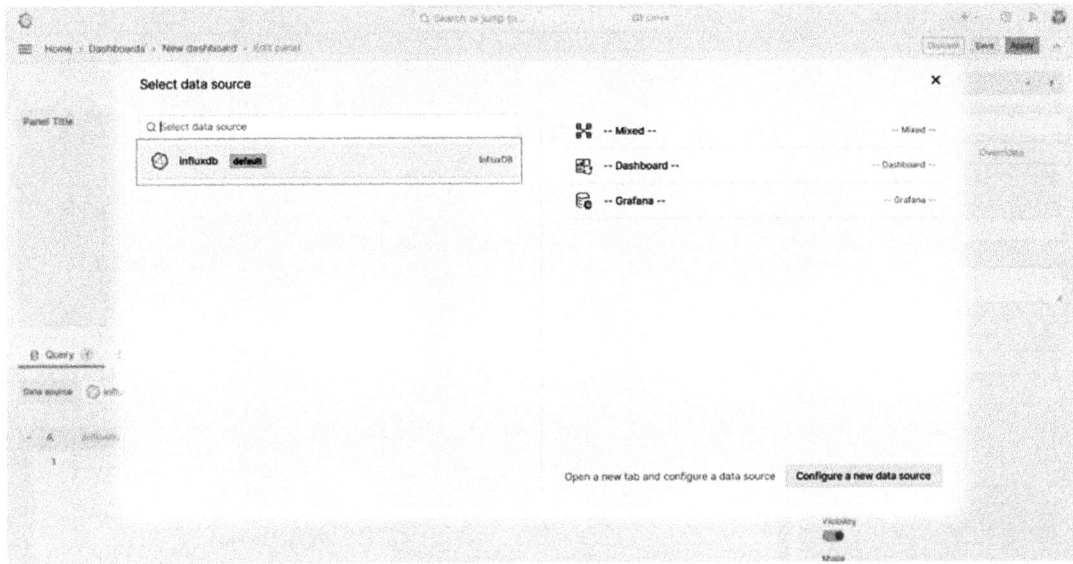

Figure 9.15: Selecting a data source

5. After selecting the data source, you will see the dashboard page, where you will be able to add visualizations (see *Figure 9.16*). Now click on the **Add visualization** button to add a new visualization panel.

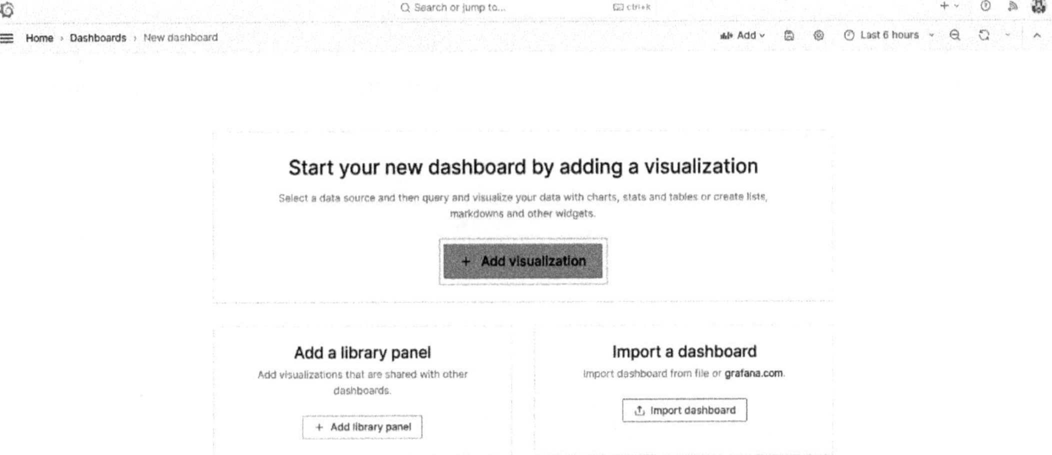

Figure 9.16: Adding a new visualization panel

6. The previous step will lead you to the page shown in *Figure 9.17*. This page has several sections. The more important are the visualization panel, the panel configuration, and the query space.

   In the visualization panel, you will see the data obtained through the queries. You can show this data in many ways, from simple tables to advanced graphics.

   In the query space, you have to enter the query to obtain the data from the data source. In our case, we will use flux scripts.

   Regarding the configuration of the visualization panel, you can use a lot of options available on the right menu. You can select, for example, different types of visualizations, titles, fields, colors, legends, etc.

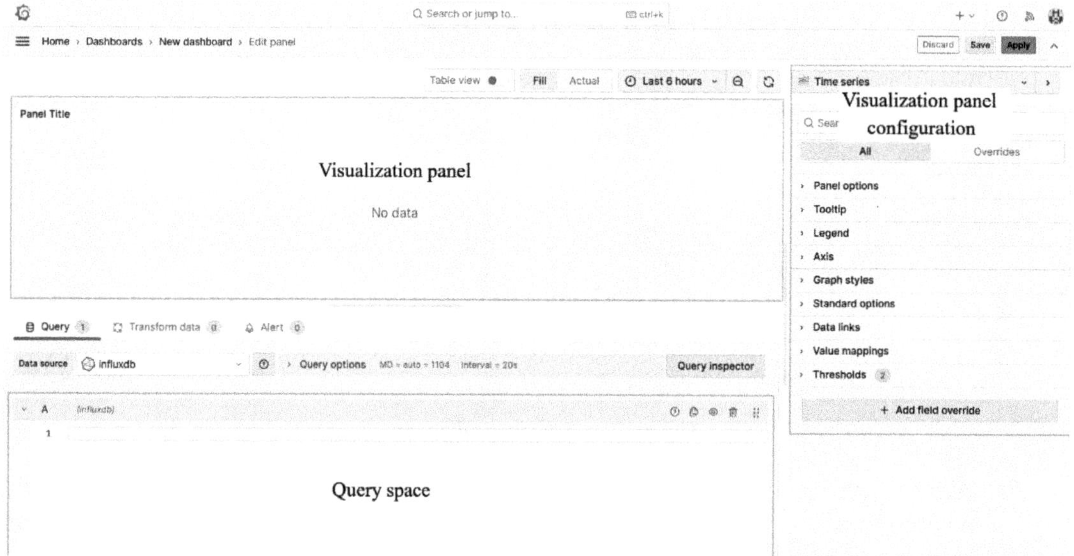

Figure 9.17: Sections of the panel editing page

7. Now go to the data explorer in InfluxDB and copy the flux script that you generated in the previous section. Then, paste the script into the query space of the visualization panel.

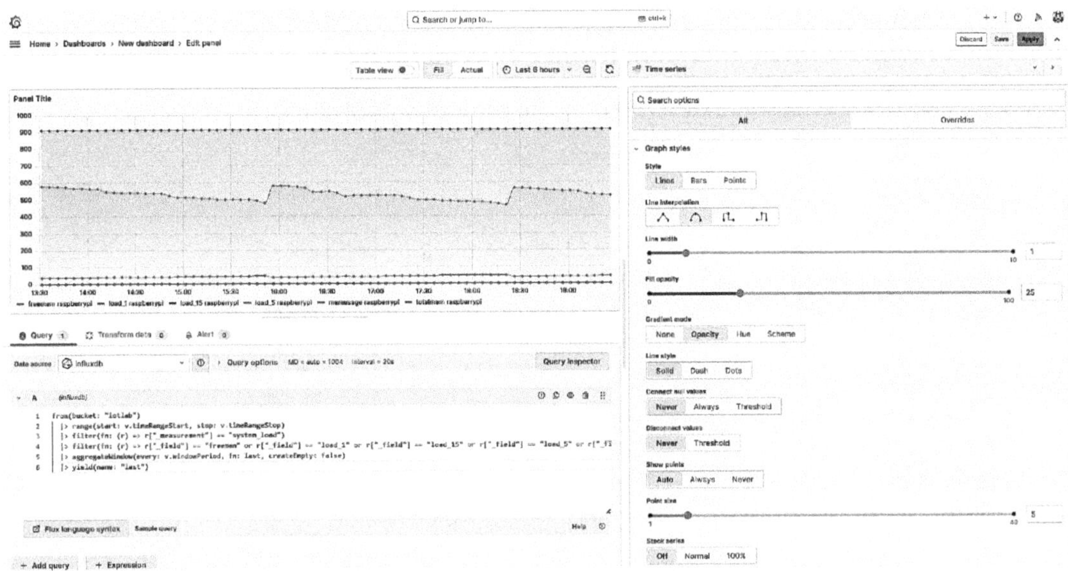

Figure 9.18: Visualizing data with a flux query

Adding visualization panels

Now that we know how to create a dashboard and query data from the InfluxDB bucket, let us see what other visualization options we have.

Grafana offers a great number of visualizations, and we cannot cover all of them in this book. However, in the section, we will see the most commonly used.

Visualization options

There are visualization options that are common to all the panel types. These are the following:

- **Panel options**: Here, you can specify the panel title and its description.
- **Tooltip**: This option, when enabled, shows you a small box with data when you hover the lines with the pointer. See *Figure 9.19*.
- **Legend**: This option lets you control the visibility and style of the data labels.
- **Axis**: Here, you can configure the appearance of the axis, including colors, labels, width, time zone, borders, etc.
- **Standard options**: This section lets you configure the data units, scale, max and min values, decimals, display names, and color schemes.
- **Value mappings**: Using this option, you can replace the values of the data with text, according to specific conditions.

- **Thresholds**: Here, you can change the color of the graphics according to the values. This is useful when you want to see if some data surpassed certain values.

Figure 9.19 shows the features described in the previous paragraph:

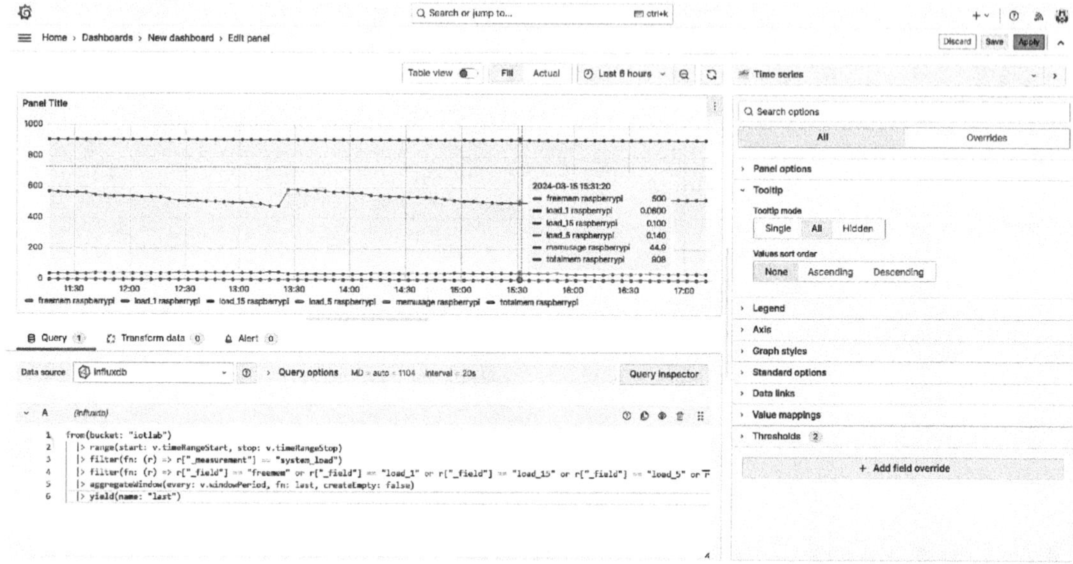

Figure 9.19: Tooltip

Continuing with the previous example, let us build some visualizations.

Time series visualization

This visualization panel is the typical time-series graphic, where you can see the evolution of the values.

This panel offers many customizations. These are some of them:

- Show the data using lines, dots, or bars.
- Choose the interpolation as linear, smooth, or steps.
- Control the line width and the opacity of the area below the lines.
- Show the point dots (or not).
- Control the dot size.

You can see an example of this type of visualization, in *Figure 9.20*:

Figure 9.20: Graph style options for the Time series panel

Gauge panels

The gauge panel allows you to show the last value of a variable, adding some contextual information, like thresholds, max and min values, colors, and units.

These panels are the best option when you want to see the status of the metrics at a glance. In the example of *Figure 9.21*, you can see the memory available in the Raspberry Pi:

Note: Many options have been set up to show the unit, a label, and two threshold values for 10 % (first left section), and 20 % (second left section) of availability.

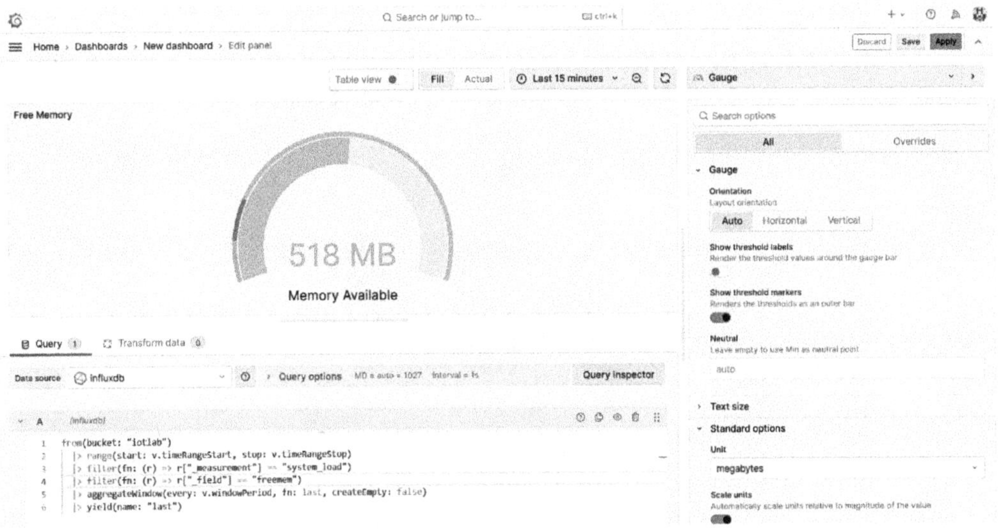

Figure 9.21: Gague visualization panel

Another type of gauge panel is the bar gauge panel. This panel, instead of showing a circular shape, uses a bar. You can apply different styles and configure many options.

In *Figure 9.22*, you can see the bar gauge using the retro **Liquid Cristal Display** (**LCD**) style:

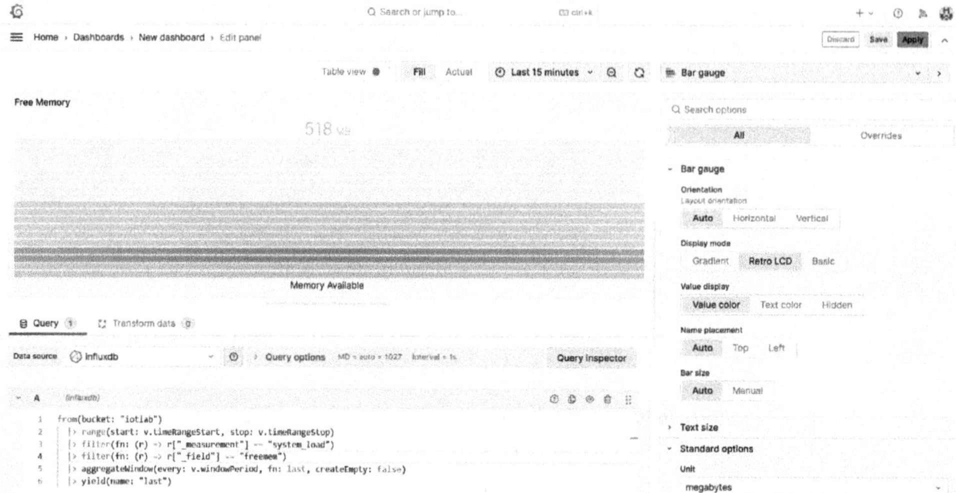

***Figure 9.22**: Retro LCD style in the bar gauge panel*

Stat panel

The stat panel is similar in functionality to the gauge panel but with a simpler graphical interface.

You can use it to show the current value of a variable and, optionally, its evolution trend.

You can see an example of a stat panel in *Figure 9.23*:

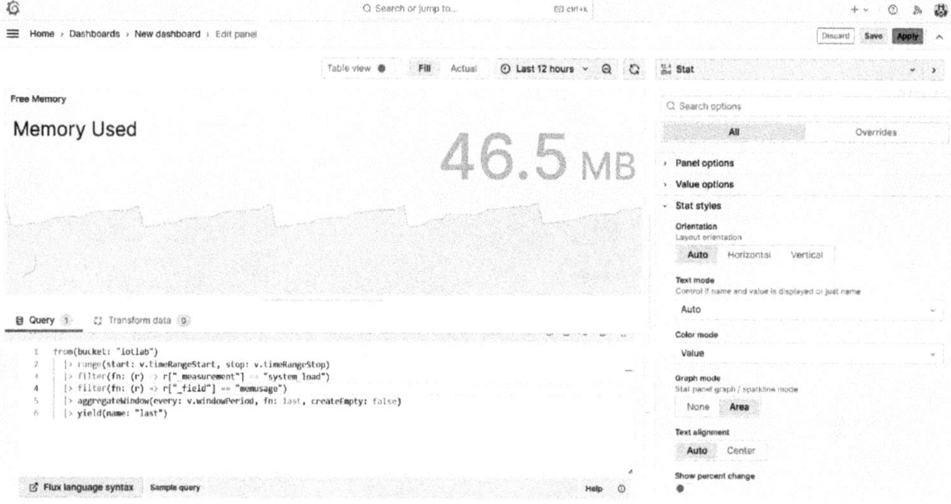

***Figure 9.23**: Stat panel*

Stat panels are also useful for showing categorical information, like the state of a relay or an on or off sensor. In these cases, you can use the mapping setting to specify the text that corresponds to each value.

Table panel

In some cases, you just need a simple table to show a list of values. This is typically the case when you want to show logs or some other textual information.

This panel will show the information with the columns available in the data structure. You can select the columns that you want to show.

Also, you can configure all the general options available in Grafana. You can see an example of a table in *Figure 9.24*:

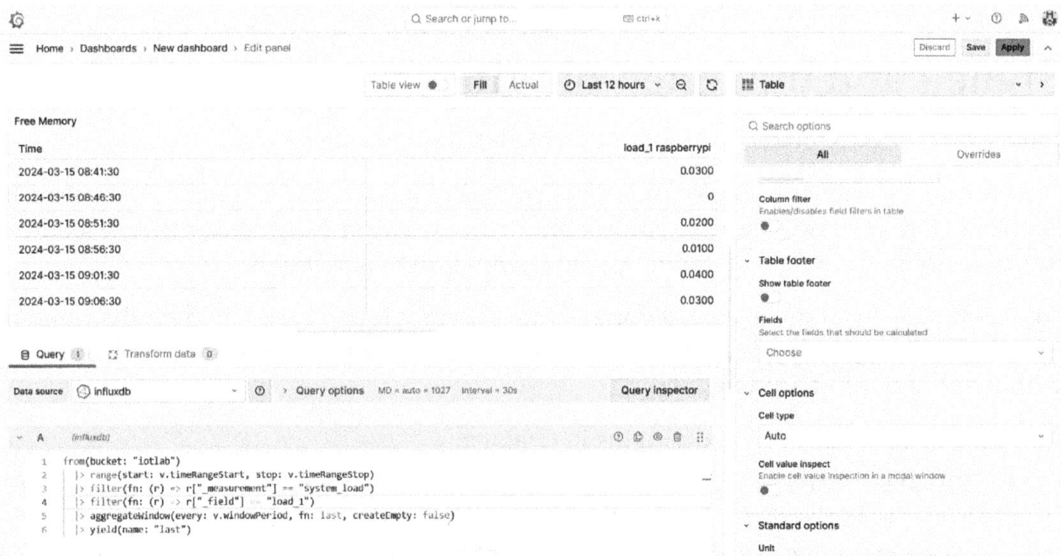

Figure 9.24: Table panel

Plugins in Grafana

Plugins are a crucial feature in Grafana, greatly expanding its capabilities. By default, Grafana offers a variety of data sources and panels, ready to use once the platform is up and running.

However, the true potential of Grafana lies in its versatility, which is where plugins come in handy.

In the plugin repository, you can find two different development sources: those developed by Grafana Labs and those maintained by a vast community.

Types of plugins

There are three main types of plugins:

- **Data source plugins**: These facilitate access to different databases, establishing communication between Grafana and these databases for seamless integration. Adding a new database is as simple as installing and configuring the corresponding data source plugin.
- **Panel plugins**: These, on the other hand, allow for the creation of specialized graphs beyond the options provided in the basic installation. While the basic installation includes panels like *time series* and *gauge*, additional plugins offer wider visualization possibilities.
- **Apps plugins**: These are intended to be used for connecting to apps and cloud services. They provide a ready-to-use approach.

Signed and unsigned plugins

When you choose a plugin, you should check if it is signed or not.

Signed plugins enhance the security, quality, and reliability of the plugin ecosystem in Grafana. They provide a more controlled and trusted environment for users to extend the functionality of Grafana while minimizing potential risks and issues.

Signed plugins in Grafana are categorized into different levels based on their distribution and usage. The signature level of a plugin determines how it can be distributed and used within the Grafana ecosystem.

There are three levels of signed plugins in Grafana:

- **Private**: Private plugins are intended for use within your own Grafana instance. They cannot be distributed to the Grafana community and are not published in the Grafana catalog. These plugins are meant for personal or internal use and are not available to others.
- **Community**: Community plugins have dependencies on open-source technologies and are not for profit. These plugins are published in the official Grafana catalog and are available to the Grafana community. They can be used by anyone who has access to the Grafana catalog.
- **Commercial**: Commercial plugins have dependencies on closed-source or commercially backed technologies. These plugins are also published in the official Grafana catalog and are available to the Grafana community. They can be used by anyone who has access to the Grafana catalog.

The different levels of signed plugins allow for flexibility in distributing and using plugins based on their intended purpose and dependencies. It ensures that plugins are properly categorized and made available to the appropriate audience within the Grafana ecosystem.

Non-signed plugins

You can certainly use non-signed plugins in your local Grafana instance.

Note: However, it is not allowed to install them in the Grafana Cloud Service.

While Grafana provides the option to allow the loading of unsigned plugins, it is strongly recommended to be cautious and thoroughly evaluate the risks before enabling this feature. It is generally best to stick with signed plugins from trusted sources to ensure the security, stability, and reliability of your Grafana environment.

Installing a plugin in Grafana

There are two approaches to installing a plugin on a Grafana instance such as, utilizing the Grafana **command line interface** (**CLI**) or opting for manual installation.

In this section, we will see how to do it in both ways. Let us start with the automatic installation.

Using the Grafana command line interface

Using the Grafana CLI simplifies the process significantly. This tool enables you to seamlessly install, upgrade, and remove plugins.

In the following, we will explore the available commands:

- To install the latest version of a plugin, execute the following command:
  ```
  $ grafana-cli plugins install <the-plugin-id>
  ```
- If you want to specify the version to install, use the following command:
  ```
  $ grafana-cli plugins install <the-plugin-id> <version>
  ```
- List available plugins for installation using the following command:
  ```
  $ grafana-cli plugins list-remote
  ```
- Check the installed plugins via the following command:
  ```
  $ grafana-cli plugins ls
  ```
- For updating a single plugin, use the following command:
  ```
  $ grafana-cli plugins update <plugin-id>
  ```
- Update all installed plugins with the following command:
  ```
  $ grafana-cli plugins update-all
  ```
- Finally, remove a plugin using the following command:
  ```
  $ grafana-cli plugins remove <plugin-id>
  ```

Now that we have explored the CLI method, let us discuss manual installation.

Installing plugins manually

Sometimes, circumstances prevent the use of the Grafana CLI. For instance, if your server lacks internet connectivity or you seek to install a plugin not listed in the official repository, manual installation becomes necessary.

To proceed with manual installation, simply copy the plugin files to the Grafana plugins directory. By default, this directory resides **`at/var/lib/grafana/plugins`**.

Plugins typically arrive in compressed (**`.zip`**) format, containing multiple files and directories. After downloading the plugin, copy it to the plugins directory and unzip it using the following command:

```
$ unzip your-plugin-0.1.0.zip -d YOUR_PLUGIN_DIR/your-plugin
```

> **Note: To verify and adjust the path to your plugin directory as specified in Grafana's configuration file. Additionally, ensure that the directory's permissions align with the default settings.**

Alerts in Grafana

Grafana comes with a very advanced and flexible alert system. In this section, we will explore its functionalities.

Grafana's alerting system is based on Prometheus Alertmanager, which offers a comprehensive set of features for defining and managing alerts. It supports complex queries, conditional expressions, aggregation, grouping, and various integrations for configuring alert notifications.

Working on alerts in Grafana

The processing of alerts in Grafana follows these steps:

1. **Alert rules**: An alert rule defines the conditions that need to be met for an alert to be triggered. It consists of one or more queries or expressions, a condition, and a duration over which the condition needs to be met. The easiest way of creating alert rules is through the graphical interface. We will see how to do it.
2. **Evaluation**: The alerting engine continuously evaluates the alert rules based on the defined conditions. It periodically executes the queries or expressions and checks if the conditions are met. If the conditions are satisfied, the alert is triggered.
3. **Alert states**: Alerts in Grafana can have different states, including OK, pending, and firing. When an alert is triggered, it transitions from OK to firing. After the condition is no longer met, the alert transitions back to OK. The pending state is used when an alert is being evaluated.

4. **Notifications**: When an alert is triggered, Grafana can send notifications to various channels such as email, slack, PagerDuty, or webhooks, to name a few. These notifications inform about the triggered alert and provide details about the issue.

Building alerts in Grafana

Now, let us see how you can build and manage alerts within Grafana.

To create a new alert rule, follow these steps:

1. Go to the left menu and click on **Alerting | Alert rules**. See *Figure 9.25*:

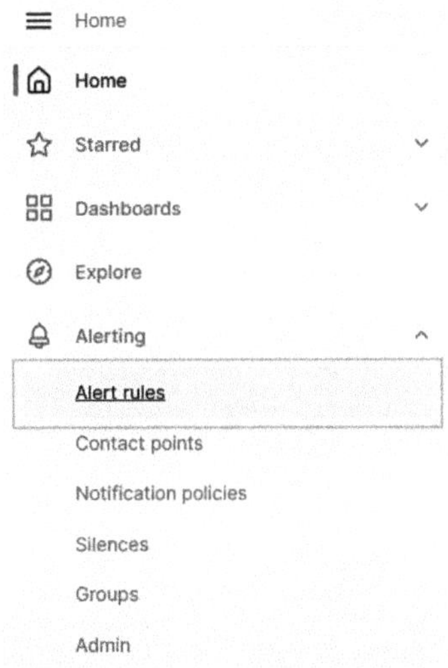

***Figure 9.25**: Alert rule menu*

2. Clicking on **Alert rules** will lead you to the alert rules page. You will see a page like the one shown in *Figure 9.26*. In this case, we still do not have rules, so nothing is displayed.

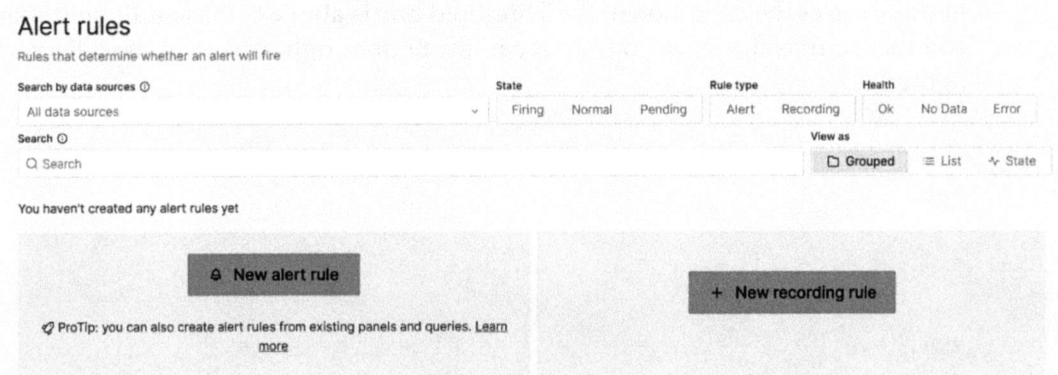

***Figure 9.26**: Alert rules page*

3. Create your first rule by clicking on the big blue button **New alert rule**.
4. In the **New alert rule** page, do the following:
   a. Give a name to the alert rule.
   b. Select the data source where you will run the query. In this case, the InfluxDB.
   c. Paste the query you obtained from the Data Explorer in the InfluxDB instance. Notice that, in this case, we are using the memusage field.

   You can see all of this in *Figure 9.27*:

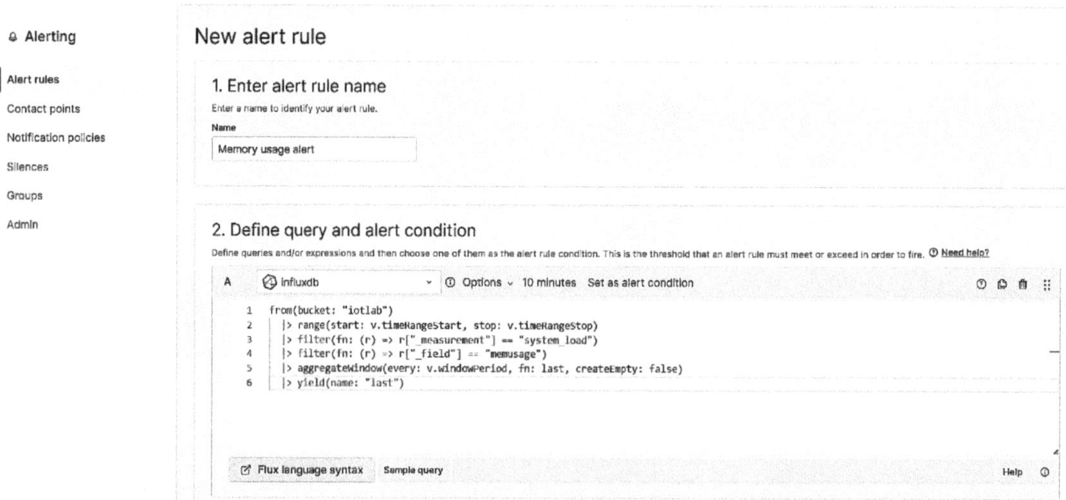

***Figure 9.27**: New query for alert rule*

5. Scroll down and look for the condition panel. You can see it in *Figure 9.28*. The two framed boxes with a red rectangle are for setting up the alarm condition. The reduce box is used to reduce the values obtained by the query to a single value that can be evaluated. The **Threshold** box is used to compare the value obtained in the first box to a threshold value.

   In this case, as the condition in the Threshold box is **above 0**, the condition is met, and the alarm is firing, as you can see in the bottom right corner of the following figure:

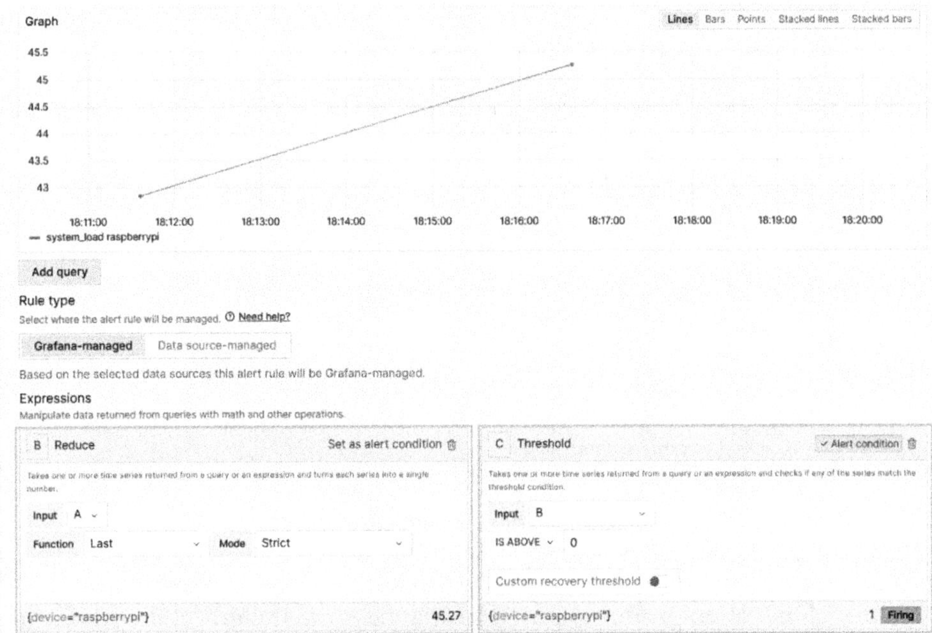

Figure 9.28: Condition evaluation

6. Now, let us change the value in the threshold box to a more useful quantity. In *Figure 9.29*, you can see a new value of 40. After clicking on the **Preview** button, you will notice that the firing event will disappear.

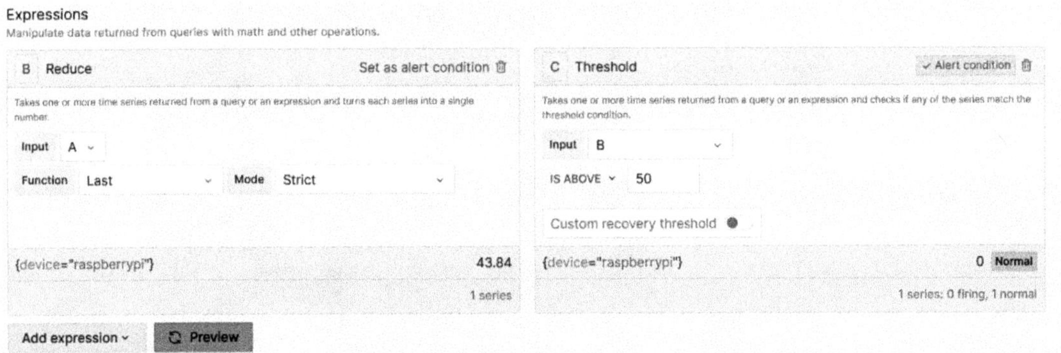

Figure 9.29: Setting up the threshold

7. Now, it is time to set the behavior of the evaluator. Scroll down to the section and click on the + **New folder** button. This will open a dialog box where you can enter the folder name.

   Alarms are stored in different folders as a first level of organization. See *Figure 9.30*:

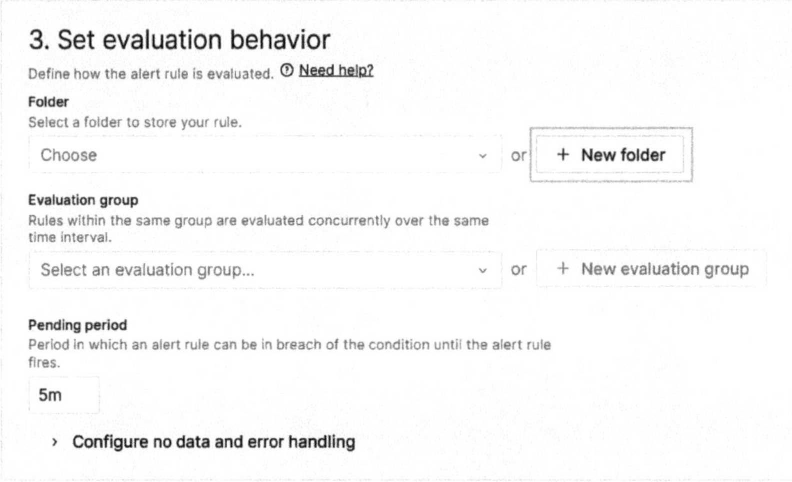

Figure 9.30: Evaluation configuration

8. Now, create an evaluation group by clicking on the + **New evaluation group** button. Evaluation groups are used to analyze similar alerts at the same time. This makes things simpler and improves efficiency. In the evaluation group, you have to specify an evaluation interval. This interval corresponds to the period that the alert manager will use to check if the alert condition is met or not. See *Figure 9.31*:

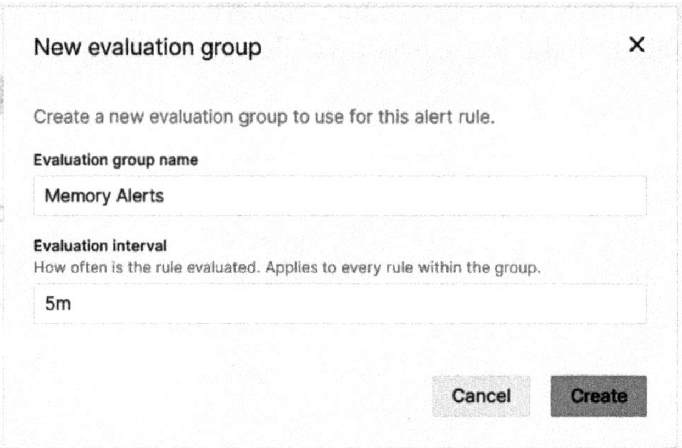

Figure 9.31: New evaluation group

9. Optionally, you can add some contextual data to the alert rule, such as a description, a summary, and some labels if available. See *Figure 9.32*:

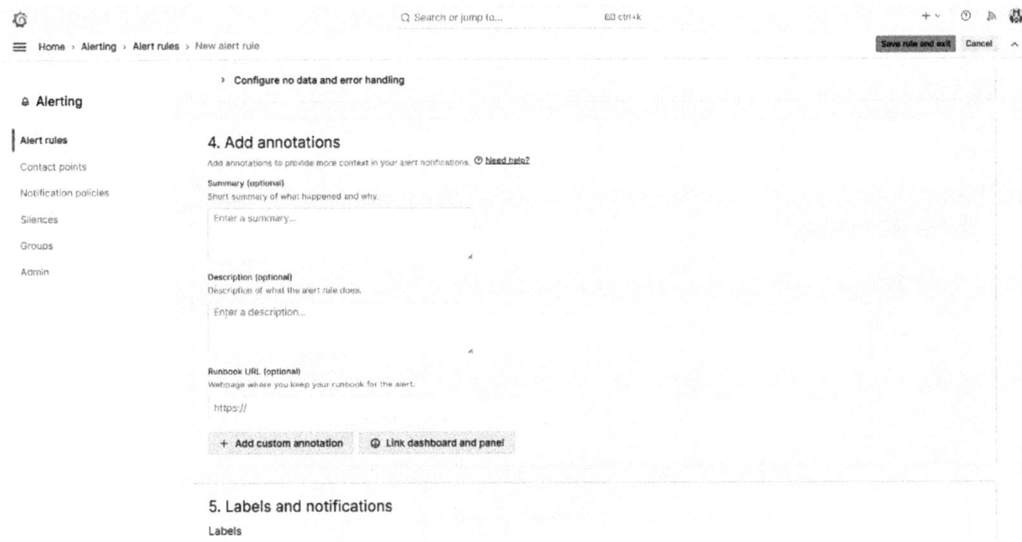

Figure 9.32: Add annotations

10. After filling in all the fields, you can click on the **Saver rule and exit** button, on the top right of the screen. This will save the new alert rule and the alert manager will start to check it. Then, you will see the rule on the alert rule page, as shown in *Figure 9.33*:

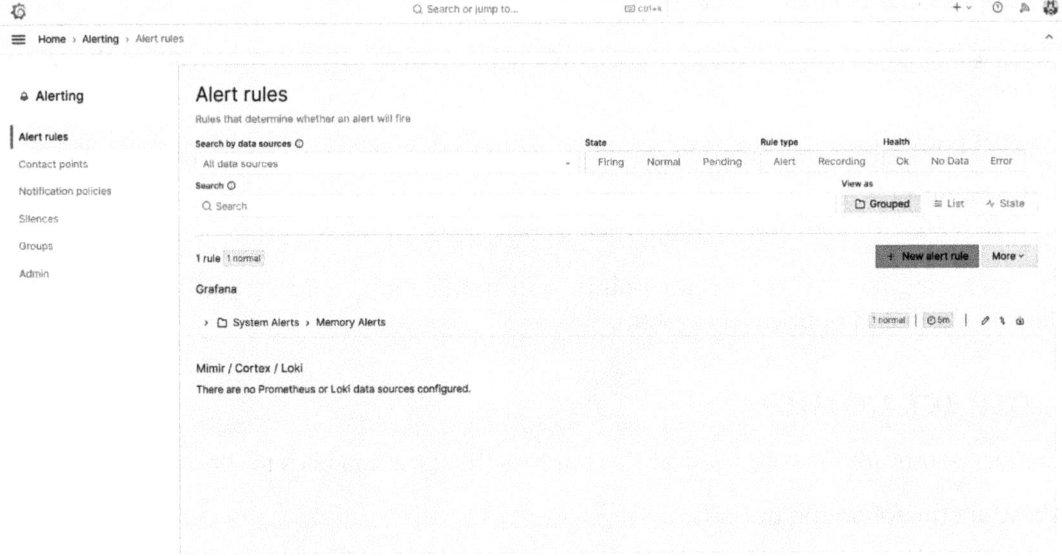

Figure 9.33: Alert rules page with the new alert rule

11. By clicking on the alert rule, you can see the alert state and its associated tags. Notice that Grafana generated some tags automatically using information from the query and the alert rule itself. Refer to *Figure 9.34*:

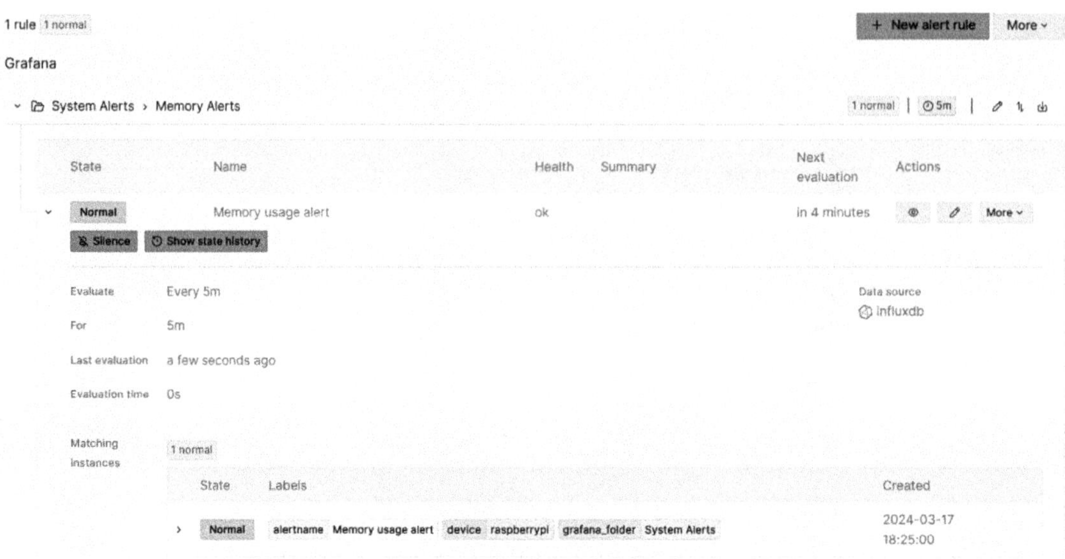

Figure 9.34*: Alert rule state and tags*

Now that you have set up your first alert rule in Grafana, let us see how you can trigger notifications.

Notifications in Grafana

Grafana has two tools for managing notifications, such as contact points and notification policies.

Contact points are the systems used to deliver notifications, like email, Telegram, etc.

Notification policies are conditions used to send a message using one contact point or another, depending on certain data, such as tags, directories, alert rules, etc.

By combining alert rules, contact points, and notification policies, you obtain a highly flexible alarm and notification system.

Contact points

Contact points are the communication channels that Grafana uses to send notifications.

These are the following options:

- Email (default contact point)
- Discord
- Slack
- Microsoft Teams

- Telegram
- Webhooks

To be able to use any contact point, you first have to create it and configure it. Now, we will use the email contact point. Although it is already created, but is not configured yet. If you try to send email using it, you will get an error. So, let us see how to set it up.

Using the email contact point in Grafana

Grafana does not come with an email server, so you have to use an external one. You could, for instance, install an email server in the Raspberry Pi or use any other server in the local network or in the cloud.

To configure Grafana to use the email server, you have to edit the configuration file of Grafana.

This file is located in **`/etc/grafana/grafana.ini`**. Open the file to edit it by running the following command:

```
$ sudo nano /etc/grafana/grafana.ini
```

The previous command will open the file, and you will be able to edit it. Go to the **`[smtp]`** section in the file. *Figure 9.35* shows what this section looks like:

```
#################################### SMTP / Emailing ##########################
[smtp]
enabled = true
host = <your-mail-server-address>:<port>
user = <username>
# If the password contains # or ; you have to wrap it with triple quotes. Ex """#password;"""
password = <password>
;cert_file =
;key_file =
;skip_verify = false
from_address = user@your-domain.com
from_name = Grafana
# EHLO identity in SMTP dialog (defaults to instance_name)
;ehlo_identity = dashboard.example.com
# SMTP startTLS policy (defaults to 'OpportunisticStartTLS')
;startTLS_policy = NoStartTLS
```

***Figure 9.35**: SMTP configuration in grafana.ini*

As you can see, you have to specify the needed parameters to connect Grafana to your email server.

At least, you have to set up the host and the port. The server may also require authentication, certificate file, key file, etc. You have to obtain this information from your email service provider.

After editing the file, save it and exit.

Then, restart the Grafana service by running the following command. This will make the changes to take effect.

```
$ sudo systemctl restart grafana-server.service
```

In the email contact point, you can configure many options for the sending of emails, as you can see in *Figure 9.36*:

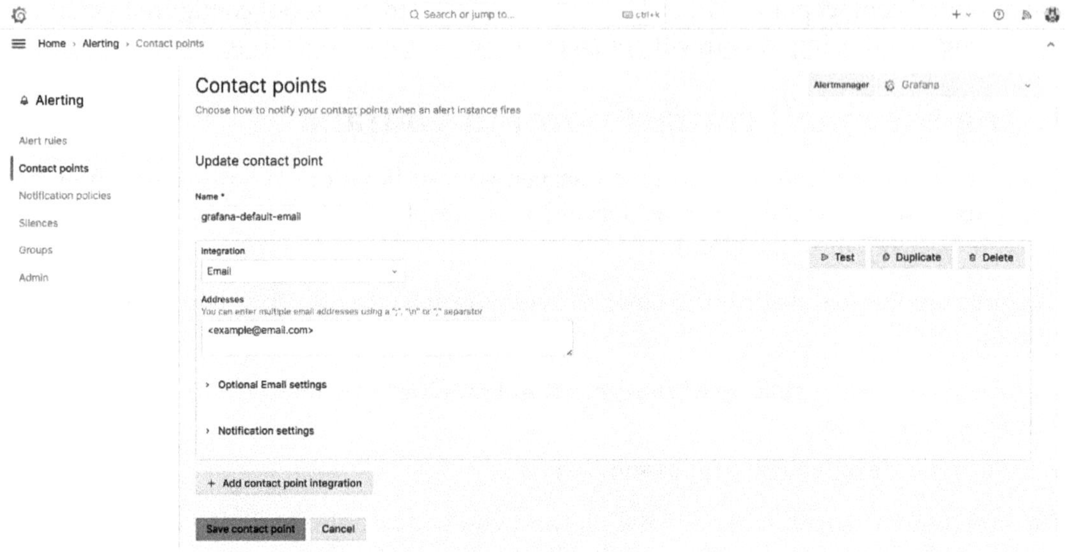

Figure 9.36: Email contact point configuration

Now that we have an email contact point, let us configure a new notification policy.

Notification policies

Grafana uses notification policies to decide whether or not to send notifications through its contact points.

A notification policy is defined according to specific alert rules, filters (tags), alert folders, and contact points.

Grafana comes with a default policy that matches any alert rule. This policy uses the email contact point. You can see this notification policy in *Figure 9.37*:

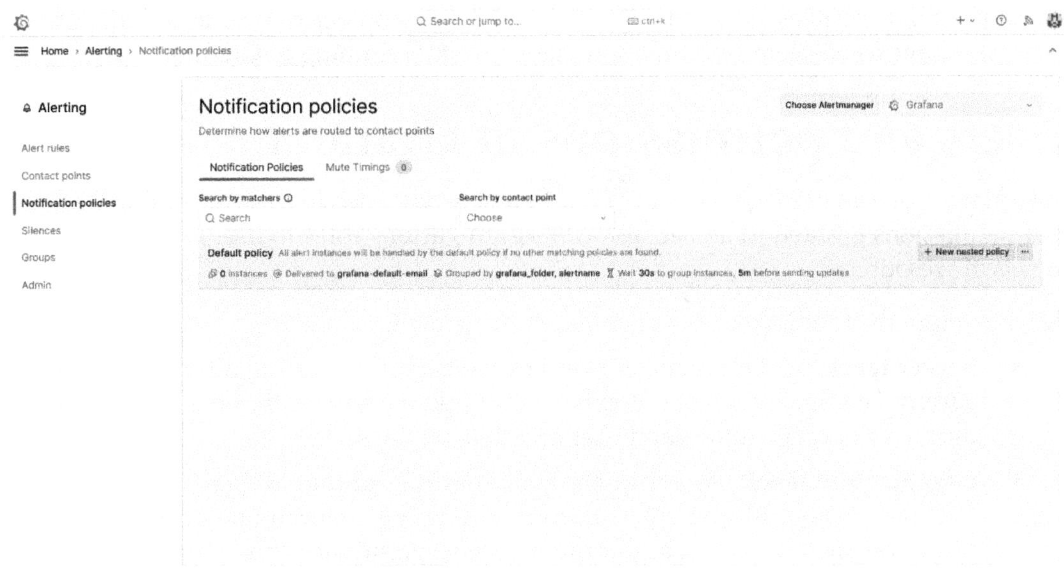

Figure 9.37: Default notification policy

Below the default notification policy, you can define new policies. To do this, click on the + **New nested policy** button and add the notification policy details, as shown in *Figure 9.38:*

In this case, we have used the alertname that we used in the alert rule we created earlier.

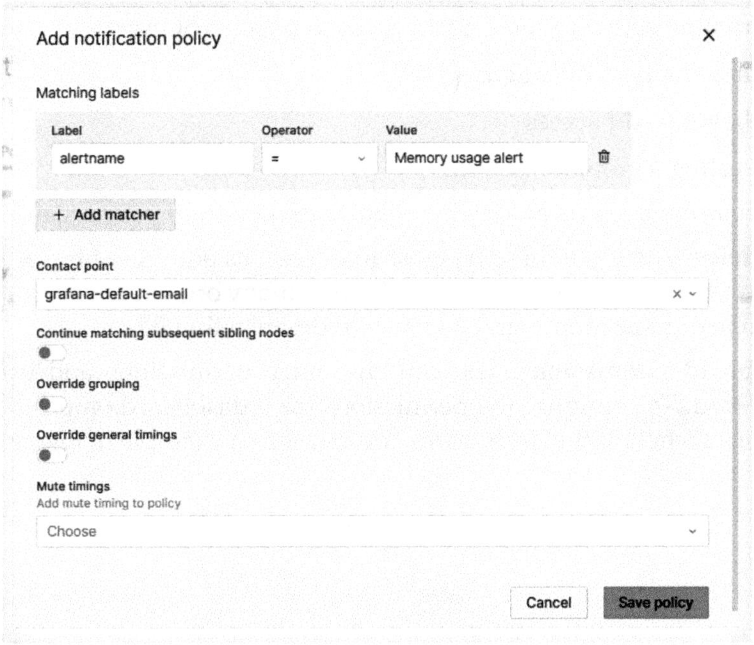

Figure 9.38: New notification policy

The notification policies close the circle of alert rules, contact points, and notifications. Now, you have a complete alert and notification system running in Grafana.

Users and permissions in Grafana

In Grafana, you can manage users across different levels, each level determining the tasks and permissions granted to a user. You can assign various roles to users, enabling access to specific resources.

Let us explore the four levels of permission management:

- **Server level**: At the broadest level lies the server, including all users within the current Grafana instance. If you have the Grafana Admin option enabled, you can oversee all organizations and user accounts on the server.
- **Organization level**: Organizations consist of user groups within a specific server. You can create multiple organizations and assign users to one or more of them. Moreover, members of an organization receive permissions based on their assigned roles. Administrators within an organization have the authority to manage users and teams within their group.
- **Teams**: You can group yourself and other users within your organization using teams. When you create a team, you can assign the same permissions to all the users that belong to it. Typically, teams are managed by organization admins. You can, for instance, create teams for the following:
    - Granting access to some dashboards to a group of users
    - Allowing read-only access
    - Allowing edit access
    - Creating a group of admins

  So, you can use teams mainly to organize users within your organization.
- **User roles**: There are three types of roles such as admin, editor, and viewer. You can define different roles for yourself across many organizations. So, you can be an admin in organization A and a viewer in organization B.
- **Dashboard permissions**: You can customize permissions and user roles for a dashboard. To configure the permissions for a dashboard, you have to go to the **Settings** section of the dashboard. You can see an example in *Figure 9.39*:

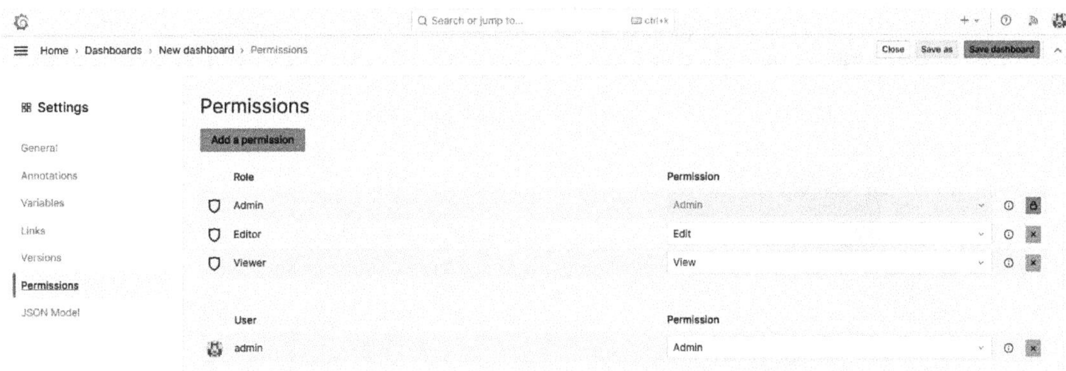

Figure 9.39: *User permissions in a dashboard*

By default, you will see the admin user and the roles of editor and viewer. That means that any user with the editor role can edit the dashboard, and any user with the viewer role can view it. These are dashboard permissions because they apply to any user in the organization.

Using Grafana Cloud Service

Grafana Cloud Service offers a quick and hassle-free alternative to the traditional installation and configuration process of Grafana.

The following is how you can get started:

1. **Registration**: Follow these steps to create an account in the Grafana Cloud Service:
    a. Visit the Grafana Cloud site at **https://grafana.com**.
    b. Go to the registration page.
    c. Enter your **Email** and **Password** or access any of the third service accounts available. See *Figure 9.40*.
    d. Confirm your registration through the email you will receive.
2. **Trial period**: You will get a trial version to try the Grafana Pro:
    a. Upon registration, you will have access to a 14-day trial of Grafana Pro.
    b. After the trial, you can choose to subscribe or continue with the free version.
3. **Configuring your Grafana stack**: Follow these steps to configure your stack:
    a. After completing the registration process, you will gain access to Grafana Cloud Services.
    b. The first step is to select a name for your stack.
    c. For free or trial versions, your domain will end with **`grafana.net`**.
    d. Paid options allow you to choose your own domain.
    e. You can use Grafana Cloud Service as you do with your local instance.

This streamlined process allows you to set up and start using Grafana in a matter of minutes, bypassing the complexities of manual installation and configuration.

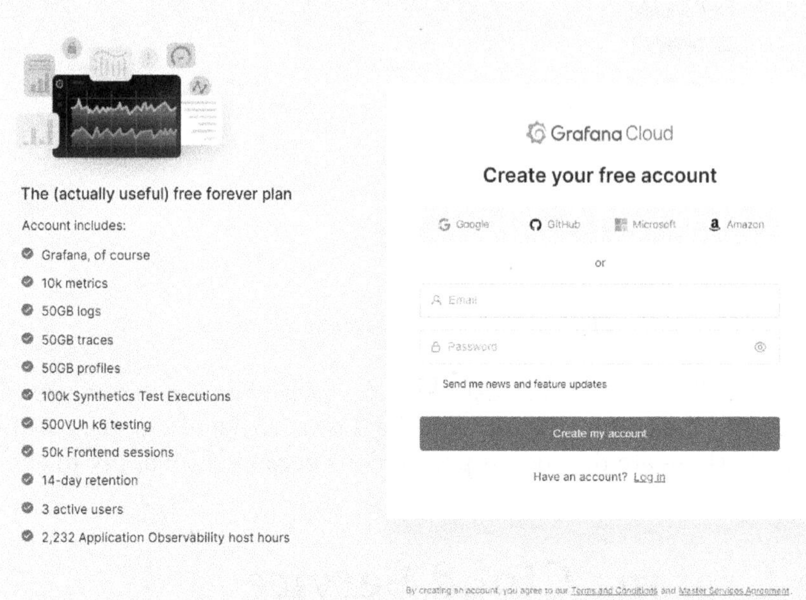

Figure 9.40: *Sign up page of Grafana Cloud.*

Pricing plans

Grafana Cloud offers various pricing plans to suit different needs and budgets. You can view the detailed pricing information on the Grafana website. These plans range from free tiers for personal use or small projects to more comprehensive paid options for larger organizations or more demanding use cases.

Conclusions

In this chapter, you have learned to install, configure, and use Grafana on the Raspberry Pi computer. You saw what data sources are and how you can use them in Grafana. Also, you learned to build a dashboard using different visualization panels. You learned about plugins, how to install them, and how to use them.

We also covered alerts and notifications. Finally, we saw the user hierarchy and the user management in Grafana. All the topics covered in this chapter give you a good understanding of Grafana and allow you to start building dashboards using this powerful visualization tool.

In the next chapter, we will use what we have learned about Grafana to build a dashboard to show weather data.

CHAPTER 10
Building a Weather Station

Introduction

In this chapter, we will use what we have learned in the previous chapters to build a weather station using a Raspberry Pi 4 and some sensors.

To build the weather station, we will first prepare the Raspberry Pi, enabling the I2C to connect to the environmental sensor.

Then, we will connect the sensor and use Node-RED to get data from it. Also, we will use Node-RED to build a dashboard for data visualization.

After that, we will store the sensor data both in a **comma-separated values** (**CSV**) file and in an InfluxDB bucket.

After having some data stored in InfluxDB, we will proceed to build a dashboard in Grafana to visualize the data in different ways.

Finally, we will see how to obtain live data from a weather cloud service.

Structure

In this chapter, we will learn the following topics:

- Preparation of the Raspberry Pi
- Using BME680 with Raspberry Pi
- Storing BME680 values
- Visualizing the data in Grafana
- Connecting to cloud weather services

Objectives

By the end of the chapter, the readers will learn to enable the I2C interface in the Raspberry Pi, connecting the BME680 sensor using this interface, getting data from the sensors using Node-RED, storing the sensor data in an InfluxDB bucket, display the data in a dashboard in Node-RED, and building a dashboard in Grafana.

Preparation of the Raspberry Pi

In this chapter, we will use an I2C sensor attached to the Raspberry Pi computer. To be able to use this serial protocol, we need to configure our Raspberry Pi.

Inter-Integrated Circuit (**I2C**) is a synchronous serial communication protocol designed for short-distance communication between integrated circuits on a single board or system.

In this section, we will learn how to configure the Raspberry Pi to enable the I2C interface. After doing this, we will be able to connect I2C sensors to the Raspberry Pi and get data from them.

Enabling I2C

Let us see the following steps for enabling I2C:

1. First, run the following commands to upgrade the system:
   ```
   $ sudo apt update
   $ sudo apt full-upgrade
   ```
2. Once you have updated your system, run the following command to access the configuration tool of Raspberry Pi:
   ```
   $ sudo raspi-config
   ```
3. The previous command will lead you to the menu shown in *Figure 10.1*. Select **Interface Options** from the menu.

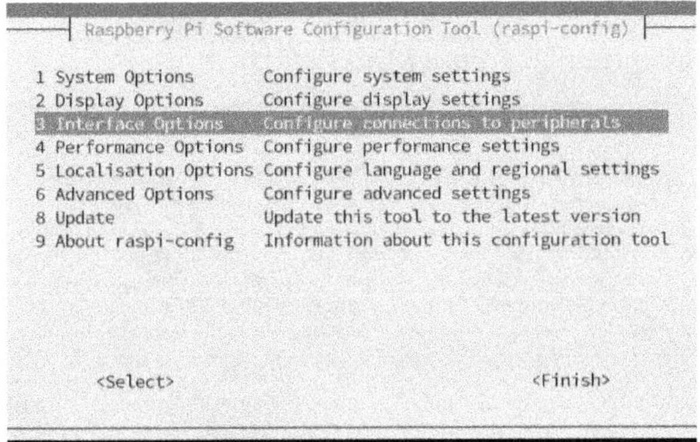

***Figure 10.1**: Raspberry PI configuration tool interface*

4. Now, you will see many options for interfacing with the Raspberry Pi. Select **I2C** to enable this serial protocol. Refer to *Figure 10.2*:

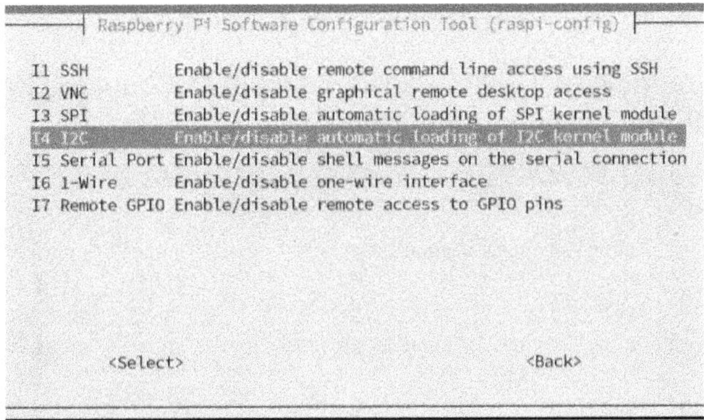

***Figure 10.2**: Selecting I2C*

5. After selecting I2C, a dialog box will emerge asking you to enable the I2C interface. Click on **Yes** to enable it, as shown in *Figure 10.3*:

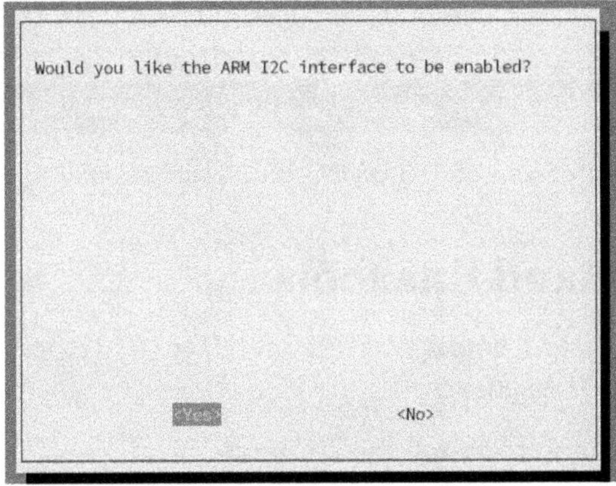

***Figure 10.3**: Enabling I2C*

6. The previous step will lead you back to the start menu. Click on **Finish** to apply the changes, as shown in *Figure 10.4*:

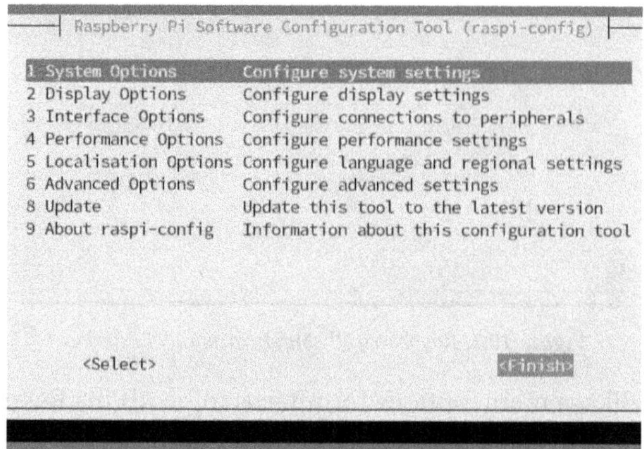

***Figure 10.4**: Applying changes*

7. The configuration tool will ask you if you want to reboot the Raspberry Pi. Answer **Yes** and wait for the computer to boot. Refer to *Figure 10.5*:

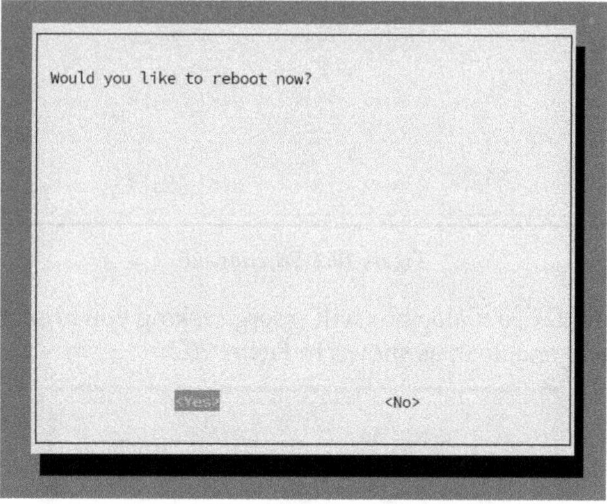

***Figure 10.5**: Applying changes and rebooting*

Installing command line tools

Now, let us install some useful **command line interface** (**CLI**) tools that you can use to test the communication with the sensors.

Run the following command to install the I2C tools.

```
$ sudo apt install -y i2c-tools
```

You still do not have any I2C device connected, so you will not see any devices yet. In the following section, we will use this tool to see if the Raspberry Pi can communicate with the sensor.

Using BME680 with Raspberry Pi 4

In this section, we will use the BME680 sensor.

The BME680 is a digital barometric pressure sensor you can use for accurate measurements of atmospheric pressure, temperature, and humidity. It is developed by Bosch Sensortec, and it employs advanced **Micro-Electro-Mechanical Systems** (**MEMS**) technology to deliver precise readings across various environmental conditions.

The BME680 sensor offers you the following features:

- **Barometric pressure measurement**: Utilize the sensor to accurately gauge atmospheric pressure, assisting you in tasks like altitude calculation, weather prediction, and environmental monitoring.
- **Temperature measurement**: The sensor also provides temperature data. You can use this to compensate and calibrate pressure values based on temperature fluctuations.
- **Humidity measurement**: The BME680 comes with humidity-sensing capabilities, enabling you to monitor ambient humidity levels alongside pressure and temperature.
- **High accuracy and resolution**: Benefit from the sensor's high accuracy and resolution in pressure, temperature, and humidity measurements, crucial for applications demanding precise environmental monitoring.
- **Low power consumption**: Operating with low power consumption, the BME680 is suitable for battery-powered devices and applications where energy efficiency is key.
- **I2C and SPI interface**: You can communicate with the BME680 sensor using standard interfaces like I2C (inter-integrated circuit) or **Serial Peripheral Interface** (**SPI**), ensuring seamless integration with your chosen microcontroller or system. We will use the I2C interface.

The following table shows the main parameters of the BME680 sensor:

Temperature accuracy	+/- 1.0 °C
Pressure accuracy	+/- 1 hPa
Temperature range	-40 to 85 °C
Humidity range	0 to 100 %
Pressure range	300 to 1100 hPa
VOC resistance	50 ohms – 50 Kohms

***Table 10.1**: Characteristics of BME680*

As you can see, you could implement a weather station using just this single sensor. However, we will see how to use other sensors as well.

Many sensor boards come with the BME680. You can use, for instance, the BME680 sensor board from Adafruit. Refer to this link **https://www.adafruit.com/product/3660**

Connecting and testing BME680

To start using the BME680, let us connect it to the Raspberry Pi 4.

The connections are as follows:

- Pi 3V3 to sensor 3V0.
- Pi GND to sensor GND.
- Pi SCL to sensor SCK.
- Pi SDA to sensor SDI (refer to the following figure):

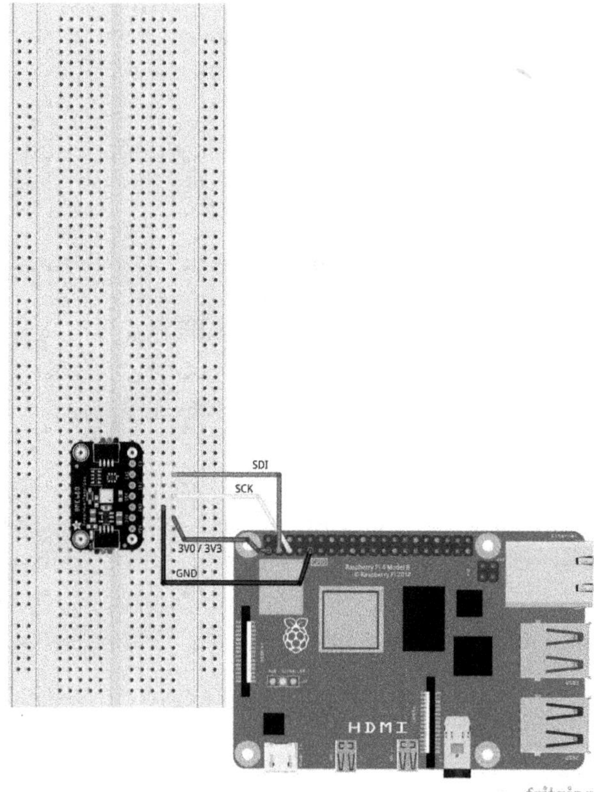

***Figure 10.6**: Connecting BME680 to Raspberry Pi 4*

Now that you have connected the sensor, you can test the connection by running the following command:

```
$ sudo i2cdetect -y 1
```

If the sensor is detected, you will see an output like the one shown in *Figure 10.7*. Notice that the last two digits are not null; instead, they show the number **77**.

```
pi@raspberrypi:~ $ sudo i2cdetect -y 1
     0  1  2  3  4  5  6  7  8  9  a  b  c  d  e  f
00:                         -- -- -- -- -- -- -- --
10: -- -- -- -- -- -- -- -- -- -- -- -- -- -- -- --
20: -- -- -- -- -- -- -- -- -- -- -- -- -- -- -- --
30: -- -- -- -- -- -- -- -- -- -- -- -- -- -- -- --
40: -- -- -- -- -- -- -- -- -- -- -- -- -- -- -- --
50: -- -- -- -- -- -- -- -- -- -- -- -- -- -- -- --
60: -- -- -- -- -- -- -- -- -- -- -- -- -- -- -- --
70: -- -- -- -- -- -- -- 77
pi@raspberrypi:~ $
```

***Figure 10.7**: Detecting the sensor with i2cdetect*

By running the previous checks, we know that the sensor is connected and it is working. Now, let us see how to get data from it.

Obtaining data from BME680 using Node-RED

We will use Node-RED to read the data coming from the BME680 sensor.

To read the sensor values, follow these steps:

1. Go to the Node-RED palette manager and install the **`node-red-contrib-bme680-rpi`** node, as shown in *Figure 10.8*:

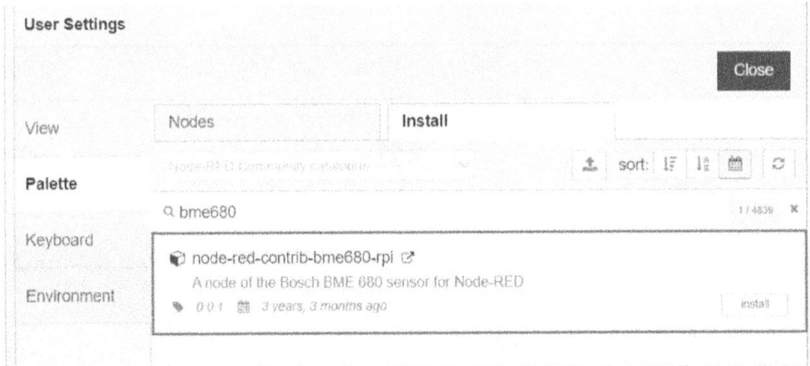

***Figure 10.8**: Installing node-red-contrib-bme680-rpi node*

2. Now, drag a **`BME680`** node from the left panel and drop it in the flow interface. Do the same for a debug node. Finally, connect them as shown in *Figure 10.9*:

***Figure 10.9**: Flow for reading a BME680 sensor*

3. Open the BME680 node, and configure it as shown in *Figure 10.10*. Select **Bus** as `1`, **Address** as `0x77`, and set the desired query interval in ms. Click on the **Done** button to save the changes and close the node configuration interface.

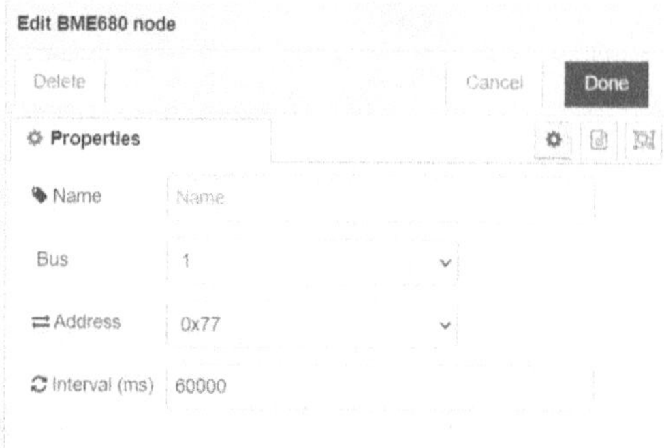

***Figure 10.10**: Configuring BME680 node*

4. Click on the **Deploy** button to deploy and execute the flow you have just created. The logic will run, and you will start to see the values coming from the sensor in the debug panel, as shown in *Figure 10.11*:

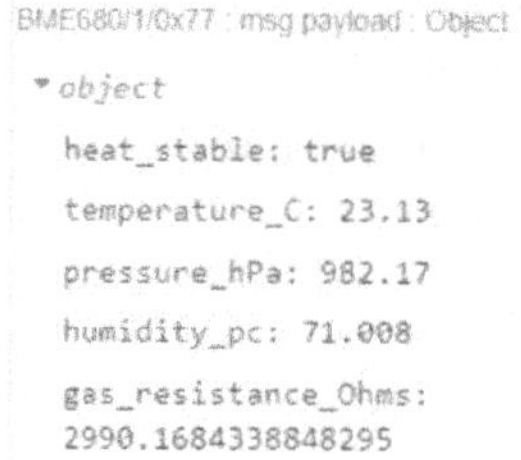

***Figure 10.11**: Debug window with sensor readings*

Building a dashboard in Node-RED

Now that we are getting data from the BME680 sensor, let us build a dashboard in Node-RED to show it.

We will use specific nodes that will allow us to build a neat dashboard, showing both current and historical values.

Also, we will manage the data to show different values in specific dashboard panels, to improve the quality of the visualizations.

Installing Node-RED dashboard 2.0

First, we need to install some nodes to be able to build dashboards in Node-RED. We will use dashboard 2.0, which is a new version of the dashboard, developed by FlowFuse.

This new dashboard comes with new features, adds more flexibility, and has a nicer interface than its predecessors.

To install it, follow these steps:

1. Click on the **Manage palette** option in the menu.
2. Look for the package **`@flowfuse/node-red-dashboard`** in the text search box, as shown in *Figure 10.12*:

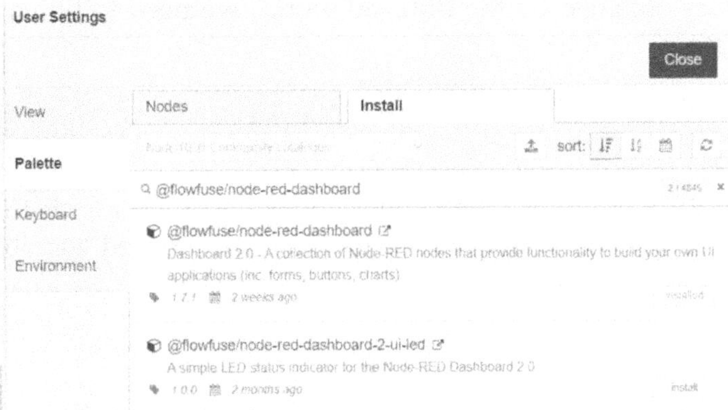

***Figure 10.12**: Installing @flowfuse/node-red-dashboard*

3. After installing the package, you will see the new nodes available in the node panel, as shown in *Figure 10.13*:

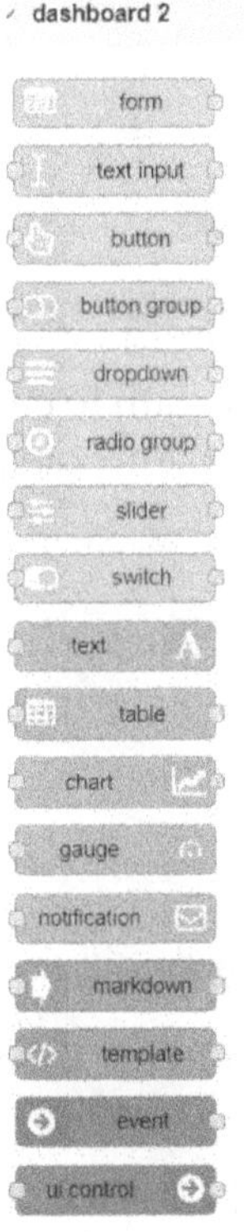

***Figure 10.13**: Nodes available in the Dashboard 2.0 package*

Now that we have the dashboard nodes, we can start building the visualizations in Node-RED.

Programming the visualization

To show the values obtained by the BME680 sensor, we need to build a small logic for processing the data.

You can see the complete flow in *Figure 10.14*.

Follow these steps to build this flow:

1. Drag and drop three function nodes and connect their inputs to the sensor node output. We will use these nodes to filter the desired variable (temperature, humidity, and pressure).

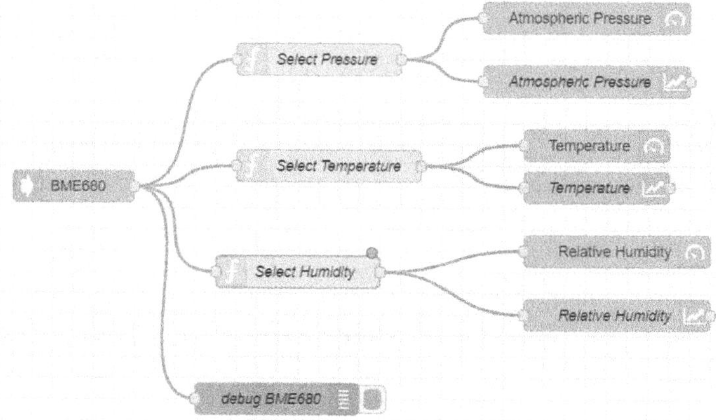

***Figure 10.14**: Flow for showing values in a dashboard*

2. From the debug panel, locate the path to each variable by clicking on the **copy path** option in the corresponding item. You can see an example in *Figure 10.15*:

```
BME680/1/0x77 : msg.payload : Object
▾ object
  heat_stable: true
  temperature_C: 24
  pressure_hPa: 1008.49
  humidity_pc: 73.434
  gas_resistance_Ohms: 26578.22067171404
```

Copy path

***Figure 10.15**: Copying the path to each item in the object*

3. Open each function block and add the following code, changing the path for each variable. Refer to *Figure 10.16*:

```
msg.payload = msg.payload.pressure_hPa
return msg;
```

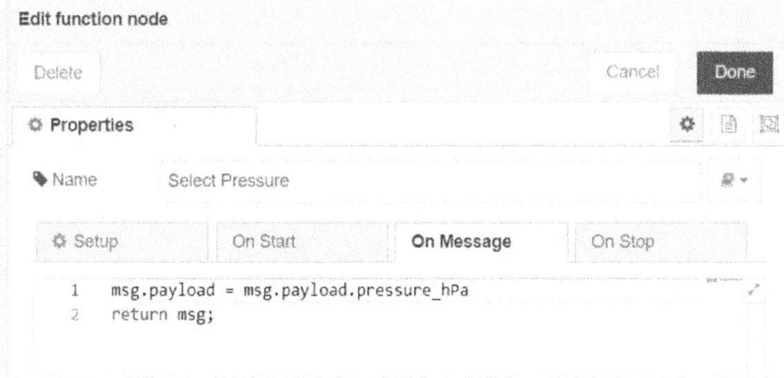

***Figure 10.16**: Selecting the pressure value*

4. Now, drag and drop a **gauge** and **chart** node for each of the variables, and connect them to each of the outputs of the function nodes, as shown in *Figure 10.14*.
5. Open each of the visualization nodes and change the **Name** and **Label** properties to represent each of the measured variables. Also, create a group for each type of visualization by clicking on the pen symbol. Then, select the group from the dropdown selection menu, as shown in *Figure 10.17*.

   Change the size of each visualization to adapt it to your dashboard size.

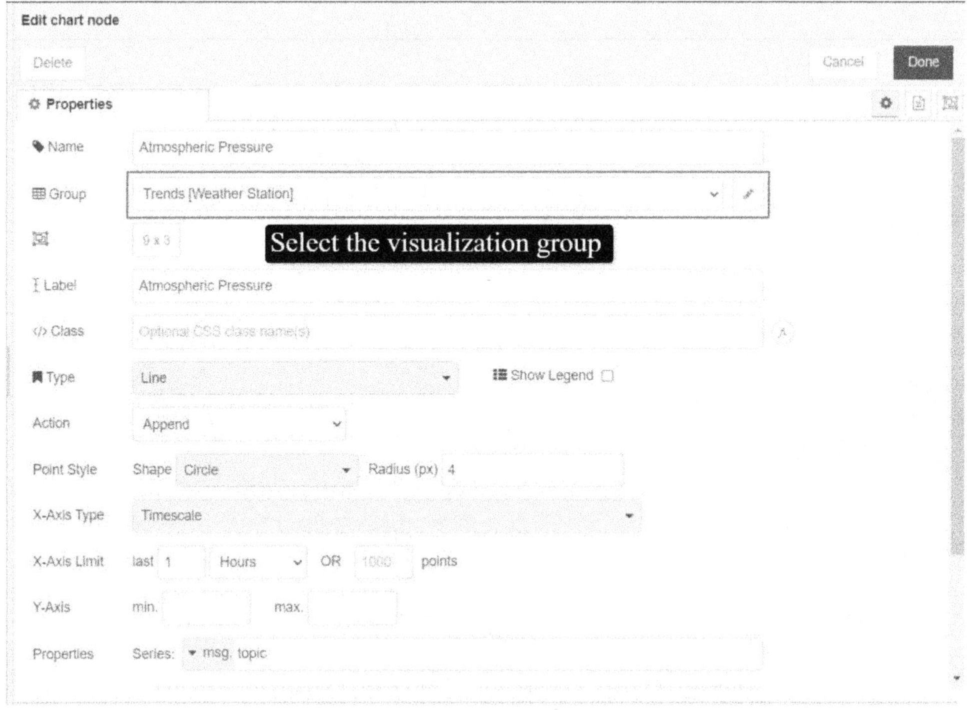

***Figure 10.17**: Configuring visualization nodes*

6. Finally, go to the **Dashboard 2.0** tab in the right panel to check the design of the dashboard and modify it as needed. Refer to *Figure 10.18*:

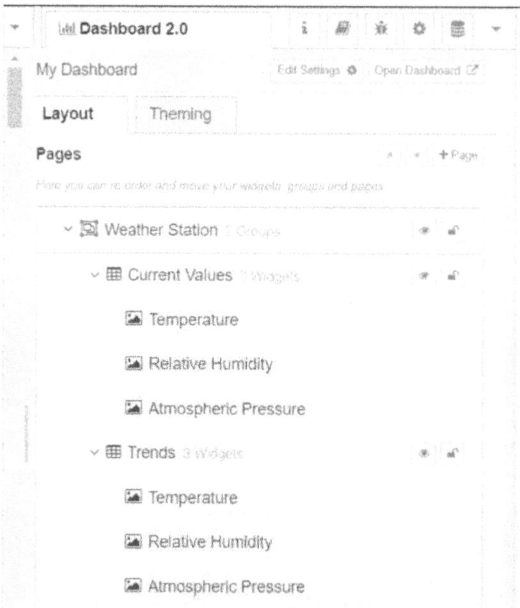

***Figure 10.18**: Designing the structure of the dashboard*

7. To go to the dashboard, click on the **Open Dashboard** button at the top of the dashboard tab in the right panel. You can also use the URL **http://your-ip:1880/dashboard**. After completing the previous steps, you will obtain a view like the one shown in *Figure 10.19*. Adjust the sizes, groups, and labels to adapt them to your needs.

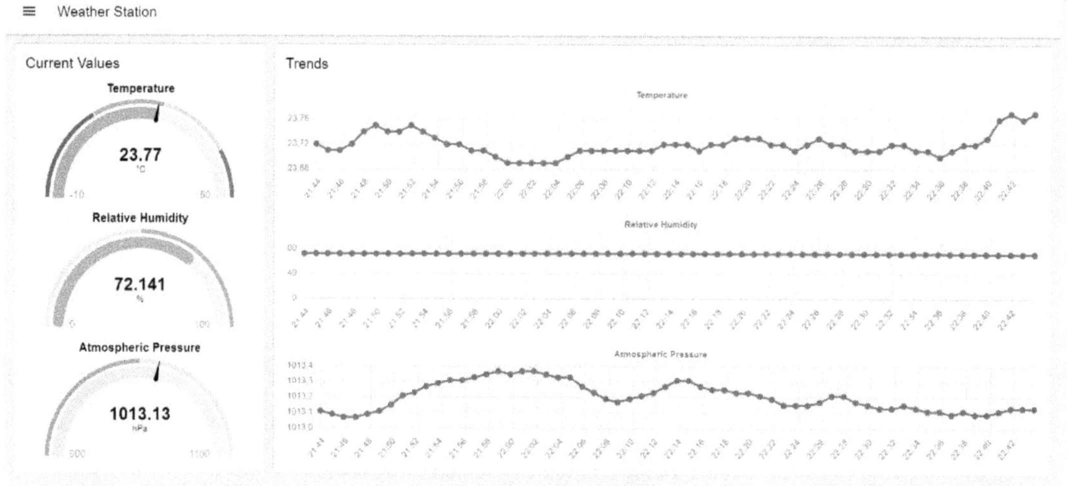

***Figure 10.19**: Complete dashboard in Node-RED*

Now we have a weather station based on the BME680 sensor and Node-RED. However, if we reboot the Raspberry Pi, we will lose all the sensor values, as they are kept in the volatile memory.

So, if we want to have historical records, we need to save the values to some kind of permanent storage. You can achieve this by using a simple text file or a database.

Storing BME680 values

In this section, we will see how to store the values obtained from the BME680 sensor. To do this, we will use two different methods: a **comma separated values** (**CSV**) file and an InfluxDB bucket.

The CSV file provides a simple but limited solution. Even when files are a light and easy option to use, they lack scalability. So, if you need to store many months of data, using a database is a better option.

On the other hand, InfluxDB is the perfect solution to store time-series data. It provides data retention policies that let you manage the time that the data will be kept. Also, InfluxDB offers many advanced tools and techniques to manage large datasets.

Let us start with the CSV file.

Writing sensor values to a CSV file

To write the sensor data to a CSV file, follow these steps:

1. Drag and drop a function node, a CSV parser node, a write file node, and a debug node.
2. Connect the nodes as shown in *Figure 10.20*:

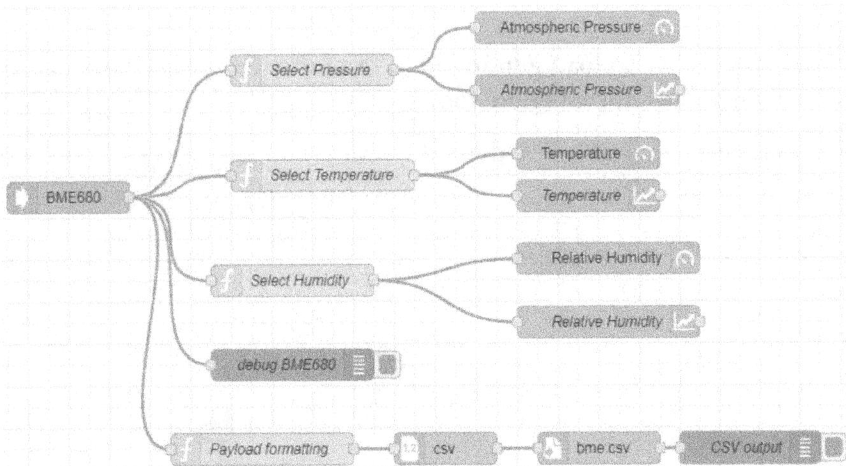

***Figure 10.20**: Connecting the CSV writing nodes*

3. In the function node, enter the following code.

```
msg.payload = {
    "temperature": msg.payload.temperature_C,
    "humidity": msg.payload.humidity_pc,
    "pressure": msg.payload.pressure_hPa,
    "device": "raspberrypi",
    "sensor": "bme680-01",
    "location": "home",
        "time": Date.now()
};
return msg;
```

   This code creates the keys for each of the measurements coming from the sensor node. Also, it adds some information such as device, sensor, location, and timestamp. You can add here any useful information.

4. Configure the CSV node as shown in *Figure 10.21*. In the **Columns** input text box, enter the following values:
   - `temperature`
   - `humidity`
   - `pressure`
   - `device`
   - `sensor`
   - `location`
   - `time`

Note: If you modify the payload generated in the function node (previous step), you will have to change the columns here too.

Leave all the other settings by default.

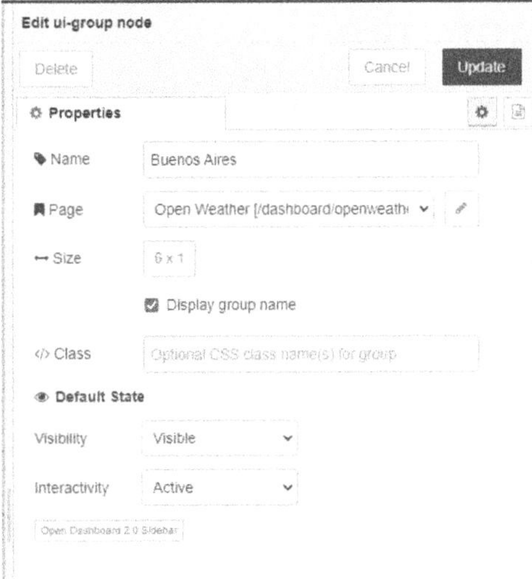

Figure 10.21: Configuring the CSV node

5. Open the write file node and configure it as shown in *Figure 10.22*. Give a name to the file and leave all the other options by default.

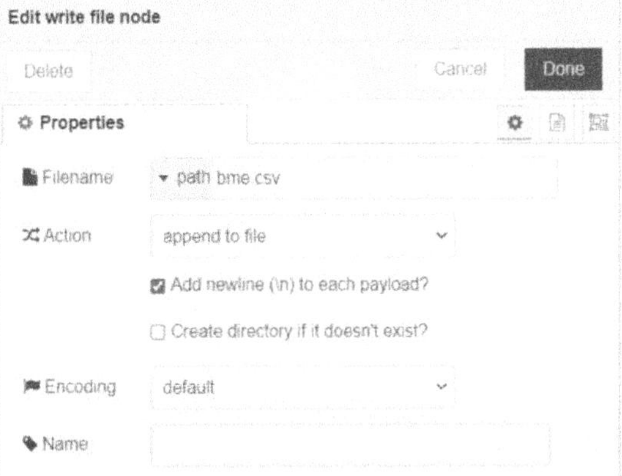

Figure 10.22: Configuring the write file node

6. Every time the sensor sends new data you should see the output from the debug node, like the one shown in *Figure 10.23*:

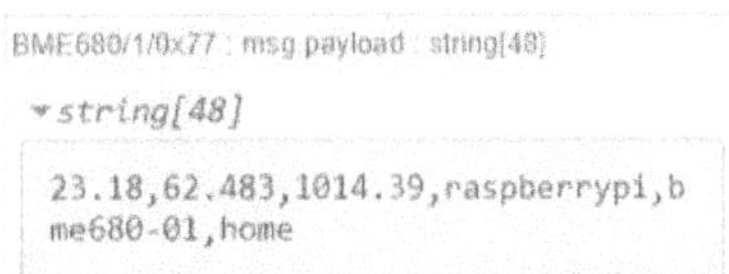

Figure 10.23: Debug data coming from the write file node

Reading data from the file

Now that you have data in the CSV file, you can read it using the **read file** node.

To implement it, follow these steps:

1. Use an inject node, a read file node, a CSV node, and a debug node, and connect them, as shown in *Figure 10.24*. For the CSV node, use the same configuration as before.

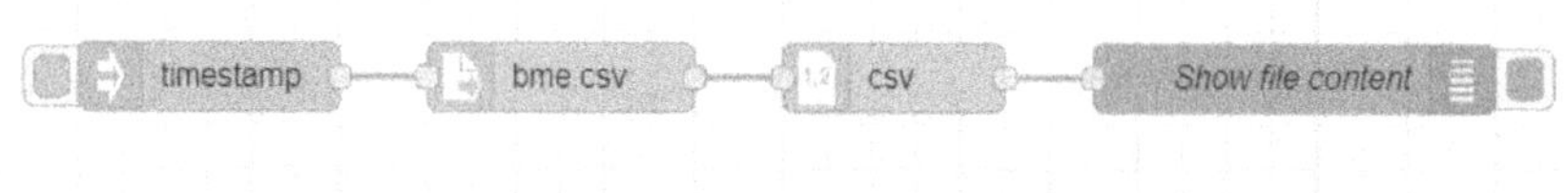

***Figure 10.24**: Reading a CSV file from Node-RED*

2. Open the read file node and enter the file name you used in the write file node, as shown in *Figure 10.25*:

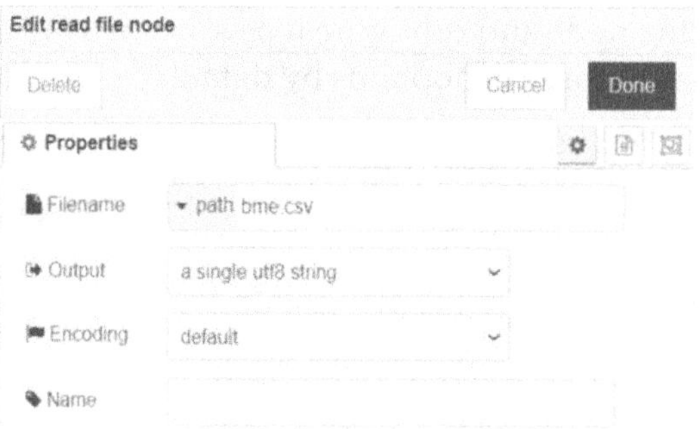

***Figure 10.25**: Specify the file name in the read file node*

3. Now, you can click on the inject node to get the contents from the **`bme.csv`** file. You can see the output in *Figure 10.26*:

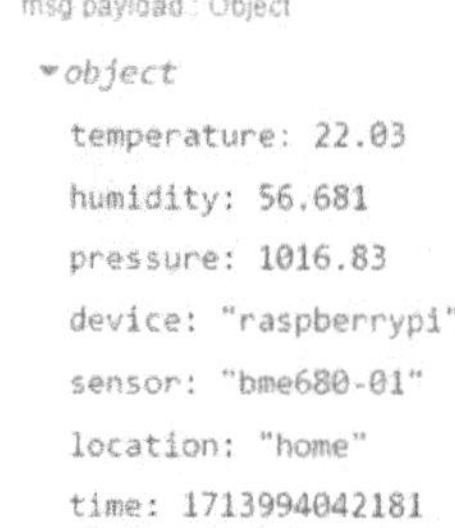

***Figure 10.26**: Output from the CSV node*

4. You can find the bme.csv file using the following command in the console terminal in the Raspberry Pi. The following command must be executed from the home directory of the pi user (**`/home/pi`**):

```
$ find bme.csv
```

The previous command will show you the following output:

```
$ bme.csv
```

Storing the values in InfluxDB

Now, let us write the values from the sensor in an InfluxDB bucket.

Follow these steps:

1. Add a function node and an influxdb-out node and connect them, as shown in *Figure 10.27*.
2. Open the function node and enter the following code.

```
msg.payload = [
    msg.payload
    ,
    {
        "device": "raspberrypi",
        "sensor": "bme680-01",
        "location": "home"
    }
];

return msg;
```

This JavaScript code will get the data from the sensor and add three parameters as tags (**device**, **sensor**, and **location**). You can add any other tags that can be useful for you.

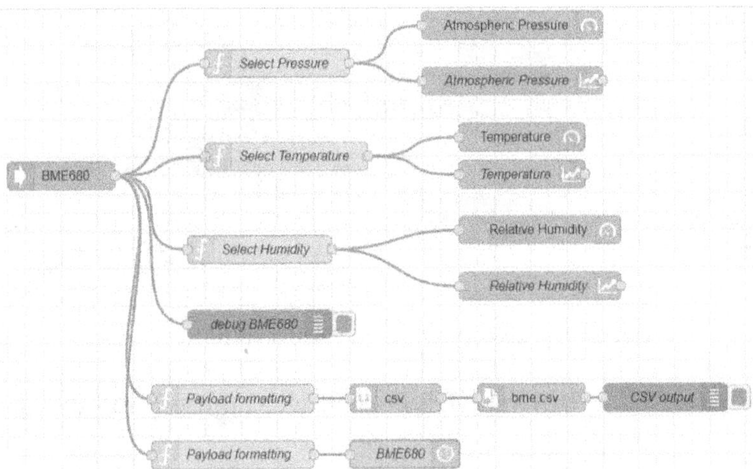

***Figure 10.27**: Adding the nodes to write in InfluxDB*

3. In the **`influxdb-out`** node, select the same configuration we created in *Chapter 8, Storing Internet of Things Data,* and give a name to the new measurement, as shown in *Figure 10.28*:

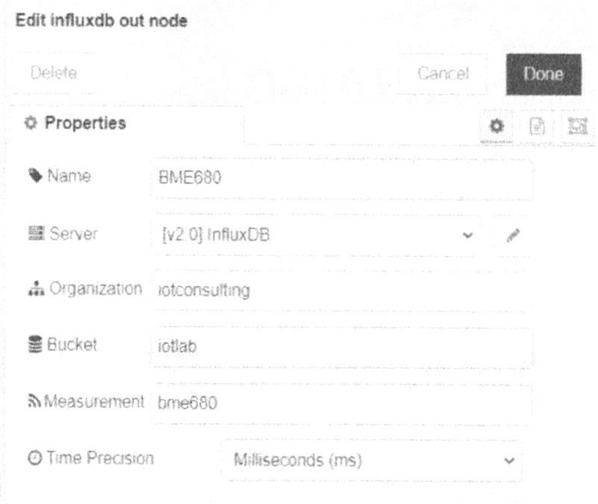

***Figure 10.28**: Configuring the influxdb-out node*

4. Deploy the flow and wait some time to have some data in the bucket. Then go to the **Data Explorer** in the InfluxDB user interface and look for the new data coming. You can see an example in *Figure 10.29*:

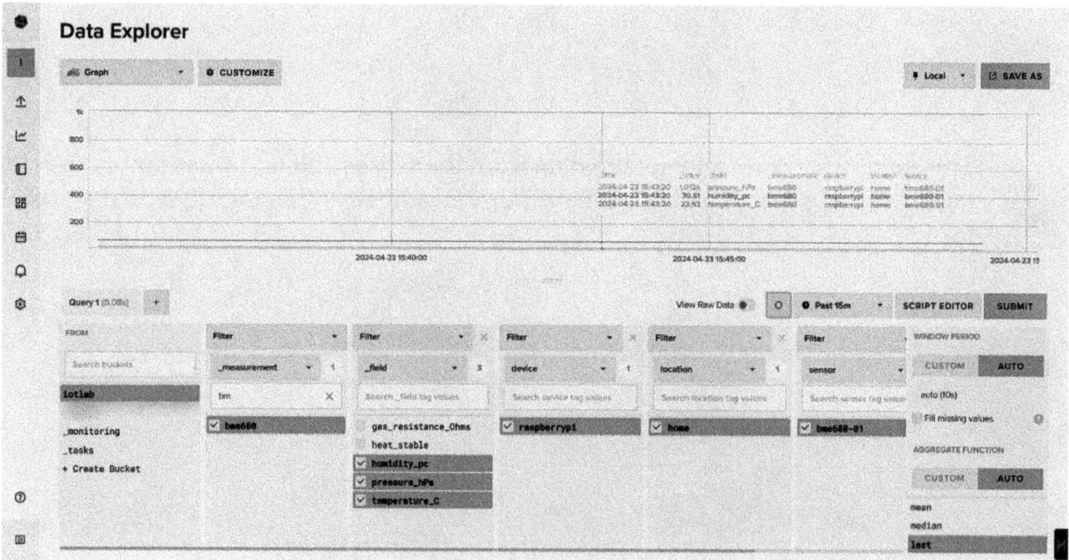

***Figure 10.29**: Exploring the new data from the BME680 sensor*

Now that we have data in the InfluxDB bucket, we can use it to build a dashboard in Grafana.

Visualizing the data in Grafana

In this section, we will use the data stored in the InfluxDB bucket to build a dashboard in Grafana.

To create a new dashboard in Grafana, follow these steps:

1. Follow the steps depicted in *Chapter 9, Visualizing Internet of Things Data,* to create a dashboard in Grafana.
2. Then, click on the + **Add visualization** button to create a new visualization panel. This will create a time series visualization panel.
3. Go back to the data explorer in InfluxDB and build a query to obtain the temperature. Refer to *Figure 10.30.*
4. Switch to the script editor using the button **SCRIPT EDITOR**. Copy the script query.

***Figure 10.30**: Build a query in InfluxDB*

5. Paste the script in the query field in Grafana, as shown in *Figure 10.31:*

Figure 10.31: Using the Flux query in Grafana

6. Modify the panel properties according to your needs and save them. Grafana will ask you for a name for the new dashboard. Enter something meaningful and click on **Save**, as shown in *Figure 10.32*:

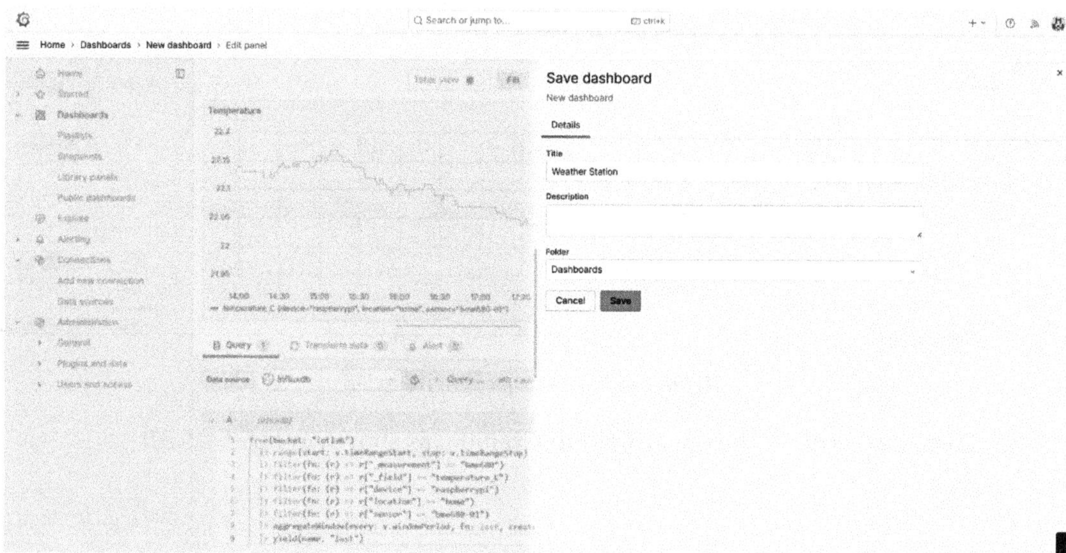

Figure 10.32: Saving the new dashboard

7. Create new panels for the humidity and the pressure.
8. Repeat the process of obtaining the queries from the data explorer in InfluxDB and paste the scripts in each of the new panels. Remember to modify the panel properties to assign them meaningful names and labels.

9. After adding these time series graphs, let us add gauge visualizations. Create a new visualization panel and select the gauge panel, as shown in *Figure 10.33*:

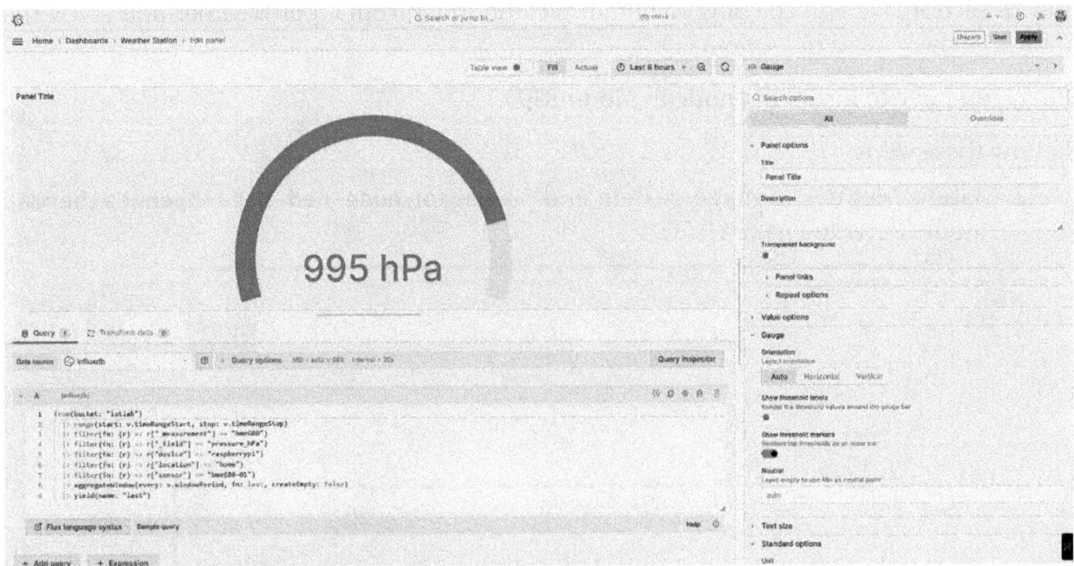

***Figure 10.33**: Adding a gauge visualization panel*

Use the same InfluxDB script we used for the time series panels and repeat the process for each of the variables. Change colors and units in the panel settings accordingly.

10. After completing the previous steps, you will obtain something similar to the dashboard shown in *Figure 10.34*:

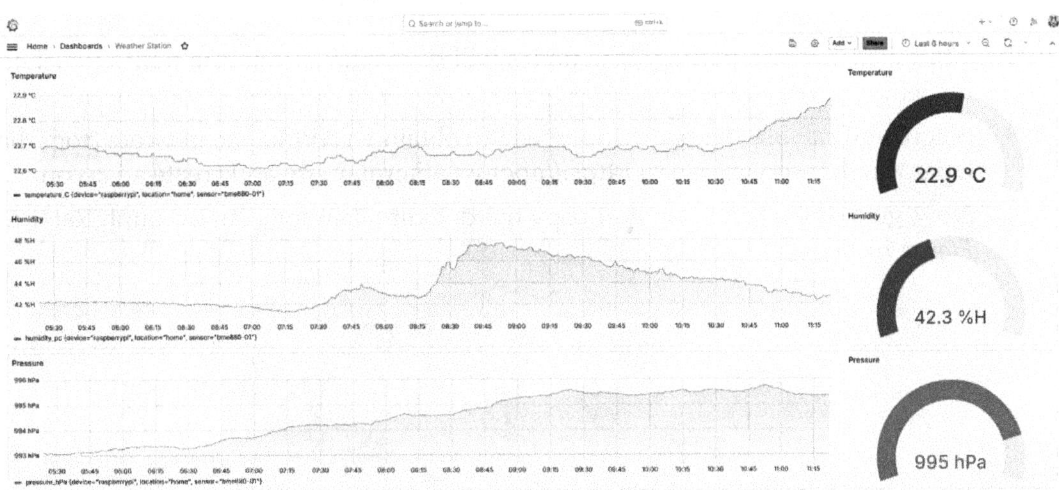

***Figure 10.34**: Complete dashboard in Grafana*

This section completes our weather station project.

Connecting to cloud weather services

In this section, we will see how to obtain weather data from OpenWeather and show the data on a dashboard in Node-RED.

First, you have to install the node in Node-RED.

Follow these steps:

1. Go to **Menu** | **Manage pallete** and search for **`node-red-node-openweathermap`** node. Refer to *Figure 10.35*:

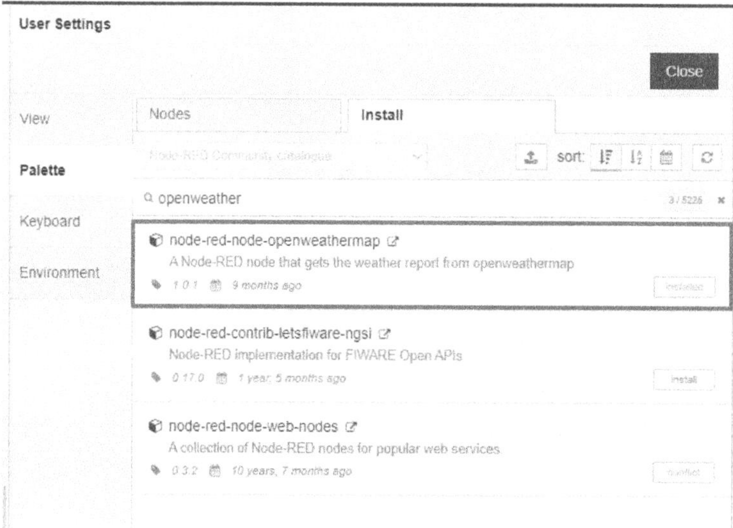

***Figure 10.35**: Installing the openweather node in Node-RED*

2. After installing the package, the nodes will be available from the nodes panel on the left.
3. Before you can use the nodes, you need to obtain an API key to get data from the OpenWeather service. Go to **https://openweathermap.org** and create an account.
4. Now, go to the API section and copy the default taken for your account. Refer to *Figure 10.36*:

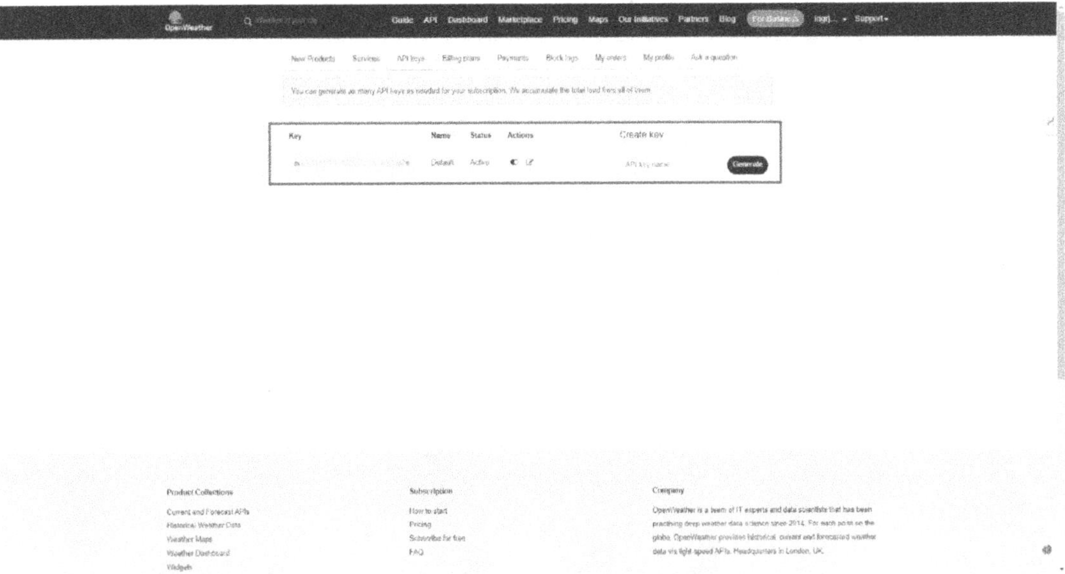

***Figure 10.36**: Getting the API token from OpenWeather*

5. Drag an OpenWeatherMap node from the palette to your workspace. Double-click the node to configure it. Give it a name, paste the token, and select the country and the city, as shown in *Figure 10.37*:

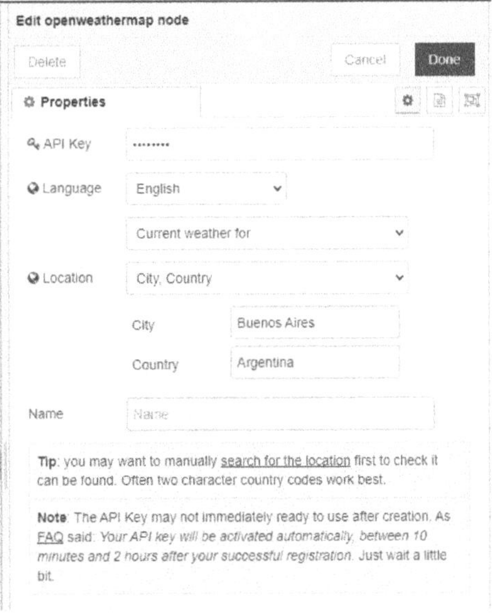

***Figure 10.37**: Configuring openweather node*

6. Add an inject node to trigger the weather request. Set it to repeat at your desired interval (for example, every five minutes). Connect a debug node to the OpenWeatherMap node to view the output. Refer to *Figure 10.38*:

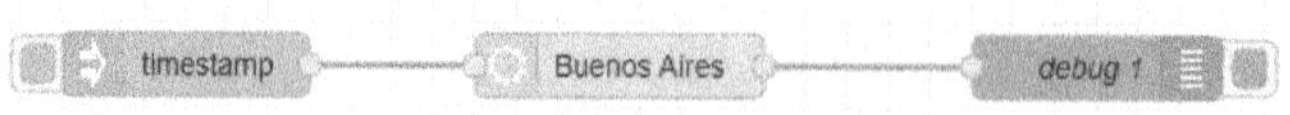

Figure 10.38: Basic flow for OpenWeather

7. Click **Deploy** to activate your flow. Trigger the inject node and check the debug sidebar for weather data. You will obtain updated data in the debug panel, as shown in *Figure 10.39*:

Figure 10.39: Data obtained from OpenWeather service

Now that we have the **`Open Weather`** node working in the flow, let us process the data and show it on a dashboard in Node-RED.

Building a dashboard for Open Weather

We will build a dashboard in Node-RED to show the Open Weather data on many visualization panels.

Let us start by creating the new dashboard in Node-RED:

1. Go to the dashboard section in the right panel and create a new page, as shown in *Figure 10.40*. Give it a name and change the path as you want. Save the new page by clicking on **Update**:

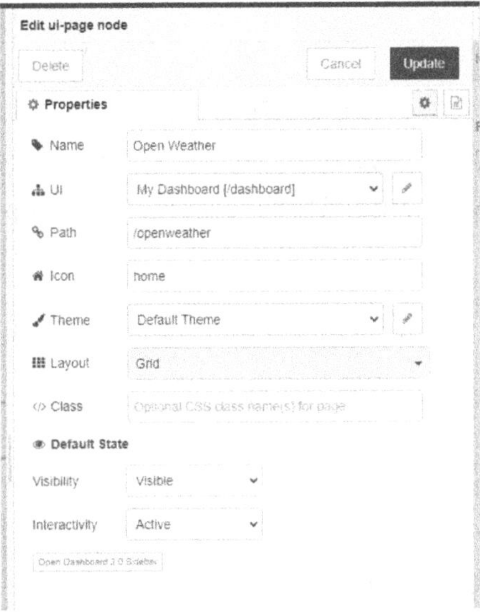

***Figure 10.40**: Creating a new page in the dashboard*

2. Create a new group on the page you have just created. See *Figure 10.41*:

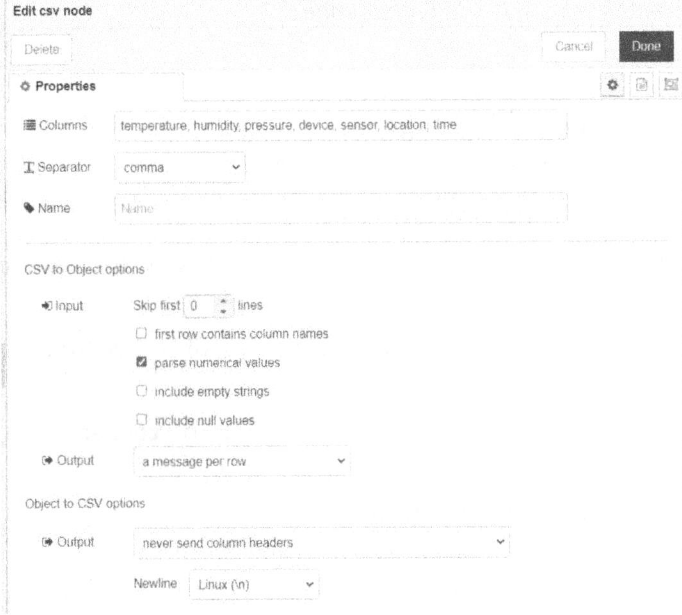

***Figure 10.41**: Creating a new group*

3. Now, we will add some function nodes for processing the data from the Open Weather node. Following are the codes for each function node:

```
# Node Get Status
msg.payload = msg.payload.weather;
return msg;

# Node Get Forecast const maxTemp = msg.payload.temp_maxc.toFixed(1);
const minTemp = msg.payload.temp_minc.toFixed(1);
msg.payload = `Max temp: ${maxTemp}°C Min temp: ${minTemp}°C`;
return msg;

# Node Get Temp
msg.payload = msg.payload.tempc;
return msg;

# Node Get Humidity
msg.payload = msg.payload.humidity;
return msg;

# Node Get Pressure
msg.payload = msg.payload.pressure;
return msg;
```

Note: Each of these function blocks extracts the variable of interest to send it to the following node, in our case a visualization node.

4. Now, add the following nodes:
   a. Two text nodes to show the outputs from the **`Get Status`** and **`Get Forecast`** nodes.
   b. Three Gauge nodes to show the values of **`temperature`**, **`humidity`**, and **`pressure`**.
   c. Three Chart nodes to show historical data of **`temperature`**, **`humidity`**, and **`pressure`**.
5. The final flow is as shown in *Figure 10.42*:

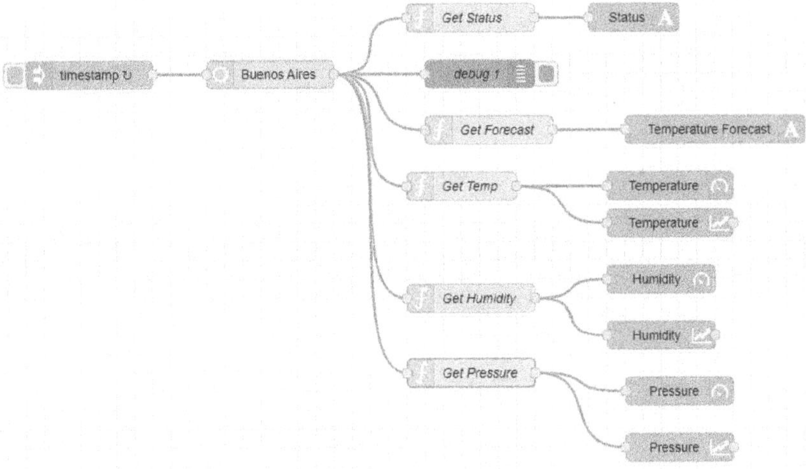

Figure 10.42: Full flow

6. See *Figures 10.43, 10.44, and 10.45* to look at configuration examples for the visualization nodes.

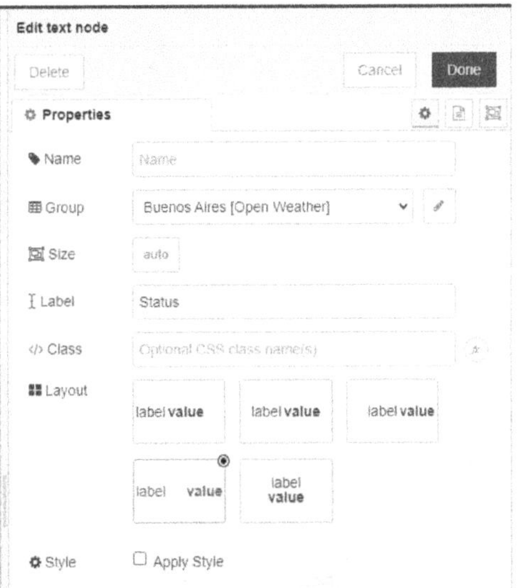

Figure 10.43: Configuring a text node

The following figure shows the configuration settings of a gauge node.

Figure 10.44: Configuration of a gauge node

7. Finally, click on **Deploy** and see the results on the dashboard page. You will obtain a dashboard similar to the one shown in *Figure 10.45*:

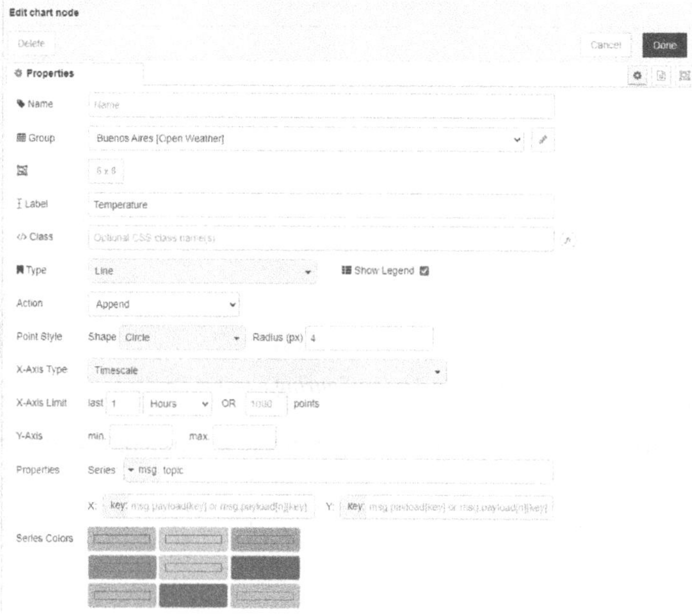

Figure 10.45: Configuration of a chart node

You can play with colors, styles, fonts and other parameters to adapt the visualizations to your needs.

Also, you can add more data from Open Weather, like coordinates, wind speed, wind direction, etc.

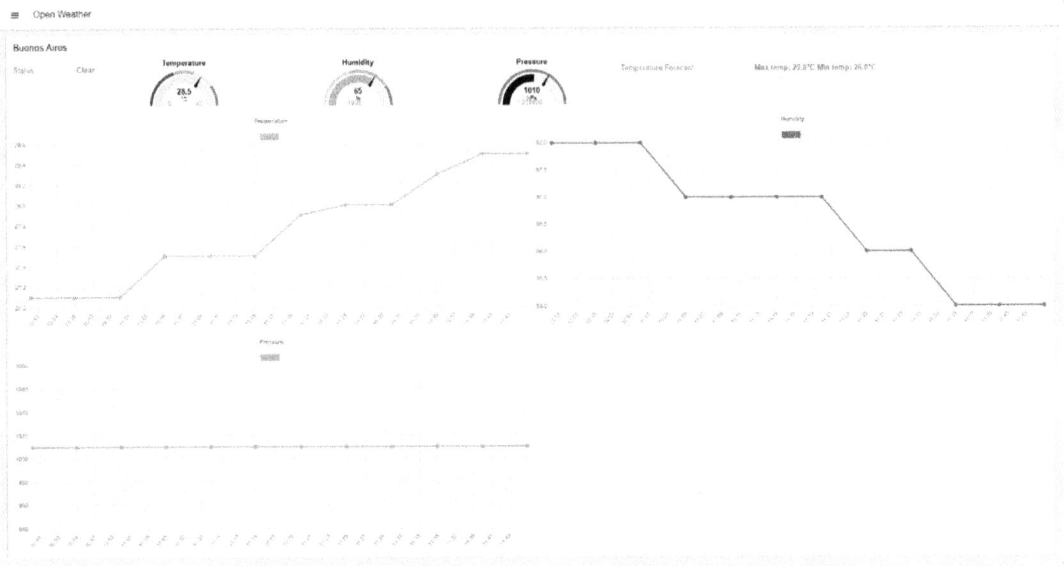

***Figure 10.46**: Complete Open Weather dashboard*

As you can see, you can obtain data from cloud services, like *OpenWeatherMap*, process it, and show it on dashboards. In this case, we used Node-RED for visualization, but you can also store the data in a database and build visualizations in Grafana, as we did with the sensor data.

All the tools used in this book provide great flexibility, and you can adapt them to fit your needs.

Conclusion

In this chapter, we have learned to use I2C with the Raspberry Pi computer. In particular, we have used the environment sensor BME680. This sensor measures all the variables needed to implement a weather station, so it is very convenient.

Using this single sensor we could obtain values from temperature, humidity, and pressure. We used Node-RED to get the data from the sensor, and we showed the values in a dashboard built in Node-RED, using the brand-new package dashboard 2.0. Then, we stored the data both in a CSV file and an InfluxDB bucket, using Node-RED to implement the logic. Finally, we used Grafana to build a dashboard by obtaining the values stored in the InfluxDB bucket.

In this chapter, we used several of the technologies and tools we covered in the previous chapters and integrated them to build a complete project.

In the next chapter, we will see how to build home automation systems using both Home Assistant and openHAB, which are two open-source systems.

Join our book's Discord space

Join the book's Discord Workspace for Latest updates, Offers, Tech happenings around the world, New Release and Sessions with the Authors:

https://discord.bpbonline.com

CHAPTER 11
Home Automation

Introduction

Home automation systems are widely used nowadays. They are useful to improve the comfort, efficiency, and security of buildings.

In this chapter, we will explore two open source systems, Home Assistant and openHAB.

These systems allow you to interact both with your custom hardware (ESP32, Raspberry PI, ESP8266, Arduino, etc) and with commercial products.

Through this chapter, we will learn the basics of installing, configuring, and using these systems.

Structure

The structure of this book is as follows:

- Using Home Assistant
- Installing Home Assitant in Raspberry Pi
- Initial setup
- Customizing Home Assitant
- Creating a Tasmota device

- Using openHAB
- Installing openHAB
- Initializing openHAB
- Creating an ESPHome device
- Integrating the ESPHome device in openHAB
- Creating an automation in openHAB
- Creating a dashboard in openHAB

Objectives

By the end of the chapter, you will be able to install, configure, and use Home Assistant and openHAB.

Also, you will learn to create Tasmota and ESPHome devices and integrate them into the systems.

In this way, you will be able to design and implement your home automation systems by combining different devices and sensors.

Also, you will learn to show data on dashboards and program automation.

After reading this chapter, you will be ready to create and manage a functional automation system.

Using Home Assistant

Home Assistant is an open-source home automation platform that focuses on local control and privacy. It is designed to integrate and control a wide variety of smart home devices and systems, providing users with a unified interface and powerful automation capabilities.

The following are some key features of Home Assistant:

- **Local control**: Home Assistant emphasizes local control and processing, ensuring that users' data stays within their home network and enhancing privacy and security.
- **Extensive integrations**: It supports a vast array of devices and services from different manufacturers, including smart lights, thermostats, sensors, cameras, and more. Integrations are continuously updated and expanded by a large community of contributors.
- **Automation and scripting**: Home Assistant includes a robust automation engine that allows users to create complex automation rules using the YAML-based configuration or through a visual editor.

- **User interfaces**: It offers customizable dashboards, allowing users to create a personalized interface to monitor and control their smart home devices. There are also mobile apps for iOS and Android.
- **Community and support**: Home Assistant has a vibrant community that contributes to its development and provides support through forums, documentation, and other resources.
- **Flexible deployment**: It can run on various hardware platforms, including Raspberry Pi, virtual machines, Docker, and dedicated home automation hubs.
- **Privacy focused**: As an open-source project, Home Assistant allows users to retain full control over their data and how it is used.

Home Assistant is highly flexible and customizable, making it a popular choice among home automation enthusiasts who value privacy and local control.

Installing Home Assistant in Raspberry Pi

There are several methods available to install Home Assistant:

- **Home Assistant Operating System**: This is the recommended method for installing Home Assistant. It provides a complete operating system with a home assistant pre-installed, making it easy to set up and manage.
- **Home Assistant Supervised**: This method allows you to install Home Assistant on a generic Linux system using Docker and Docker Compose. It provides more flexibility than the Home Assistant operating system but may require more technical knowledge to set up.
- **Home Assistant Container**: This method allows you to run Home Assistant in a Docker container on any system that supports Docker. It is a lightweight and portable option for running Home Assistant.
- **Home Assistant Core**: This method allows you to install Home Assistant Core, which is the core functionality of Home Assistant without the user interface. It can be installed on a variety of systems, including Raspberry Pi, Windows, and macOS.

We will use the Home Assistant **Operating System** (**OS**). By choosing this method, we can focus on the use of Home Assistant and the implementation of the home automation system itself.

Let us see the steps to install the Home Assistant OS:

1. Download and install Raspberry Pi Imager on your computer from **https://www.raspberrypi.com/software/**. We used this software in *Chapter 1, Meet the Boards* to install the Raspberry Pi OS.
2. Insert the SD card into your computer. An SD card with a minimum of 32 GB is recommended.

3. Open Raspberry Pi Imager and select your Raspberry Pi device (Raspberry Pi 4 in our case). Refer to *Figure 11.1*:

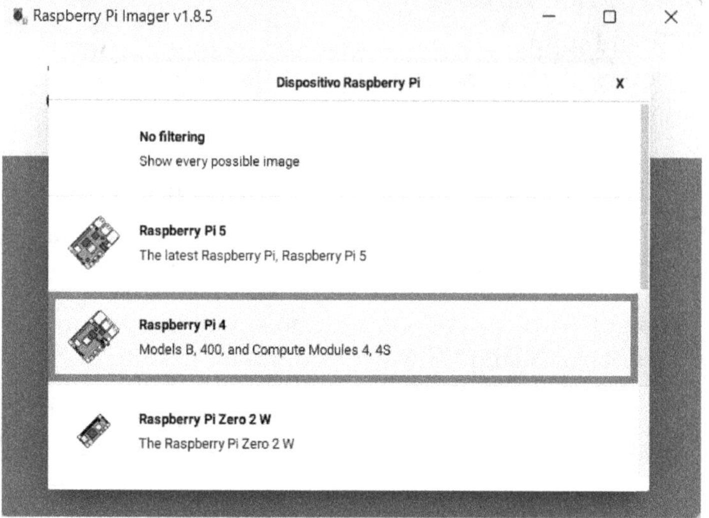

***Figure 11.1**: Selecting Raspberry Pi 4*

4. Choose the OS by selecting **Choose OS**.
5. Navigate to **Other specific-purpose OS** | **Home assistants and home automation** | **Home Assistant**. Refer to *Figures 11.2, 11.3, and 11.4*:

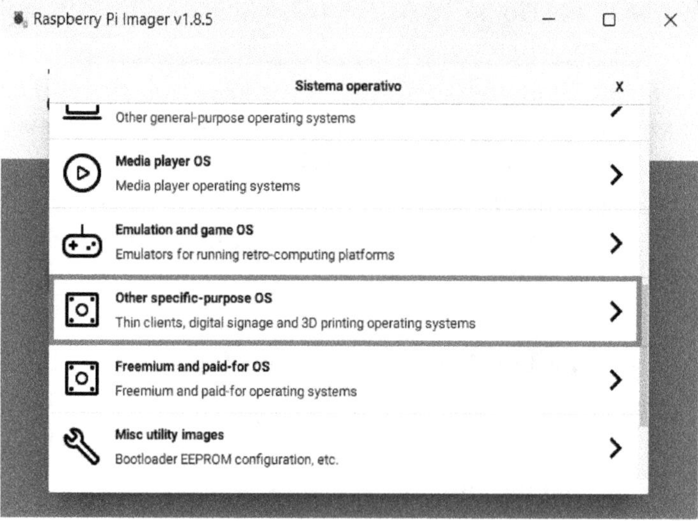

***Figure 11.2**: Selecting the OS*

The following figure shows the **Home assistants and home automation** option:

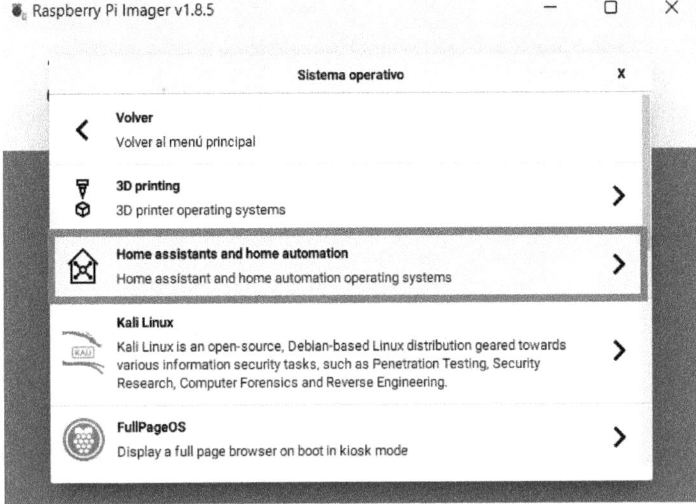

Figure 11.3: Selecting home automation OS

The following figure shows the **Home Assistant** option:

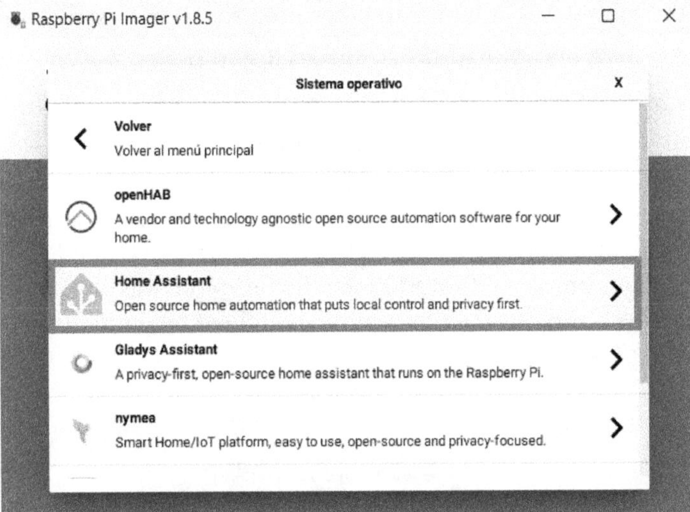

Figure 11.4: Selecting Home Assistant OS

6. Select the **Home Assistant OS RPi 4/400**. Refer to *Figure 11.5*:

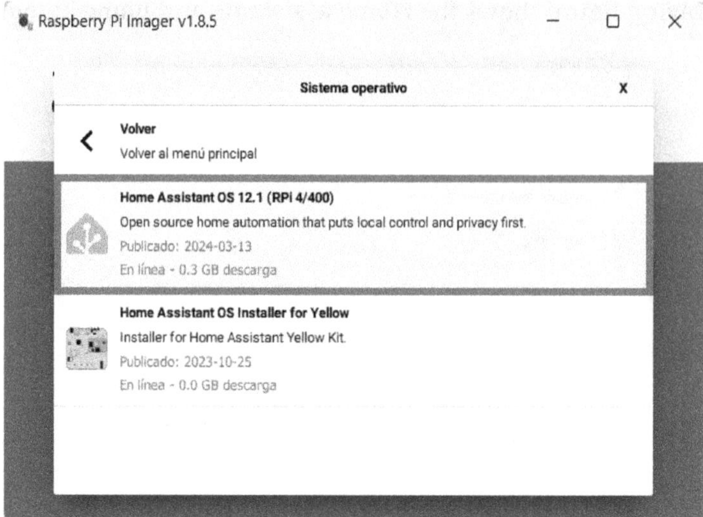

Figure 11.5: Selecting Home Assistant OS for Raspberry Pi 4

7. Choose your SD card within Raspberry Pi Imager.
8. Start writing the installer onto the SD card by selecting **Next**.
9. Wait for the Home Assistant OS to be written to the SD card.
10. Eject the SD card once the writing process is complete.
11. Insert the microSD card into your Raspberry Pi and power it on.
12. Wait for the initial boot process to complete. The time it takes depends on the speed of your internet connection, as it downloads many packages before starting the system. You can access the Home Assistant web interface by navigating to **http://homeassistant.local:8123** in your web browser. In case that address does not work, try with **http://homeasistant:8123** or **http://<your-raspberry-ip-address>:8123**. You will see a screen like the one shown in *Figure 11.6* while the system is installed:

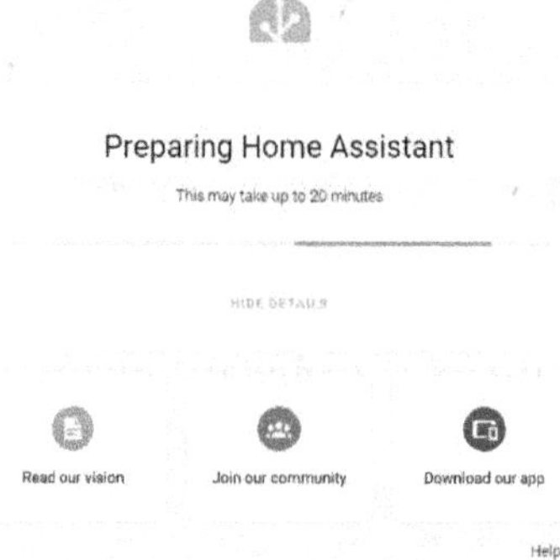

Figure 11.6: Initializing Home Assistant

13. Follow the on-screen instructions to set up your Home Assistant instance, including creating an account and configuring your preferences.
14. Once the setup is complete, you can begin customizing and configuring your Home Assistant installation to meet your needs.

Initial setup

When you first access **Home Assistant** (**HA**), you will be asked to make some initial configurations.

Let us see each of the steps:

1. When you access HA for the first time, you will see a page similar to the one shown in *Figure 11.7*. Click on the big blue button **CREATE MY SMART HOME**.

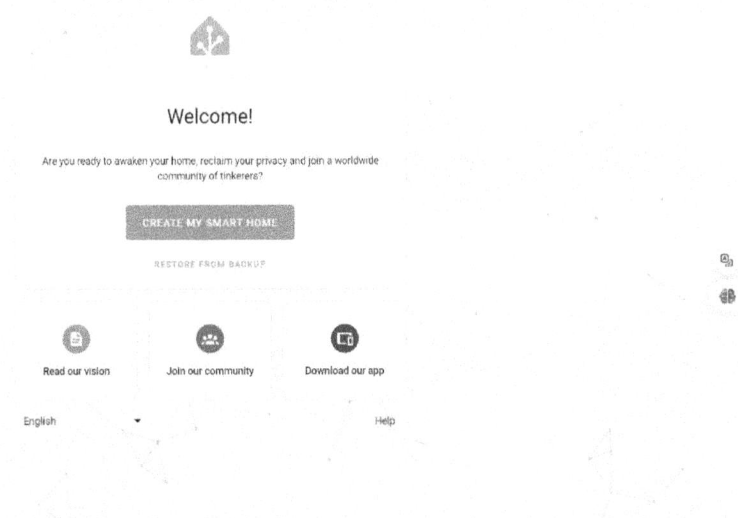

Figure 11.7*: First access page of HA*

2. In the following step, create a user and enter a password. Refer to *Figure 11.8*:

Figure 11.8: Creating user and password in HA

3. In this step, you can optionally enter your location. Refer to *Figure 11.9*:

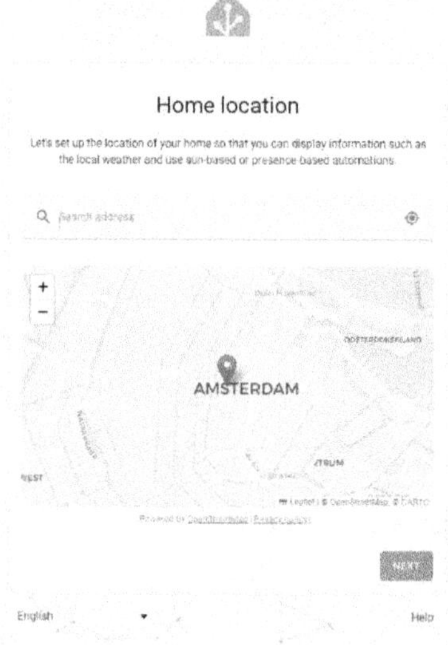

Figure 11.9: Entering location in HA

4. On the next screen, you can optionally enable the statistics of use. Refer to *Figure 11.10*:

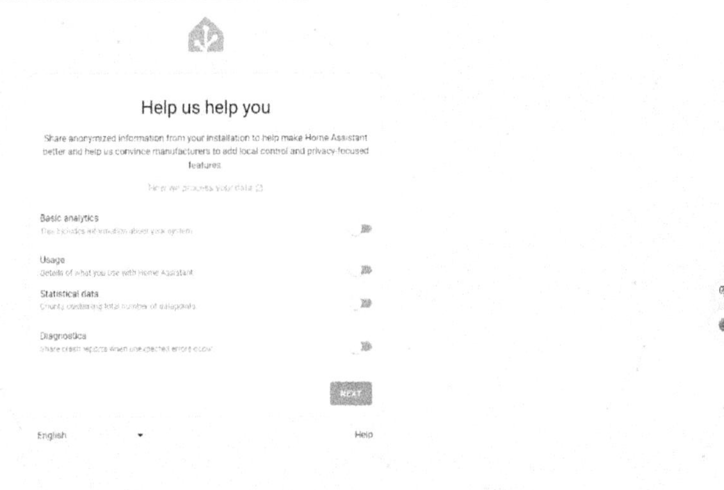

Figure 11.10: Enabling statistics in HA

5. As you are running HA in a Raspberry Pi 4, HA will discover your **Bluetooth Low Energy** (**BLE**) interface, as shown in *Figure 11.11*:

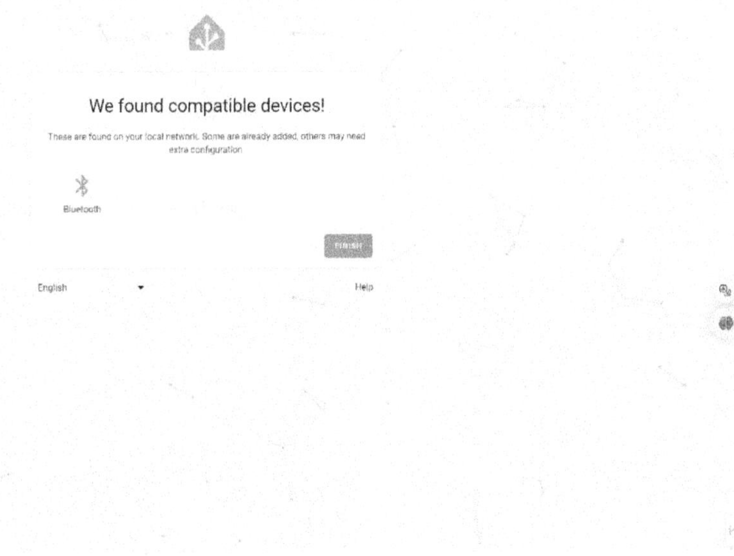

Figure 11.11: Discovering the BLE interface

6. After finishing the setup procedure, you will see a page like the one shown in *Figure 11.12*:

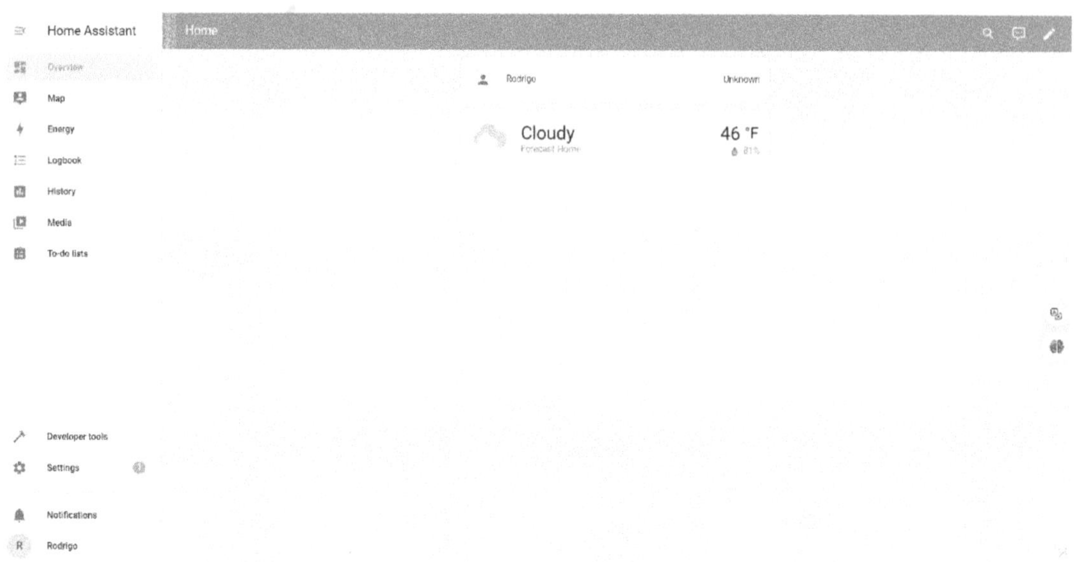

Figure 11.12: Home page of HA

Now, let us see how to add some useful tools to our HA instance.

Customizing Home Assistant

Home Assistant brings a lot of possibilities through its integrations and plugins. This is because of the great community that helps to develop and maintain a large variety of packages.

In this section, we will install some packages to enable very useful features, like the **Secure Shell** (**SSH**) add-on, the file editor, and others.

Installing SSH add-on

Let us start by installing an SSH server, so we can access HA from the console.

To install an SSH server, follow these steps:

1. Click on the **Settings** option in the left menu page. Then click on the **Add-ons** button, as shown in *Figure 11.13*:

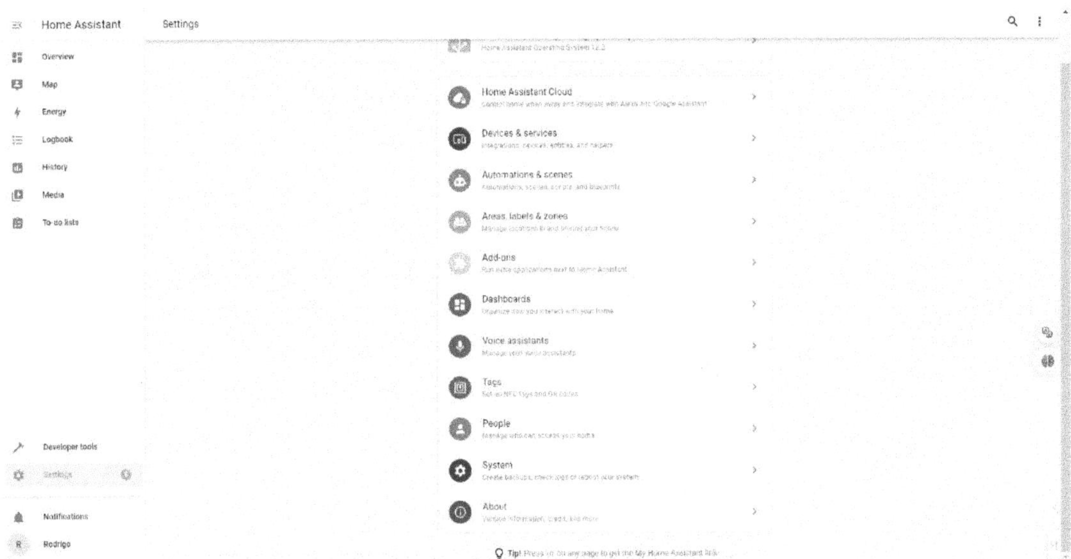

Figure 11.13: Settings page

2. The previous step will guide you to an empty page. Click on the **ADD-ON-STORE** button that appears at the bottom right of the page. This will lead you to the store where you can choose among many packages and applications. Refer to *Figure 11.14:*

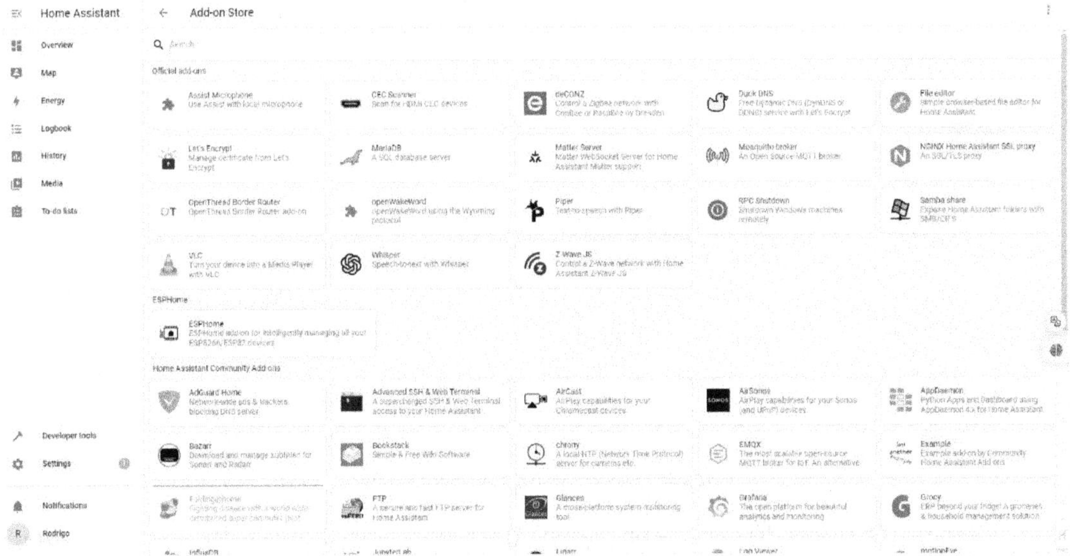

Figure 11.14: Add-on store

3. In the add-on store page, click on the **Advanced SSH & Web Terminal** add-on. You will reach the installation page of the add-on. Refer to *Figure 11.15*. Click on the **Install** button to install the add-on in HA.

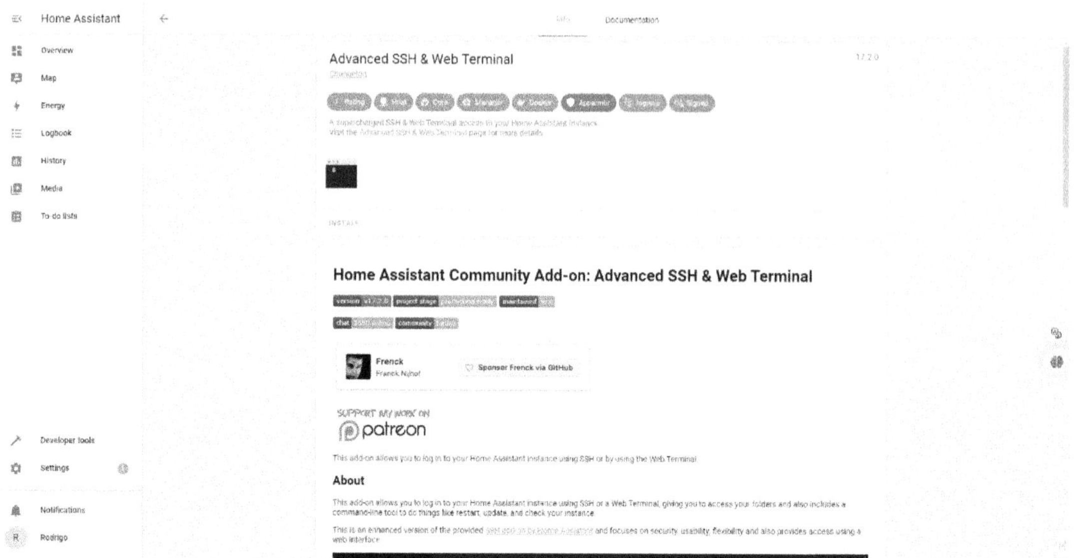

Figure 11.15: Installation page of the add-on

4. Now go to the management page of the add-on and click on the **Configuration** tab. There, enter the **`username`** and the **`password`** of HA, so the web SSH client can connect to the system. Refer to *Figure 11.16*:

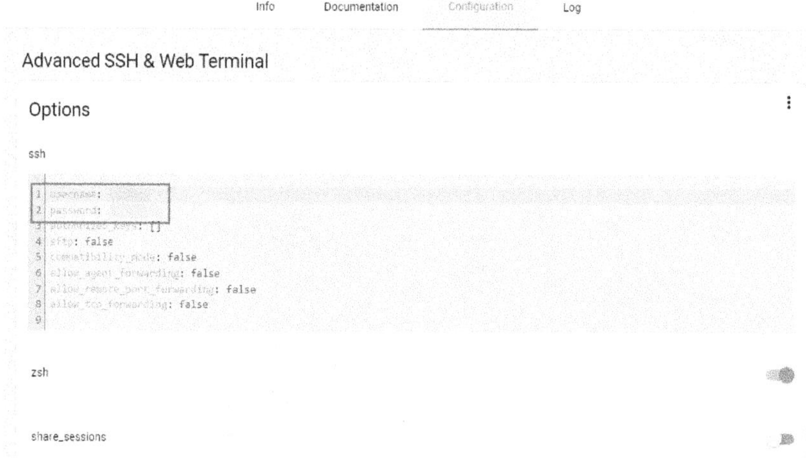

Figure 11.16: Configuring the add-on

5. Finally, go back to the management page and start the service using the **Start** button.

Note: You can enable or disable many options.

Refer to *Figure 11.17*:

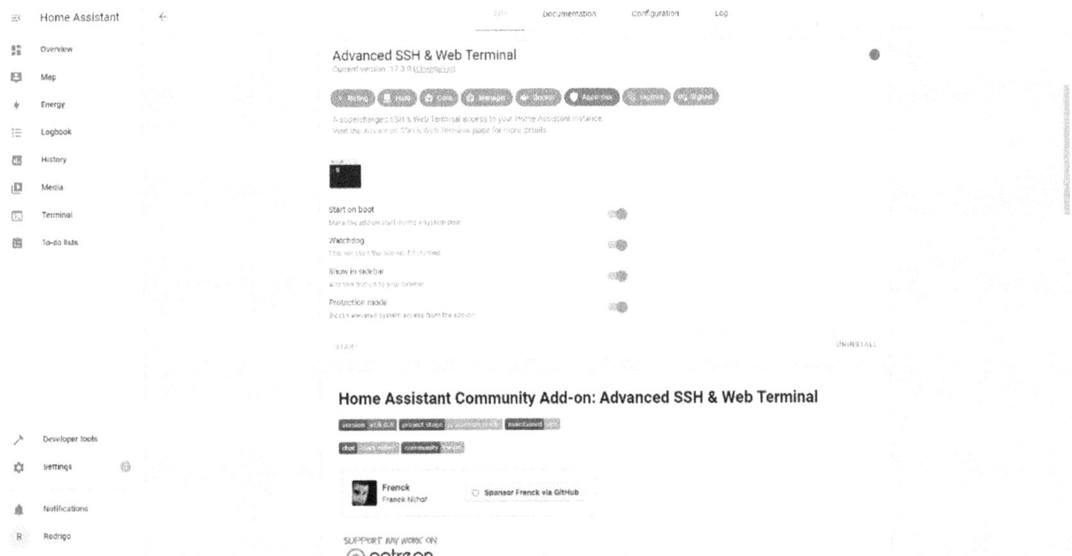

Figure 11.17: Starting the add-on

6. Now, you can access HA using SSH. You can use an SSH client or directly from the browser, as shown in *Figure 11.18*:

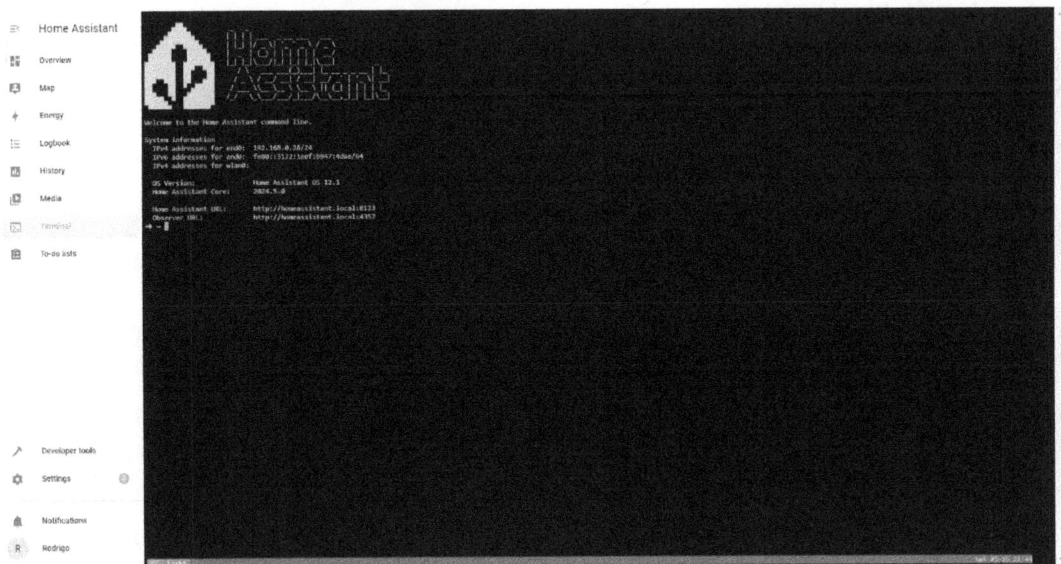

Figure 11.18: Accessing HA through SSH from the web browser

Now, let us install other useful add-ons.

Installing the file editor

The file editor add-on is a very convenient tool for editing configuration files directly from the browser.

To install it, follow these steps:

1. Go to the add-on store again and click on the **File editor** button. This will lead you to the installation page of the add-on, as shown in *Figure 11.19*:

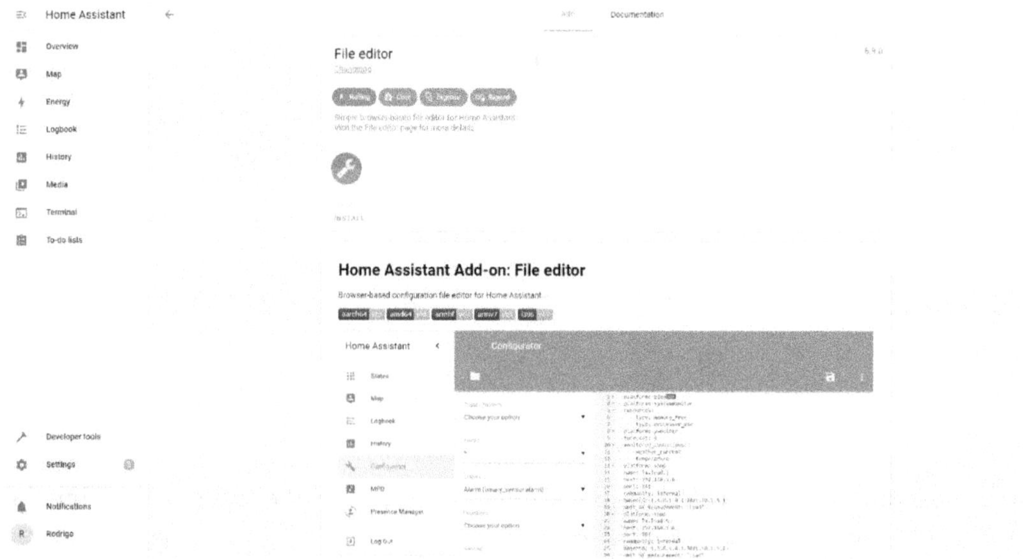

***Figure 11.19**: Installing the file editor*

2. Once it is installed, start it. You can enable the options **Start on boot**, **Watchdog**, and **Show in sidebar**, as shown in *Figure 11.20*:

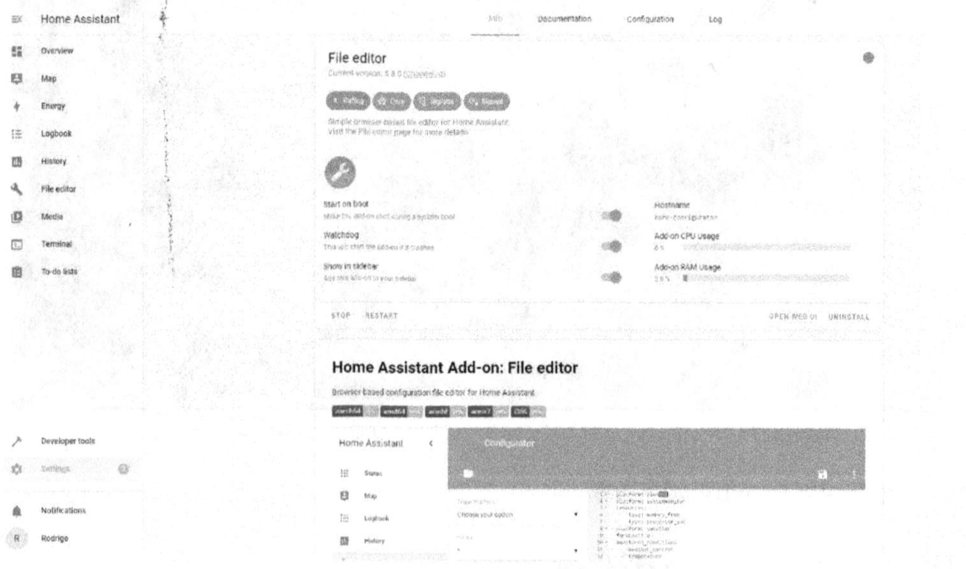

***Figure 11.20:** Managing file editor*

3. Now, you can open and edit the files in HA, as you can see in *Figure 11.21*:

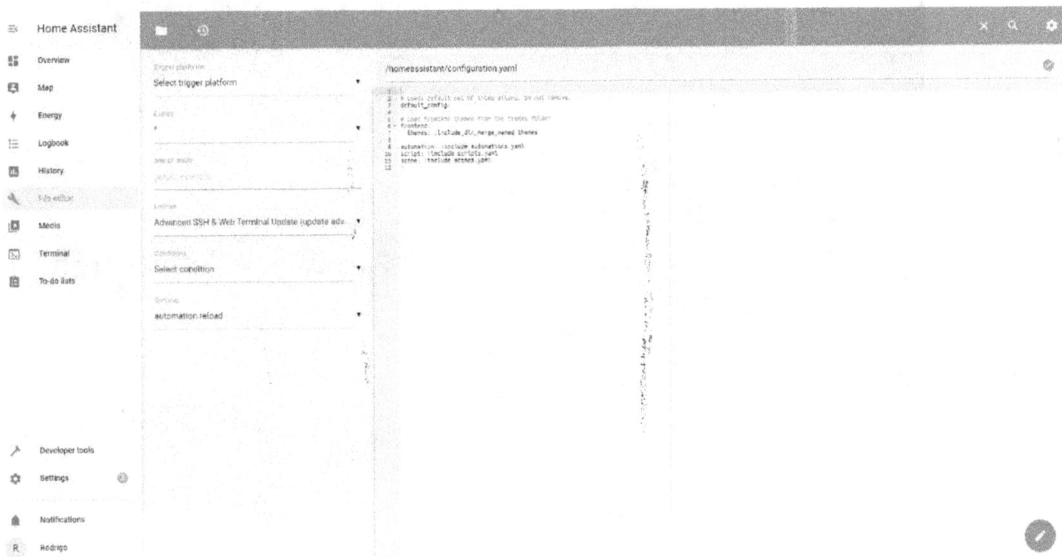

Figure 11.21: Opening the filed editor

Installing Home Assistant Community Store

By installing the **Home Assistant Community Store** (**HACS**), you can take advantage of many community-developed plugins, integrations, scripts, themes, and services.

To install HACS, follow these steps:

1. Open a new terminal by using the advanced SSH and web terminal you already installed.
2. Copy the following command in the terminal and press enter. This script will download all the required packages and install them in the system. Refer to *Figure 11.22*:

```
$ wget -O - https://get.hacs.xyz | bash -
```

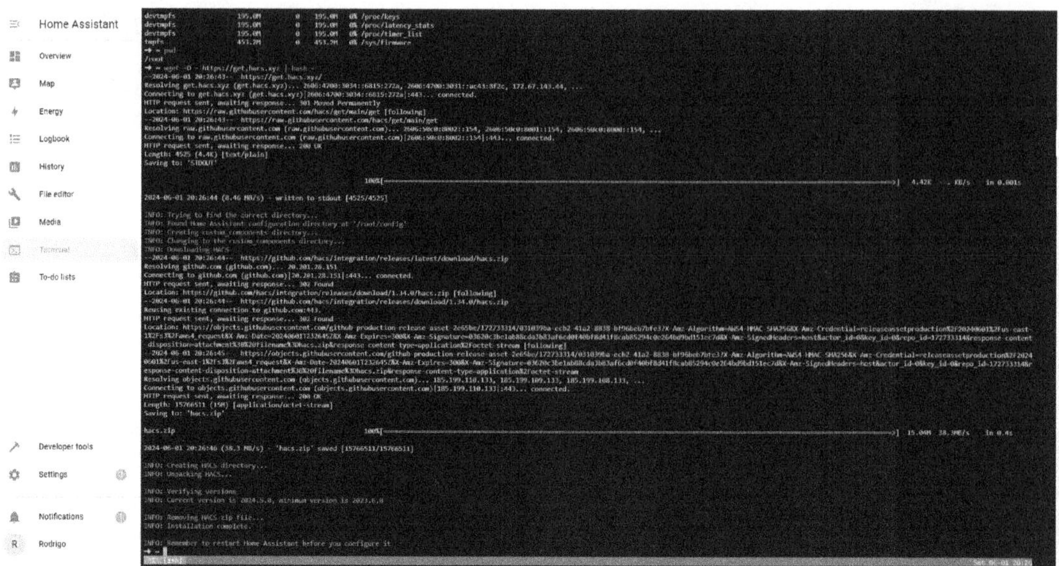

Figure 11.22: Installing HACS

3. After installing HACS, run the following command to reboot HA:

```
$ reboot now
```

4. Go to the **Settings** page in Home Assistant.
5. Go to **Devices & Services** and the **Integrations** tab in the HA. Then, click on the + **Add Integration** button and search for HACS, as shown in *Figure 11.23*:

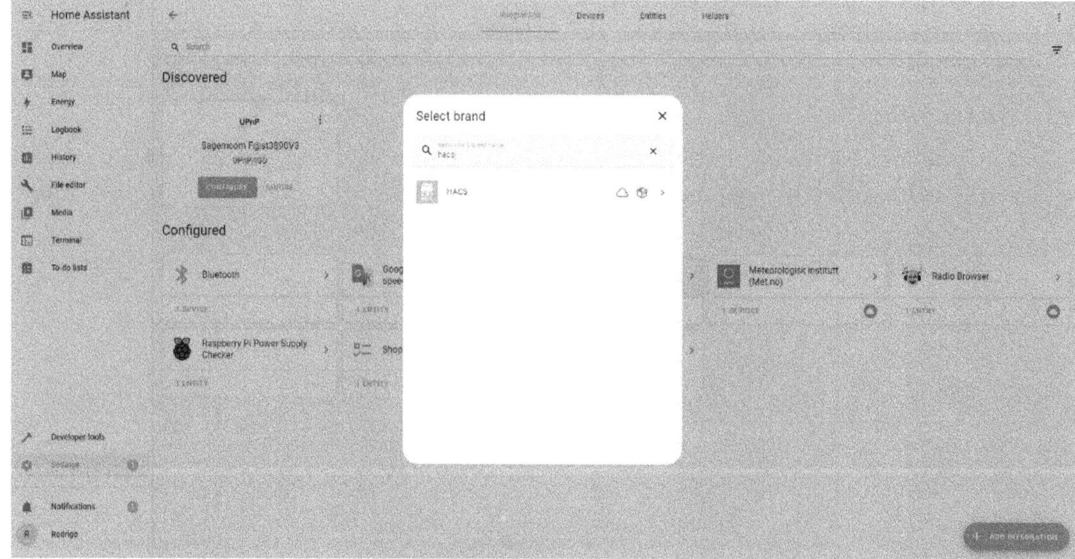

Figure 11.23: Enabling HACS in HA

6. Click on the **HACS** item. A window with several options will appear. Click on all of them, as shown in *Figure 11.24*:

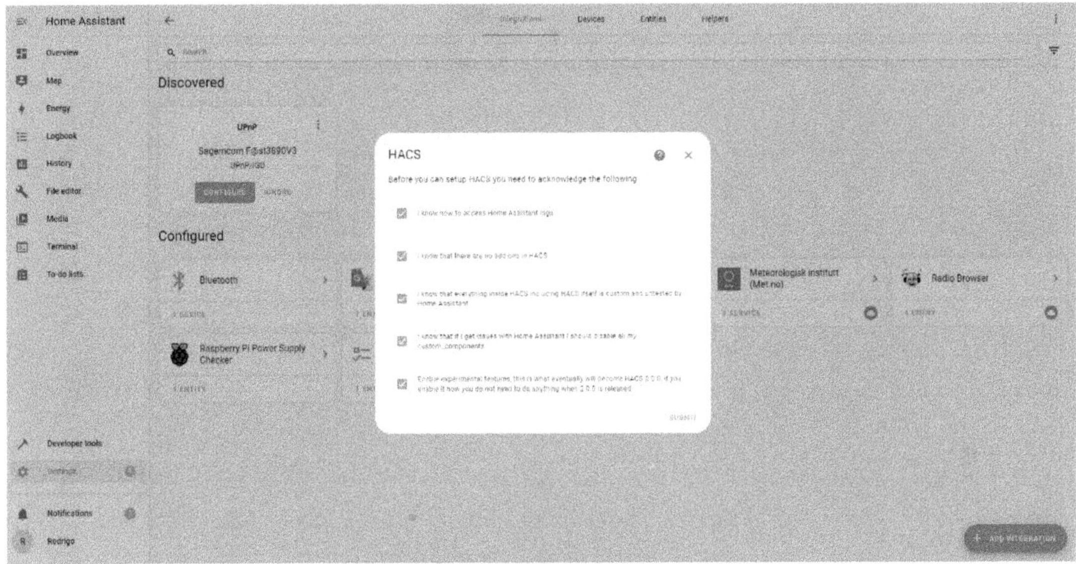

Figure 11.24: Accepting conditions in HACS

7. HA will show you a code that you have to enter on **https://github.com/login/device** to authenticate the device on GitHub. Enter the code in the fields, as shown in *Figure 11.25*:

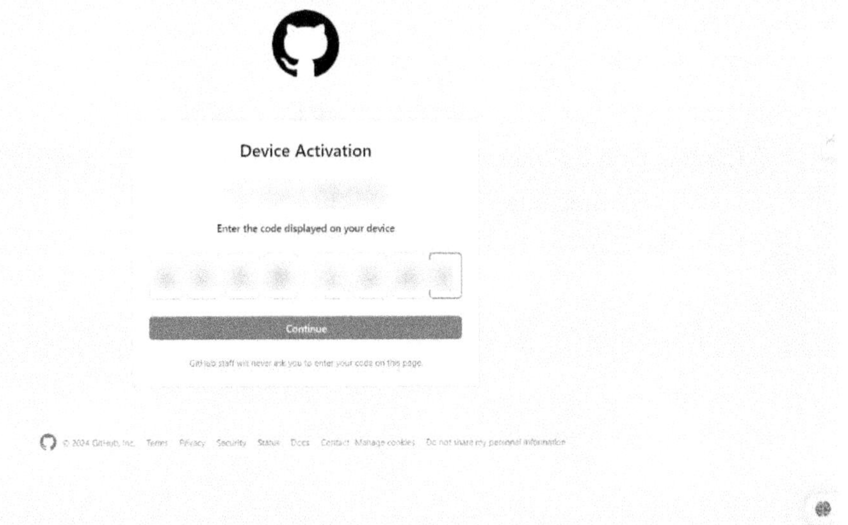

Figure 11.25: Entering the code in GitHub

8. Finally, authorize the application (HACS) as shown in *Figure 11.26*:

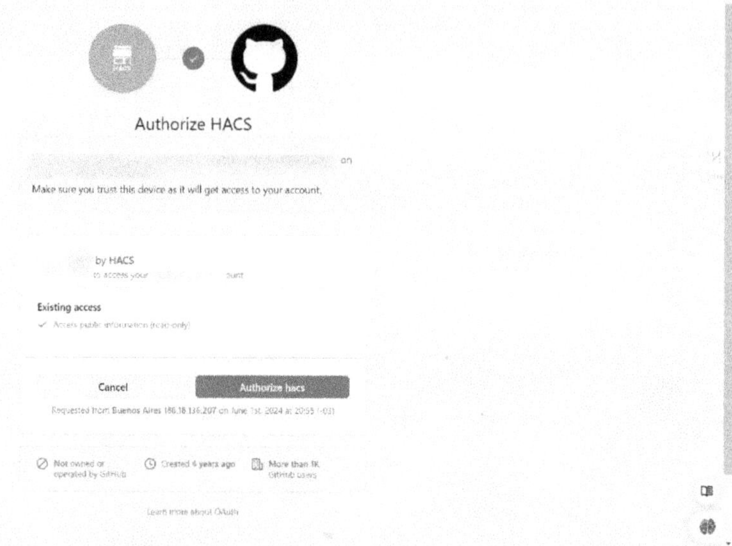

***Figure 11.26**: Authorizing HACS in GitHub*

Now that you have installed HACS, you can install some useful packages maintained by the community.

Installing and using Mosquitto in Home Assistant

In this section, we will see how to install and configure Mosquitto using the Home Assistant add-on.

To install the add-on on your system, follow these steps:

1. In your Home Assistant interface, go to **Settings** | **Add-ons** | **Add-on Store**.
2. Locate the Mosquitto broker add-on and click on it.
3. Press the **INSTALL** button. Refer to *Figure 11.27*:

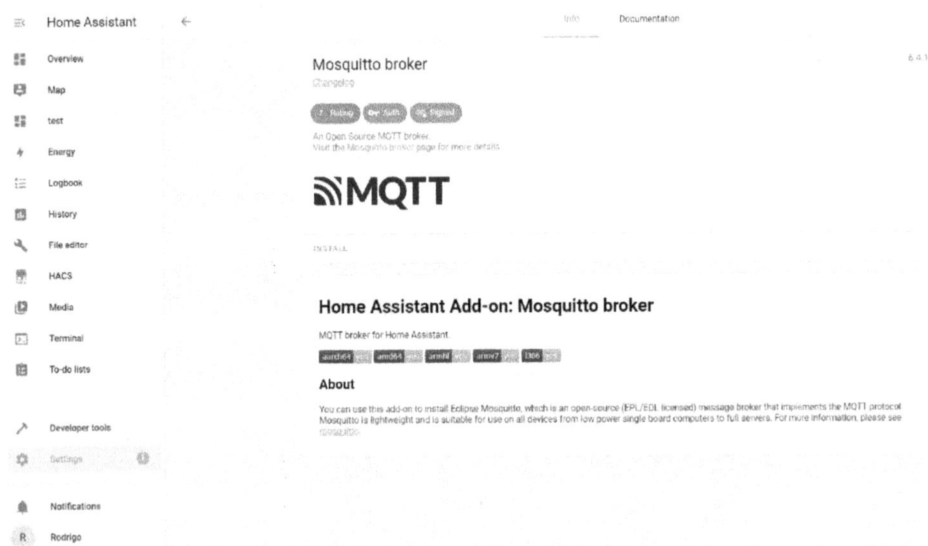

Figure 11.27: Installing Mosquitto broker add-on

The add-on includes several options.

To get it up and running, follow these steps:

1. Start the add-on. Refer to *Figure 11.28*.
2. Be patient and wait for a few minutes.
3. Review the log output of the add-on to check the results.
4. Create a new user for **Message Queuing Telemetry Transport** (**MQTT**) through the Home Assistant interface by navigating to **Settings** | **People** | **Users**

Note: That this should not be done in the Mosquitto Configuration tab.

Refer to *Figure 11.29*.

Please notice the following:

- The username cannot be **homeassistant** or **addons**, as these are reserved.
- If you do not see the option to create a new user, ensure that Advanced Mode is enabled in your Home Assistant profile.

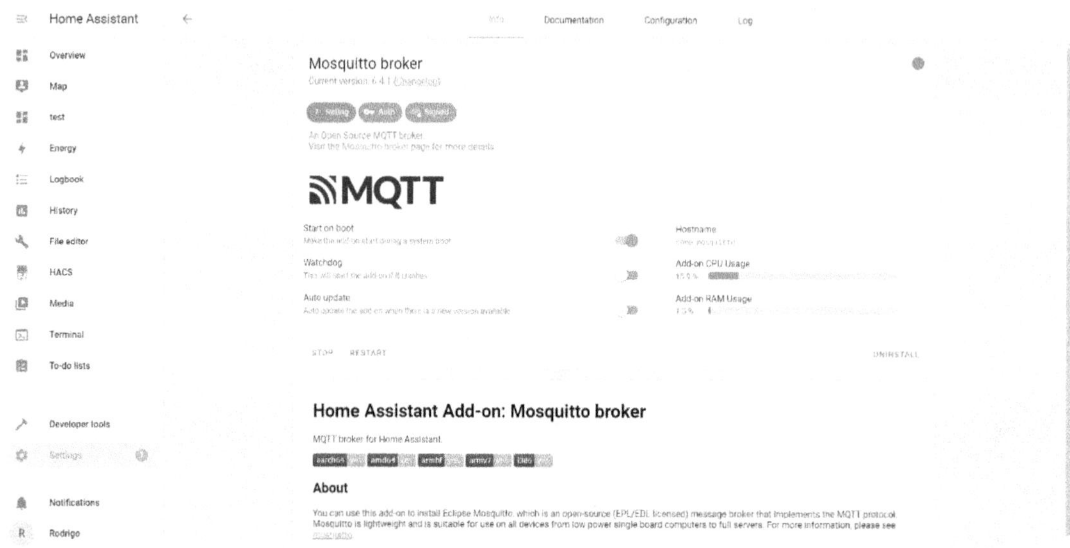

Figure 11.28: Start the Mosquitto broker

The following figure shows the configuration of a MQTT client:

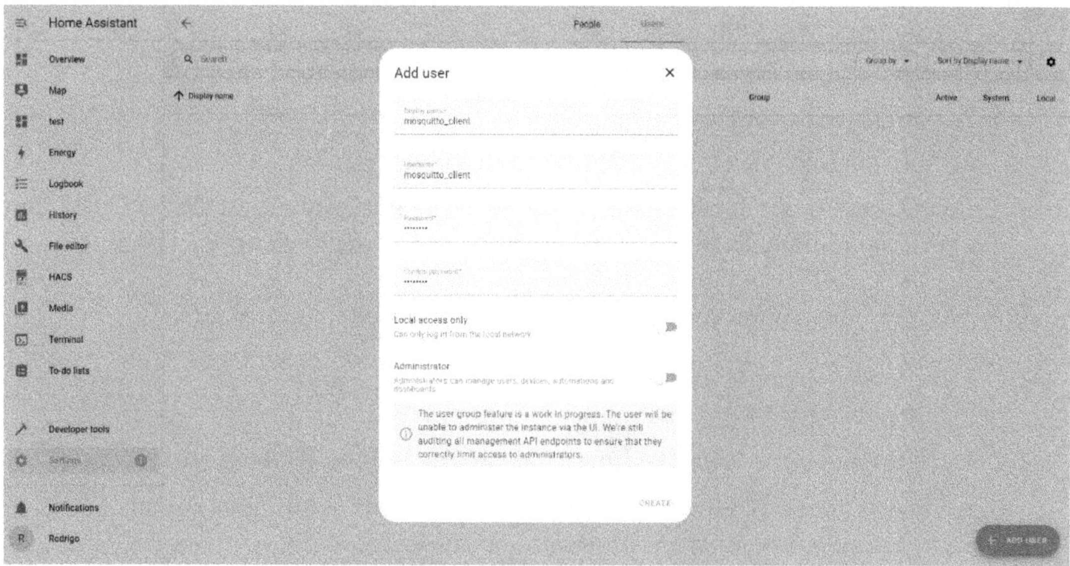

Figure 11.29: Adding a user for the Mosquitto broker

To utilize Mosquitto as a broker, go to the integration page and install the configuration with a single click. Follow these steps:

1. In your Home Assistant interface, navigate to **Settings** | **Devices and Services** | **Integrations**.

2. MQTT should appear as a discovered integration at the top of the page. Refer to *Figure 11.30*.
3. Select it, check the box to enable MQTT discovery if you wish, and click **Submit**.

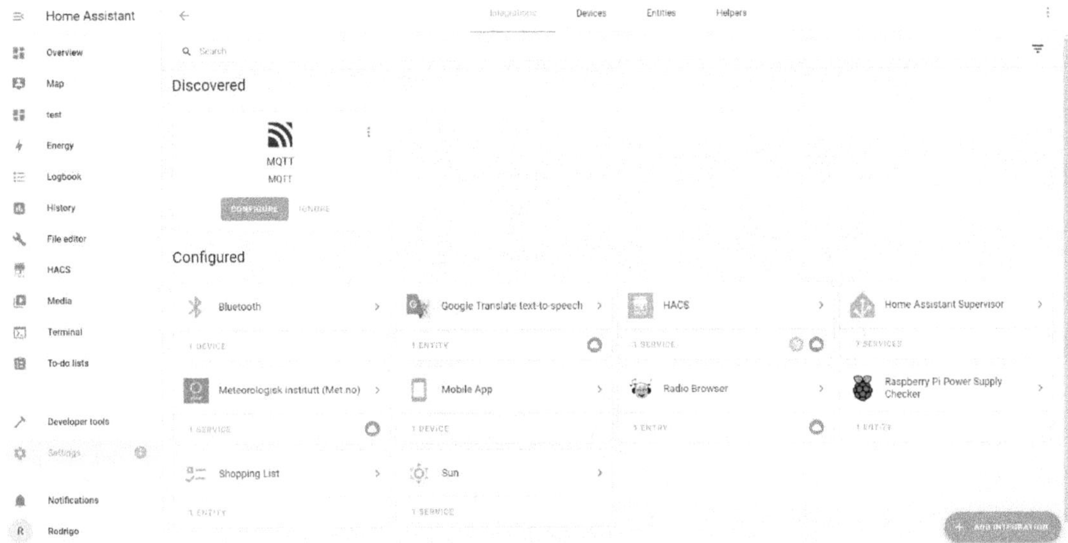

***Figure 11.30**: MQTT integration discovered*

Creating a Tasmota device

Tasmota is an open-source firmware designed to operate on ESP8266 and ESP8285 based devices, commonly used for **Internet of Things** (**IoT**) applications. It provides a robust, feature-rich alternative to proprietary firmware on various smart devices, enabling users to take full control of their devices without relying on cloud services.

The key features of Tasmota include the following:

- **Device control**: Users can control devices like smart plugs, light bulbs, sensors, and switches directly through web interfaces, MQTT, HTTP, or serial communication.
- **Customization**: Tasmota allows extensive customization of device functions, enabling users to set up their own automation rules, scripts, and configurations.
- **Home automation integration**: It supports integration with popular home automation platforms like Home Assistant, openHAB, and Domoticz.
- **Local control**: Tasmota emphasizes local control over devices, enhancing privacy and reducing dependence on external servers.
- **Community support**: Being open-source, Tasmota has a large and active community that contributes to its development and provides support to users.

Building a thermostat

Any hardware and software platform can be used to build an IoT device. However, for this specific example, we will use the ESP32 Dev Kit V1 along with the Tasmota firmware. We will build a thermostat using a relay and a temperature sensor.

The board will be connected to a DS18B20 temperature sensor and a relay, as shown in *Figure 11.31*:

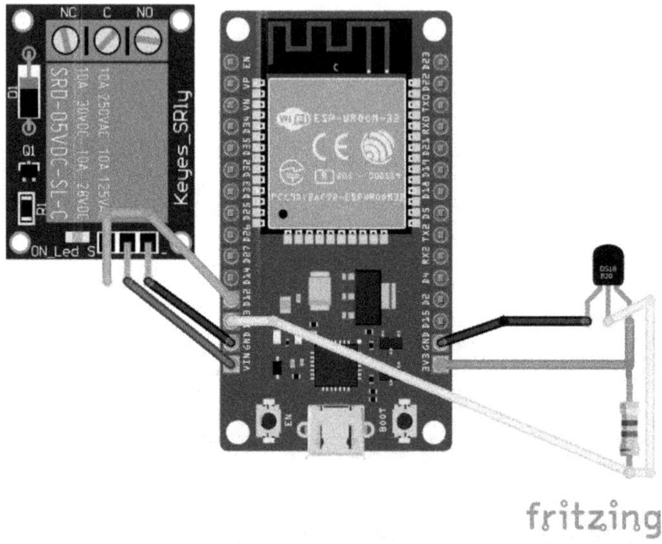

***Figure 11.31:** Tasmota device based on ESP32*

Programming the device

To program the device using the Tasmota firmware, follow these steps:

1. Connect the device to your computer using a USB cable.
2. Identify the port where the device is attached.
3. Use the web installer at Tasmota getting started.
4. Select **Tasmota** and click on **CONNECT** (refer to *Figure 11.32*).
5. The firmware will be downloaded, and the device will reboot.
6. After the installation is complete, click on the **NEXT** button. The installer will search for available Wi-Fi networks and automatically connect to the strongest one. Choose the desired network from the dropdown menu, enter the Wi-Fi password when prompted, and wait for the configuration process to finish. Then, click on **CONTINUE**.

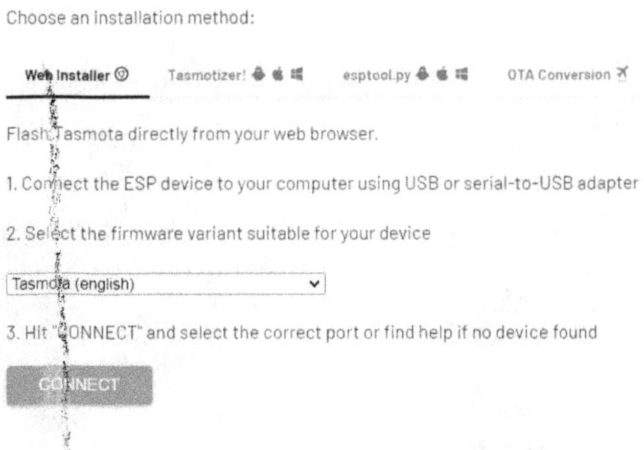

Choose an installation method:
Web Installer
Tasmotizer!
esptool.py
OTA Conversion
Flash Tasmota directly from your web browser.
1. Connect the ESP device to your computer using USB or serial-to-USB adapter
2. Select the firmware variant suitable for your device
Tasmota (english)
3. Hit "CONNECT" and select the correct port or find help if no device found
CONNECT

***Figure 11.32**: Programming a device with Tasmota*

Connecting to the MQTT broker

Now that the device has been programmed with the Tasmota firmware, it is time to configure it. Follow these steps:

1. Navigate to the home page and click on the **Configuration** button (refer to *Figure 11.32*).
2. Locate the MQTT configuration section and enter the necessary settings, as shown in *Figure 11.33*. You will need to specify at least the IP address of the broker (your Raspberry Pi IP), the port, the username, and the password.

Tasmota
Configuration
Information
Firmware Upgrade
Console
Restart

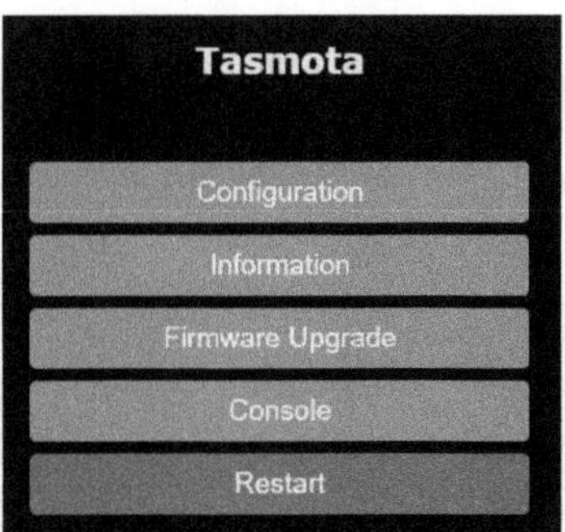

***Figure 11.33**: Tasmota home page*

The following image shows the MQTT configuration of the Tasmota device.

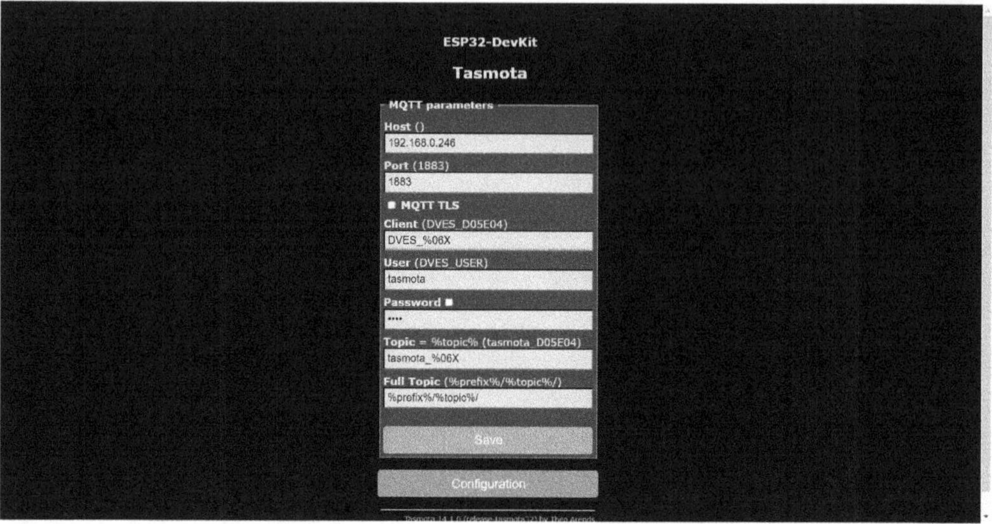

Figure 11.34: Configuring MQTT in the Tasmota device

Configuring the relay and the sensor

To enable the sensor and the relay, follow these steps:

1. Go to **Configuration** | **Configurate Template**.
2. Change the configurations of the pins to **Relay** and **DS18B20**, as shown in *Figure 11.35*.
3. Save the changes.

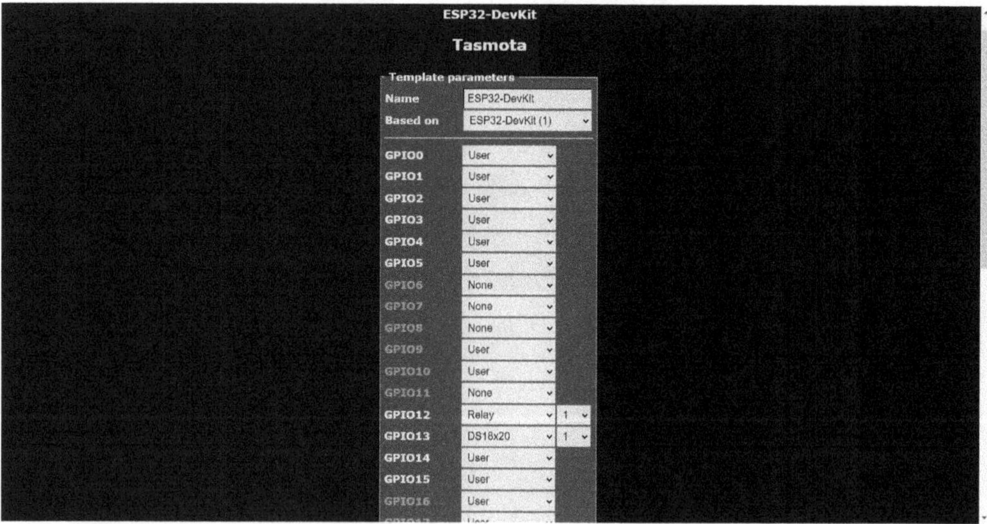

Figure 11.35: Template configuration page

Finishing the configuration

We will finish the Tasmota configuration by applying the following steps:

1. Go to **Configuration | Other Configuration**, and enable the **Activate** option in the **Template** section, as you can see in *Figure 11.36*:

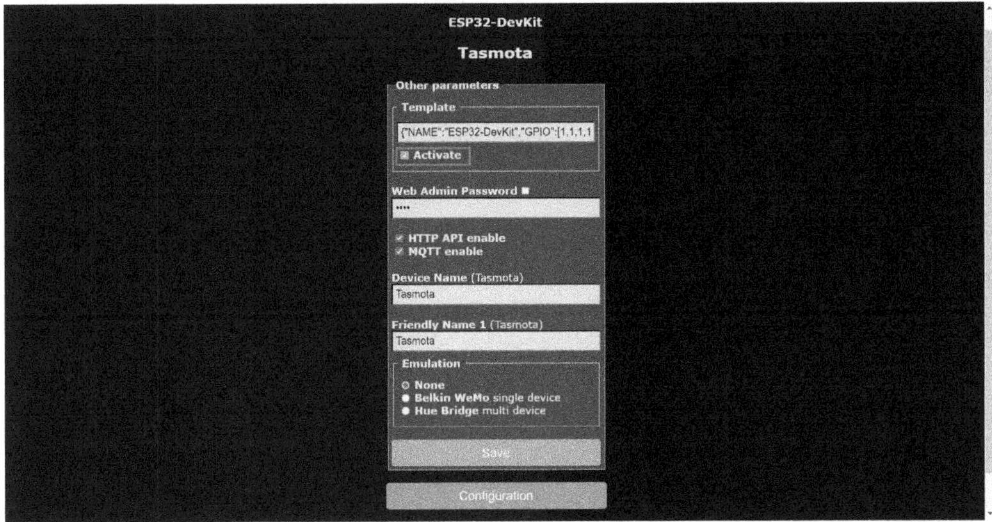

Figure 11.36: Enabling the template

2. Finally, go to **Tools | Console** and enter the following command:

   ```
   SetOption19 0
   ```

   This will allow the Tasmota integration in Home Assistant to discover the device. See *Figure 11.37*:

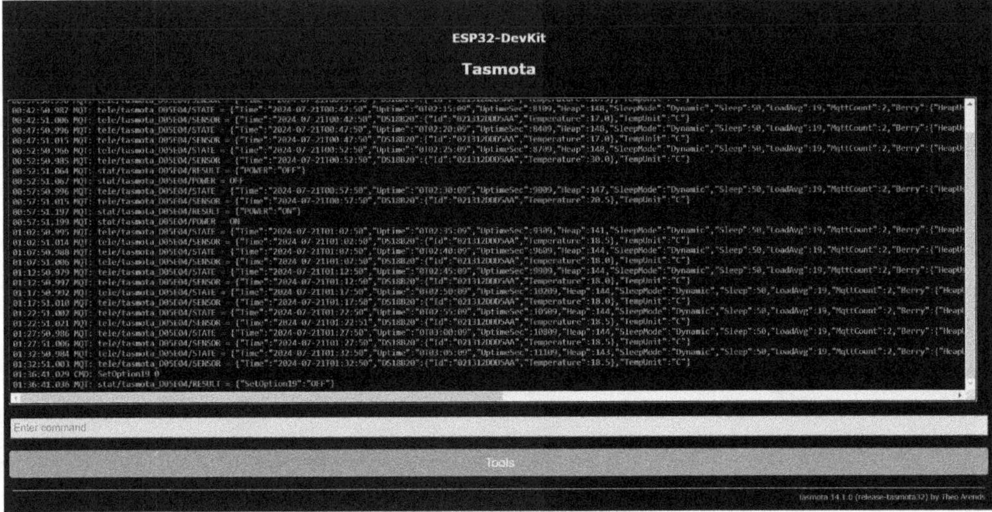

Figure 11.37: Tamsota console

Now we are ready to install the Tasmota integration in Home Assistant.

Adding the Tasmota device to Home Assistant

To add the device to Home Assistant, follow these steps:

1. Access the web interface of Home Assistant.
2. Go to **Settings | Devices & Services.**
3. You will see a new device discovered, like the one shown in *Figure 11.38*.
4. Click on the new device to see the details. Refer to *Figure 11.39*:

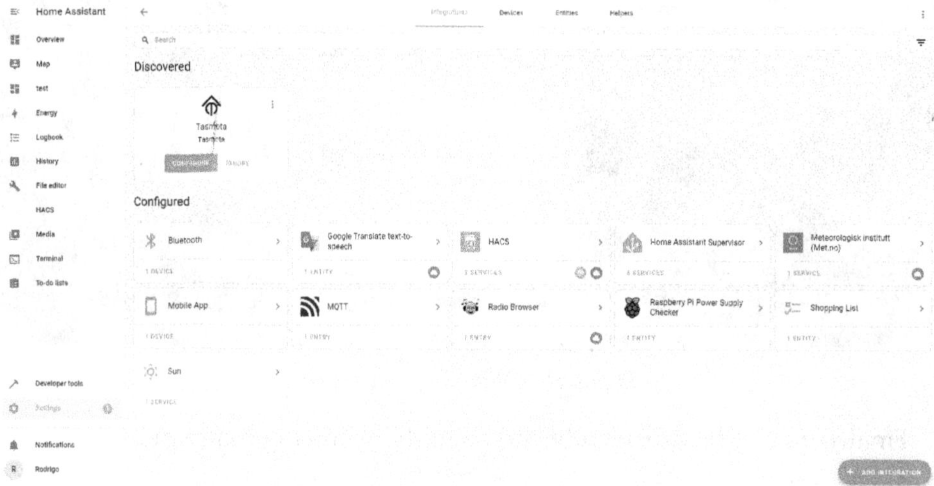

Figure 11.38: *New Tasmota device discovered*

The following figure shows the details of the Tasmota device:

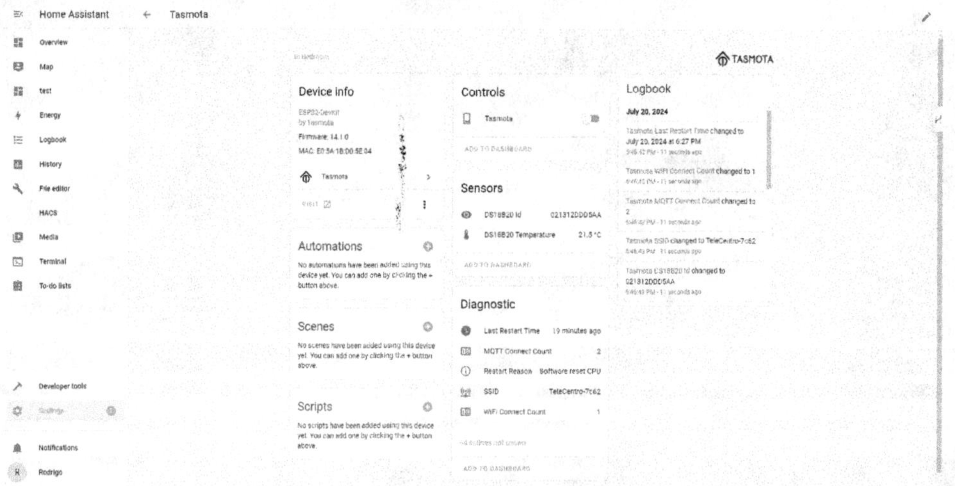

Figure 11.39: *Device details*

Creating an automation

Let us build an automation using the device we just created:

1. Click on the + button in the **Automations** card to create an automation. Refer to *Figure 11.40*.
2. Create a new automation like the one shown in *Figure 11.41*. This automation triggers the relay when the temperature is lower than 19 degrees.
3. Create a new automation like the one shown in *Figure 11.42*. This automation turns off the relay when the temperature exceeds 24 degrees.

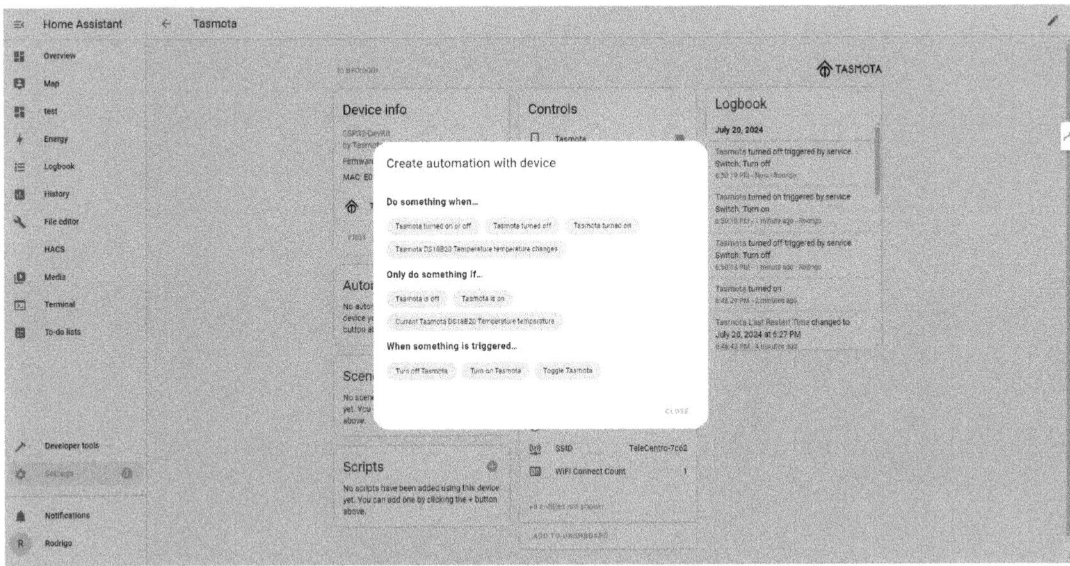

***Figure 11.40**: Create an automation*

The following figure shows the configuration settings of the automation:

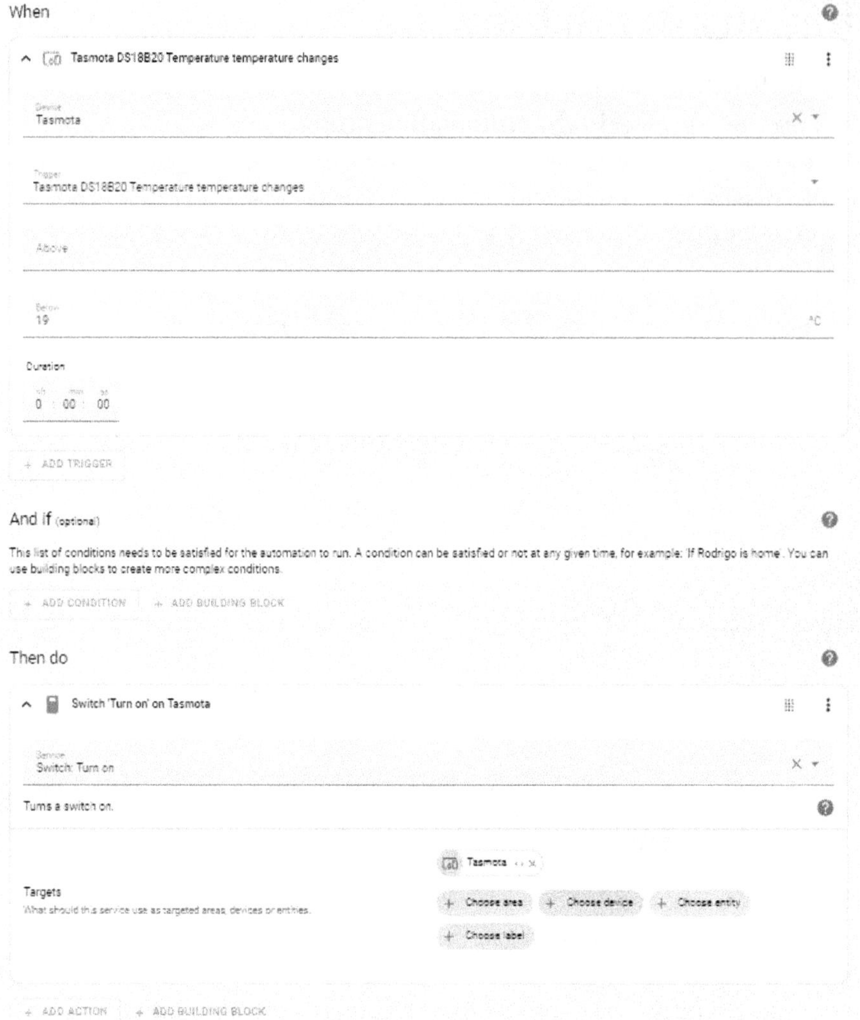

***Figure 11.41**: Turn on the switch when the temperature is low*

The following figure shows the automation when the temperature is high.

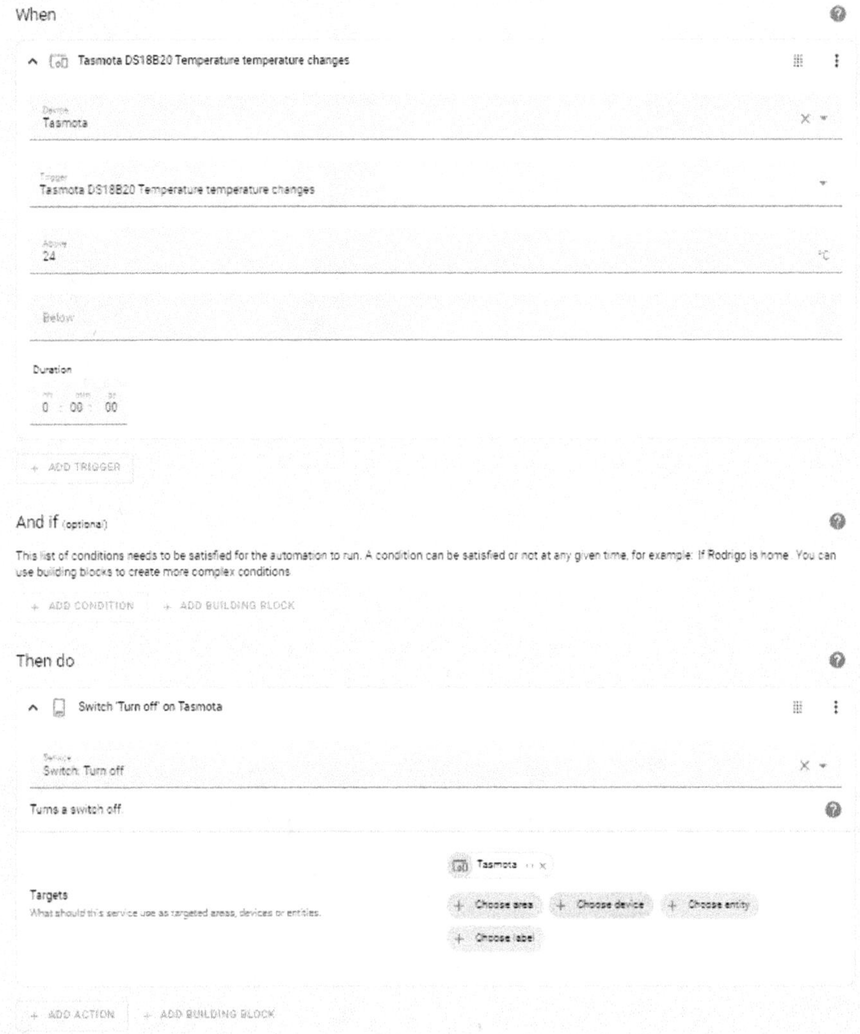

***Figure 11.42**: Turn off the switch when the temperature is high*

Add the new device to the dashboard

The final stage of this project consists of adding the Tasmota device to the Home Assistant dashboard.

Follow these steps to add the card to the dashboard:

1. Go to the **Overview** page and click on the pencil icon, on the top right of the screen. This will enable you to edit the dashboard.
2. Click on + **ADD CARD** button, on the bottom right of the screen. This will open the dialog box shown in *Figure 11.43*:

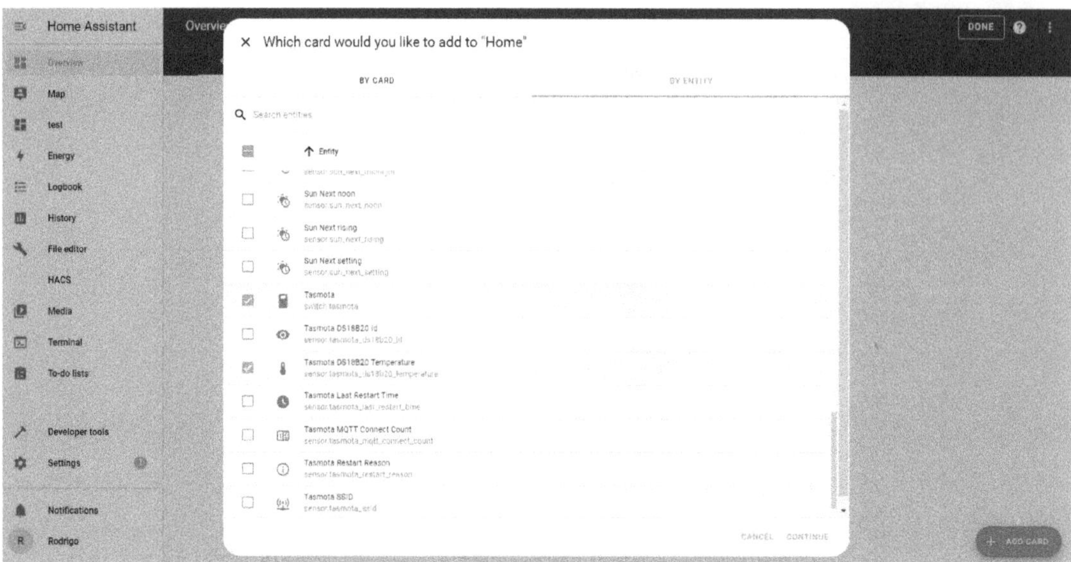

Figure 11.43: Select the switch and sensor entities of the Tasmota device

3. Select the entities you want to show on the new card. In this case, the switch and temperature entities are shown in *Figure 11.43*.
4. Add the new card to the dashboard. Refer to *Figure 11.44* and *Figure 11.45*:

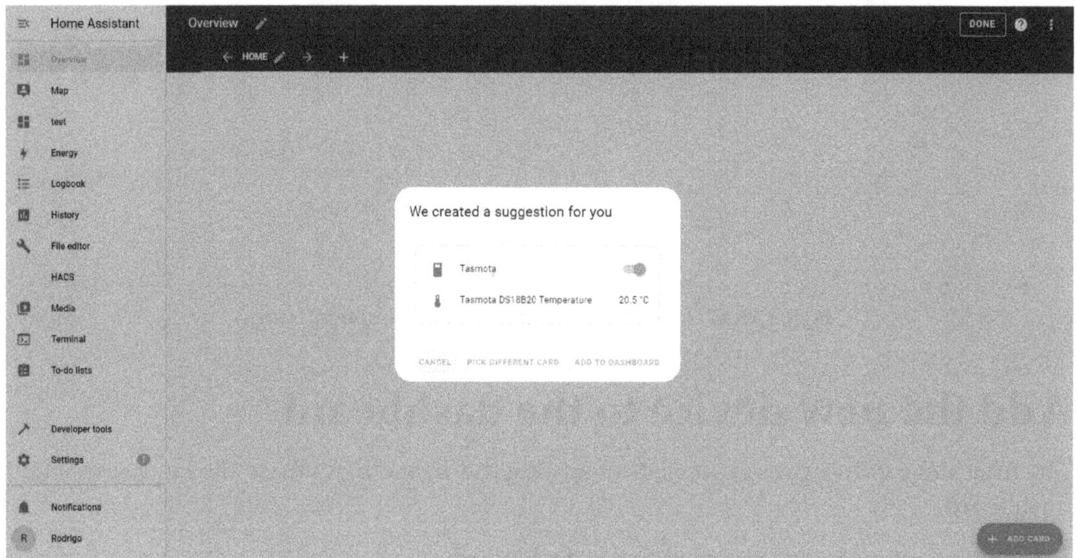

Figure 11.44: Add the device card to the dashboard

The following figure shows the card that you just added to the dashboard.

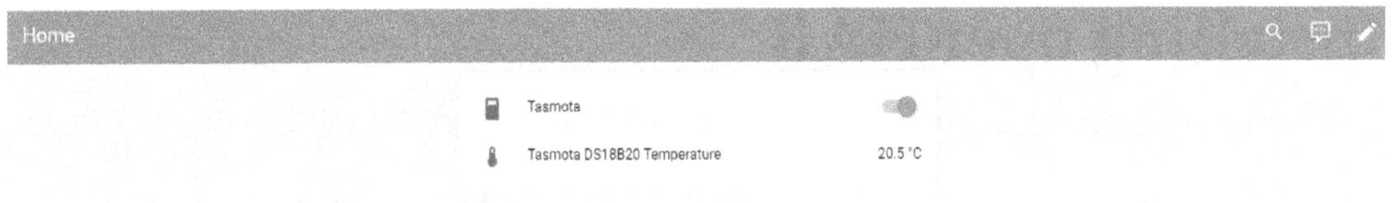

Figure 11.45: Card added to the dashboard

Using openHAB

Open Home Automation Bus (**openHAB**) is an open-source platform designed for integrating and automating smart home devices and systems. It provides a unified approach to control a wide variety of smart home technologies, regardless of the manufacturer or protocol. Here are some key features of openHAB:

- **Vendor-independent**: openHAB supports numerous devices and technologies from different manufacturers.
- **Extensible**: The platform is highly extensible, with a large number of add-ons available to support various devices and services.
- **Rules engine**: openHAB includes a powerful rules engine for automating smart home devices based on various conditions and events.
- **User interfaces**: It offers several user interfaces, including web-based, mobile apps, and voice control through integration with assistants like Alexa and Google Assistant.
- **Community and support**: openHAB has a robust community and extensive documentation, providing support and resources for users and developers.
- **Data privacy**: As an open-source project, openHAB allows users to have full control over their data and how it is managed.

openHAB can run on various hardware platforms, including PCs, Raspberry Pi, and other dedicated home automation hubs. It supports integration with many smart home standards like Z-Wave, Zigbee, MQTT, and others, making it a versatile choice for home automation enthusiasts.

Installing openHAB

In this section, we will see how to install openHAB on the Raspberry Pi 4.

Note: The procedure is quite similar to the one we used to install Home Assistant.

To create the image, follow these steps:

1. Download and install Raspberry Pi Imager on your computer from **https://www.raspberrypi.com/software/**. We used this software in *Chapter 1, Meet the Boards,* to install the Raspberry Pi OS.
2. Insert the SD card into your computer. An SD card with a minimum of 32 GB is recommended.
3. Open Raspberry Pi Imager and select your Raspberry Pi device (Raspberry Pi 4 in our case).
4. Choose the operating system by selecting **Choose OS**.
5. Navigate to **Other specific-purpose OS** | **Home assistants and home automation** | **openHAB**. Refer to *Figure 11.46*.
6. Select the openHABian (64 bit). Refer to *Figure 11.47*.
7. Choose your SD card within Raspberry Pi Imager.
8. Start writing the installer onto the SD card by selecting **Next**.
9. Wait for the openHAB to be written to the SD card.
10. Eject the SD card once the writing process is complete.
11. Insert the microSD card into your Raspberry Pi and power it on.
12. Connect the Raspberry Pi to Ethernet or configure Wi-Fi (do not attach a keyboard), and power on the device.
13. Wait 15 to 45 minutes for the installation process to complete, which you can monitor in your browser at **http://openHABian:81**. If you cannot connect using the hostname, enter the IP address of your Raspberry Pi (**http://<ip-address>:81**). Refer to *Figure 11.48*.
14. Once installed, access the openHAB user interface at **http://openHABian:8080**, connect to Samba network shares, and view logs using the openHAB Log Viewer at **http://openHABian:9001**. Use the IP address of the Raspberry Pi if the hostname does not work.

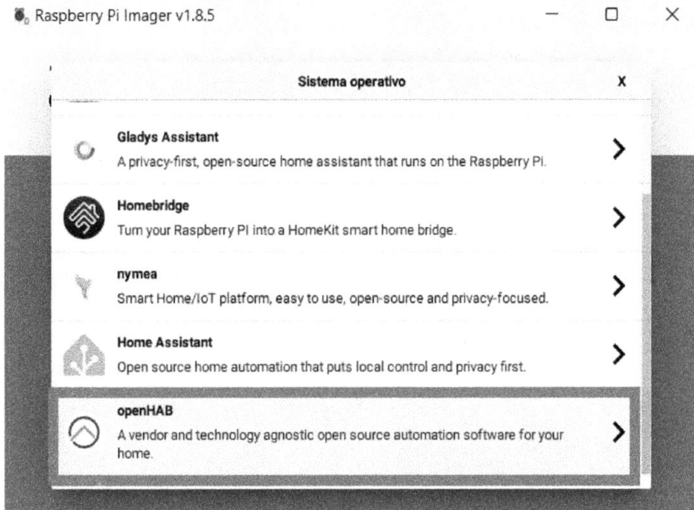

Figure 11.46: Select openHAB

The following figure shows the openHABian operating system option:

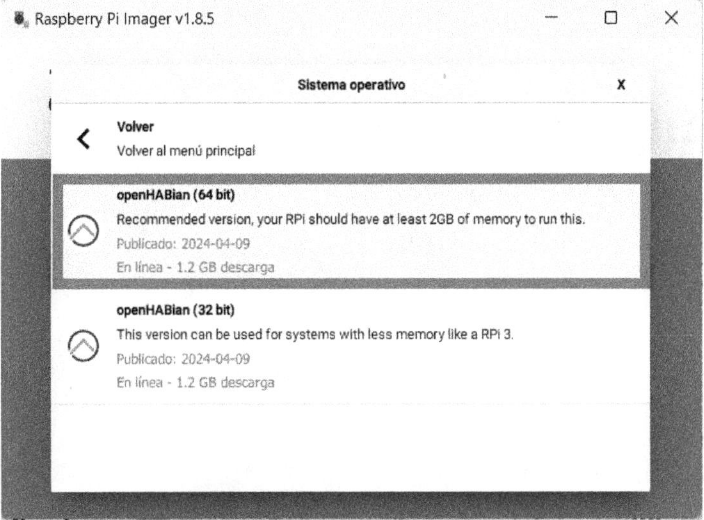

Figure 11.47: Select the 64 bit version

In the following figure, you can see a screen capture from the installation process.

openHABian Installation Status

The log will be refreshed automatically every 10 seconds.

```
2024-03-15_15:09:20_UTC [openHABian] Starting the openHABian initial setup.
2024-03-15_15:09:20_UTC [openHABian] Storing configuration... OK
2024-03-15_15:09:21_UTC [openHABian] Starting webserver with installation log... OK
2024-03-15_15:09:26_UTC [openHABian] Changing default username and password... SKIPPED
2024-03-15_15:09:26_UTC [openHABian] Setting up NetworkManager and Wi-Fi connection... 2024-04-09_00:00:00_UTC [openHABian] Ensuring network connectivity... OK
2024-04-09_00:00:00_UTC [openHABian] Waiting for dpkg/apt to get ready... OK
2024-08-06_15:08:24_UTC [openHABian] Updating repositories and upgrading installed packages... OK
2024-08-06_15:13:21_UTC [openHABian] Updating myself from https://github.com/openhab/openhabian, openHAB branch... OK
2024-08-06_15:13:24_UTC [openHABian] Starting execution of 'openhabian-config unattended'... OK
2024-08-06_15:13:24_UTC [openHABian] Checking for root privileges... OK
2024-08-06_15:13:24_UTC [openHABian] Updating Linux package information... \ ␛[2D| ␛[2D/ ␛[2D- ␛[2D\ ␛[2D| ␛[2D/ ␛[2D- ␛[2D\ ␛[2D| ␛[2D/ ␛[2D- ␛[2D\ ␛[2DOK
2024-08-06_15:13:31_UTC [openHABian] Loading configuration file '/etc/openhabian.conf'... OK
2024-08-06_15:13:31_UTC [openHABian] Adjusting swap size to 1814 MB... OK (reboot required)
2024-08-06_15:13:31_UTC [openHABian] Setting timezone based on openhabian.conf... OK (Europe/London)
2024-08-06_17:13:33_CEST [openHABian] Setting locale based on openhabian.conf... OK (reboot required)
2024-08-06_17:13:52_CEST [openHABian] Setting hostname of the base system based on openhabian.conf... OK
2024-08-06_17:13:52_CEST [openHABian] Setting the GPU memory split down to 16MB for headless system... OK
2024-08-06_17:13:52_CEST [openHABian] Enabling Audio output... OK
2024-08-06_17:13:52_CEST [openHABian] Installing basic can't-be-wrong packages (screen, vim, ...)... OK
2024-08-06_17:15:30_CEST [openHABian] Installing additional needed packages... OK
2024-08-06_17:16:13_CEST [openHABian] Installing additional Python packages... 2024-08-06_17:16:13_CEST [openHABian] Installing python3 serial package... OK
2024-08-06_17:16:27_CEST [openHABian] Installing pigpio package... OK
2024-08-06_17:16:29_CEST [openHABian] Installing additional bluetooth packages... OK
2024-08-06_17:19:55_CEST [openHABian] Adding slightly tuned bash configuration files to system... OK
2024-08-06_17:19:55_CEST [openHABian] Adding slightly tuned vim configuration file to system... OK
2024-08-06_17:19:55_CEST [openHABian] tailscale VPN installation... SKIPPED (no preauthkey defined)
2024-08-06_17:19:55_CEST [openHABian] Applying miscellaneous system settings... OK
2024-08-06_17:19:55_CEST [openHABian] Downloading FireMotD... OK
2024-08-06_17:19:58_CEST [openHABian] Installing FireMotD... OK
2024-08-06_17:19:58_CEST [openHABian] Generating FireMotD theme... OK
2024-08-06_17:20:36_CEST [openHABian] Setting up FireMotD apt updates count service... OK
2024-08-06_17:20:50_CEST [openHABian] Fetching OpenJDK 17...
```

***Figure 11.48**: Installation logs*

In the next section, we will see how to initialize openHAB.

Initializing openHAB

After openHAB finishes its installation, you have to configure a few things.

Follow these steps to initialize openHAB:

1. Choose an admin user and set the password. Refer to *Figure 11.49*:

***Figure 11.49**: Set the admin user and its password*

2. Specify the language and the location. Refer to *Figures 11.50 and 11.51*:

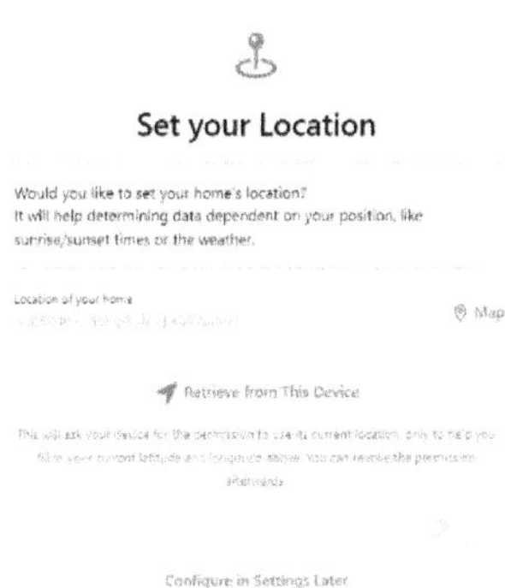

Figure 11.50*: Set the location*

The following figure shows the region, language, and time zone configuration. You can change these settings after the installation:

Figure 11.51*: Set language and time zone*

3. Install persistence add-ons and optionally additional add-ons. Refer to *Figures 11.52* and *11.53*:

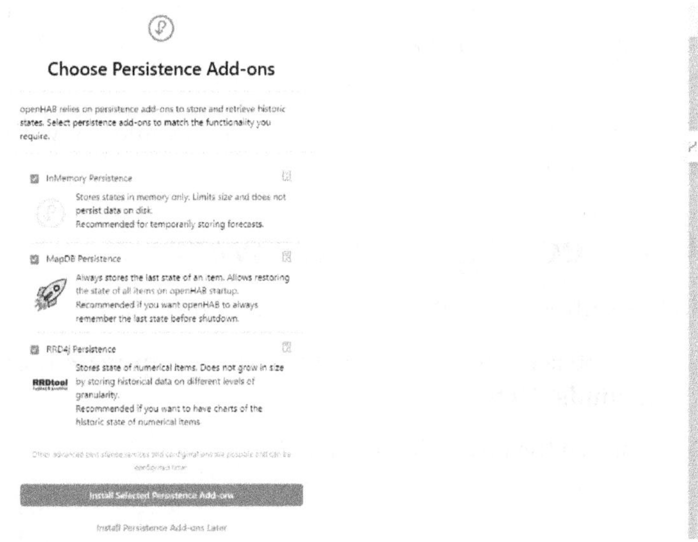

Figure 11.52*: Install persistence add-ons*

Finally, in the next screen the system will ask you to install some add-ons.

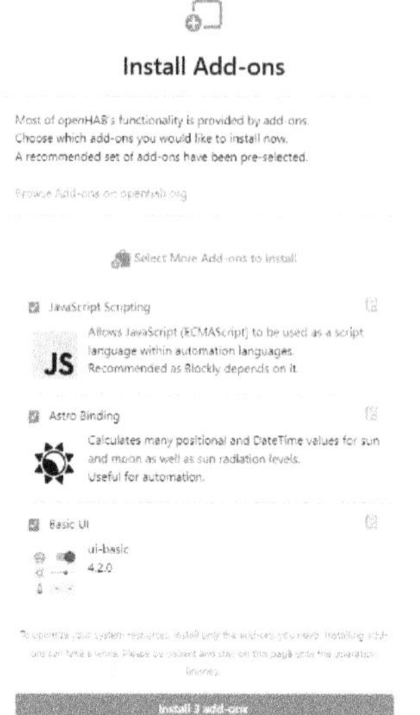

***Figure 11.53**: Install additional add-ons*

Now that we have a working instance of openHAB, let us start using it.

Creating an ESPHome device

ESPHome is a platform that helps you easily create custom firmware for ESP8266, ESP32, and Raspberry Pi Pico microcontrollers (among others).

With ESPHome, you can configure devices like sensors, lights, and switches using simple YAML files. Once you have set up your configuration, ESPHome compiles it into firmware that you can upload to your microcontroller.

This allows you to integrate your devices seamlessly with home automation systems like Home Assistant, openHAB, etc.

Connecting the hardware

In this section, we will create a device using a Raspberry Pi Pico W, and a SGP30 sensor.

The SGP30 is a sensor capable of measuring **equivalent CO2 (eCO2)** and **volatile organic compounds** (VOC).

You can see the device in *Figure 11.54*:

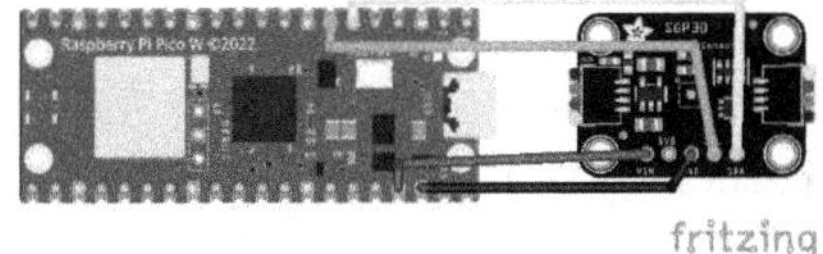

Figure 11.54: Raspberry Pi Pico W with SGP30 sensor

Programming the firmware

We will use the ESPHome Python script to build and upload the firmware to the device.

To use ESPHome follow these steps:

1. First, run the following commands to install the required Python modules:

```
pip3 install wheel
pip3 install esphome
```

2. Create a YAML file with the following content:

```
esphome:
   name: "rpipicow"

wifi:
  ssid: Your-WiFi
  password: Your-WiFi-Key

api:

rp2040:
  board: rpipicow
  framework:
    platform_version: https://github.com/maxgerhardt/platform-
raspberrypi.git

i2c:
  sda: 4
  scl: 5

sensor:
  - platform: sgp30
    eco2:
      name: "Workshop eCO2"
      accuracy_decimals: 1
```

```
tvoc:
  name: "Workshop TVOC"
  accuracy_decimals: 1
store_baseline: yes
address: 0x58
update_interval: 1s
```

For a description of each part of the code, visit **https://esphome.io/components/**

3. Connect the Raspberry Pi Pico W to the computer using the USB cable.
4. Run the following commands to compile, build, and upload the firmware to the device. Execute the command from the directory where the YAML file is located.
   ```
   esphome compile your-file.yml
   esphome upload your-file.yml
   ```
5. The previous step will upload the firmware to the device, and it will start working.

Now that you have the device, let us go back to openHAB to integrate it.

Integrating the ESPHome device in openHAB

The first thing we have to do is install the ESPHome add-on.

Follow these steps to install the add-on

1. Go to **Add-on Store** in the left menu and search for ESPHome.
2. Click on the add-on and click on the **Install** button to install it. Refer to *Figure 11.55*:

Figure 11.55: Installing the ESPHome add-on

3. After installing the add-on, a new device will appear in the **Things** section, as shown in *Figure 11.56*:

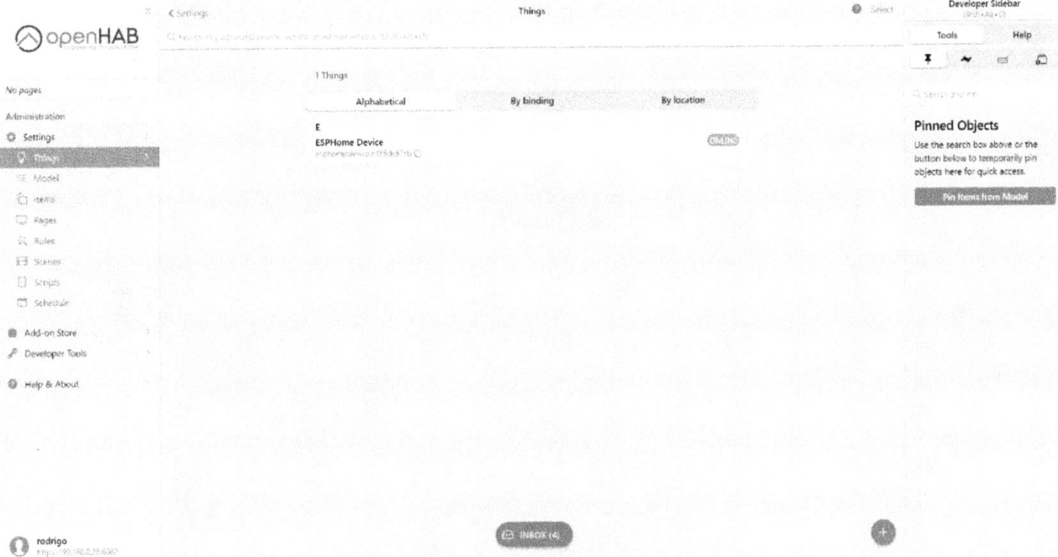

***Figure 11.56**: New ESPHome Thing*

4. Click on the **Thing** to see the details, as shown in *Figure 11.57*:

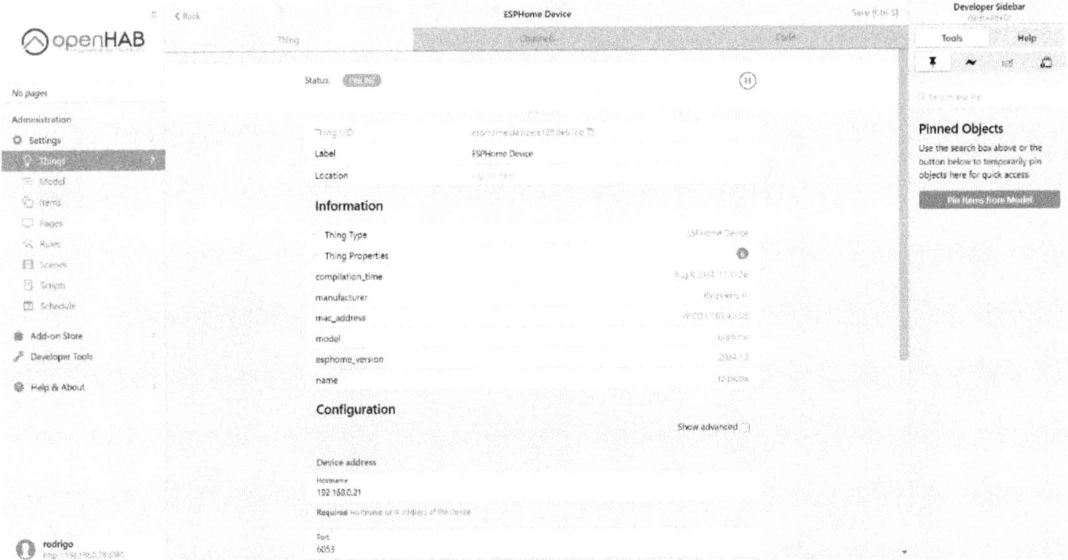

***Figure 11.57**: Thing details*

5. Go to the **Channels** tab to create a new item and link it to the device's channel. Select one of the channels and click on **Add Link to Item**.

6. In the **Link Channel to Item** page, select **Create a new Item** and fill in the details like **units, labels**, etc. Refer to *Figure 11.58*:

Figure 11.58: Create a new item

The following figure shows the channel with the new item:

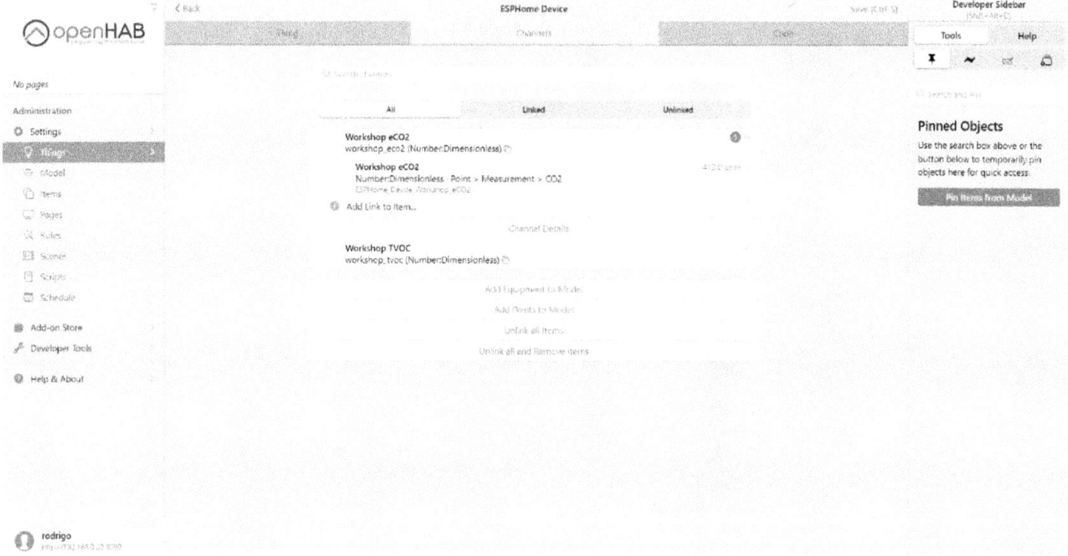

Figure 11.59: Channel with a new item

7. After finishing the process, you will see the new item on the **Channels** page, as shown in *Figure 11.59*.

Now you can use these items to show the values on a dashboard, run rules, etc.

Creating an automation in openHAB

In this section, we will create an automation using the values of the CO2 sensor. Every time the sensor surpasses 800 ppm, the system will produce a sound alarm.

Notice that for testing this automation, you will have to connect the audio output of the Raspberry Pi to an external speaker.

In openHAB, automation can be implemented using rules, scenes, scripts, and schedules. In this case, we will use rules.

To build the rule, follow these steps:

1. Go to **Settings** | **Rules** in the left menu and click on the + blue button at the bottom right of the screen. This will create a new rule. Refer to *Figure 11.60*.
2. In the trigger section of the rule, click on **Add Trigger** in the **When** section of the rule.

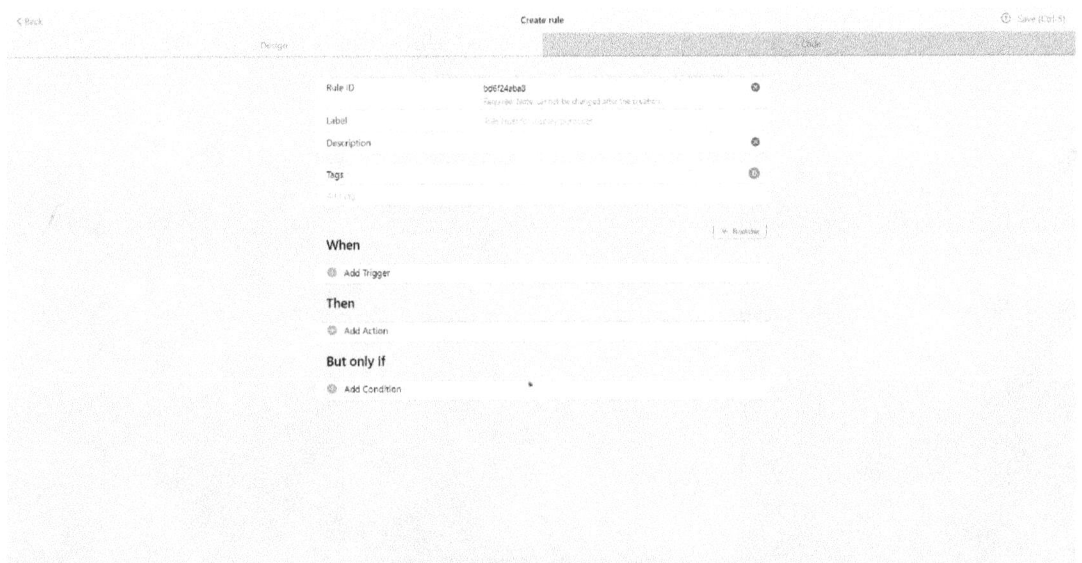

Figure 11.60: *New rule*

3. Select **Time Event** in the **Add Trigger** window, as shown in *Figure 11.61*:

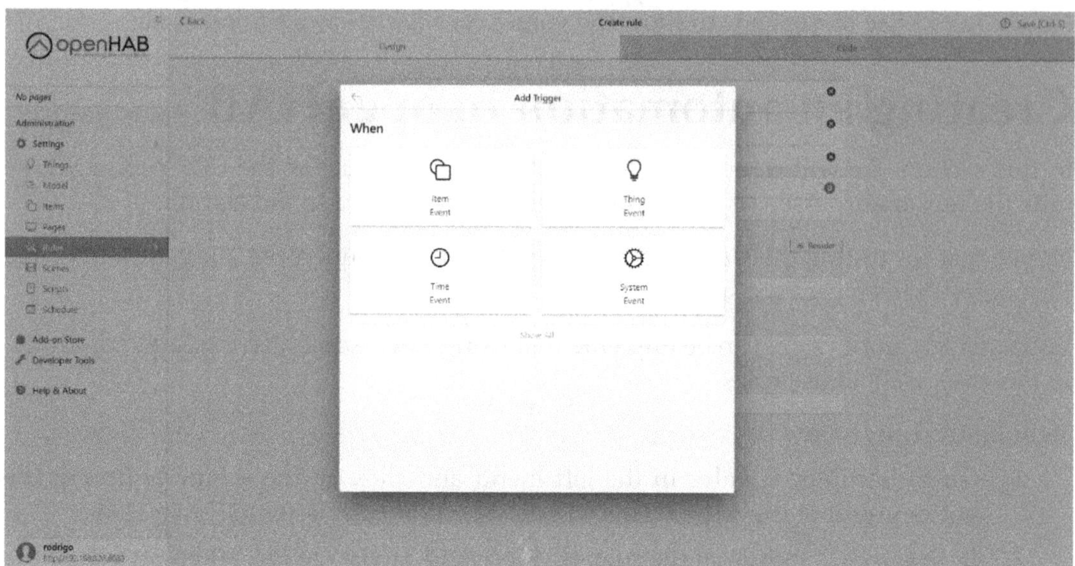

Figure 11.61: Select the item for trigger

4. Create a cron trigger, and select the time schedule. Refer to *Figures 11.62 and 11.63*:

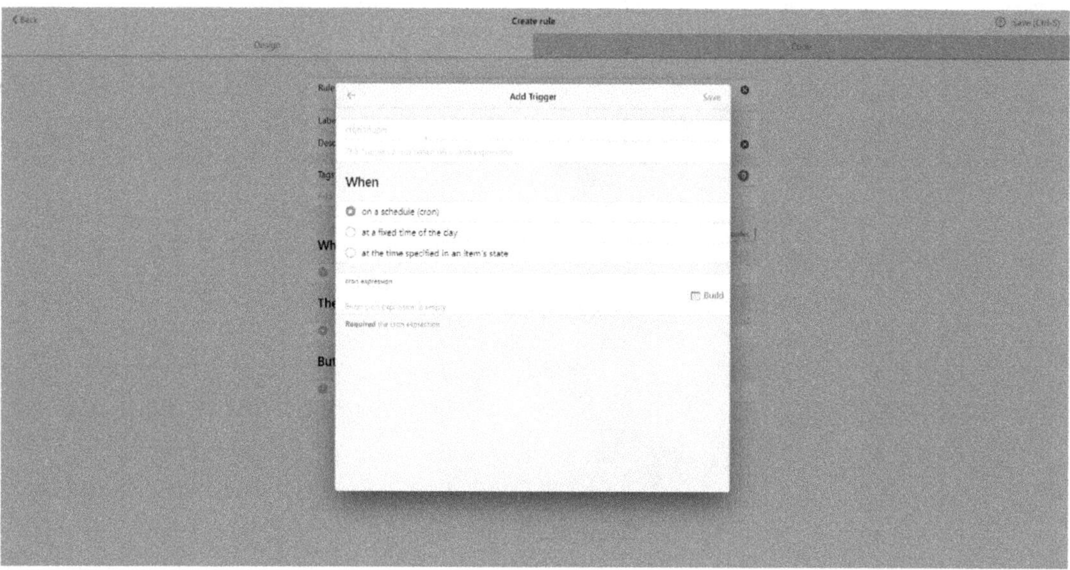

Figure 11.62: New cron event

The next figure shows the configuration panel of the cron event.

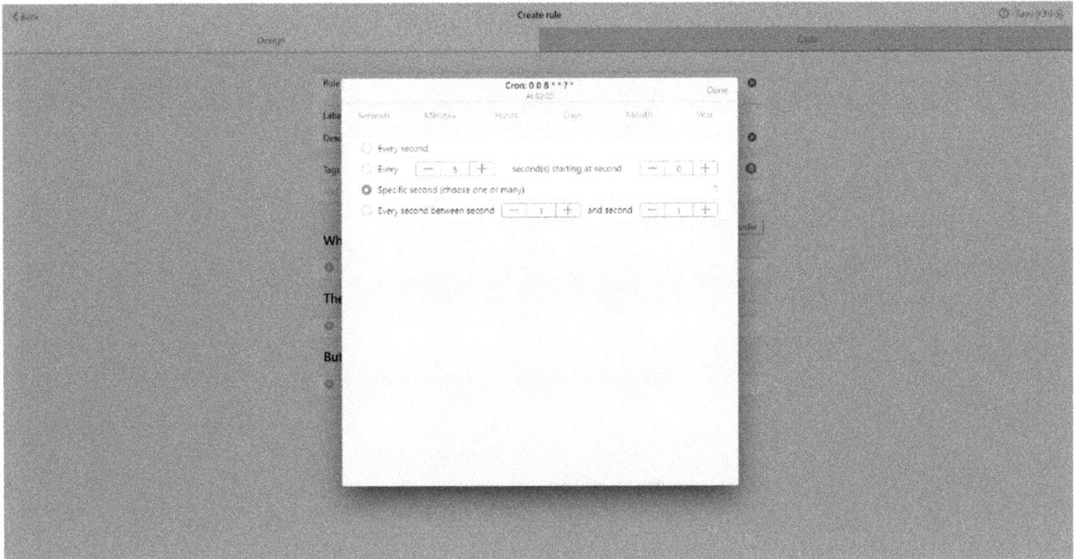

Figure 11.63: Configure cron event

5. Now, on the rule page, in the **Then** section, click on **Add Action**. In the **Add Action** window select **Audio & Voice**. Refer to *Figure 11.64*:

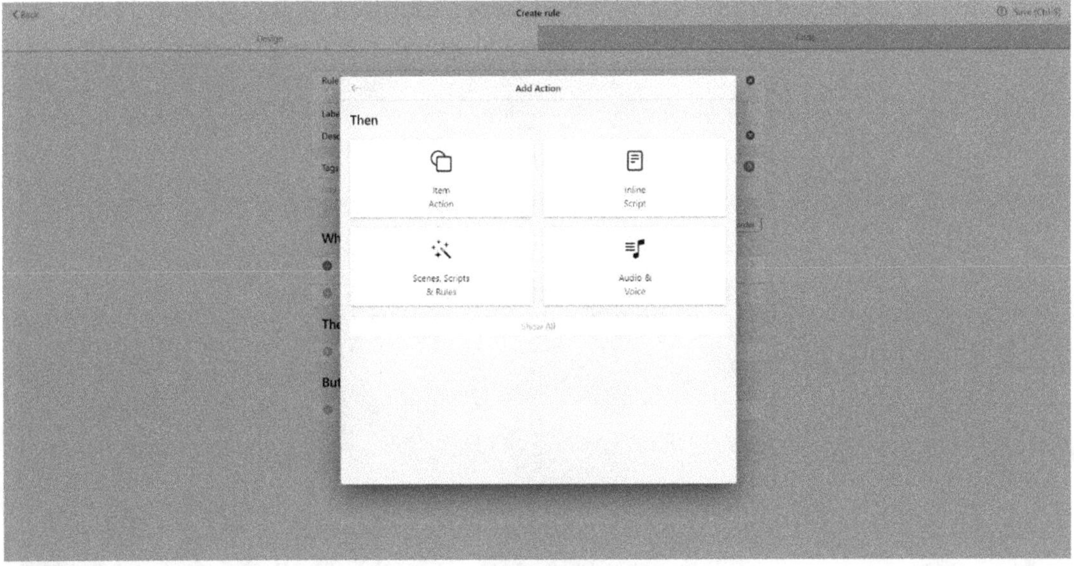

Figure 11.64: Audio action

6. Select the type of audio action that you want to use. In this case, we will use an alarm sound to reproduce it in an external speaker. Refer to *Figure 11.65*:

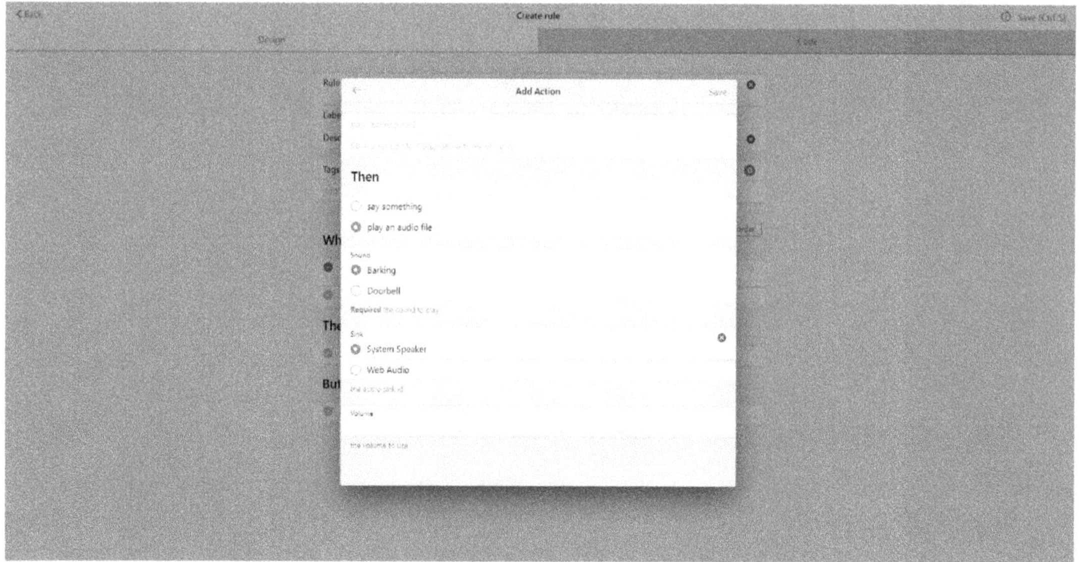

Figure 11.65: Configuring the audio action

7. Finally, we will create a rule condition. On the rule page, click on **Add Condition** in the **But only if** section.
8. In the **Add Condition** window, select **Item Condition**. Refer to *Figure 11.66*:

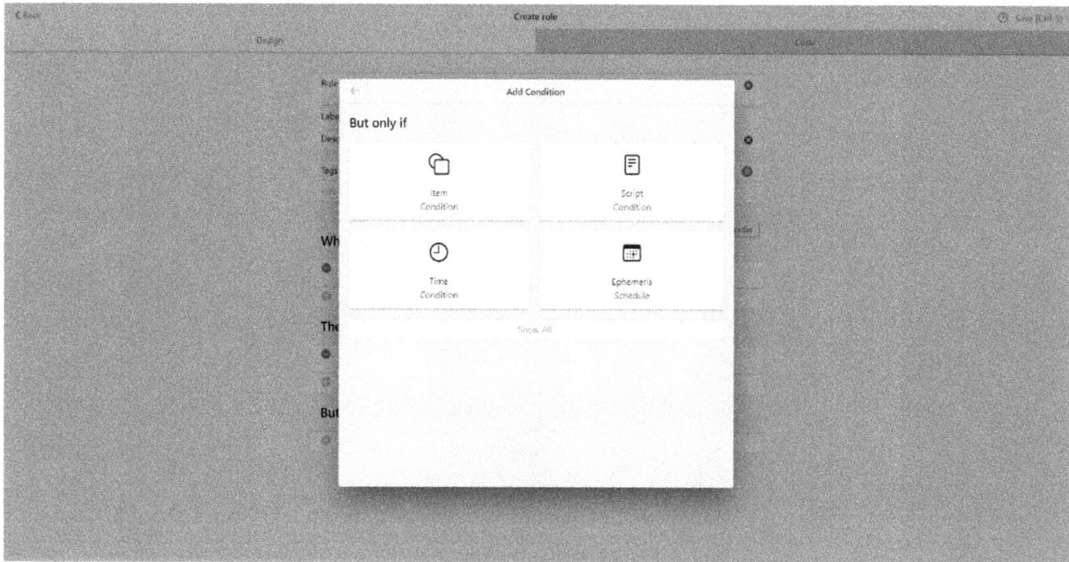

Figure 11.66: Selecting the type of condition

9. In the condition window, select the item, the conditional, and the value, as shown in *Figure 11.67*:

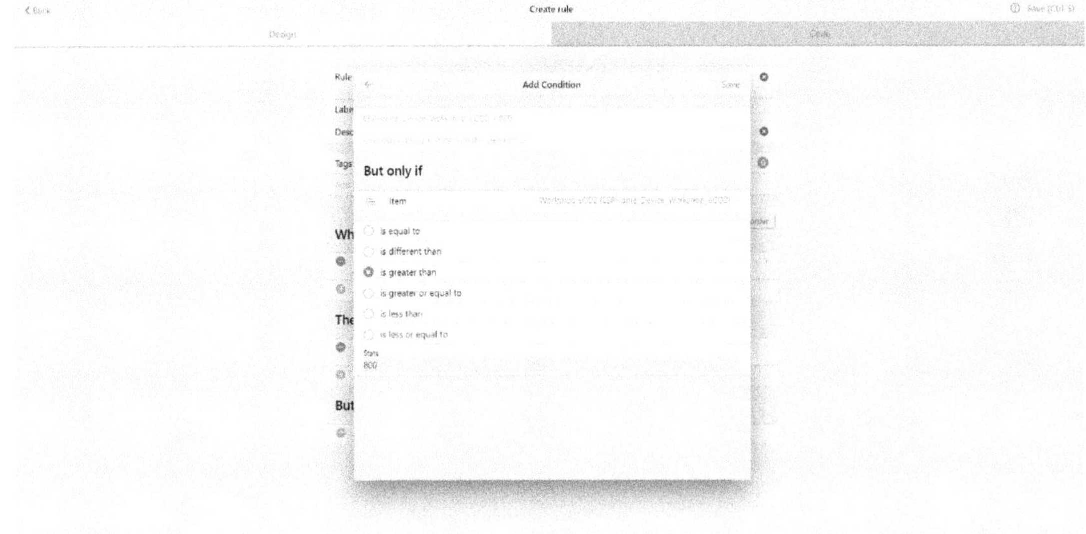

Figure 11.67: Configuring the condition

10. With this last step, we have completed the automation, and you can save the rule. Every time the CO2 sensor goes beyond 800 ppm, a sound will be played in the speaker.

Note: You can combine different types of events, schedules, actions, and conditions. The system is very flexible and admits a lot of variations.

Creating a dashboard in openHAB

Now, we will create a dashboard for the home page of openHAB.

To create the dashboard, follow these steps:

1. Go to **Settings** | **Pages** on the left menu and click on the **Overview** default dashboard. Refer to *Figure 11.68*:

Figure 11.68: Default dashboard

2. On the dashboard page, click on the big + sign to add a new widget. Then select the type of widget you want to use. In this case, we will use a gauge. See *Figure 11.69*:

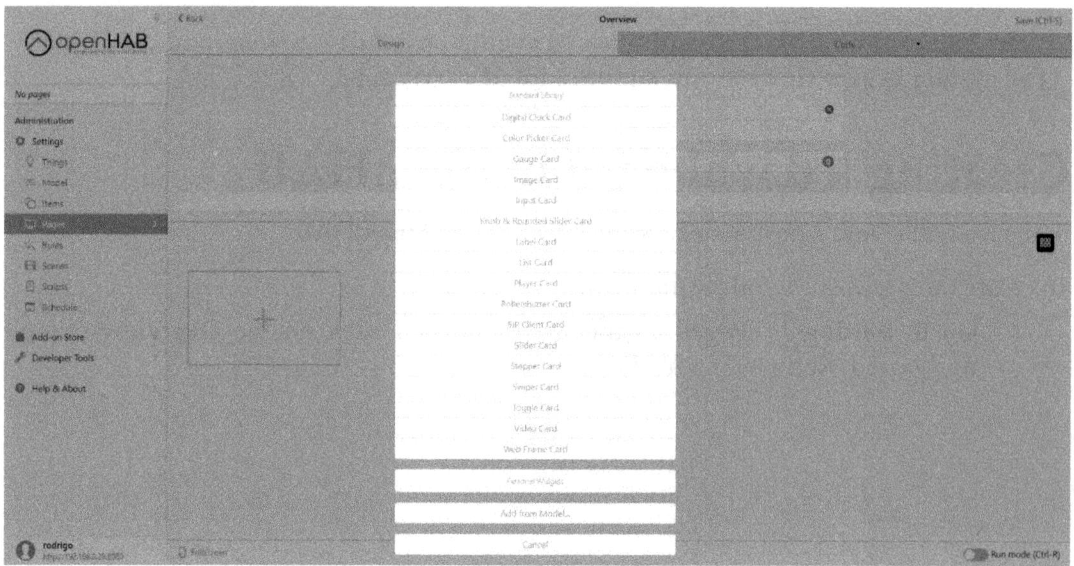

Figure 11.69: Selecting a gauge

3. Now, click on the small rectangle on the top right of the widget and select **Configure Widget**, as shown in *Figure 11.70*:

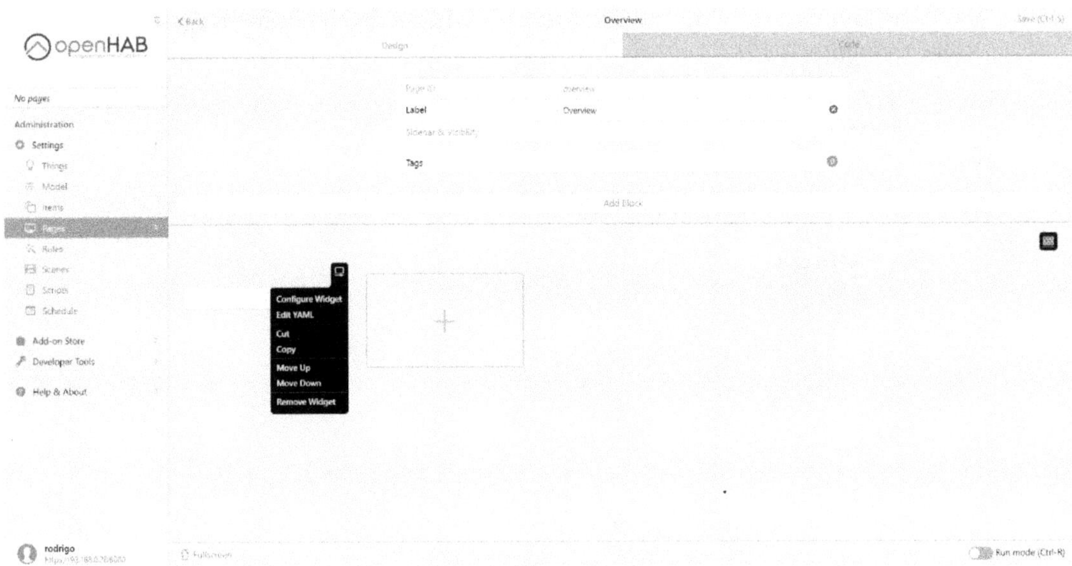

Figure 11.70: Widget menu

4. In the configuration windows of the widget, select the item you want to show and modify the properties according to your needs. Refer to *Figure 11.71*:

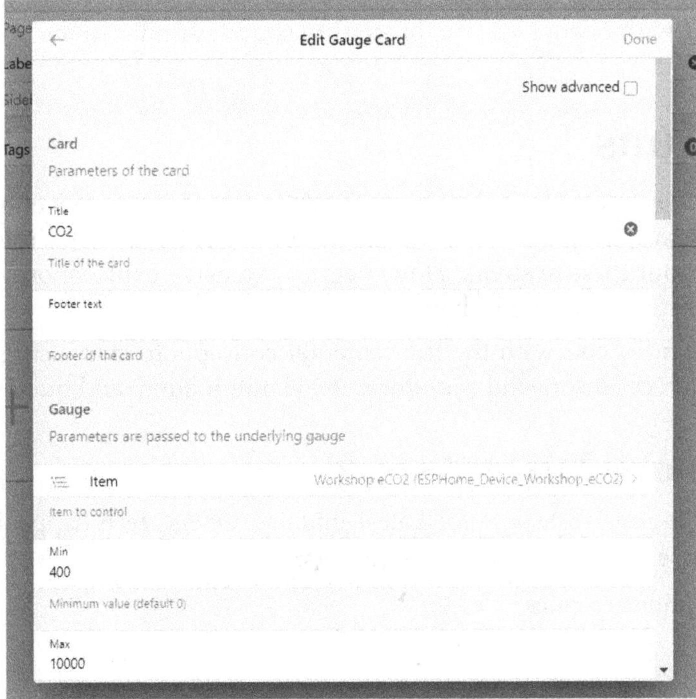

Figure 11.71: Widget properties

5. Save the layout, and you will see the new widget on the home page of openHAB. Refer to *Figure 11.72*:

Figure 11.72*: openHAB dashboard*

Now you have a working dashboard in openHAB. You can add more widgets to show data and interact with openHAB. The procedure is quite similar to the one we have used in this case.

Conclusions

In this chapter, we have covered the basics of the two most used open source home automation systems. They are Home Assistant and openHAB. Certainly, there is much more to cover about these systems. However, an extensive exploration would require a complete book instead of a single chapter.

This chapter provides you with the fundamental concepts to start using these systems. You can now connect sensors and actuators, create automation, and build dashboards.

Join our book's Discord space

Join the book's Discord Workspace for Latest updates, Offers, Tech happenings around the world, New Release and Sessions with the Authors:

https://discord.bpbonline.com

Index

C

D

E

G

H

I

J

K

L

M

N

O

P

R

S

www.ingramcontent.com/pod-product-compliance
Lightning Source LLC
Chambersburg PA
CBHW061758210326
41599CB00034B/6808

* 9 7 8 9 3 6 5 8 9 2 6 5 9 *